THE INDIAN CHIEF  AS T

THE INDIAN CHIEF AS TRAGIC HERO

NATIVE RESISTANCE AND THE LITERATURES OF AMERICA, FROM MOCTEZUMA TO TECUMSEH

GORDON M. SAYRE

THE UNIVERSITY OF NORTH CAROLINA PRESS   Chapel Hill

© 2005 The University of North Carolina Press
All rights reserved
Manufactured in the United States of America
Set in Quadraat and Othello types
by Keystone Typesetting, Inc.

The paper in this book meets the guidelines for
permanence and durability of the Committee on
Production Guidelines for Book Longevity of the
Council on Library Resources.

Frontispiece: From Henry Trumbull, History of
the Discovery of America (1830).

Library of Congress Cataloging-in-Publication Data
Sayre, Gordon M. (Gordon Mitchell), 1964–
The Indian chief as tragic hero : native resistance and the
literatures of America, from Moctezuma to Tecumseh /
Gordon M. Sayre.
     p. cm.
Includes bibliographical references and index.
ISBN 0-8078-2970-6 (cloth: alk. paper)
ISBN 0-8078-5632-0 (pbk.: alk. paper)
1. American literature—History and criticism. 2. Indians in
literature. 3. Indians of North America—Kings and rulers—
Biography—History and criticism. 4. Indians of North
America—Wars—Historiography. 5. American drama
(Tragedy)—History and criticism. 6. Indians of North
America—Historiography. 7. Heroes in literature. I. Title.
PS173.16S288 2005
810.9′352997—dc22   2005008005

cloth   09 08 07 06 05   5 4 3 2 1
paper   09 08 07 06 05   5 4 3 2 1

To my mother

Constance Mitchell Sayre Epstein

25 January 1940–6 September 2003

CONTENTS

ILLUSTRATIONS

ACKNOWLEDGMENTS

I began this project during a sabbatical year at the University of Oregon and continued it with support from a summer research award and a fellowship from the Humanities Center there. I wish to thank my colleagues at Oregon, especially Lowell Bowditch, Matt Dennis, Stephanie Wood, Leah Middle-brook, and the Early Modern Research Group. The Knight Library and its staff, including Deb Carver, James Fox, and Karen Munro, and was a first-rate research venue. Oregon has been a wonderful place to teach and to write.

Friend and colleague Ralph Bauer has been an inspiration to me and to others working on comparative colonial American literature. In addition to organizing conferences where I met and exchanged ideas with Ibero-American specialists, Ralph read drafts of parts of this book. Thanks also to Barbara Fuchs, Laura Murray, Phil Round, and Ed White for advice on sources and resources and for invitations to share my work. Other scholars in early American literature—particularly Kristina Bross, Jonathan Elmer, Sandra Gustafson, Karen Kupperman, Carla Mulford, David Shields, Scott Manning Stevens, and Ned Watts—have nurtured my career as mentors and peers. Faculty at the University at Buffalo, especially Neil Schmitz and Dennis Tedlock, have fostered my work ever since graduate school there.

Hal Cannon, Harry Epstein, and Jake Page helped me to track down information about the annual reenactment of the Pueblo Revolt's fleet-footed messengers, and Peggy Seltzer of the Quinault nation alerted me to the annual ride of the Sioux and inspired my teaching of Native American literature at Oregon. Tricia Oman was my diligent indexer.

Ben Saunders and Eugene Vance helped me learn more about René Girard. George Milne shared some of the results of his research in Paris archives on the Natchez and French Louisiana. Among the small community of experts on colonial Louisiana, Shannon Dawdy was a valuable resource, as were Jim Barnett, Patricia Galloway, and Jennifer Lamonte.

I did archival research for this book at the New York Public Library, the Firestone Library at Princeton University, the Hill Library at Louisiana State

University, and most extensively at the Newberry Library in Chicago. For my visits to Princeton and New York, I thank Margo Baender and Laura Sayre.

I am grateful to the Newberry for a short-term research fellowship in 2002 and to the library and the National Endowment for the Humanities for supporting my visit to teach as part of the 2003 summer institute "French Colonial Travel Writing, 1500–1800." Sara Austin and the rest of the staff there were always helpful, and Carla Zecher was the tireless and generous organizer both of the institute and of the subsequent project to edit and publish Dumont de Montigny's manuscript memoir. In my ongoing project to translate portions of Le Page du Pratz's book, Nicole Degli Esposti has been a superb research assistant.

Part of chapter 3 was published in *Arizona Quarterly* 60:2 (2004), and part of chapter 6 appeared in *Early American Literature* 37:3 (© 2002 by the University of North Carolina Press; used by permission of the publisher).

My family of fellow scholars—Laura, Nathan, and Robert Sayre—have been perhaps my best teachers, providing an ongoing interdisciplinary seminar in history, geography, literature, and environmental studies. Marsha, Joshua, and Hannah have offered joy and love every day.

CHAPTER 1 / FROM ENEMY TO HERO

Metacom, the Wampanoag chief called King Philip by New England colonists, was regarded as a demonic villain during the bloody war of 1675–76, "a Salvage and a wild Beast" to be "hunted by English forces through the Woods" (Hubbard 1:265). Yet in the early 1800s, numerous histories, novels, plays, and orations portrayed Metacom as a brave leader fighting for native independence. Black Hawk, who was pursued and captured in 1831–32 by an army of U.S. troops, was subsequently taken east to meet President Andrew Jackson. In Baltimore, the "Indians and the president attended the theatre the same night, and it was remarked, that the attention of the house was pretty nearly equally divided between them. . . . Considerable inconvenience was experienced from the meeting of two such conspicuous characters as the president of the United States and Blackhawk, at the same time, in populous places"—so much "inconvenience" that the Sauk leader's departure for Philadelphia was delayed so that President Jackson might go ahead unchallenged. Later, when Black Hawk reached New York and Albany, the crowds wishing to see him were so thick that he could scarcely proceed from the ferry landing into the city.[1] Tecumseh led the native resistance to the U.S. military invasion of the Old Northwest in 1810–11 and fought with the British in some of the largest battles of the War of 1812, yet shortly after his death in 1813, a Dayton, Ohio, newspaper called him "perhaps the greatest Indian general that ever lifted a tomahawk" (*Dayton Republican*, 25 October 1812, qtd. in Sugden 395), and in 1820 a Vincennes, Indiana, newspaper published a letter declaring that "every schoolboy in the Union now knows that Tecumseh was a great man. . . . As a statesman, a warrior and a patriot, take him all in all, we shall not look upon his like again" (*Indiana Sentinel* qtd. in Josephy 131). By the 1840s, Tecumseh had been memorialized in dozens of poems, plays, and biographies.

How did these fierce enemies of the Anglo-American colonists become revered heroes? Why did some men who had faced these native leaders in combat, who might well have been killed by their uprisings, publish texts that not only attested to the power of the defeated Indian leaders but celebrated their nobility and valor? In more recent U.S. history, one can find a degree of macabre fascination with enemy leaders, from Adolf Hitler to Osama bin Laden and Saddam Hussein, and there is an undeniable political advantage to be gained by U.S. politicians who demonize these foes and even exaggerate their power. But to express a genuine admiration for these modern enemies is an act of radical dissent. Native American resistance leaders, from King Philip's War to the early nineteenth century, were treated quite differently. While they may have been demonized in war propaganda, they were often warmly celebrated soon thereafter. Miami war leader Little Turtle led Native American warriors in the defeat of Governor Arthur St. Clair in 1791, the U.S. military's most costly battle in all of its frontier Indian wars. Thirty-eight officers and 593 soldiers were killed (Thatcher, *Indian Biography* 2:249). Historian Richard White describes Little Turtle as "perhaps the greatest Algonquian war leader" of all (*Middle Ground* 495). Nevertheless, in 1798 Little Turtle traveled to Philadelphia, where he petitioned Congress and Quaker missionary organizations for aid to his tribe and was introduced to Thomas Jefferson, Polish patriot Tadeusz Kościuszko, and French geographer and historian Constantine Volney, who praised Little Turtle as an embodiment of the philosophical ideal of the noble primitive.[2] One can hardly imagine the enemies of twentieth-century wars being so received. What explains such sudden transformations in the receptions of these Indian chiefs, from enemy to hero, from savage foe to noble friend?

The answer, I believe, is that Indian leaders of wars of resistance against European invaders were the tragic heroes of America. The Indian leaders' nobility, ambition, and courage as well as their flaws and their demises were portrayed with all the dignity accorded the greatest characters of the classical and Renaissance tragedies by Aeschylus, Racine, and Shakespeare, the most elevated literature of the time. As Volney wrote after his exchange with Little Turtle, "In the personages of Homer's *Iliad*, I find the manners and discourse of the Iroquois and Delawares. Sophocles and Euripides portray, most faithfully, the opinions of the *red men*, on necessity, destiny, and the miseries of human life" (410). This vision was realized by the publication of epic poems and stage tragedies that cast resistant Indian chiefs as their heroes. Metacom, Pontiac, Tecumseh, and Logan, each of whom is the topic of a chapter in this book, became the heroes of stage tragedies written by Anglo-American authors between 1766 and 1836. The United States saw a craze for such Indian dramas in the 1830s. In his anthology, *Dramas from the American Theatre*, Richard Moody cites thirty-five such works written in the two decades following the 1829 premiere of the most popular work in the genre, John Augustus Stone's dramatization of Metacom's uprising, *Metamora; or, The Last of the Wampanoags*. Priscilla Sears counts forty Indian dramas written between 1820 and 1860, of which only seventeen are extant.

There may have been many more than forty, for in the barnstormy world of nineteenth-century American theater, many plays were hastily written and staged, closed not long after they opened, and were never printed, pub-

 lished, or revived.

This book is not a study simply of the Indian dramas, however, but of the culture that produced and watched them. It constitutes an analysis of the entire phenomenon of North American native resistance struggles and the leaders who organized them as represented not only in dramas, epic poems, and historical novels but also in popular histories such as Francis Parkman's *The Conspiracy of Pontiac* (1851), in the transcribed speeches by these native leaders, and in the documents created by soldiers, traders, and missionaries directly involved in these conflicts from the conquest of New Spain through the War of 1812. The ethos of the Indian tragic hero was articulated not only in stage tragedies but also in gothic novels, verse romances, travel narratives, and ethnographic texts by famous, obscure, and anonymous authors writing in English, French, and Spanish.

The dynamic of the Indian chief as tragic hero was consistent with the social functions of tragedy as established by Aristotle and still current in the eighteenth century. In the *Poetics*, Aristotle proposes that a "perfect tragedy" should "imitate actions which excite pity and fear," where "pity is aroused by unmerited misfortune, fear by the misfortune of a man like ourselves" (55). The tragic hero was at once close to and distant from the experience of the commoner, from "ourselves" in the audience of the Greek or the contemporary theater: "He must be one who is highly renowned and prosperous—a personage like Oedipus, Thyestes, or other illustrious men of such families," yet he is not a man of godlike virtues, Aristotle writes, for his misfortune arises "by some error or frailty," his tragic flaw. Roy Harvey Pearce, in his classic 1953 study *The Savages of America* (later revised and retitled *Savagism and Civilization*) perceives how this peculiar blend of sameness and difference, of admiration and condemnation, also characterizes the attitude toward Native Americans in the early United States. Pearce writes that "as doomed noble savage the Indian could be pitied; and American literary men, sensitive to the feeling of their readers, cultivated such pity. But he also had to be properly censured, and his nobility denied or qualified as to be shown not really to be nobility" (169–70). My father, Robert Sayre, in *Thoreau and the American Indians*, published in 1977, when I was twelve, cites Pearce and remarks that "pity and censure are also very close to the classic tragic emotions of pity and terror, and 'The Indian' was the most popular tragic figure in early nineteenth-century America" (6). Because Pearce is at pains to correct the myth of the Noble Savage and to discredit the French and English writers who embraced it, he is reluctant to admit that early American writers such as Thoreau not only pitied Indians but genuinely admired their virtues and feared their power. Perhaps because his exhaustive reading of literature about American Indians from 1609 to 1851 included such a great number of insipid and preposterous works by authors who had little or no knowledge of actual Native Americans, Pearce fails to do justice to many fascinating texts by men who knew the Indians well, such as Joseph Doddridge, Robert Rogers, and Robert Navarre, whom we will meet in the chapters that follow.

The European colonial invasion of America, followed by the expansionist wars of western settlement, led to the killing of millions of Native Americans. Colonizers recognized, at some semiconscious level, their responsibility for these deaths but summoned up complex responses to assuage or dismiss this responsibility. Perhaps the most pervasive was a sense of precious melancholy about the death of the Indians. In the first half of the nineteenth century, expressions of melancholic grief for the "vanishing Indian" became so commonplace, such a hackneyed trope of public discourse, that it is impossible to quote a single canonical statement of it.[3] President Andrew Jackson's remarks from his second annual address may be the best epitome, as he bears the most direct responsibility for Indians' death and dispossession during the period when the Indian tragedy reached its greatest popularity:

> Humanity has often wept over the fate of the aborigines of this country, and Philanthropy has been long busily employed in devising means to avert it, but its progress has never for a moment been arrested, and one by one have many powerful tribes disappeared from this earth. To follow to the tomb the last of his race and to tread on the graves of extinct nations excite melancholy reflections. But true philanthropy reconciles the mind to these vicissitudes as it does to the extinction of one generation to make room for another. (qtd. in Pearce 57)

Jackson acknowledges an emotional response of tears and grief arising from his Indian policies and attempts to justify the policies and dismiss the emotions by making both part of a natural process, a process as inevitable as death and the progress of time. These "melancholy reflections" and the tears wept over the Indians' fate are sentimental responses to the Indians' suffering, where sentimentality is defined as an affective response to the suffering of another that one cannot or will not alleviate. Although the vanishing Indian complex was most pervasive in the nineteenth century, it has not vanished any more than have the Indians themselves. An updated version is the trope of "imperialist nostalgia" as identified by Renato Rosaldo in his 1989 book, *Culture and Truth*. Rosaldo observes that "agents of colonialism . . . often display nostalgia for the colonized culture as it was 'traditionally' " and that anthropologists share with colonial officers and missionaries this "mourning for what one has destroyed" (69).[4] His capsule definition, "a person kills somebody, and then mourns the victim" (69), applies perfectly to Jackson's speech. Rosaldo's critical goal aligns itself with postmodern anthropology's self-conscious examination of its complicity in colonialism. He admits to feeling imperialist nostalgia in his fieldwork with his wife, Michelle, among the Ilongot "headhunters" of the Philippines, and he elicits his readers' grief in writing of his wife's death during that fieldwork as the result of an accidental fall off a cliff. *Culture and Truth* simultaneously invites and deplores sentimentality. It is symptomatic of other scholarly critiques of imperialist nostalgia and the vanishing Indian insofar as it fails to clear up the contradictions between the ideological and emotional components of these tropes. We may be able to stop ourselves from reasoning like Andrew Jackson and bring ourselves to oppose the continuing dispossession of Indian lands and culture, but what if we still feel the melancholy he acknowledged? Emotions, by definition, defy rational control, and non-Indians' emotional responses to Indians remain very powerful. I can recognize the manipulative strategies of the 1970s public service ad that featured an actor in Plains Indian regalia weeping at the sight of roadside litter, but I still cannot stop myself from crying when I see it on TV (see Berkhofer 138 illustration 11).

Analyzing the resistance of Native Americans to colonization as a tragedy and its leaders as tragic heroes yields a better explanation of these phenomena than do the concepts of the vanishing Indian or of imperialist nostalgia—phenomena caused by both the historical patterns of Indian uprisings and the responses of their participants. While "melancholy" describes the paradox of pleasing sorrow or sweet grief, it remains a description of the passive observer or at least of one who disavows involvement in the death and dispossession of the Indians. In this manner, David Murray has described the reception of Indian eloquence in speeches such as Logan's as a sympathy for Indians that was "turned into an aesthetic, rather than a moral, sensation" (40). Aesthetics pertains to the responses of the audience rather than the actor, of the poet more than the soldier, and we need to deal here with soldiers, even if some of the soldiers were also poets. The Indian chiefs and warriors examined in the following chapters could not be described as vanishing: they were powerful and genuinely threatened those who fought against them. If we want to understand the exhilaration of these warriors and soldiers in the midst of battle and their grief or relief in its aftermath, we cannot aestheticize it as nostalgia or melancholy. The emotional process of Indian tragedy is instead catharsis, for only catharsis reconciles the contradictory reactions of enmity and admiration, pity, fear, and censure and articulates the responses of both historical agents and distant audiences. As Northrup Frye puts it,

Catharsis implies that the emotional response to art is not the raising of an actual emotion, but the raising and casting out of actual emotion on a wave of something else. We may call this something else, perhaps, exhilaration or exuberance. . . .

It is impossible to understand the effect of what Milton called "gorgeous tragedy" as producing a real emotion of gloom or sorrow. Aeschylus's *The Persians* and Shakespeare's *Macbeth* are certainly tragedies, but they are associated respectively with the victory of Salamis and the accession of James I, both occasions of national rejoicing. (93–94)

Athenians watching Aeschylus's *The Persians*, which as we shall see is particularly relevant to the American Indian tragedies, might sympathize with the Persian leader, Xerxes, amid his defeat but would also revel in the Greek victory over him. Apropos of *Macbeth*, Frye suggests that although tragedies by Shakespeare and Racine may have been set in the classical or medieval past, they often were understood as allegories for contemporary events. The affect of the audience was not aesthetic distance or disavowal but political relevance. Indian tragedies did not have to be so allegorical, for they used a classical form but often showed contemporary characters, Indian leaders who in some cases had been defeated only a few years earlier. Hence, the catharsis they inspired could be even more politically ambivalent than Frye allows.

Robert Rogers's play about Pontiac's rebellion, *Ponteach*, begins with a satire of the greed and racism of the British colonial officers for whom Rogers fought. If the play was performed in the 1760s (and it is not certain whether or not it was), London theatergoers would have been invited to identify with a rebel hero who had besieged English forces at Detroit for several months in 1763. As a young boy, Joseph Doddridge had fled with his family from Logan's storm of vengeance on the western Pennsylvania back settlers who had killed Logan's family. Fifty years later, Doddridge wrote a tragedy about Logan that declares in its preface, "The tear of commiseration is due to Logan. Like Wallace he outlived the independence of his nation. Like Cato, 'he greatly fell with his falling state.' Like Ossian, he was the last of his family, all of whom, but himself, had fallen by assassinations, which, for their atrocious character, are scarcely paralleled in history." As a pioneer white settler in western Pennsylvania and as a refugee from an Indian rebellion, Doddridge might be expected to express the necessity of imperial conquest and Indian removal, to mourn its victims only in a perfunctory manner, as Thomas Jefferson and Andrew Jackson did. But although Dod-

dridge did weep the "tear of commiseration" like Jackson, he also unequivocally denounced the slaughter of members of Logan's family, and in his *Notes
on the Settlement and Indian Wars Of the Western Parts of Virginia and Pennsylvania,*
Doddridge called Lord Dunmore's War, the retaliatory strike on Logan's
Shawnee allies, "a dishonorable blot on our national history" and hoped that
his writings would teach his "descendants to show justice and mercy to the
Indians" (171). His evocation of Cato and Ossian might be dismissed as
imperial nostalgia, but to group them with William Wallace, who in 1297 led
a band of Scottish peasants to a stunning defeat of the invading English,
suggests that Doddridge was questioning U.S. imperial expansion into the
trans-Allegheny west from Dunmore's War through the 1820s.[5] Doddridge
portrays Logan as a violent foe, and Doddridge and his family suffered from
this violence, but at the same time, his historical writings compare the early
settlers of the region, such as himself, to the local natives who had lived
nearby. Both peoples were "early settlers" whose memory demanded respect. The catharsis of this Indian tragedy is not simply the purgation of the
sentimental pity and literal fear that audiences felt toward Indians who had
recently been defeated; it is the resolution of a wrenching moral and political
ambivalence with regard to the Indian hero.

Such cathartic ambivalence was best resolved indirectly, through rituals
whose symbolic meaning was not immediately understood by all involved.
In chapters 2 and 5 I develop an interpretation of frontier Indian warfare that
draws on René Girard's concept of sacrifice. Girard's *Violence and the Sacred*
reads Greek tragedy alongside the rituals of primitive societies as symbolic
reenactments of an originary sacrificial crisis, a moment when cycles of
violent vengeance were resolved by the designation of a sacrificial victim.
Girard asserts that "in the final analysis, the sole purpose of religion is to
prevent the recurrence of reciprocal violence" (55).[6] Girard's ancient and
"primitive" sources should not diminish the relevance of his ideas to the
early modern period. The world of the trans-Allegheny frontier in the mid–
eighteenth century, the world of Pontiac and Logan, was plagued by cycles of
vengeance—what Girard calls reciprocal violence. The stated goal of colonial
armies was to "pacify" the region, generally by killing the Indian leaders
who were blamed for the killings of white settlers. Today, the Indians would
be called "terrorists." Such wars failed to stop the bloodshed, of course, but
only continued the cycles of retaliation, as Pontiac's rebellion was followed
by the battles of Logan's Shawnee allies in Lord Dunmore's War and then by
battles in the Ohio Territory in the 1790s and Tecumseh's resistance before
and during the War of 1812. But in the writings by someone such as Joseph
Doddridge or by eulogists of Pontiac and Tecumseh, the Indian tragedy
serves as a ritual and the Indian hero as a sacrificial victim, possibly bringing

about a cure for reciprocal violence. Reconnecting the Athenian city-state with the primitive and the theatrical with the medical significations of the Greek root behind the words "cathartic" and "catharsis," Girard writes that "in describing the tragic effect in terms of katharsis [Aristotle] asserts that tragedy can and should assume at least some of the functions assigned to ritual in a world where ritual has almost disappeared" and that in Aristotle's *Poetics*, "the qualities that make a 'good' tragic hero are precisely those required of the sacrificial victim" (*Violence* 290, 291). The Indian chief fits these qualities perfectly. As a "red" man, he came from outside colonial society, yet the process of war, defeat, and captivity brought him within it, as Black Hawk and Geronimo became celebrities and were exhibited at spectacles such as the St. Louis Columbian Exposition. Indian tragedies such as Doddridge's *Logan* or Stone's *Metamora* and elegiac verse romances such as James Wallis Eastburn and Robert Charles Sands's *Yamoyden* and Sarah Wentworth Apthorp Morton's *Ouâbi* staged this ritual of the capture and sacrifice of an Indian leader as a symbolic means for securing a social compact that would replace frontier violence and the bitter racial and political factions behind it with a new civil order.

This may seem like an awfully portentous claim to hang on some obscure verse epics and a small corpus of dramas, some of which were never performed. To most modern readers, as to Roy Harvey Pearce, the hero of a play such as *Metamora* represents a most egregious example of the Noble Savage, a romanticized caricature of Native American magnanimity and bravery concocted out of myths of the classical Golden Age and the French Enlightenment. The Indian tragic hero on stage is noble; his elite status was required by the formulas of both Aristotelian tragedy and nineteenth-century melodrama. But fundamental differences exist between the myths of the Indian tragic hero and of the Noble Savage. The best literary expressions of the Noble Savage are eighteenth-century French portrayals of semifictional characters such as the Baron de Lahontan's Adario, Chateaubriand's Chactas, or Diderot's Orou who have traveled to Europe and can make a satiric attack on the failings of European society compared with the honest virtues of primitive life. These men are not chiefs, for their words emphasize their societies' nonhierarchical organization, and they are not rebels, for, like Chactas in *Les Natchez*, they generally advise their tribes against attacking the colonizers. Most importantly, the primitive virtues they extol are utopian and egalitarian, shared by their culture as a whole rather than confined to its noble leaders. In the terms of Herodotus's *Histories*, the Noble Savages are more like the Scythians (as François Hartog explained) than Xerxes and his Persians. The Indian tragic hero, conversely, like Xerxes, leads an enemy people against a society that structurally is not so different from his own. His warriors are a motley crew, often including renegade Europeans or members of a hostile group of colonizers, such as the British fighting alongside Tecumseh or the French with Pontiac. The Indian tragic hero does not come from a utopian society: he knows the wide spectrum of social class and virtues. His warriors may be ruthless demons ready to torture a captive, but the heroic chief will step in and enforce a higher law of honor.

In his essay "The Noble Savage Theme as Fetish," Hayden White argues that the "Noble Savage was a concept with which to belabor 'nobility,' not to redeem the 'savage.'" As a radical idea, it sought to "undermine the very concept of 'nobility' or at least the idea of nobility tied to the notion of genetic inheritance" (130). The political purpose of the Indian tragic hero may have been anticolonial, but it was not radical in the sense of leveling social castes. As Harry Liebersohn shows, Chateaubriand, Tocqueville, Maximilian von Wied, and other aristocratic refugees of the Age of Revolution in Europe came to America to try to establish their affinity and common interest with American Indians, who were also being dispossessed of their land by republican imperialists. And like Chateaubriand, a few American authors of Indian romances, such as Sarah Wentworth Apthorp Morton, came from elites who believed they had been victimized by a populist mob. The meaning of Indian "nobility" changed profoundly during the Age of Revolution.

In the seventeenth century, the idea that Indian chiefs were kings was considered self-evident. In 1608, the Jamestown colonists under Christopher Newport organized a "coronation of Powhatan," a ceremony intended to secure him and all those under his rule as tributaries to King James I of England. But the effort failed. John Smith writes of "the foule trouble there was to make him kneele to receive his crowne, he neither knowing the majesty nor meaning of a Crowne, nor bending of the knee" (2:184). In spite of this farce, after Powhatan's daughter, Pocahontas, was captured and taken to England, Smith wrote to Queen Anne that because "Lady Pocahontas" had married Englishman John Rolfe and borne a child by him, "this Kingdome might rightly have a Kingdome by her meanes" (2:260). Two royal houses could make a dynastic alliance by marriage that would result in an imperial advantage for England, Smith claimed. The New England Puritans were not such royalists as the Jamestown colonists, yet they dubbed Metacom "King Philip" and after killing him in 1676 sent his "royalties" to the king of England. By the 1760s, however, the notion that Indian leaders were hereditary monarchs had faded.[7] Many ethnographers had by then observed that chiefs could not pass their mantles on to their children and that the nature of their authority over their tribes was closer to that of a republic than a monarchy.

A sense of Native American societies as republics did not, however, make its people citizens of postcolonial nations such as the United States. Even when an Indian rebel leader was perceived as having led a revolution to defend his sovereignty against royalist colonizers, as Metacom was in several texts from the 1820s and 1830s, the respect accorded the chief did not extend to Native American people as a whole. Karen Kupperman and Francis Jennings have observed how in the sixteenth and seventeenth centuries, English colonists, some of whom had experience with the colonization of Ireland, expected Native Americans to behave like peasants. This prejudice can be said to have persisted through the nineteenth century, as removals, surveys, and enclosures turned Indians into a landless proletariat. The celebrity to which captured native leaders were treated—for example, the publicity tours of Little Turtle and Black Hawk—contrasts with the abuse and neglect of their tribespeople, who were often denied the land and annuities promised to them in treaties. This double standard is consistent with the ethos of tragic drama, which shows us only the elite class of the rulers, not the subaltern subjects being slaughtered by the thousands in offstage battles. It is also consistent with the historiography of the early nineteenth century, a period of transition from classicist traditions to the "great man" paradigms of romantics such as Thomas Carlyle. Histories of colonial conquest and Indian resistance in Spanish America had been written in a classicist style by sixteenth- and early-seventeenth-century authors such as Peter Martyr, Francisco Gomara, and the Inca Garcilaso de la Vega. Their grand *cronicas* often dramatized the violent encounters between the conquistadors and the Indians by writing long heroic speeches for the native leaders, much as the barbarians of northern Europe defied the Roman Caesars in Tacitus's *Germania* and *Agricola*. Although these historians generally supported the Spanish conquistadors, they often portrayed the Indian victims as dignified and stoic, undeserving of the brutal treatment so often meted out to them. Anglo-American colonial histories such as that of John Smith did not aim for such a high style but nonetheless often included brief orations by the Indian leaders. In the nineteenth century, this rhetorical feature was revived and combined with a more didactic mode of biography in the tradition of Plutarch and of Cotton Mather's exemplary lives of the New England colonial founders, resulting in edifying educational books that sought to inculcate the values of civil society by presenting the virtues of Native American leaders.

In 1832, when the craze for Indian stage tragedy had just taken off, there appeared two large books entitled *Indian Biography*, one in New York, in two volumes, written by B. B. (Benjamin Bussey) Thatcher, and the other in Boston by Samuel Gardner Drake.[8] Both were hugely successful. Thatcher's work saw thirteen editions by 1870, and Drake's reached its fifteenth, "revised by Prof. H. L. Williams," in 1880, five years after Drake's death. Several different publishers in New York, Boston, and Philadelphia released the books, most often in inexpensive editions designed to reach a broad audience. Drake's initial effort took the form of a biographical dictionary, beginning with Accompanet, followed by Adario, and ending with Wittuwamet on page 348. At twenty-six pages, the entry for King Philip (Metacom) was the book's longest, reflecting the fact that Drake had in 1825 published Benjamin Church's history of King Philip's War with an extensive critical commentary. Readers seem to have been more inclined to read Indian biographies as historical narratives than as reference works, however, because in the second edition Drake not only changed his title to avoid the confusion of two books titled *Indian Biography* but also changed the format, making it more like Thatcher's. Thatcher's text began as an 1831 article in the *North American Review* that was recycled in the first volume of *Indian Biography* as several chapters on Massassoit through King Philip's War. This first volume was devoted to the Indians surrounding the seventeenth-century English colonies in Virginia and New England. The second followed the Iroquois and the Algonquians of the Ohio Valley, including two chapters on Pontiac and three on Tecumseh. The whole was written in an engaging, accessible style, sympathetic toward the Indians but with few strident criticisms of the colonists and including eloquent addresses by the Indian leaders wherever a source for such speeches could be found. Drake seems to have been stunned by this competitor, whom he quickly imitated. In the September 1833 preface to his second edition, published under the title *The Book of the Indians of North America*, Drake explained, "The method of books and chapters was adopted, mainly for the benefit of combining history with biography. . . . It was not expected that a work of this kind would meet with a ready sale; but such was the case, and the very favorable reception with which the first edition met, was the cause of the early appearance of this."

The second edition was so successful that just two months later he released a third, with fifty pages of new material, *Biography and History of the Indians of North America*. Drake organized his work into five books, the first an essay on the ethnography of the Indian tribes and their prehistoric origins, the second and third on New England, the fourth on the "southern Indians," and the fifth on the Iroquois or Five Nations and other western tribes (west of Boston, that is). Even after Thatcher died in 1840, Drake did not rest but continually revised the work. Subsequent editions bore various titles, including *The Aboriginal Races of North America*, and through the 1830s and 1840s Drake kept up with the unfolding history of the bloody Creek and Seminole Wars by adding chapters to the book on the southern Indians, portraying Osceola as a hero every bit as valiant as Metacom or Tecumseh. Drake's republicanism may have reflected the politics of his New England base, but it was nonetheless militant and topical: he attacked Jackson and the Indian Removal Bill in his 1830s editions and the Southern Confederacy in the 1860s and 1870s.

Although they are almost entirely ignored by American scholars today, Thatcher and Drake wrote histories as serious and as carefully researched as those by more famous nineteenth-century romantic historians Francis Parkman, William Hickling Prescott, and George Bancroft.[9] And because thousands of American households owned copies of Drake and/or Thatcher, readers absorbed much of their knowledge of the nation's past not through a celebration of imperial conquest and its white leaders but from portraits of Indian leaders. In Drake's later editions, the names of all the colonial officers are italicized, but the names of the Indians appear in all capital letters. The books may have served as textbooks for schools, for Thatcher also published a juvenile version, *Tales of the Indians, being prominent passages from the history of the North American natives taken from authentic sources* (1831). In the preface to his first edition, Drake belittled Thatcher on this score, proclaiming, "There is no work before the public upon this subject, unless, indeed, some juvenile performances be so considered, recently published in New York." Nonetheless, Thatcher's *Tales of the Indians* was reprinted many times, and the genre endured into the twentieth century with works like the anonymous *Boy's Book of Indian Battles and Adventures* (1861) and Edwin Sabin's *The Boy's Book of Indian Warriors* (1918).

A third multivolume work of Indian biography also appeared in the 1830s, Thomas McKenney and James Hall's *The Indian Tribes of North America with Biographical Sketches and Anecdotes of the Principal Chiefs*. McKenney served as the superintendent of the Indian Trade Bureau until 1822 and then became the first head of the Bureau of Indian Affairs when Congress created it in 1824. As Indian leaders came to Washington to ratify treaties that expropriated their land, McKenney arranged for many of them to sit in Charles Bird King's studio for portraits, which he then hung in his office. As he traveled through the Great Lakes and Upper Mississippi regions in the 1820s, he sought out more native subjects, and at major councils such as Fond du Lac, Wisconsin, in 1826, James Otto Lewis, an apprentice of King's, painted more portraits that joined the gallery in Washington. McKenney's sympathetic stance toward the Indians did not fit with Andrew Jackson's removal policy, and McKenney was dismissed in 1830. He then turned his attention to publishing a lavish large-format edition of these portraits, an "elephant portfolio" of Indian specimens much like Audubon's contemporary elephant folio of his paintings and "ornithological biographies," *Birds of America*. Although the enterprise nearly drove McKenney bankrupt, two volumes containing 120 portraits were published in Philadelphia in 1836 and 1838, with biographies penned by Hall, a frontier jurist and journalist who also worked with Benjamin Drake. In 1844 a third volume appeared, consisting of two lengthy "Histories of the Indians" by McKenney and by Hall.[10] Although their work perhaps better deserved the title "Indian Biography" than Thatcher's did, it was not so historically comprehensive, and its much higher price limited its influence. The 120 Indians include only a few of the many major chiefs who were deceased by the 1820s: Joseph Brant and Cornplanter are included but not Metacom or Pontiac. The tribes that McKenney visited, including the Sioux, Sauk and Fox, and Chippewa, were also overrepresented in the selection. The portraits are compelling, however, and are less obviously romanticized than those of George Catlin, which were already attracting many visitors to galleries by the time McKenney's books appeared. The 120 also included many women and men of modest status. Catlin's portraits introduced a new iconography of Indian chiefs centered on the Plains tribes, with their buckskin leggings, feathered headdresses, and horseback Bison hunts, and this iconography still dominates twentieth-century Western art and popular savagism. This was quite different from the visual style of McKenney and Hall's collection and from the textual tropes of the Indian as tragic hero. Drake's and Thatcher's encyclopedic Indian biographies were the essential handbooks for this earlier literary tradition, and I will refer to them frequently in this volume. Let us now turn to this literary history of Indian tragedy.

Indian Drama as Literary and Performance Genre

In his 1955 history of the theater in the United States, *America Takes the Stage*, Richard Moody noted that "there were practically no native dramas until after the Revolution" (25) but that even in the absence of original dramatic works written and staged by the colonists, a form of theater nonetheless existed in eighteenth-century North America:

The numerous treaty meetings between the Indians and white men were essentially the first indigenous American dramatic expression. These "theatre-in-life" dramas recorded by various secretary interpreters, were solemn and serious in intent; and although the conflicts and problems treated were in the nature of life and death struggles, they were filled with theatrical and dramatic details: the exchanging of wampum belts and strings, the processionals to the treaty, the formal, stage-like form of address, the participation of the spectators as a kind of chorus, and the highly ingenious and romantic figures of speech. (78–79)

Life-and-death struggles certainly did hang on the speeches and decisions made at these meetings, and the fact that Native American communities were so often deceived by colonizers and the resulting treaties violated only enhances the sense of these meetings as real-life tragedies. Fifty years later, Daniel Richter also has discussed Indian diplomacy as a formulaic performance (137–49). Praise for the gravity and eloquence of oratory by native leaders was a commonplace in colonial accounts, and treaty speeches were not only printed for the public record but reprinted for general readers in histories and collections such as Cadwallader Colden's *The History of the Five Indian Nations*. In her study of oratory and performance in early America, Sandra Gustafson remarks on how Benjamin Franklin's published proceedings of the 1744 Lancaster Treaty between the Five Nations Iroquois and the colonies of Virginia, Pennsylvania, and Maryland "created the effect of performance on the printed page by employing a playlike format that emphasized the theatrical dimensions of the proceedings," including "a list of participants resembling the dramatis personae of a playbill" (121). Franklin printed more than a thousand copies and distributed them throughout the colonies and to Britain, reaching an audience far wider than merely those people interested in the treaty's legal stipulations. Not only was (and is) the treaty speech a popular oratorical genre among Anglo-American audiences, but it also was just one of many performance genres among the predominantly oral cultures of Native America.[11]

Another was "chanson de mort," or "death song," which a man sang to his tribe to arouse its warriors' martial spirit and sang to his enemies if he were captured and tortured. The captors expected and relished the warrior's recitation of defiant threats and past battlefield successes because it proved the bravery of the man they had defeated. This bravery would then be symbolically incorporated into the captors' tribe, particularly in Iroquois society, through a ritual cannibalism that involved eating small pieces of the victim's heart. The appropriation of the power of the Indian tragic hero into colonial society involved a similar symbolic process. The death song genre was adopted into colonial dramatic literature in such instances as "The Son of Alknomook," included in Royall Tyler's *The Contrast* (1787) and in the first opera composed in the United States, Ann Julia Hatton's *The Songs of Tammany* (1794).[12]

The diplomatic protocol of frontier treaty conferences allowed native leaders such as Pontiac and Tecumseh to speak in their own languages even if they knew French or English. And because colonial officials at such councils rarely understood local languages, these meetings were less diplomatic conversations than a series of performances. Many at these councils had to focus on the speaker before the interpreter made it possible for them to understand his speech, and as Colden wrote, "I suspect our Interpreters may not have done Justice to the Indian Eloquence" (xi). The impression of eloquence came largely from the speaker's tone, pace, and gestures. For most Euro-Americans, frontier treaty meetings were akin to watching an opera without subtitles. There is thus a certain logic in the fact that Hatton's opera was an Indian pageant, although it was not in the Lenape language of its hero, the Delaware chief Tamenund (Tammany). For their part, natives often remarked that Europeans spoke poorly or failed to respect the more eloquent native orators, too frequently interrupting them. Men such as Tecumseh's foe, William Henry Harrison, negotiated from a position of military strength but faced a strong challenge if they wished to match the eloquence of their counterparts. As we shall see in chapter 8, Harrison's recorded speeches rose to this challenge by using the Indians' diplomatic metaphors, such as covenant chains and buried hatchets.[13]

Treaty negotiations offered a setting for intercultural performances in which both natives and Euro-Americans were simultaneously actors and audience. Native Americans who were taken to Europe or to East Coast cities played unwitting (and generally unwilling) roles in a quite different sort of theatrics. Americans taken to Europe in the sixteenth century were often compelled to dramatize their lives in spectacles mounted for the entertainment of the transatlantic navigators' kingly patrons, and paintings and engravings of these spectacles constitute some of the earliest European art depicting Native Americans. In Toledo, Spain, in 1528, Christoph Wieditz drew the juggling and ball-playing performances of Mexicans brought by Cortés to King Charles V (Honour 59–61). In Rouen in 1550 a corps of fifty Brazilians portrayed themselves in a mock village constructed on the banks of the Seine for the occasion of a state visit by King Henri II (Honour 63). Another spectacle in Rouen in 1563 afforded Michel de Montaigne the chance to speak with Tupis captured in Brazil by Nicolas Durand de Villegagnon, an encounter that inspired Montaigne's famous essay, "On Cannibals." American Indian captives were presented to European monarchs both as imperial prizes and as entertaining novelties. The iconography of these spectacles associated them with luxury products obtained from their homelands, such as feathers and dyewoods, and the spectacles resembled the court masques that also employed leading dramatists such as Ben Jonson. Native American "kings" and "princesses" were expected to play up to this royal status, either as a masque or farce or as a genuine diplomatic confrontation. The 1710 visit of the four Iroquois "kings" to London is perhaps the best known of such encounters. William Davenant dedicated a performance of his musical version of Macbeth to the Iroquois who attended it at the Queen's Theatre in the Haymarket, and when the audience demanded a better view of the "kings," they were moved from their box to seats on the stage. During a 1765 visit to London, Mohawk emissaries were so offended by being constantly put on display that they appealed to the House of Lords, which passed a resolution prohibiting the "unbecoming and Inhuman" practice of "making a public shew of Indians" (qtd. in Dowd, *War* 68).

A similar commotion occurred when "a large delegation of Western Indians" attended a performance of *Metamora* at the Tremont Theater in Boston and "were so excited by the performance that in the closing scene they rose and chanted a dirge in honor of the death of the great chief" (Alger 1:240). Contemporary journalists and later theater historians relished such moments both for the way they suggested the theatrical or imaginary status of the Indian "kings" and, conversely, as in the case of Metamora, for the implication that the stage portrayal of Metacom received a stamp of authenticity from "real" Indians. Colonizers were always anxious to see their preconceptions of Indians confirmed. When John Ross, Cherokee leader and a wealthy owner of a plantation and slaves, came to Washington in 1836, he was taken to see a production of the Indian drama *Pocahontas; or, The Settlers of Virginia*, at the National Theater. A local newspaper reported that "Ross and his 'merrie men' . . . performed their real Indian war dance, exhibiting hate, triumph, revenge, etc., and went through the agreeable ceremony of scalping, all of which seemed to give great satisfaction to a crowded house." Ross wrote a letter of rebuttal to the paper (*Globe*, 13 February 1836, qtd. in Bank 67). He suggested that non-Cherokee actors had been hired to disrupt the performance as a publicity stunt (Scheckel 59). Later in the nineteenth century, many Plains Indians took jobs portraying Indians in Buffalo Bill Cody's Wild West Show, a spectacle that white audiences actually took quite seriously as edifying and educational. Sioux autobiographer Black Elk joined Buffalo Bill's show in the belief that by doing so, he would be teaching audiences about his culture.

These scenes of dramatic encounter between Native American and Euro-American peoples—at frontier treaty councils, in theaters, or in open-air spectacles—support a definition of cultural and racial identity as performative. In spite of the nineteenth century's pervasive rhetoric of race as blood, as essentialist and hierarchical, the representation of racial identity was often a question of performance. The Indian tragedies profoundly affected the popular conception of Native Americans, even though the authors and actors were not Indians. Indians generally could not respond to these plays with hostile reviews, but their appearances on the stage of the "theatre-in-life," to use Moody's term, constituted an intercultural reply that was not limited to print publications. Hence, in this study I will redress a critical paradigm in American studies that has long valued narrative literature, especially the novel, over dramatic literature such as the Indian tragedies and the oratory of treaties and councils. One consequence of this paradigm is that a small corpus of published writings by Native American authors prior to 1850 has been held up as virtually the sole manifestation of the native "voice" in American literature of the period, while oratorical performances by the likes of Pontiac and Tecumseh are relegated to a secondary, uncertain status. A second consequence is that the early American novel receives a disproportionate share of critical attention, while early American drama remains a tiny scholarly subspecialty in spite of the fact that stage versions of novels (Cooper's *The Wept of Wish-ton-Wish*, Bird's *Nick of the Woods*, and Richardson's *Wacousta* are three that we will examine in this volume) often had wider success than the novels themselves.

In chapters 4, 5, and 8 I will focus in part on the orations of Pontiac, Logan, and Tecumseh and on the Indian tragedies written about them within a lifetime after their uprisings. I shall concentrate on Indian dramas about those three men as well as about Metacom, but I must acknowledge that the genre has a long history. Most scholars of English and American literature cite John Dryden and Richard Howard's *The Indian Queen* (1664) and Dryden's sequel, *The Indian Emperor; or, The Conquest of Mexico by the Spaniards* (1667) as initiating the tradition of Indian plays. Don Wilmeth indicates that his research "has identified over six hundred plays that fit this category from 1606 to the present" (2). Wilmeth's count must include the many Indian plays in other European languages. In the 1780s and 1790s, when Royall Tyler, Susannah Rowson, and William Dunlap began writing original plays for the American stage, German playwright August von Kotzebue was perhaps the most popular in the transatlantic theater, and two of his most successful works were set amid the Spanish conquest of Peru: *Die Sonnenjungfrau* (1791) and its sequel, *Die Spanier in Peru; oder, Rollas Tod* (1795). The two plays turn on a love triangle involving Cora, an Inca "virgin of the sun" (see Vega, *Royal Commentaries* 195–203); Rolla, a noble and heroic Inca; and Alonzo, a virtuous Spaniard opposed to Pizarro. Eugene Jones cites "at least eight versions of *The Virgin of the Sun* and not fewer than eleven adaptations of *The Spaniards of Peru*" (9), including William Dunlap's and Richard Sheridan's, which were both titled simply *Pizarro*. In addition to Kotzebue's works about early colonial America, his countryman, Johann Wilhelm Rose, wrote a play about Pocahontas (1784), and a Frenchman, Le Blanc de Guillet, wrote one titled *Manco Capac* (1763) (Chinard, *Amérique* 404, which also cites several more French Indian dramas). The Incas of Peru were particularly popular in the eighteenth century, as in Françoise de Graffigny's *Lettres d'une Peruvienne* (1747), and Jean-François Marmontel's novel of the conquest, *Les Incas* (1777), which originated the story adopted by Kotzebue and took a strong anti-Spanish stance.

The Spanish corpus of Indian drama is even richer and, as we shall see in the next chapter, offers evidence that Indians in the Americas may have been exposed to European tragic drama from early in the 1500s, making possible a syncretism of imperial dramatic forms. As Gordon Brotherston has observed, the Spanish sought to expose the Indians to Golden Age plays, but the native converts who translated and performed these works often shifted the language and staging to invert their original religious and ideological intent. As one example, Brotherston cites "Calderón's El gran teatro del mundo (1641), whose doctrinal content is distinctly reformulated in the Nahuatl of Bartolomé de Alva Ixtlilxochitl, a descendant of the house of Tezcoco" (Book of the Fourth World 314), a family that also included a sixteenth-century native historian of the conquest, Fernando de Alva Ixtlilxochitl. Aesop was also translated into Nahuatl, and Virgil and Racine into Quechua. Tragedy does not appear to have held any preeminence over other genres, as all kinds of elite European literature have been translated into native languages in Spanish America, and natives have creatively subverted the imperial messages contained in many of these texts. By the early-nineteenth-century era of revolutions in Latin America, Indian tragedies supported nationalist movements there as they did in North America. I will examine Xicoténcatl, an anonymous text about the conquest of Mexico, in chapter 2, and Columbian author José Fernández Madrid penned the plays Atala (1822) and Guatimoc (1827) (the former an adaptation of Chateaubriand's novella).

Although Dryden's works thus claim primacy in the English literary history of the Indian drama and mark a rare contribution to the genre by a canonical author, they are not of central interest for our purposes. Dryden set his works in Mesoamerica, the first just prior to and the second in the midst of the Spanish invasion, but the setting is exotic rather than historical. The Indian Queen begins with a battle between the Mexica and the Incas, which of course never took place, and names some of its characters after Mexican city-states (Zempoalla, Traxalla) in a fashion that bears no relation to those cities' historical roles. "Montezuma" fights for the Incas. Elaborate costumes and sets, including feather headdresses brought from Surinam by Aphra Behn (see Oroonoko 2), provided the exotic American interest. The epilogue appealed to wit and the audience for approval, for "considering the cost / Tis a true voyage to the Indies lost" if the production failed, and Joseph Addison quipped in The Spectator that the "ordinary method of making an Heroe is to clap a huge Plume of feathers upon his head" (qtd. in Roach 130). The Indian Emperor dramatizes the conquest of New Spain led by Cortés and his henchmen and represents some of the key events of this history that we will examine in the next chapter, such as a love interest between Cortez and Montezuma's daughter and the torture of Montezuma in an effort to compel him to reveal more golden treasures. "Pizarro," however, does the dirty work, while Cortez remains a hero too noble for such tactics. At the close of the play, Montezuma does not die but departs with his people for the northern wilderness. This could be the Aztlan of his primitive ancestors, but it is also a convenient Indian removal that leaves Mexico and its riches to the Spanish conquerors, a colonialist denouement similar to that of such nineteenth-century novels about seventeenth-century New England as *Hope Leslie* and *Hobomok*. Richard Slotkin has observed that in contrast to Dryden's Montezuma, "Rogers's Ponteach, on the other hand, is clearly the rightful possessor of his soil" (240). Rogers provides a more dignified treatment of his hero not only, as Slotkin has suggested, because of the fashion for neoclassical stoicism in eighteenth-century theater, for we shall see that this became a hackneyed trope of Indian tragedy. Ponteach's genuinely heroic figure arises, I believe, from the fact that Rogers was there. He met Pontiac and fought against his rebels, and his play bears the mark of this experience. If the *Monthly Review* called *Ponteach* "one of the most absurd productions we have ever seen" (qtd. in Moody, *America Takes the Stage* 85), this merely suggests that European audiences did not appreciate the value of this experience.

The element that most strongly links Dryden's Indian plays to those of the nineteenth-century United States that portrayed Tecumseh, Metacom, and Logan also appears in classical tragedies—the use of dreams and omens that foretell the destiny of the tragic heroes. In *The Indian Queen*, Zempoalla, the female ruler of Mexico, tells of a dream in which she held a lion by a thread. A dove came and pecked through the thread, and the lion "presently turned all his rage on me." The lion evidently represents Montezuma, the Inca warrior she holds captive, but Zempoalla must defer to the interpretation of the dream made by her priest, Ismeron. In *The Indian Emperor*, Montezuma consults a high priest who informs him,

A Nation loving Gold must rule this place,
Our temples Ruine, and our Rites deface
To them, o King, is thy lost sceptre given. (act 2, scene 1)

Although Montezuma replies, "I'le scorn my destiny" and ignores the omen, the priest persists and even seeks confirmation from another priest, Kalib.

As Priscilla Sears has commented in one of two published monographs on the U.S. Indian dramas, the heroes and their priests "interpret natural events as supernatural signs; vengeance is generally assumed to be a divine commandment" (53). But these signs often foretell the failure of the natives' resistance. In Stone's *Metamora*, the soothsayer priest, Kaneshine, does not tell Metamora the results of the prayer of augury to Manito, the Algonquian Great Spirit, until act 5, when the hero is already at war with the English. Kaneshine "beheld gasping under a hemlock, the lightning had sometime torn, a panther wounded and dying in his thick red gore. I thought of the

tales of our forefathers who told us that such was an omen of coming evil"
(94). The omen is even worse than he knows, for in the play's opening scene,
the heroine, Oceana, tells of how Metamora saved her life by slaying, with a
lightning-like arrow, a panther that was about to attack her. The panther
stands for Metamora's violent rebellion, and his virtuous character obliges
him to protect all friendly English settlers. The omen that foretells Ponteach's demise also involves symbolic animals and, as in *The Indian Queen*,
comes to the Indian leader in a dream. In a scene with his two sons, Chekitan and Philip, and his aide, Tenesco, Ponteach says,

> my last Night's Dream I will relate,
> Which much disturb'd my weary anxious Mind,
> And must portend some signal grand Event
> Of good or Evil both to me or mine.
> On yonder Plain I saw the lordly Elk
> Snuffing the empty Air in seeming Sport,
> Tossing his Head aloft, as if in Pride
> Of his great Bulk and nervous active Limbs,
> And Scorn of every Beast that haunts the Wood.
> With mighty Stride he travelled to and fro,
> And as he mov'd his Size was still increas'd,
> Till his wide Branches reached above the Trees,
> And his extended Trunk across the Plain. (204)

The other animals, including "Wolves, Panthers, and Porcupines," attack
"with Force united," but the giant Elk "trampled and spurn'd them with his
Hoofs and Horns" (204). The function of the trope of dream omens in this
play is more complex than in most Indian tragedies. Chekitan, whose loyalty
to his father's rebellion is compromised by his love for Monelia, daughter of
the pro-English Mohawk chief, Hendrick (the name of an actual Mohawk),
tells his father, "I fear these Things portend no Good to us" (205). But Philip
contends,

> It ne'er was counted ill to dream of Elks,
> But always thought portentous of Success,
> Of happy Life, and Victories in War. (205)

Angry at his brother for having sold away a captive Illinois girl, Donanta,
with whom Philip was in love, Philip later kills Monelia out of jealousy.
Ponteach's tragic hubris therefore comes not from a superstitious dread of
the omen or from a stubborn defiance of it but simply from his decision to
follow the martial confidence of one son rather than the cautious warnings
of the other. Each son is in his own a way a traitor, and Ponteach's decision is

conscious and rational, not bound to superstition. The dream follows the trope without diminishing the free will of Ponteach's character. Its lines of elegant pentameter enhance the play, and its resemblance to actual native legends of a past era, when game animals were much bigger—legends that may reflect memories of the Pleistocene megafauna—suggest that Rogers may have based it on tales he heard from tribal storytellers.

Such omens and the heathen priests who interpret them have been a common ingredient of hubris since the dawn of tragedy. Aeschylus's *The Persians* is in fact the earliest drama in the Western tradition, composed in 472 B.C. and based on the Battle of Salamis in 480 B.C., in which Aeschylus fought. The tragic hero, Xerxes, was emperor of the Persians, whose invasion of Greece Herodotus describes in much greater detail (books 7–9). The play focuses on the floating bridge that Xerxes ordered built across the Hellespont and how his retreating soldiers fell from it into the water. Although the Aristotelean unity of time limits the action to the day when Xerxes receives news of the defeat, his mother, Atossa, foretells the arrival of this bad news when she recounts a dream. She dreams of two women, one Greek and one Persian, whom Xerxes tries unsuccessfully to yoke together to his chariot. When she awakens, she goes to an altar to make a sacrifice, only to witness a conflict between animals that seems to recapitulate the dream and to confirm it as an ill omen for her son's military expedition:

> But there I saw an eagle flying toward the hearth
> Of Apollo's altar; speechless I stood in fear, my friends.
> A moment later I saw a hawk circle about,
> Then rush at the eagle with flapping wings and tear his head
> With its claws. The eagle did nothing more than cower and yield
> To the hawk. A dreadful sight this was for me to see. (lines 206–10)

Other elements of *The Persians* also contribute to an analysis of nineteenth-century Indian dramas, and while full consideration of the historiography of the Persian War is impossible here, a structural comparison to the Indian tragedy is straightforward. The Persians stand as the barbaric Other to classical Greece, and the Hellespont forms a symbolic and geographic separation between Europe and Asia, enlightenment and superstition, freedom and tyranny. In Aeschylus's tragedy, "The gods are keeping the Goddess Pallas' city [Athens] safe" (line 347), yet Xerxes is nonetheless the hero and is likewise the central character of books 7 and 8 of Herodotus (which some scholars believe were originally intended to form a separate work; see 21). In the nineteenth-century Indian plays as well, the enemy leader becomes the literary hero. Aeschylus's experience fighting against Xerxes enhances this interest as well as Aeschylus's bona fides as author of the work. Xerxes' ultimate defeat forecloses any actual fear that Greek audiences might have of him, and the tragedy thus facilitates a subversive fascination with the Persian foe. Aeschylus's tragedy casts Xerxes as the hero who is condemned to defeat but at the same time subverts this imperial ideology by inviting the audience to embrace the Persian and his cause. Moreover, as Herodotus acknowledges, the ranks of the Persian army include a good number of Greeks. The polarization between East and West, self and Other, civilization and barbarism is not as absolute as one might assume.

The one thing missing in Aeschylus that became essential to the nineteenth-century Indian tragedy was the same ingredient that historical novels and dramas from Sir Walter Scott to Hollywood have always included—a love interest, particularly liaisons between Native Americans and Europeans. This, after all, is the theme of the Pocahontas story, which generated several plays: Joseph Croswell's A New World Planted (1802) had a heroine named "Pocahonta," but she was the daughter of New England's "King Massassoit," not of Powhatan. James Nelson Barker's The Indian Princess; or, La Belle Sauvage (1808), a musical or "operatic melo-drame" (with a score that has survived), was the first in the U.S. theater to dramatize the legend of the rescue of John Smith. During the heyday of the Indian plays, several more Pocahontas vehicles appeared: George Washington Parke Custis's Pocahontas; or, The Settlers of Virginia (1830), Robert Dale Owen's Pocahontas, A Historical Drama (1837), and Charlotte Barnes Connor's The Forest Princess; or, Two Centuries Ago (1848) as well as Powhatan: A Metrical Romance, in Seven Cantos (1841) by Seba Smith. By the 1850s, the theme—and the Indian drama as a whole—was ripe for parody, and John Brougham provided it with Po-ca-hon-tas; or, The Gentle Savage (1855) and Metamora; or, The Last of the Pollywogs (1847). It is noteworthy that Barker was mayor of Philadelphia; Owen was a congressman and then founder of the utopian community at New Harmony, Indiana; and Custis was the grandson of Martha Washington and therefore the closest descendant of the infertile Founding Father. The Pocahontas myth lent itself to a patriotic stage treatment of national origins, and to be associated with such an Indian hero or heroine might advance one's political career, as vice presidential candidate Richard Johnson did in hiring Richard Emmons to write Tecumseh; or, The Battle of the Thames, a National Drama as a campaign puff piece for the 1836 election. The Pocahontas legend was distinctly a romance, however, not a tragedy. In these plays as in the 1995 Disney feature film, Powhatan has no opportunity for tragic heroism but is consigned to a secondary role as the blocking father of the heroine. Pocahontas must avert a marriage to an Indian named Kocoum (Disney), Matacoran (Custis), or Miami (Barker) to find her love and happiness with John Rolfe (see the Disney sequel). As Susan Scheckel points out in her analysis of the Pocahon-

tas plays, the spurned lover of the heroine has the tragic role in these romantic comedies. Matacoran in particular is "the defeated but proudly defiant
noble savage who futilely resists the advance of 'civilization' " (65).

The familiar contrast between romance and tragedy can help to organize the corpus of nineteenth-century American Indian dramas. At the tragic
extreme lie plays such as Joseph Doddridge's *Logan, the Last of the Race
of Shikellemus, Chief of the Cayuga Nation*, discussed in detail in chapter 5.
This work includes only one female character and focuses on the struggles
and strategies of Logan and the Shawnee warriors before the 1774 battle of
Point Pleasant. The Spartan, masculine severity of these tragedies reflects an
ethos in which martial duty outweighs even familial—much less romantic—
affection and in which the rhetorical flourish "Better to perish thus than
breathe as slaves" speaks of a very real dilemma.

That particular line is from *Carabasset: A Tragedy, in Five Acts*, published in
Portland, Maine, in 1830 by Nathaniel Deering. The play is based on the
killing of French Jesuit missionary Sebastien Rasles and members of the
Norridgewock tribe by New England troops in 1724 (see Samuel Drake,
Aboriginal Races 312). This history became central to William Carlos Williams's *In the American Grain*, and Deering's Indian tragedy, like the novels and
plays about King Philip's War examined in chapter 3, demonstrates how
already in the 1820s a revisionist critique of New England Indian wars was
well developed. The heroine of this play is Adelaide, a daughter of the Baron
Castine, a French colonial officer who was infamous in seventeenth-century
New England for having gone native and married the daughter of an Abenaki
chief. The villain is Ravillac, an orphan of French parents who has been
adopted by Ralle (as Rasles's name is spelled in the play). Ravillac threatens
the chastity of Adelaide, who is protected by Ralle, and tries to avenge his
parents' death by inciting the Norridgewocks to attack the English. Carabasset is weary of the violence of Queen Anne's War and declines French
requests to mount another battle: "Let the pale faces spill each other's
blood" (24), he says. But then Ravillac murders Carabasset's wife, Rena, a
convert of Ralle's, and contrives to have the English blamed for the killing.
Carabasset's lines to Ralle echo Logan's speech, which inspired Doddridge's
play, and include another hackneyed simile for the vanishing Indian:

> Who mourns for Carabasset? Is he not
> Like the scath'd pine on which the flame hath fed,
> Till it is sapless, naked and decaying. (31)

The fifth act portrays the assault by two hundred New England soldiers
under Joseph Moulton, who kills Rasles and destroys "a handsome church,
on which the English committed a double sacrilege, first robbing it, then

setting it on fire," as Samuel Drake describes it (*Aboriginal Races* 311), drawing on François-Xavier de Charlevoix's *Histoire de la Nouvelle France* to rebuke the New Englanders and celebrate the martyred Rasles, over whose mutilated body, Charlevoix claimed, the Norridgewoks had shed many tears. In the play, Carabasset and his warrior, Taconet, refuse to flee for their lives, instead staying to guard Ralle and a refugee Englishwoman named Agnes. Ravillac then kills Ralle, and Carabasset delivers his final defiant speech, enters battle against the English, and then jumps off a cliff before they can slay him.

Although its hero is now obscure, *Carabasset* is typical of the Indian tragedy genre. Carabasset earns our admiration by upholding ethical principles that transcend the sordid frontier violence in which he is caught up. He favors neither the French nor the English side but like Rasles offers shelter to refugees from both sides. He fights only in self-defense and refuses to be made a prisoner or a slave. That Deering should write, stage, and publish in Portland, Maine, a play strongly criticizing this bloody attack on the local Indian peoples a century earlier suggests that many Mainers wished to disavow the same colonial processes that had created their society and sympathized with one of its victims, Carabasset. This may seem like hypocrisy, but if so, it is no greater than that of many American readers today who buy books such as Dee Brown's *Bury My Heart at Wounded Knee*, Peter Matthiessen's *In the Spirit of Crazy Horse*, or novels by many of the most popular contemporary Native American authors. *Carabasset* promoted a sense of cathartic ambivalence, and although Deering did not put it in the title, Carabasset of course is, as he declares in his climactic speech, "The last of all the Norridgewocks—a race / Who die in battle" (54). For unlike Powhatan and other chiefs in Indian romance dramas, Carabasset has no daughter—indeed, has no surviving heir when the curtain falls. Adelaide plays the role of a melodrama heroine whose virtue is threatened by the villain, but she has no lover, so the play lacks any romance subplot.

John McWilliams has observed in *The American Epic* that epic historical romances about American Indians break into two traditions, one, including Magua and Pontiac, that "led writers to imagine the Indian as hard, solitary, unyielding, aged, and doomed" and a second, including Yamoyden and Uncas, that "led writers to imagine the Indian as graceful, generous, pliable, young, and equally doomed" (127). Notably, Eastburn and Sands's epic poem on King Philip's War, *Yamoyden*, includes both types. As chapter 3 will demonstrate, the titular hero, Yamoyden, who has no historical basis, is in love with the English heroine, Nora, while Philip plays the rigid tragic hero who cannot tolerate such a "soft" romantic betrayal by one of his warriors. McWilliams's two categories match closely my definition of the tragic and romance strains of Indian drama.

Werner Sollors's analysis in *Beyond Ethnicity* offers more insight on the Indian dramas and their ideology of form. Sollors discusses *Carabasset*, *Metamora*, Richard Emmons's *Tecumseh*, and Lewis Deffebach's *Oolaita; or, The Indian Heroine* (1821) and observes how "the conflict between parentally arranged marriage and romantic love is connected to the Indian theme" (109). In *Oolaita*, the heroine's father, Sioux chief Machiwita, wants her to marry the elderly Monoma, but she is in love with a young Sioux warrior, Tululla. Monoma sends warriors to kill his rival, but Tululla defeats them. At the same time, Oolaita intervenes to protect Stephen and Eumelia, white captives who had eloped across the frontier and married against their parents' wishes. Machawita still refuses to give his consent for his daughter's love marriage, and she commits suicide by jumping from a locally famous "Lovers' Leap" near Lake Pepin on the Upper Mississippi River. *Oolaita* typifies the romance version of Indian dramas insofar as the sacrifice of life or love by the Indian hero or heroine helps to secure life and love for white colonist(s). The love interest is heightened when it is a crossracial love affair, as in *Ouâbi; or, The Virtues of Nature: An Indian Tale* (1790), a dramatic verse romance by Sarah Wentworth Apthorp Morton. Morton's work drew on some of the same history as *Carabasset*: she acknowledged that her white hero, Celario, was based on the Indianized Frenchman Saint-Castin. Celario saves the life of an Illinois chief, Ouâbi, after he is captured by enemy Hurons, and Ouâbi in return divorces his beloved wife, Azakia, so that she can marry Celario instead. Sollors, writing several years before Jay Fliegelman published *Prodigals and Pilgrims: The American Revolution against Patriarchal Authority*, calls attention to the politics of romance and marriage in the early republic and proposes that the plots of these Indian dramas reflect a conflict between legitimacy and republicanism: "The legitimate rule of the Indians, based on descent and long residence, was threatened and overthrown by republican immigrants. In the period from the American Revolution to the Civil War, this process was perceived as parallel to that of European bourgeois revolutions against indigenous aristocracies" (102). The plots of *Oolaita*, *Ouâbi*, and *Metamora* suggest a reconciliation between these principles, as the Indian chief/monarch fails to impose his will on his daughter and/or facilitates the love marriage of a white immigrant hero(ine). Although Sollors does not discuss *Metamora* at length, his theory of "red-white fusion, of the newcomers becoming one with the continent, of gaining legitimacy through love and in defiance of the greed for gold and the ruthless politics which were sometimes logically associated with white fathers" (127) fits the interpretation of that play I propose in chapter 3. *Metamora* not only protects the heroine, Oceana, from her evil suitor and blocking father but symbolically adopts her as a daughter and bestows his legitimacy on her marriage to the hero, Walter, and the republican future of their New England home. The severity of the Indian tragedy is softened by a melodramatic love story, and this formal blend of tragedy and romance accomplishes a political reconciliation of Indian sovereignty and colonial settlement, of republican values and imperial history. Scheckel makes a similar argument for the Pocahontas plays.

These plays thus worked to reconcile political and ethnic differences in the interests of a hegemonic U.S. national purpose. Other dramas and epics—the ones McWilliams would place at the "hard" end of his spectrum— emphasize the virtues of masculine self-discipline in the tradition of republican tragedy. Julie Ellison has traced the origins of this neoclassical stage genre to the Whig exclusion crisis in England in the 1680s, and she collects several of its founding works, notably John Dennis's Liberty Asserted (1704) and Joseph Addison's Cato (1712), under the term "Roman Plays." Liberty Asserted was loosely adapted from the history of King William's War between the British and French and their Iroquois and Huron allies but used the North American setting as a political allegory to exploit "the swell of national feeling following Marlborough's victory [over the French] at Blenheim in August 1703" (77). These dramas are notable for African, Native American, or mixed-blood characters who subordinate their romantic or familial bonds to a homosocial loyalty to Roman or English father figures. From Addison's hero, Juba, to Robert Rogers's Ponteach, Ellison traces how "tragedy in the Roman vein still served in London as a vehicle for the exemplary Indian. This figure had long been conflated with the doomed republican and descended as well from the neoclassical glamour of the suffering native heroes in Dryden's Indian Emperor (1665) and Behn's Oroonoko (1688)" (92). I wish to extend Ellison's work to the Indian tragedies of nineteenth-century America, for, as we shall see, Metamora, like Liberty Asserted, proposes a complex analogy between North American and English politics. The Indian tragic heroes embody the republican virtues that J. G. A. Pocock has argued were so important to the political theory of the U.S. Founding Fathers, but the heroes ultimately must sacrifice their lives and the future of their tribes to the imperial designs of that same United States. As Philip Gould has written, "Metamora's death belies a political paradox at the heart of the 'Indian' melodrama: the Native American hero exhibits republican virtues that implicitly legitimate claims both for Native American citizenship and public identity, but these claims are ultimately erased by either his death or his disappearance" ("Remembering" 119). For the Indian heroes of republican tragedies, the hubris of defending their people is not only a tragic flaw but a republican virtue, yet it nonetheless dooms them to defeat.

There is one constant in the Indian dramas. From "hard" tragedy to "soft" romance, the Indian chief must die at the end—or, in a few cases, such as Dryden's Montezuma, remove himself across a frontier to make way for European conquest. Critics' interpretations of the Indian dramas, most of

which focus on the genre's epitome, Stone's *Metamora*, have therefore read Native American resistance as being thoroughly contained in the plays and the audience's potentially subversive identification with the heroes as strictly limited. Several recent books and articles (surveyed in chapter 3) read *Metamora* as endorsing President Andrew Jackson's Indian removal policy, which was proposed at the time the play premiered, and read its hero as emblematic of the vanishing Indian. In the last scene, Metamora's son is shot by the English, he stabs his wife to keep her from the "white man's bondage," and he finally takes a bullet from "Church" (representing the historical Benjamin Church, who tracked Metacom down in August 1676). Thus, the English triumph in King Philip's War was reenacted on stage. But as I will argue at length, to interpret the ending of this and other Indian tragedies as unequivocally triumphalist, anti-Indian, and proremoval ignores both important contextual evidence and a rich literary tradition. The tradition appears in Metamora's final lines, when he threatens, "Murderers! The last of the Wampanoags' curse be on you! May your graves and the graves of your children be in the path the red man shall trace! And may the wolf and the panther howl o'er your fleshless bones" (98). Did the audience pity, fear, or laugh? Did they scoff at such threats from a dying enemy? Or did they sense that the curse still haunted them and that it was being fulfilled in the form of frontier wars such as those in progress in the 1830s and 1840s against the Seminoles in Florida? McWilliams refers to "the mixture of awe, fear, and guilt with which white audiences contemplated the possibility that the controlling Indian response to dispossession would be the unchecked rage of an Achilles or a Turnus" (131). Sollors raises the question of why "American audiences liked even the 'anti-white' curse scenes in the Indian plays as if they had been blessings!" The best answer Sollors can offer, however, is that "Freud illustrated the antithetical sense of primal words; and the relationship of curses and blessings is the related case of an affinity between antithetical concepts" (124). We have to do better than that.

Indian Resistance and Imperial Epic

The defiant curse that the dying Indian leader invokes on his conquerors accentuates the ideological ambivalence that I have argued is characteristic of catharsis in the Indian tragedy. It also follows an epic topos traceable to the blinded Polyphemus's curse on Odysseus, and, as David Quint has shown, revived in Spanish epics about Indian wars in the Americas. Both

Quint and José Rabasa discuss the curse delivered by defeated Acoma Indians at the end of one of the few full-blown epic poems written about
colonial Indian wars in North America, Gaspar Perez de Villagrá's *Historia de
la Nuevo Mexico* (1610). Their contrasting readings of the scene put into relief
these issues of sympathetic identification and (anti)colonial politics. Villagrá
took part in Juan de Oñate's 1598 expedition to extend the northern frontier
of New Spain by conquering and converting the Pueblo Indians. His title is
somewhat overstated, for although his first few cantos relate the Aztec myth
of origin in Aztlan, which was vaguely located in New Mexico, and something of Cabeza de Vaca's journey through the area a half century earlier,
the second half of the work concentrates on a single vicious battle against
the Pueblo of Acoma, led by their heroic chief, Zutacapán. As in many of the
Indian tragedies and poems we will examine in this volume, dissenters
within the tribe, including the chief's son, Zutancalpo, and a 120-year-old
elder with the unfortunate name of Chumpo, challenge their leader's martial resolve and thereby aid the invaders. Oñate's victory was decisive and
brutal—of the six hundred surviving Acomans who surrendered, he sentenced all men over the age of 25 to have one foot amputated. Villagrá's
account does not precisely follow other documentary sources and was written in part as an effort to defend Oñate against the criminal charges of which
he was convicted in 1614, so the final curse should not be taken as fact. We
need to read it as a trope.

Two Acoma warriors, Tempal and Cotumbo, flee the scene of surrender
and hole up in a kiva for three days. Rather than surrender, they accept
Oñate's offer of two ropes with which to hang themselves. The two warriors
announce their departure for the afterlife just before they leap from the
branch of a tree, but they threaten the Spaniards that "if we can return to
avenge ourselves, no sons born to Castilian or Indian mothers in the whole
wide world will be as wretched as you" (Quint 101). Rabasa focuses on the
lines that follow, where Villagrá observes that foam spurts out of the hanged
men's mouths, followed by "their hidden tongues, now all swollen / And
tightly clenched between their teeth" (Rabasa 158), one of countless gory
details in the text. For Rabasa, "Villagrá's poem exemplifies an aesthetic of
colonial violence that draws its legitimacy from an ideology of just war
against Indians, but whose force of representation resides in the use of
grotesque images that rob indigenous peoples of all dignity, even in death"
(158). Such grotesque violence is customary in epic (while it is difficult to
represent on stage), but its repetition helps "keep the audience from em-
pathizing with suffering" (Rabasa 139). I agree with Rabasa inasmuch as
Villagrá's work fails to grant the Acoma warriors more than the barest shred
of the respect accorded Indian heroes in other colonial North American

epics and tragedies, but Rabasa does not allow that Tempal and Cotumbo's self-sacrifice might confer on them a certain dignity of suffering that carried a good deal of weight for contemporary Spanish readers. The Spanish colony of New Mexico that Oñate established eventually made the conversion of the Pueblo Indians its primary justification, and many of the Franciscan missionaries there, much like their Jesuit contemporaries in New France, dreamed of heroic martyrdom as the ultimate pious sacrifice. In the Pueblo Revolt of 1680, which we will examine in chapter 7, the twenty-one martyred missionaries were not just victims but sacrifices to the cause of conversion. The sacrifice of Tempal and Cotumbo must be considered in this context, for the cruelty of the conquistadors might, as in the works of Bartolomé de las Casas, make their victims not demonic heathen but chosen people of God.

As a New World epic, *Historia de la Nuevo Mexico* stands in contrast to its predecessor, Alonso de Ercilla's *La Araucana*, published in three long installments in 1569, 1578, and 1589. Ercilla fought for eight years against the Araucana Indians of Chile, whose determined resistance continued into the nineteenth century. If I had the space and scope in this volume to consider South America, *La Araucana* would be a key text, for it has become the national epic of Chile, and its heroic portrayal of Indian leaders is of the highest order. Don Francisco de Villagrá, the chief conquistador of Chile, was a relative of Gaspar Perez, who may even have drawn the suicide of the two Acomans after a similar scene in Ercilla's poem. Such extremes of stoic valor are common in portrayals of Native American life even aside from colonial wars; in scenes of torture, cannibalism, and sacrifice; and in the martyrologies of missionary priests and their native converts. Such gruesome suffering thus had both religious and military modes of representation. In the military or secular context, Rabasa suggests that Tempal and Cotumbo do the conquistadors' work for them, that resistance in such a form is pointless. Quint, however, suggests that "their curse raises the specter of a real future retribution, one that will take the shape of periodic insurrections, renegade raids, and acts of sabotage by a people that can never be reconciled to colonial rule" (104). Such an insurrection did arise some seventy years after Villagrá's poem in the form of the Pueblo Revolt, probably the most successful Indian uprising in North American history. That rebellion was eventually overcome, but Quint's words nonetheless ring true, for today the pueblo of Acoma remains atop its mesa, the Spanish no longer rule New Mexico, and a grand equestrian statue of Juan de Oñate erected near Espanola, New Mexico, has fallen victim to symbolic guerrilla attacks: Indian protesters have several times removed his foot with a blowtorch. Now that a thirty-six-foot-tall bronze equestrian statue of Oñate is planned for installation at the El Paso, Texas, airport, the controversy is sure to continue.

If epic poems about Indian wars had taken hold as a distinct genre of Anglo-American colonial literature to the degree they did in Spanish writing, then the shape of imperial form in the representations of native resistance might be quite different, and this book might have a different title. Two epics in French about the Natchez Massacre are discussed in chapter 6, but of works in English I shall discuss at length only one, Eastburn and Sands's *Yamoyden*, and it is perhaps closer to a verse romance than a true epic. The reasons for this absence follow from Quint's theory, put forth in *Epic and Empire*, of two distinct traditions in the genre. The dominant strain includes the major epics of national formation such as the *Iliad* and *Aeneid*—the epics of the winners. A dissenting strain is the epics of the losers, which Quint traces out of Lucan's *Pharsalia*, the story of Caesar's defeat of the Roman republicans led by Brutus and Pompey. Quint connects Persians Darius and Xerxes to these two epic traditions when he notes how according to Plutarch, Alexander visits Achilles' grave, invokes him as a model, and takes the *Iliad* when he invades Asia as well as how in Lucan's epic Caesar in turn invokes Alexander. Thus, the epic of the Greeks came to be co-opted by Roman tyrants and the resistant heroism of Xerxes was embraced by republican partisans such as Lucan. The French colonial ethnographer and historian Bacqueville de La Potherie also sought to correct these imperialist tendencies of epic as they were applied to the American Indians: "The cruelty the Indians use in war, is deservedly held in abhorrence; but who ever has read the history of the far famed heroes of Greece and Rome, will find them little, if at all better, even in this respect. Does the behaviour of Achilles to Hector's dead body appear less savage! But Achilles had a Homer to blazon forth his virtues; not so with the unlettered Indian; every pen is dipped in gall against him" (qtd. in McIntosh 304–5).

The glory that was Greece was founded on violence just as savage as that of the American Indian warriors. A triumphalist epic of the winners written about the Anglo-American colonial experience in North America would have to be anti-Indian and antirepublican. And although some such works were written—for example, Roger Wolcott's early-eighteenth-century poem on the history of Connecticut or Edward Johnson's *Wonder Working Providence*—none earned enough respect from the literati of the early republic to be considered as an epic of U.S. national foundation. As a republic, the nation would need a republican epic, but this genre would have to make the defeated Indian its hero as much as the minuteman of the revolutionary war, and the two could not easily share the role. Hence, when Joel Barlow set out in *The Columbiad* to write such a work, the Native Americans to whom he gave the largest roles were not the Iroquois victims of the genocidal attack of General John Sullivan—were in fact not members of any North American tribe—but the

Incas, the victims of Spain's epic conquest of Peru. In book 3, drawing on Vega's *Royal Commentaries* and some of the many popular eighteenth-century plays and novels about the Incas, Barlow represents Manco Capac and his son, Rocha, as enlightened deists who civilize by conquest the barbarian tribes of the Amazon basin. Barlow is acutely conscious of the two divergent epic traditions, just as Quint presents them. Barlow praises Lucan in the preface as the only republican among epic poets and refers in the endnotes to "the works of Homer, which have caused more mischief to mankind than those of any other" (194). However, Barlow's effort at republican epic did not succeed as well in the market as the republican tragedies about Indian resistance leaders.

The republican epic lacks the sense of closure that supports national and imperial myths, for the only solace it can offer partisans of the defeated is some hope for survival and a future uprising, and this characterizes the position of American Indians as at Acoma. In *La Araucana*, Quint suggests, "the losers who attract our sympathies today would be—had they only the power—the victors of tomorrow" (18). This, likewise, is the catharsis of the Indian tragedy. Readers and playgoers living in an imperialist state can indulge in a sympathy for the native leaders whom that state has defeated and dispossessed. This sympathy may take the form of a pointed political dissent, a vague millennial vision of justice, or a more local cause. It was all the more powerful in Indian tragedies because the hero's role was nearly always played by a white actor, embodying the fantasy of appropriating the pity and valor of the defeated victim while retaining the advantages of the imperialist victor. In *Playing Indian*, Philip Deloria has shown how white men in the early republic dressed themselves in Indian outfits and adopted Indian oratorical styles in support of populist and republican goals, such as the Boston Tea Party and the Whiskey Rebellion. Deloria takes quite seriously both the ideology of these movements and the exploitative nature of their racial appropriations. But he devotes only a page to "the Indian plays that gained special popularity in the decade 1828–1838," dismissing them as "examples of the ideological force of the vanishing Indian" (64). As I have shown, the ideology of the Indian tragedies was not simply a staging of the vanishing Indian trope. Although Edwin Forrest, the biggest star actor in the nineteenth-century United States, built his career playing Metacom in the title role of Stone's *Metamora*, he also starred in other roles, such as Spartacus, popular with working-class males protesting against a corrupt elite. Romantic individualism and its sympathy for the underdogs of history embraced defeated Indian leaders as an expression of dissent, even if that dissent was sometimes redirected toward the support of established political leaders. Appearing within a half century of the American Revolution, Indian tragedies such as *Metamora* and *Carabasset* were anticolonial works protesting the actions of the invading English in the seventeenth and early eighteenth centuries. And the appropriation of native rebellions for anti- or postcolonial nationalism happened not only in the United States but also in Mexico, as we shall see in the next chapter, and in Canada with Tecumseh, as the final chapter explains.

If *Metamora* or one of the other Indian tragedies were to be staged today in the United States, it would likely be regarded as theatrically wretched and historically embarrassing: the bombastic, overwrought style of the hero's lines could only be played as camp, as an ironic amusement for viewers aware of the unfortunate history of Indian relations in this country. But in spite of any such smug irony, Americans may not have learned our lessons as well as we believe, for the emotional and political power of the heroic Indian chief still functions much as it did 175 years ago. White Americans still enjoy the chance to sympathize and identify with the romantic cause of Native Americans in the glory of their resistance, and Indian leaders—particularly those from the nineteenth-century such as Crazy Horse, Chief Joseph, or Chief Seattle—retain much of their prestige in spite of some efforts to debunk the myths that have grown up around them. The heroism of these figures is no longer conveyed through verse epics or stage tragedies but instead is portrayed in television documentaries and popular histories such as Alvin Josephy's *The Patriot Chiefs* or Ian Frazier's *The Great Plains*, with its compelling biography of Crazy Horse, or even on T-shirts and bumper stickers such as those featuring Chief Seattle's oration (see Kaiser; Furtwangler).

The strongest appeal of the resistant Indian chiefs today is as a vehicle of protest against modern society. Chief Seattle's oration has been adopted as a kind of liturgy for environmentalist causes because by invoking so many of the clichés of nineteenth-century vanishing Indian rhetoric, by insisting that "day and night cannot dwell together. The Red Man has ever fled the approach of the White Man, as the morning mist flees before the morning sun" (Vanderwerth 100), the oration opposes nature against culture, red against white, and verdant past against polluted present. All white people—indeed, all of modernity—are lined up against Seattle; hence, his image is equally accessible to anyone desiring an emblem of protest.[14] The gesture is easy to make because the binary oppositions are so stark. Chief Seattle's speech does not, like Pontiac, appeal to his allies, the French, to take up arms against his enemies, the British; does not, like Tecumseh, side with the British-Canadians against the Americans; does not, like the Natchez, reproach the Choctaw for fighting with the French; and does not, like Xicoténcatl, appeal to Tlascalans to resist the offers of alliance with the Spaniards against Tenochtitlán. In reading or hearing Seattle's speech, we are hailed as either "white" or "red," not, for example, as the mixed-blood child of a Salish mother and a French-Canadian fur trader. People of such mixed ancestries and divided loyalties were common around Puget Sound in 1854, when Seattle supposedly delivered his oration, and in the regions of the uprisings examined in this book. Many of these people had to make difficult choices about which side to take. Their perspectives are too often ignored now. Because the colonial wars of North America are now so far in our past, it is easy for most of us to ignore the more messy and complex allegiances and divisions of these wars and instead see "white" versus "red," greedy imperialists versus romantic victims. And by adhering to a misconception of Native American wars of resistance as a clash of civilizations driven by absolute cultural differences, it is easy to deny the ways in which literary and artistic expressions of the resistant native are often not voices of the Other heard from across a cultural divide but rather an imperial culture employing its own timeworn tropes of dissent. As Barbara Fuchs demonstrates in her fine study, *Mimesis and Empire*, literary expressions of the American Indian cause against Spanish colonialism, notably *La Araucana* and Vega's *Royal Commentaries of the Inca*, adopted the most prestigious genres of European imperial writing, epic poetry and classicist historiography. By creating an image of the Inca state that resembled the Roman and the Spanish colonial empires and by portraying Araucanian (or Villagrá's Acoman) leaders in imitation of the warriors of Troy, the mestizo Vega and other writers challenged Spanish claims regarding the superiority of Renaissance European culture.

The most compelling form of anticolonial protest in imperial society is not one of cultural difference but of cultural mimesis. The giant relief sculpture of Crazy Horse on Thunderhead Mountain in South Dakota, the life's work of artist Korczak Ziolkowski, is not so much an antithetical protest against the nearby portraits of four U.S. presidents on Mount Rushmore as a mimicry of them. Ziolkowski was in fact a pupil of Rushmore carver Gutzon Borglum until they had a falling out (Lame Deer 84), and by reshaping a mountain in the Black Hills to resemble Crazy Horse, Ziolkowski delivers no more tangible benefit to the Sioux than Borglum did harm. But the cultural politics of mimesis are tremendously powerful. In the eyes of Ziolkowski and of thousands of visitors who donate money to a project that after fifty years remains far from completion, the best response to the desecration of Mount Rushmore is to carve up another mountain to honor the spirit of Crazy Horse.

Theories of literature such as Aristotle's *Poetics* that emphasize the mimetic faculty have long been out of favor. But theories of cultural mimesis such as Homi Bhabha's and Michael Taussig's have recently come into vogue

in the fields of postcolonial literature and anthropology. This book attempts
to combine the two, to create a hybrid of literary and historical methodolo-
gies. And while the word "hybrid" is also in vogue, its genetic etymology
suggests a useful creature that is unfortunately sterile, an evolutionary dead
end. I hope my arguments will prove fertile and inspire further study, but the
question that haunts my crossbreed offspring of literary genre studies and
Native American ethnohistory is whether the literary expressions of the Indian tragic heroes actually convey anything of Native American experience. If
tragedy is a genre unique to the Western (Mediterranean-European) tradition, as George Steiner has argued, what relevance can it have for Indian
resistance except as an imperial form that prescribed defeat? Epic may be a
nearly global genre, but a Native American epic such as the Maya *Popol Vuh* is
nonetheless an epic of the winners that celebrates the defeat of surrounding
peoples who were incorporated into the Quiche Maya empire. At what level
and from what perspective can one claim that Native Americans' resistance
to European conquest was structured as a tragedy? In one attempt, Arnold
Krupat draws on Hayden White's concept of emplotment to propose divergent views of Cherokee removal:

> The story of Indian savagery must be structured as a tragedy because the
> story of Euroamerican civilization . . . was structured as a comedy. Com-
> edy is the name the West gives to stories that organize images in terms of
> a progress toward reconciliation and integration. . . . If comedy is an in-
> tegrative structure which cheerfully reconciles and unites its characters,
> tragedy is a dispersive structure which fearfully casts out and severs its
> characters from the places and persons they would be near. Terrible
> as such exile is, still, it is tragedy's insistence, it is just. (*Ethnocriticism*
> 134–35)

In another book and about another genre, Krupat observed that "victory is
the ennobling condition of western autobiography, defeat is the ennobling
condition of Indian autobiography" (*For Those* 48), suggesting that even from
the Indian autobiographer's point of view, loss confers a sense of dignity.
But is this tragic melancholy simply a result of the sorrows of history as
examined from the imperialists' perspective, or does it truly reflect indigenous storytelling traditions?

"Historical situations are not *inherently* tragic, comic, or romantic," wrote
Hayden White in a famous essay on the "Historical Text as Literary Artifact."
"How a given historical situation is to be configured depends on the histo-
rian's subtlety in matching up a specific plot structure with the set of histori-
cal events that he wishes to endow with a meaning of a particular kind"
(*Tropics* 85). White's essays from the mid-1970s introduced poststructuralist

theory to historiography by emphasizing the constructed, literary nature of histories as written texts. White built on the work of Giambattista Vico and Northrup Frye, who had sought to explain the transhistorical, deeply mytho-

poeic existence of genres and their power to explain not just literary texts but the patterns of human behavior and understanding. Because the validity of totalizing theories such as Jung's collective unconscious had come into doubt during the rise of poststructuralism, White did not suggest that historical events themselves followed any genre or that the historian in representing them followed a generic formula subconsciously. Rather, the historian chose a certain genre archetype from among those available in his culture, "a plot structure with which he is familiar as a part of his cultural endowment" (86). It was bold enough for White to challenge the notion of history as a positivist, objective production of knowledge by revealing its figurative and literary basis.

White's concept of "emplotment," of "the encodation of the facts contained in the [historical] chronicle as components of specific kinds of plot structures, in precisely the way that Frye has suggested is the case with 'fictions' in general" (Tropics 83) is an important part of my methodology. Francis Parkman chose to portray Pontiac as a tragic hero largely because, as White has argued, the tragic plot structure is characterized by a "mode of metonymy" and "a mechanistic causal connection as the favored mode of explanation" (128). For Parkman and other nineteenth-century Anglo-Americans who believed that the Indian was doomed to vanish, the tragic mode was an obvious choice for representing acts of resistance doomed to failure. Yet as we shall see in the chapter on Pontiac, Parkman's portrayal of his tragic hero was ambivalent. Pontiac's leadership was in Parkman's view alternately despotic and democratic, opposed to the manifest destiny of the American republic yet inspirational for it.

The greatest weakness in White's concept of historical emplotment is not that the array of genres or plots available to historians may be too limited or too culturally specific to explain the events at issue but rather the separation that White maintains between historians and the people who took part in these events. Historians are said to work on an epistemological plain far above the matter of their research. White's subsequent analogy between history and psychoanalysis makes this clear. The neurotic patient knows the facts, the events, of his life, but needs the analyst "to 'reemplot' his whole life history in such a way as to change the meaning of these events for him" (87). The analogy does have a certain appeal. The traumatic events of frontier warfare must have haunted many of those who had lived through them, and the Indian tragedies such as Doddridge's Logan may have functioned for him and readers from his region as a kind of therapeutic working out of this history. But Doddridge and the other authors who most interest me were historians and dramatists of wars in which they themselves had fought or suffered: they were simultaneously patients and analysts. The division between writers of history and history's "writees" is no more valid than the notion that oral indigenous cultures such as the North American Indians had neither any history nor any historians to tell it.

My methodology therefore emphasizes the hybrid, intercultural nature of Indian resistance movements and of the historiography about them. I will employ the lenses of literary genres to read not only the historical literature but also the events themselves. Although I will leave open the question of whether the genre of tragedy exists in Native American culture and literature, I contend in the following chapter that Mexica students trained at the Collegio de Santa Cruz de Tlatelolco may have influenced the portrayal of Moctezuma as a tragic hero in Diego Durán's *History of the Indies of New Spain*. And in chapter 6, we will examine Wole Soyinka's *Death and the King's Horseman* as a provocative application of classical tragedy to the practice of retainer sacrifice in West African and Natchez Indian cultures. If archetypal plots or genres function on a deep collective level before or behind textual productions, we must recognize that they can operate not only as literary traditions but also in a folkloric manner and that they operated in both Native American and colonial societies. It is wrong to oppose literate Euroamerica to oral Native America as mutually exclusive cultures and modes of communication. It is likewise false to suppose a clean separation between historians and their subject matter. In the histories of Indian rebellions at issue here, we shall see that even historians with no literary pretensions still followed the tragic and epic formulas, that men who participated in these wars sometimes felt inspired to attempt literary works even if they had no talent, and, most important, that eyewitnesses' oral statements and memories of Indian rebellions often fell into certain dramatic patterns, such as the counting tokens that I examine in chapter 7. There I will argue that the trope of the "surprise attack betrayed" shaped the way the colonizers wrote stories of Indian uprisings and their suppression as well as how these tales were not only written but also told by soldiers and sailors widely separated across North America during several centuries. In Native America, the oral circulation of news and stories may have at certain times created a transcontinental movement of resistance, such as the revolts that took place from New England to New Mexico to Virginia and South Carolina in 1675–80.

Native resistance struggles in North America show a continuity of strategies across thousands of miles and hundreds of years. Prior to the European invasion, natives of separate nations and separate languages had no sense of their common identity, and even after Columbus they did not quickly gain a sense of their common interests. This of course is why Cortés could conquer Mexico with only a few hundred soldiers. An uprising or war of resistance therefore depended on establishing a sense of common purpose. For colonizers and their historians, this often took the form of a "conspiracy" such as that which Parkman ascribed to Pontiac. For Indians, it often involved a nativist revival, an effort to mobilize spiritual powers in defense of a common way of life. As Gregory Dowd has explained in A Spirited Resistance, Tecumseh's brother, Tenskwatawa, the "Shawnee Prophet," elaborated key features of the phenomenon—"that the movement was intertribal, that it integrated the religious and the political, and that it spanned generations" (xv). He modeled his efforts after those of Pontiac, who had invoked the spiritual vision of a Delaware prophet named Neolin. In chapters 4 and 8 we shall examine these men.

Among the common elements of nativist spiritual movements was a quasi-millennial prophecy: if Indians followed a certain code of behavior, often involving the rejection of European influences such as alcohol, guns, or flint and steel, the invaders might be dispersed and the Indians' land restored. Plans for a militant uprising might be encouraged by the prophet's claims of a magical resistance to the invaders' guns and bullets. So spoke Tenskwatawa before the battle of Tippecanoe, and such was the supposed power of the special shirts worn by initiates of the Ghost Dance religion at Wounded Knee in 1890. Similarly, Moravian missionary David Zeisberger wrote that Delaware Indians had a magical "beson" that was supposed to protect against gunshots (127). According to John Smith, the conspiratorial mastermind of the massacre of Virginia colonists at Jamestown in 1622 was Nemattenow, who "for his courage and policy, was accounted amongst the Salvages their chiefe Captain, and immortall from any hurt could be done him by the English" (2:294; Steele 46 says it was magic body oil). After being shot by two English boys, Nemattenow reportedly pleaded with them not to allow his body to be returned to his tribe and not to "make it known he was slaine with a bullet" (John Smith 2:294). One cannot be certain about the authenticity of this "bulletproof" myth, which has also arisen in slave revolts and peasant rebellions around the world. Likewise, one cannot be sure of the degree of continuity or coordination among various rebellions in native North America in the seventeenth and eighteenth centuries. The search for "authentic" Native American resistance strategies is chimerical anyway, because, like guerrilla fighters the world over, Indians learned many of these spiritual and political strategies from their enemies. Pontiac's speeches were particularly shrewd in manipulating the figural language of patriarchy and the republican responses to it. Later, when Tecumseh and his brother faced invasions by men from the seventeen states of the United States, they seem to have sensed how this federalist alliance might offer a model for their own pantribal alliance against the United States. We shall also see how the doctrines of nativist movements were influenced by Christian revivals and millenarianism as spread by missionaries and itinerant preachers among both native and colonial converts during the Great Awakening. The tales of separate origins or separate afterlives for Indian and white peoples that loomed large in the prophetic visions of Tenskwatawa and his precursors such as Neolin cannot have been pristine preconquest legends. They are complex spiritual responses to colonization, syncretic spiritual road maps for political rebellion. The syncretic political strategies of Pontiac and Tecumseh are perceivable through their recorded speeches, and those of early published American Indian authors such as William Apess are even more obvious. With Apess in chapter 3, John Oskison in chapter 8, and George Stiggins in chapters 6 and 8, I discuss histories of Indian rebel leaders written by Native Americans themselves.

Many of the lessons colonizers learned from the Indians represent the converse of the same process. A good case study of this cycle of political exchange (or appropriation) is the debate over the possible influence of the confederalist political structures of the Iroquois on the Articles of Confederation and subsequently on the U.S. Constitution. Based in part on pamphlets written by Benjamin Franklin, who as we have seen published the proceedings of several major conferences with the Iroquois, and on the Albany Plan of Union, which he drafted in 1754, several scholars in the 1970s and 1980s argued that the Iroquois League was an inspirational model for American democratic institutions.[15] They cited some propitious, if anachronistic, coincidences, such as the roll call of fifty sachems who attended councils of the League. Elizabeth Tooker pointed out in a 1988 article that these sachems were not representatives of tribal constituencies and that the Iroquois system of consensus differed sharply from the votes of a legislative body. Nonetheless, the fact that Iroquois leaders themselves called the early United States "the thirteen fires" and recognized its republican system as in some ways similar to their own and that Tecumseh later called it "the seventeen fires" (when there were seventeen states) proves that this political syncretism is not just an invention by recent academics who are enamored of Indians but that it existed two centuries ago. Colonists learned from natives not so much about federal political structures as about charismatic revolutionary leadership, both its virtues and its horrors.

Sympathetic identification with the Indian tragic heroes was, after all, not based simply on their inevitable defeat or romantic martyrdom. Colonial leaders who fought against Tecumseh, Metacom, or the Natchez not only feared dying in battle but also depended on their Indian foes for political survival. They needed to consolidate and demonize the threat of native rebellion into the figure of its leader, because they wanted to receive the power and support to do battle with this enemy. If a single Indian chief could be identified who had the power to sign treaties of surrender or cessions of land or to bring miscreants in for punishment, the colonizers' job became much easier. The status of native leaders could be even more important to colonists after violent conflicts broke out. At Detroit, Natchez, and elsewhere, native rebellions were quickly assumed to reflect a great conspiracy among a number of tribes, and one leader was believed to be the mastermind behind these conspiracies. We see this imperialist political dynamic all the more sharply in the early twenty-first century as the specter of Osama bin Laden drives so much of U.S. foreign policy. One of my major aims is to elucidate the complex of myths that grew up around this fearsome imagination of Indian conspirators, such as the part-European ancestry of Tecumseh and of the Natchez Sun St. Cosme, or the myth of token sticks in what I call the trope of the surprise attack betrayed. I hope that as Richard Slotkin's *Regeneration through Violence* offers a commentary on American culture in the time of the Vietnam War, this study may help bring about a recognition of the mythic foundations of U.S. imperialism in the time of the so-called war on terrorism.

Slotkin followed his landmark 1973 book with two sequels, carrying his analysis of American frontier conflict through the twentieth century. Although I have no plans to write one, a sequel to this book would be possible as well. Some readers may by this point already have wondered how the analysis of the Indian chief as tragic hero might be applied to Black Hawk, Osceola, Geronimo, or Chief Joseph or why those figures are not discussed herein. This study draws its chronological limit at 1841, when Benjamin Drake published his biography of Tecumseh, William Henry Harrison was inaugurated as U.S. president after campaigning on his notoriety as the man who had defeated Tecumseh, and both men died. Also at around that time, the Indian dramas, after growing in popularity for nearly twenty years, had begun to seem hackneyed and false, and soon after John Brougham wrote his hilarious parodies. The popularity of Indian biography, such as the books by Thatcher and the two Drakes, grew so great in the 1830s and 1840s that thereafter any Indian rebel leader such as Black Hawk or Geronimo was eagerly sought out by frontier journalists and asked to tell his story (for the profit of the journalists), and the publication of these books rendered any dramas, poems, or novels about them seem secondary and less authentic. Moreover, the neoclassicist literary style that informed both the Indian tragedies and the histories, filled with defiant speeches by Indian leaders, was in decline by 1840. Populist, sensational styles of writing no longer betrayed

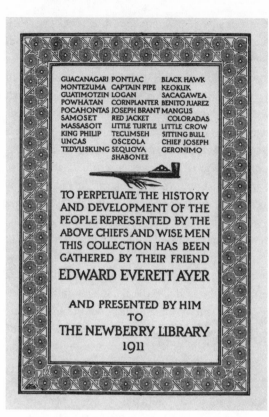

FIGURE 1.1. This bookplate is pasted on the inside cover of every book held in the Edward E. Ayer Collection of Americana and American Indians at the Newberry Library. With more than 130,000 books, it is the largest such collection in the world. Courtesy of the Newberry Library.

any bashful consciousness of their inferiority, and the Indian leader's stoic nobility no longer carried the same gravitas as it had in the early Indian dramas. After all, Black Hawk's resistance posed no real threat to the U.S. military, as Tecumseh had, even if the two men were celebrated in much the same manner. And although biographer John B. Patterson advertised in 1834 that he was writing a tragedy based on Black Hawk's life and intended to act in the drama himself, the work was evidently never written or staged (Schmitz 75).

This is not to say that Americans no longer perceived the elite virtues of Indian rebel leaders. Some presidents, such as Theodore Roosevelt, continued to seek the company of Indian leaders and to write on frontier history as a means of burnishing their political credibility, and early-twentieth-century civic leaders such as Ernest Thompson Seton, cofounder of the Boy Scouts, adopted Indian cultural symbols for the purpose of training young Anglo-American manhood. But by the late 1800s the phenomenon of the Indian tragic hero became more attenuated, more self-conscious, than it had been in the 1830s. Native American resistance became more distant and more desperate, and the heroes of the past and the writings about them perhaps seemed more authentic than those of the present. Edward E. Ayer, a Chicago businessman and early trustee of the Newberry Library, donated to it in 1911 his collection of seventeen thousand books and objects that formed the core of what is now the world's largest collection of materials on American Indian history. Ayer wrote that he was inspired to collect Native Americana after reading William Prescott's tragic portrait of Montezuma in *History of the Conquest of Mexico*. A bookplate placed inside the cover of every Ayer Collection book bears Ayer's proclamation, "To perpetuate the history and development of the people represented by the above chiefs and wise men," and lists thirty Indian leaders from the 1520s to 1890s, eight of whom we will study in the chapters that follow (figure 1.1). The bookplate does not mention "American Indians" but instead lists the chiefs' names as representative of them and implies that as a business and civic leader, Ayer bears a relation to them not only as "their friend" but as their equal, that he might smoke with them the calumet pictured and put an end to the cycle of frontier violence in his region.

The chapters that follow are only roughly chronological, for each one concludes with an analysis of key literary and historical texts published in the 1810s to 1830s. At this time, the United States formulated a nationalist historiography to give meaning to its revolution of fifty years earlier, Mexico saw the first major rebellions that led to its independence from Spanish rule, and British Canada defended itself against the United States and began to recognize a distinct national identity that was codified with Confederation in 1867. The history of Indian rebellions and the figures of the heroic leaders behind them were foundational in all three of these processes. The stories and myths of these seven Indian rebellions are deeply ingrained in the national myths of the three nations of North America. We must begin where Ayer did, with Moctezuma and the conquest of Mexico.

CHAPTER 2 / MOCTEZUMA

The conquest of New Spain is the best epic story in North American history. The contest between Hernan Cortés and the Aztec leader Moctezuma, culminating in the siege of Tenochtitlán, epitomizes the heroic colonial wars that gave rise to the literary-historical phenomenon to which this book is devoted, and the subject was of great interest during the period when this phenomenon thrived. William Prescott's monumental *History of the Conquest of Mexico* (1843) was among the great nineteenth-century popular histories published in the United States, offering a model that Francis Parkman emulated in his studies of Pontiac and of the French colonies in the New World. As John McWilliams observes in *The American Epic*, other literati of the period wrote fictional literature about colonial Mexico, including "Zeuma" by James Ralph (best known as the quixotic friend of the young Benjamin Franklin), and *Calavar* (1834) and *The Infidel* (1835) by Robert Montgomery Bird. The fall of Tenochtitlán and its ruler, Moctezuma, was all the more attractive a subject for these authors because they could freely criticize the Spanish conquistadors without casting aspersions on the motives of English colonizers. Such anti-Spanish sentiments became part of a jingoistic propaganda campaign at midcentury during the Mexican War. However, this campaign was so easy only because, as I demonstrate in the following chapter on King Philip's War, a postcolonial critique of English imperialism in North America had already become quite common in the 1820s and 1830s. Books by McWilliams, David Levin, and Eric Wertheimer have already done much to explain how nineteenth-century American authors portrayed the Aztec and Inca empires conquered by the Spanish. In this chapter I analyze not so much the perspectives of Anglo writers on the conquest of Mexico as the indigenous and Spanish-American literature and historiography of the events of 1519–21, both in the sixteenth century and in the early 1800s, during the initial Mexican insurgency against Spanish colonial rule.

An indigenous historiography of Mexico is accessible to us in a way that it really is not for North American tribal history. For our study of Moctezuma and the events of 1519–21, we are not limited to textual research but can consult a rich record of pictographic works, painted by natives of the valley of Mexico. These people maintained elaborate historical and genealogical documents, painted or written in bright colors on cotton rolls by a specially trained cadre of artists, using a semiological system called *tlacuilolli*, a mixture of hieroglyphic and iconic symbols unique among world languages (Brotherston, *Painted Books* 12). Nearly all of these traditional books or screenfolds, called codices by specialists in the field, were destroyed by the Spanish invaders. The *tlacuilolli* method survived, however, in a hybrid form, as postconquest artists created new records of their cities, often telling the history of the conquest and their peoples' role in it. Franciscan friar Bernardino de Sahagun, working at the Collegio de Santa Cruz, a school for indigenous boys established by his monastic order at Tlatelolco, adjacent to the Aztec capital of Tenochtitlán, beginning in the mid-1500s employed his students to paint hundreds of illustrations for his exhaustive ethnographic project on native culture, the *Historia géneral de las cosas de Nueva España*. This great work was suppressed by his church superiors and was not published until the nineteenth century. The last of its twelve books (which forms the thirteenth volume of Anderson and Dibble's English translation) tells of the Spanish conquest. The text includes small illustrations that constitute a pictorial narrative resembling the native practice of hieroglyphic writing. This narrative offers additional insights on the relationship between Moctezuma and his foe, Cortés.[1] The sequence of images in book 12 begins with one that shows the Spaniards unloading their ships on the Gulf Coast near modern Veracruz. Then come eight illustrations depicting the eight omens of the conquest seen in the previous years, phenomena we will analyze closely. Panel 19 (in the enumeration added by Anderson and Dibble) shows the Mexican leader listening to a description of the newcomers delivered by two messengers who have "flying tongues" in front of their mouths—the *tlacuilolli* symbol for important spoken information (figure 2.1). Moctezuma strikes the characteristic pose used for rulers: he is sitting on a throne beneath a decorated roof, a reverse C-shaped enclave that closely resembles the Aztec year-sign House. His right arm is raised with index finger pointed, and his left arm extends slightly downward.[2] It may be significant that whereas in the two earlier images of Moctezuma he was clean shaven, in this one he sports a beard, just as Cortés and nearly all the Spaniards do (though some other Mexicans, including Cuauhtémoc in image 141, are also shown with beards). The first explicit image of Cortés, image 12, as well as images 100 and 101 show him as he receives messengers in a pose quite similar to the iconic one assumed by Moctezuma in panel 19, except that Cortés appears on the left side of the frame, wears a hat or helmet, and sits on his own Spanish-style curule chair instead of a throne. Thus, these native artists used some of the same conventions to represent the rule of Cortés as they had

FIGURE 2.1.
Bernardino de Sahagun, *General History of the Things of New Spain*, a.k.a. the Florentine Codex, book 12, panel 19. In the original codex, the illustrations appear as small illuminated section headings amid the text and are in color. Courtesy of the Biblioteca Medicea Laurenziana, Florence, Italy.

used to depict his predecessor and victim, Moctezuma. An image from the *Lienzo de Tlascala*, a book produced by artists from Tlascala, a city that provided crucial military assistance to the Spaniards, shows the situation after the conquest. Cortés still sits on a Spanish-style chair, "which came to symbolize authority in post-conquest indigenous documents" (Schwartz 124), but now he sits beneath the iconic roof just as Moctezuma did and holds his hands in a similar pose (figure 2.2). His mistress and interpreter, Doña Marina (Malinche), stands behind him. Moctezuma sits in another curule chair directly facing him. Stephanie Wood has documented how in the colonial period "caciques felt it appropriate for them to adopt the curule chair, substituting it for their own thrones" (55). But Moctezuma and his three advisers are shown perched in midair, no longer real men but only icons of tribute, like the birds and deer shown in cages just below. Many such tribute records appear among surviving sixteenth-century native Mexican texts. They were used both as contracts—to show the terms of payment—and perhaps as a form of imperial art by the recipients.

To the postconquest painters, Cortés had replaced Moctezuma, and although the details of clothing and furniture styles had changed, the basic icons of power remained the same. Because he was familiar with absolute despotism and the role of tributary vassals, the cunning Spanish leader usurped rather than defeated his foe. Cortés was very fortunate to succeed, and part of his good fortune resulted from the fact that he had encountered a ruler whose style and structures of power resembled the absolutist monarchy under which Cortés lived. In the chapters in this volume on Metacom, Pontiac, and Logan, we will see that the heroic power of those native leaders was constructed and legitimated through republican political theory. They

FIGURE 2.2. *Lienzo de Tlascala*, plate 11. This scene, one of eighty-seven plates in this pictorial history of the conquest of Mexico, shows Moctezuma first welcoming Cortés, whom Moctezuma still suspected was the returning Quetzalcoatl. Tlascalans painted this *lienzo* (tapestry) around 1550, in large part to remind the Spaniards of their city's crucial assistance during the conquest. From *Homenaje a Cristóbal Colón: Antigüedades mexicanas* (1892). Courtesy of the Architecture and Allied Arts Library, University of Oregon.

came from decentralized societies of hunters and subsistence farmers and possessed the primitive virtues of egalitarian independence and martial valor. Although Metacom was the son of a sachem, Massassoit, he, Pontiac, and Logan all had built their influence through exploits on the field of battle and through charismatic leadership in councils. Their legacy came to be bound up with the formation of an American republic and its search for distinctly American models. The key adversaries of these North American Indian leaders, Robert Rogers, Benjamin Church, and even Edwin Forrest, were of modest origins and remain obscure today. Like Cortés, they attempted to use the heroic status of their Indian rivals to promote their political ambitions. But because the political context was republican rather than absolutist, their success had a much more modest scope. They did not dream of gaining the kind of despotic power that Cortés obtained over a major city-state, one of the wealthiest and most populous in the world at the time.

Thus the confrontation between Cortés, a subject of King Charles V, and Moctezuma II, *tlatoani* of Tenochtitlán since 1502, brought together two despotic rulers of advanced and far-flung empires that had grown quickly in previous years and whose legitimacy rested on a grandiose but fragile super-structure. Only in 1492 did the Castilian monarchs conquer Grenada and consolidate control of the Iberian Peninsula. Charles V had come to the throne in 1517, and when Cortés wrote the second of his *cartas* (letters) to the king in 1520, he had just added the title of Holy Roman Emperor and was traveling to Germany. Moctezuma II was the ninth ruler of Tenochtitlán, which less than a century earlier had consolidated its control of the valley of Mexico by forming the Triple Alliance with the cities of Texcoco and Tacuba. In 1473 the alliance had reduced the neighboring city of Tlatelolco, on the northern end of the island they shared in Lake Texcoco, to the status of a tributary subject. The Aztec kingdom now stretched from the Gulf Coast south to the Pacific, east to the isthmus of Tehuantepec, and west to frontiers with Tarasco and Michoacan.

Both of these empires had refined techniques for supporting their power through symbolic, spectacular displays of wealth and obeisance. The Mexica demanded from their conquered subjects tribute in the form not of military service as much as of food, gold, feathers, rare animals, and other luxury goods as well as in sacrificial victims. The spectacle of human sacrifices, chiefly to the war god and Mexica patron deity, Huitzilipochtli, was a fear-some spectacle indeed, as the victim's still-beating heart was torn from his chest and his blood poured on an image of the god. The Spanish colonizers expressed their horror at Aztec human sacrifice, but their monarch was equally adroit at an absolutist monopoly on violence. The Inquisition was empowered to torture and mutilate its victims, and public executions of criminals were routine. The *conversos* and *moriscos*, subjects who had been forced to convert from Judaism or Islam, came under intense scrutiny in a state that maintained an ideology of racial and religious purity. The Mexica also practiced a rather paranoid despotism. As Inga Clendennin has ob-served, displays of brutal power scarcely concealed the Aztecs' notion of "living on a razor's edge" (29), of the instability of their lives and influence. The island metropolis in the brackish lake was home to as many as 150,000 people, but it was vulnerable to drought, crop failure, and, as Cortés quickly perceived, to the disruption of its freshwater supply, carried by an aqueduct from springs at Chapultepec many miles away.

Cortés appears to have instinctively focused his violent designs on Moc-tezuma, so closely as to transform him from an evil nemesis into a kindred spirit, what René Girard calls a mimetic rival, bound by a common desire for imperial power over Mexico. Cortés's politically brilliant move was not to destroy the legitimacy of Moctezuma's absolute power, for an absolutist monarch offers no basis for such a challenge, but instead to appropriate it, to suggest that the two regimes were really the same all along. Cortés enjoyed an inherent advantage over his rival. Because this was the first European invasion of continental North America, Moctezuma had no familiarity with Spain to answer to Cortés's quickly acquired knowledge of native America. Moctezuma was not able to adroitly turn the rhetoric of European politics and diplomacy against his foes or to ally with one colonizing power against another, as did subsequent leaders of Native American resistance such as Pontiac and Tecumseh.

Had he had more time to learn, Moctezuma might have discovered that he was already familiar with what he found in Spanish political customs. The prevalent rhetorical model of Spanish colonial writings, as in Cortés's *Letters*, was the form of petitions and letters to the king. The king was the "fountainhead of justice" (J. H. Elliot, introduction to Cortés xv), the first and last resort of the wronged, the oppressed, and the dissatisfied. Such an extreme centralization of power had its own fragility, for every provincial official or missionary felt empowered to appeal to the top and no deputy was safe from such a challenge.[3] Cortés was writing in this mode. He was a vassal who had blatantly disregarded orders from his superior, Cuban Governor Diego Velazquez, and appealed over Velasquez's head directly to the king, blithely excusing this insubordination and promising tribute in the form of gold too lavish to be refused. Cortés portrayed himself alternately as Charles's servant and his equal, his emissary and his replacement. Cortés cleverly manipulated the contradictions implied by a world supporting numerous imperial, absolutist monarchies. For example, on the way toward Tenochtitlán in the fall of 1519, Cortés wrote of an encounter with a local cacique, probably at Zautla, "After I had spoken to him of Your Majesty and of the reason for my coming to these parts, I asked him if he was a vassal of Mutezuma, or owed some other allegiance. And he showed surprise at my question, and asked who was not a vassal of Mutezuma, meaning that here he is the king of the whole world. I replied by telling him of the great power of Your Majesty and of the many other princes, greater than Mutezuma, who were Your Highness's vassals" (56). This expresses a smug assertion of a European's sense of superiority and the rhetoric of flattery from a subject, but it also reveals a certain twisted logic. An absolute monarch must be total, tolerating no rival anywhere, and therefore must have knowledge of the whole world, as the whole world must acknowledge him. To pay tribute to a different ruler is not only treason but unthinkable. Cortés may have recognized the absurdity of this logic, which posits Mexico as part of Spain or Spain as part of Mexico even though most people in each place knew nothing of the other, and sensed his power to exploit it in spite of its absurdity. If "Your Majesty" Charles is the absolute ruler, Moctezuma must be "Your vassal," and Cortés implies that he need only secure tribute from Moctezuma to himself, "Your servant," to make himself the absolute ruler of this place. The two speeches by Moctezuma that Cortés wrote into his second "Letter" effect this transfer of power by bringing this mythical totalitarianism to fact. From our perspective, these speeches seem fabricated, but it is important to recall that Cortés's letters were the first published account of the conquest and that Moctezuma's orations fit a style of classical and Renaissance historiography that seemed natural at the time.

At the rivals' first meeting, Cortés wrote, Moctezuma "bade me sit on a very rich throne, which he had had built for him," and then sat on another throne and began speaking:

> For a long time we have known from the writings of our ancestors that neither I, nor any of those who dwell in this land, are natives of it, but foreigners who came from very distant parts; and likewise we know that a chieftain, of whom they were all vassals, brought our people to this region. And he returned to his native land and after many years came again, by which time all those who had remained were married to native women and had built villages and raised children. And when he wished to lead them away again they would not go nor even admit him as their chief; and so he departed. And we have always held that those who descended from him would come and conquer this land and take us as their vassals. So because of the place from which you claim to come, namely, from where the sun rises, and the things you tell us of the great lord or king who sent you here, we believe and are certain that he is our natural lord, especially as you say that he had known of us for some time. (85–86)

These lines, written by Cortés yet ventriloquized through the man whose name he spells "Mutezuma," blend two complementary myths, the Mexican myth of Quetzalcoatl and the European myth of a prior discovery of America. Versions of the latter had circulated since Columbus, building on medieval stories of Prester John and of the apostle St. Thomas's travels into India and on classical references in Plato and other texts to a lost Carthaginian colony of Atlantis. The most germane to Cortés's account, however, was that of the legendary Spanish King Hesper, who had supposedly sent an expedition across the western sea to the Isles of the Hesperides. This story was based on a spurious document fabricated in 1497 by Friar Jacobo Annius, apparently with the intent of bolstering Spanish claims to the New World against the competing Portuguese, who by the papal bull of 1493 had been granted claims to the eastern part of all newfound lands in America. Gonzalo Fernandez de Oviedo, in his *Historia general y natural de las Indias* (1535–50), the first comprehensive Spanish history of the Americas to be published, repeated this story even as he criticized Cortés (Brading 36–38). Such a "lost colony," be it Hesperides or Atlantis, was an irrefutable theory, for as Mutezuma explains, its descendants would have forgotten their origins, just as Europe preserved only vague recollections of sending the expedition out. This fantasy offered a claim of sovereignty over Mexico into which Cortés might easily insert himself.

The myth of Quetzalcoatl is, however, the more obvious allusion behind this first oration of Mutezuma. A great deal has been written on this topic, and the myth's validity remains hotly debated. The many sources, both textual and archeological, make it difficult to pin down. Quetzalcoatl translates as "plumed serpent" or "feathered serpent" and was one the major deities in the large and complex Aztec pantheon. He was associated with the wind and storms (a manifestation known as Ehecatl) as well as with writing and the arts. He had been the tutelary god of the civilization of the Toltecs at Tula (Tollan), which thrived between 900 and 1200 C.E. According to the epic history of the Nahua people, their ancestors had come from frontier regions to the north, home to primitive peoples called the Chichimecs. These people overran the region around the valley of Mexico, including Tula, and founded new cities atop the ruins of the old. As for the Mexica of Tenochtitlán, extant painted books depict their northern origins in the mythical seven caves of Aztlan and the path they followed from there toward the valley of Mexico.

At roughly this time lived a ruler of the Toltecs named Topiltzin, who adopted the name of the city's deity. Topiltzin Quetzalcoatl had been born to a virgin mother, Chimalman, in the year Ce Acatl (1 Reed) and was honored as a master craftsman and as builder of four temples at Tula. Postconquest texts by anonymous native authors, the *Anales de Cuauhtitlan* and the *Leyenda de Soles*, recount various episodes in the career of this warrior-priest and culture hero. Some versions emphasize that he wished to abolish the practice of human sacrifice and that this innovation brought him into conflict with followers of the god Tezcatlipoca, forcing Topiltzin to flee Tula. According to an early-sixteenth-century text by a Spanish missionary translated by French cosmographer André Thevet, Topiltzin passed through other cities, including Cholula and Cempoala, during a period of hundreds of years. The key event for the myth, however, is the enigmatic departure of Topiltzin Quetzalcoatl across the sea toward the east. His fall and departure are represented variously as the result of a scandalous episode of incest with his sister, as a defeat by supporters of human sacrifice, or as a righteous self-imposed exile. In the more symbolic or cosmological version, Quetzalcoatl commits self-sacrifice by burning himself and rises into the sky as the morning star, a fate resembling that of the hero twins Hunahpu and Xbalanque in the Mayan *Popol Vuh*. In a more earthly historical version, to which Mutezuma's speech alludes, Topiltzin departed toward the east in the year 1 Reed: "Such was the life, in its entirety, of him who was called Quetzalcoatl. He was born in 1 Reed. And he also died in 1 Reed, and so it is reckoned he lived for fifty-two years" (*Anales de Cuauhtitlan* qtd. in Carrasco 34). The carved stone year glyphs so common in Mesoamerican temples confirm this date. Much has been made of the prophetic significance of the fact that 1519, the year of the Spanish landfall at Veracruz, was also a 1 Reed year. According to Clavigero (1:89), Topiltzin Quetzalcoatl ended his reign at Tula in 1052, 468 years (nine 52-year cycles) before the arrival of Cortés. The Aztecs evidently practiced a typological historiography not unlike that of New Englanders, who made much of the coincidence between King Philip's uprising in 1675–76 and the American Revolution one century later.

The Mexican reaction to the Spanish as related in Sahagun's account attributes to Moctezuma a speech that parallels the one from Cortés. It is possible that the friar's Tlatelolcan informants, having learned the ideology justifying Cortés's claim to power, dutifully echoed his words: "Thou hast come to arrive on earth. Thou hast come to govern thy city of Mexico; thou hast come to descend upon thy mat, upon thy seat, which for a moment I have watched for thee, which I have guarded for thee. For thy governors are departed—the rulers Itzcoatl, Moctezuma the Elder, Axayacatl, Tizoc, Auitzol, who yet a very short time ago had come to stand guard for thee" (13:44). This version of the speech adopts the paratactic style characteristic of Sahagun's Nahuatl text and lists the five *tlatoani* (rulers) who had preceded Moctezuma II on the throne. But although it implies that Moctezuma believes Cortés to be a *teotl* or *teule* (god), it does not identify him as the returning Quetzalcoatl, just as Cortés's version does not. That identification appears only in earlier passages in the volume, where the appurtenances or costume of that god were given to the Spaniards when still on board their ships. The word "Quetzalcoatl" does not appear anywhere in Cortés's five *Letters* or in Bernal Díaz's history, even though the outline of the myth of prophetic departure and return to reclaim the throne comes up several times in his text. The god's name is suppressed, like a third term in a triangle of desire between Moctezuma and his rival, Cortés. Moreover, the status of the Aztec ruler as a monarch who was worshipped as a god by his people becomes part of the ambiguous transference linking the two men. For although Moctezuma's first speech in Cortés's second Letter links Cortés to the "chieftain" of long ago, a mythical ruler who like Topiltzin Quetzalcoatl appears to have been regarded as semidivine, it also refutes the idea that Moctezuma enjoyed that status:

> "I know [Moctezuma's subjects] have told you that the walls of my houses are made of gold . . . and that I was, and claimed to be a god, and many other things besides. The houses as you see are of stone and lime and clay."
>
> Then he raised his clothes and showed me his body, saying, as he grasped his arms and trunk with his hands, "See that I am of flesh and blood like you and all other men, and I am mortal and substantial. See how they have lied to you?" (86)

Moctezuma asserts that he is mortal "like you" and connects the mistaken belief in his divinity to the fantasy of a city of gold that so many conquistadors would sustain for years to come as they thrashed around North and South America seeking Quivira and El Dorado. The divinity of Moctezuma is no more real than the divinity of Cortés, and vice versa. We can be sure only that they are on the same level. Cortés embraces Moctezuma as a friend, a brother, a rival. As Aristotle specifies (56), the tragic conflict best evokes terror and pity if the rivals are not sworn enemies but friends, kin, or allies. René Girard's study of tragedy in *Violence and the Sacred* updates the classical terms with Freudian psychodynamics, enriching the understanding of how political rivalries are often grounded not in ideological differences but in mimetic desires. And however much it may fly in the face of cultural differences, Girard's concepts explain the rivalry between Cortés and Moctezuma. Cortés wants what Moctezuma has from the moment the Spaniard learns of the Mexica's existence, even before learning the precise location or extent of his kingdom. "The rival desires the same object as the subject," Girard writes; "Rivalry does not arise because of the fortuitous convergence of two desires upon the same object; rather the subject desires the object because the rival desires it" (145). Cortés wants to be a god, a manifestation of Quetzalcoatl, not because it is the only way to achieve the conquest but because Moctezuma is shrouded in this mythical status.

If we consider the confrontation from Moctezuma's perspective as well, the two rivals become doubles of one another, and the rivalry is played out on a semidivine plane through the myth of Quetzalcoatl. "To say that the monstrous double is a god or that he is purely imaginary is to say the same thing in different terms," says Girard (*Violence* 161). Cortés and Moctezuma, I believe, are monstrous doubles of one another—the stark cultural difference that separates them scarcely conceals their alternating fate and common interest. The absolutist throne of power that they dispute becomes a position they share. Girard writes of classical tragedy (and specifically of Sophocles' *Oedipus Tyrannus*) that the plot's antagonists are bound into a reciprocal relationship of alternating *kudos* (fortune): "When one of the 'brothers' assumes the role of father and king, the other cannot but feel himself to be the disinherited son. That explains why the antagonists only rarely perceive the reciprocal nature of their involvement" (158). The myths of Quetzalcoatl promoted by Cortés and Sahagun indeed made Cortés and Moctezuma kin. In the "native" version, the Mexica rulers claimed Quetzalcoatl as their ancestor and identified Cortés as his descendant; in Cortés's version, the unnamed chieftain from the east is their common ancestor. Moreover, the subsequent events of the conquest follow an alternation of *kudos* among Moctezuma, Cortés, and their successors, including Cuauhtémoc. In the first "act," Cortés entered Tenochtitlán, was received graciously by Moctezuma, and then took his rival captive, holding him for weeks in the palace under Spanish guard. But Moctezuma's power diminished the longer he remained a hostage, and his death, in disputed circumstances we shall examine subsequently, removed the influence of his pacifying authority over the city's residents and exposed the Spaniards to the 30 June 1520 attack known as the *noche triste*, when Moctezuma's people struck back and hundreds of Spaniards and thousands of Tlascalans were killed. Cortés was acutely aware that his fortunes lay in usurping the monarch of Mexico, but his initial success only left him vulnerable to retaliation from the Mexican population and to the same sort of challenge from other Spaniards.

While holding Moctezuma captive in Tenochtitlán, Cortés learned that his rival in Cuba, Diego Velázquez, had organized an expedition, led by Panfilo de Narváez, to sail to Veracruz and remove Cortés. Moctezuma, too, learned of this from his messengers and supposedly began plotting a revolt against Cortés. In the second of the *Letters from Mexico*, just a few pages after he reports receiving the rich tribute accorded Moctezuma, Cortés writes, "Narváez had sent these men to Vera Cruz to speak to the people there on his behalf and see if they could win them over to his purpose and make them rise against me" (116). Replace "Narváez" with "King Charles," and these could be lines written by Moctezuma on receiving news of the Cortés's arrival at Vera Cruz to attempt to win over Moctezuma's subjects and topple his empire. Cortés expresses shock that Narváez would send "letters of inducement to the people, whom I, in the service of your majesty, had in my company, to rise against me and join him as though one of us were a Christian and the other an infidel or as if one were Your Highness's vassal and the other his enemy" (117). Cortés then accuses Moctezuma of doing exactly the same thing after learning that Moctezuma has been communicating with Narváez. Cortés then rushes back to the Gulf Coast and wins over Narváez's men with promises of gold and power. The putative difference between Cortés and Moctezuma, between Christian and infidel, is erased, and there is finally no difference between the rival claimants, successive plunderers of Mexico. As Girard says of the Oedipus-Tiresias rivalry, "Each sees in the other the usurper of a legitimacy that he thinks he is defending but that he is in fact undermining" (*Violence* 71).

Cortés further suggests the fundamental equivalence of the Spanish and Aztec regimes through his efforts to assimilate the natives by anointing hereditary rulers. While preparing for the final siege of Tenochtitlán, Cortés learns that the leadership of the city of Texcoco is in dispute. As Bernal Díaz tells it, Cortés convened a meeting of chieftains and decided that "it should go to a certain youth who at that time became a Christian with much religious pomp, and was named Don Hernando Cortés, for our Captain was his godfather. They said that this youth was the legitimate son of Nezahualpilli, the Lord and King of Tezcoco" (343; Nezahualpilli will be discussed again later in this chapter). A native leader not only must pledge allegiance to Cortés but must also take his name, like a legitimate son. Moreover, after the conquest, the families of Moctezuma and those of Cortés and some of his leading henchmen became allied, specifically through Tecuichpotzin, a.k.a. Isabella, the legitimate daughter of Moctezuma II (figure 2.3). (Moctezuma is believed to have had more than a hundred illegitimate children as well.) After her father's death, Tecuichpotzin married an Aztec nobleman, who soon died, and then Cuauhtémoc, who led the fierce resistance to the Spanish during the siege of Tenochtitlán in the summer of 1521. Cuauhtémoc had seized power by imprisoning and killing Asupacaci, Moctezuma's only surviving legitimate son, and marrying the legitimate daughter consolidated Cuauhtémoc's claims. When Cuauhtémoc was captured in August, he pleaded to the Spaniards to have mercy on his wife. She was baptized Isabella and over the next three years married three conquistadors in succession, Alonso de Grado, Pedro Gallego, and finally Juan Cano de Saavedra. In between the first two, however, Cortés bedded Isabella, and the union produced her first child, Leonor Cortés Moctezuma. Isabella's granddaughter through Leonor married Juan de Oñate, the brutal conqueror of New Mexico. Cortés also awarded Isabella feudal title to the town of Tacuba and the income of its tribute and stressed that her father had been helpful, even loyal, to Cortés's cause. But Isabella also staged a limited rebellion against her conqueror. In the 1530s and 1540s, lawsuits were brought in Mexico and petitions filed in Spain demanding that Isabella and her husband be restored the lands that had been unjustly taken from Moctezuma. When she died in 1550, the conflicts passed to her children and widower, who continued to squabble over Tacuba's tributes.[4]

GENEALOGY of the MEXICAN KINGS.

Deduced from the Beginning of the Thirteenth Century.

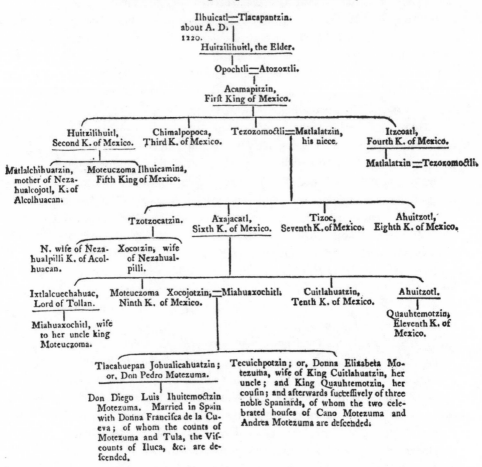

FIGURE 2.3. Francesco Saverio Clavigero's genealogy of the rulers of Mexico. At bottom right is "Donna Elizabeta" (Isabella Motezuma), "of whom the two celebrated houses of Cano Motezuma and Andrea Motezuma are descended." Clavigero was a Jesuit priest in Mexico until his order was expelled from the Spanish colonies in 1767. He fled to Italy and published a history of Mexico in Italian in 1780–81. From Francesco Saverio Clavigero, *History of Mexico* (1787), 1:241.

Omens of Conquest and the Myth of Quetzalcoatl

Most readers and students today regard the conquest of Mexico as a stark confrontation between two powerful and sophisticated civilizations that were radically different and that until the 1510s had had no knowledge of one another. But, ironically, this fact actually poses a barrier to understanding the logic that guides the events—their historiography or plot, depending on whether we view it as a history or a drama. Most scholars and historians take the cultural divide an a priori fact, an assumption that obscures common techniques in the mythification of the conquest by historians from both sides. As a case study, let us consider the famous omens of the conquest, events in the years before 1519 that the Mexica supposedly received as doomsday prophecies. These appear in many sources but are best known from the list of eight (a significant number for the Aztecs) as it appears in Sahagun. First came a comet, "like a tongue of fire . . . it was there to the east when it thus came forth at midnight" (13:1–2). Second, the *cue* or temple of Huitzilopochtli spontaneously burned, and "when they cast water upon it, when they tried to put it out, all the more did it flare up" (2). Third, a temple at a place called Tzonmulco was struck by lightning. Fourth, another comet or falling star was seen: "It began there in the west, and it traveled there to the east as if showering glowing coals. . . . And when it was seen, great was the outcry." Fifth, the water of the lake surrounding Tenochtitlán foamed or boiled up, flooding and destroying some houses. "A sixth evil omen: often was heard a woman going weeping, going crying out. Loudly did she cry out at night. She walked about saying: 'My beloved sons, now we are about to go!'" (2–3). Seventh, and most provocative, an ash-colored bird, like a crane, was found and brought to Moctezuma, who saw on its head a mirror and in the mirror the stars of a constellation called the Fire Drill: "And Moctezuma took it as an omen of great evil when he saw the stars and the Fire Drill. And when he looked at the bird's head a second time, he saw, a little beyond, what was like people coming massed, coming as conquerors, coming girt in war array, Deer bore them upon their backs" (3). Finally, there were found monstrous "thistle-men" with two heads, who, when shown to Moctezuma, magically disappeared (3).

The recounting of these omens in the first chapter of Sahagun's history of the conquest of Mexico lends them a powerful air of authority. Other historians, such as mestizo Tlascalan Diego Muñoz Camargo (qtd. in Léon-Portilla 7–11) repeat them as well. The aura of superstition around them and the hints at culturally specific meanings of thistle-men, the Fire Drill, and the crane invite Euro-Americans to approach these omens as deeply significant yet impenetrable. In *The Conquest of America*, Tzvetan Todorov places a great deal of emphasis on the Aztecs' preoccupation with such omens and auguries. It is a central piece of evidence supporting his contention that "Indians and Spaniards practice communication differently" (63), that while the former communicate primarily with the gods or with nature, the latter favor communications between humans, such as the military intelligence that was so important for Cortés. Todorov also traces "accounts, proceeding from peoples very remote from each other" (including the Tainos, Mayans, Incas, and Tarascans), all "striking in their uniformity: the arrival of the Spaniards is always preceded by omens, their victory is always foretold as certain" (74). The same pattern appears in some native histories of North American colonial invasions and the anticipation of and resistance to them.[5] Yet although Todorov acknowledges that at least one European colonizer, Christopher Columbus, shared with the Indians this mystical or superstitious style of thinking, Todorov still insists on an essential cultural difference in the practices of communication by the two cultures. The Indians are wedded to ritual, to narrative oral eloquence, to a cyclical view of time, and to a focus on the past. The Spaniards, epitomized by Cortés, practice improvisation, interpretation, a linear view of history, and they plan for their future success.

In his effort to make Cortés and the Spanish emblematic of modern semiological sophistication, Todorov (except for his remark about Columbus) disregards the superstitious and millenarian beliefs of the European colonizers, both Spanish and English, in the sixteenth and seventeenth centuries and recapitulates the prejudices of missionaries and historians who branded the Indians as being in thrall to the devil or to superstition. Comparative study of the history of Indian uprisings in North America reveals that omens of impending war preoccupied colonists as well as natives. New England Puritans of all ranks were deeply concerned with the interpretation of natural phenomena as indications of divine providence, and their historians recorded ominous signs of King Philip's War. For example, William Hubbard wrote of the opening days of that conflict,

> On the 26th of June [1675] a Foot Company under Capt. *Daniel Henchman*, with a Troop under Capt. *Thomas Prentice*, were sent out of *Boston* towards *Mount Hope*; it being late in the Afternoon before they began to March, the central Eclipse of the Moon in *Capric*[orn] hapned in the evening before they came to *Naponset River* . . . Some melancholy Fancies would not be perswaded, but that the Eclipse falling out at that Instant of Time was ominous, conceiving also that in the Centre of the Moon they discerned an unusual black Spot, not a little resembling the Scalp of an *Indian*; As some others not long before, imagined they saw the Form of an *Indian*

Bow, accounting that likewise ominous (although the mischief following was done by Guns, not by Bows). (1:67–68)

Hubbard's nineteenth-century editor, Samuel Drake, expressed surprise that Cotton Mather, the prominent Boston minister who combined scientific ambitions with evangelical superstitions, omitted any mention of these omens even though his *History of King Philip's War* refers to the same detachment of militia. Mather, however, reported,

> In a clear, still, sunshiny morning, there were divers persons in Maldon who heard in the air, on the south east side of them, a great gun go off, and presently thereupon the report of small guns like musket shot, very thick discharging, as if there had been a Battel. This was at a time when there was nothing visibly done in any part of the colony to occasion such noises; but that which most of all astonished them was the flying of bullets, which came singing over their heads, and seemed very near to them, after which the sound of drums passing along the westward was very audible, and on the same day, in the Plymouth colony, in several places invisible troops of horses were heard riding to and fro. Now reader, prepare for the event of these prodigies, but count me not struck with a Livian superstition in reporting prodigies, for which I have such incontestable assurance. (Drake, *History* 52)

As we will see in chapters 7 and 8, eclipses and earthquakes added an ominous supernatural power to the resistance led by Tecumseh and the Shawnee Prophet in 1810 and 1811. And in his *History of Louisiana*, discussed in chapter 6, Le Page du Pratz describes three separate celestial phenomena that some people perceived as omens of the uprisings of the Natchez nation between 1722 and 1729. The first is a fireball in the sky, much like the comets seen in Mexico. The third he describes as a particularly spectacular sunset, but his friends, among both the Indians and the colonists at Natchez, are greatly alarmed: "The Natchez did not take it this way. All that I could tell them did nothing to dissuade them from the idea they had that the red men were menaced by some bad luck because, they said, the sky had looked red and as though it were angry" (3:225). And although Le Page du Pratz is skeptical, the local settlers remain convinced that "it was a phenomenon that announced something sinister for Louisianans. And though the massacre of the French establishment at the hands of the Natchez would not come until almost four years later, most of those who escaped it, are still persuaded that this was a warning of that disaster" (3:225).

The belief that catastrophic events such as these colonial wars had been foretold by omens is not a product of a primitive worldview, as Todorov claims. It is, rather, an interpretive strategy of the histories that record the events. Historians—European, native, and mestizo—all relied on these tropes to emplot their narratives. Todorov admits that "everything suggests that the omens were invented after the fact" (74), and prominent historian of Latin America Stuart Schwartz agrees that the omens were an ex post facto elaboration by Sahagun's Tlatelolco informants, "who wished to please the Spaniards or who resented the failure of Moctezuma and of the warriors of Tenochtitlán to provide leadership" (29–30). In Todorov's estimation, for the Aztecs, "the present becomes intelligible and at the same time less inadmissible, the moment one can see it already announced in the past" (74). But is this manner of thinking really so foreign to Europeans? The retrospective analysis of portents and predictions is an integral part of historians' art: they look for forces and causes of events that may have escaped the notice of those who lived through them or that may have been misunderstood. For colonials trained in classical history, as were Hubbard, Mather, and many Spanish priests, omens were not only wonders of a visible world but rhetorical devices of historiography and epic. Hence Mather's defensive comment about Livy, historian of Rome's mythic foundation, who believed in Romulus and Remus as literally as Mather believed the stories of Jonah and the whale or Moses and the burning bush. In Lucan's Pharsalia, Caesar's invasion of Rome is foretold by a hyperbolic list of omens that makes the Mexicans' list of eight seem modest: meteors, lightning, eclipses, volcanic eruptions, the extinguishing of the vestal flame, monstrous births, and several more. The passage (book 1, lines 522–600) seems designed not so much to insist that the fall of the Roman republic was magically foreseen as to measure the significance of the event by the number and magnitude of its portents. Lucan, after all, objected to the Homeric epic machinery of the gods' frequent intervention in earthly events. The Annals of Tacitus are also filled with the analysis of omens and portents for the events of Roman history. Historians, whether Todorov, Mather, Lucan, Sahagun, or one of Sahagun's native informants, play a role with respect to their readers somewhat analogous to the role of astrologers, soothsayers, or, as we call them today, military intelligence officers, with respect to the leader they serve and on whom the burden of interpretation and responsibility falls. For even when the providential sign is, like a comet, something that can be established with scientific certainty today, extant evidence of the immediate reaction to the sign is always partial, always that of one voice among many. The test of the power of an omen is not so much whether it turns out to be accurate as whether the leader to whom it is addressed heeds or defies the warning. The outcome on the battlefield is usually less definitive than the commander's immediate response.

Cortés was also concerned with omens, if only because his soldiers were. During one of the desperate initial battles against the Tlascalans, when Spanish victory was very much in doubt, "the horses were struck with something like gripes and fell to the ground. . . . The Spaniards began saying to [Cortés], 'Sire, this is a bad sign, and it would better to wait for daylight; then we can see our way.' But he said: 'Why do you heed omens? I shall not give up the march, because I sense that much good will come of it this night' " (Andres de Tapia in Fuentes 30). Todorov cites this scene as evidence that Cortés "refuses to see divine intervention—or else it can only be in his favor, even if the signs seem to say the contrary" (108). Cortés's supposedly secular mind exploits the notion of divine favor in a cynical, Machiavellian manner. Yet in his second Letter, Cortés recounts the scene differently: "Five of the horses fell and would go no further, so I sent them back. And although all those who were with me in my company urged me to return, for it was an evil omen, I continued on my way secure in the belief that God is more powerful than Nature" (62). The power lies with the leader, who in the case of Cortés is also the historian, to interpret the sign, even if he must interpret it paradoxically. Cortés's soldiers "say that if I was crazy enough to go where I could not return, they were not" (63), but he replies that he is confident that "God is on our side." As he wrote this letter, dated 30 October 1520, Cortés had not yet begun to conquer Tenochtitlán. The outcome would prove him more prophetic than his fearful soldiers. However, a leader's defiance of omens could just as easily be tragically flawed as courageously modern.

Diego Durán's *History of the Indies of New Spain* tells the story of Moctezuma's reaction to the omens of his defeat with much greater dramatic detail than Sahagun or any of the other sixteenth-century sources. Durán's magisterial work, consisting of the *History* and two separate volumes on the Aztec pantheon, festivals, and calendar (published together in translation as *Book of the Gods and Rites and the Ancient Calendar*), is a masterpiece of colonial ethnohistory and is still underappreciated because it remained in manuscript until the late nineteenth century. Although he wrote in the late 1570s, after Sahagun's work was nearly complete, Durán also interviewed natives who had witnessed some of the events of 1519–21 or their descendants who had preserved the local memory of the catastrophe. He may also have collaborated with Sahagun and the students of the Colegio at Tlatelolco (Bernal in Durán, *History* 568). Although born in Seville, Durán lived in Texcoco from the age of about six until entering the Dominican order at age nineteen, and he spoke Nahuatl fluently. Mexican scholars have given him the honorary title of "mestizo." Most important, however, Durán based much of his *History* upon a now-lost document, a source that he cites frequently as the

"Crónica" (although Doris Heyden translates this as "Historia" rather than "Chronicle"). This narrative, which may have been written partly in Nahuatl and complemented by pictographs, was also used as a source by Jesuit Juan de Tovar and by native Texcoco historian Fernando Alvarado Tezozomoc. Specialists now call it the *Cronica X*. Ignacio Bernal believes that it may have been the work of Father Andrés de Olmos, a Franciscan who in the 1530s did ethnographic research similar to Sahagun's and to whom is also attributed a document preserved and translated by French cosmographer André Thevet quoted earlier (see also Lafaye 145). Drawing on the *Crónica X*, Durán becomes a historian of the Aztecs from their own perspective, in no way reducing them to the status of victims of the Spaniards. He also expresses a sardonic skepticism about details that support a triumphalist pro-Spanish history of the conquest, even if Sahagun or Bernal Díaz had affirmed them. "I have heard it said, though I do not find it in [the *Crónica X*] that Moctezuma and the other rulers offered to give an enormous amount of wealth to Cortés if he would return to his own country" (*History* 533; see Díaz 188). This passage continues with a comment about the poetic justice meted out to the conquistadors, many of whom, Durán writes, now live in poverty and go through the streets begging. The existence of this source lends Durán's history an authority that its dramatic, literary qualities, notably the characterization of Moctezuma, might otherwise encourage modern readers to deny it. For in Durán, Moctezuma is a fully tragic hero.

In many of the nineteenth-century Indian tragedies, including the most successful of them, *Metamora*, the native leader receives symbolic omens of the impending war, suggesting that he will lose. Joseph Doddridge's *Logan, the Last of the Race of Shickellemus* portrays the reaction of the Indians and of the colonial soldiers to the same celestial phenomena. This too is the dramatic opening of Durán's account of the conquest from Moctezuma's point of view. After recounting for hundreds of pages the mythic origins of the Mexica in Aztlan, their migration into the valley of Mexico, the establishment of the Aztec empire, and its succession of rulers, Durán comes to the 1502 election of Moctezuma II (Moctezuma Xocoyoltzin) as the ninth ruler and his subsequent conquests of nearby states. The narrative shifts in chapter 61 when the leader of Texcoco, Nezahualpilli, son of the famous lawgiver, Nezahualcoyotl, and an elder statesman who had supported the election of Moctezuma, comes with a warning:

> You must be on your guard, you must be warned, because I have discovered that in a very few years our cities will be ravaged and destroyed. We and our children shall be killed, our subjects humbled. Of all these things you must not doubt. In order to prove to you that I speak the truth,

you will see that whenever you wage war on Huexotzinco, Tlaxcala, or Cholula, you will be defeated. You will always be overcome by the enemy and will suffer great losses of your officers and soldiers. I shall add this: before many days have passed you will see signs in the sky that will appear as an omen of what I am saying. . . . I shall not see these calamities and afflictions because my days are numbered. That is why I wished to warn you before my death. (452)

We find a similar passage in Hubbard's history of King Philip's War. Passaconaway, a Niantic "bashaba" (which Hubbard defines as a sachem of sachems or chief of chiefs) on the Merrimack River, told his people in 1660 just before his death, "Take heed how you quarrel with the English, for though you may do them much mischief, yet assuredly you will all be destroyed." Hubbard adds that "this Passaconaway was the most noted Pawaw and Sorcerer of all the Country" (1:48–49), just as Durán reports that Nezahualpilli "possessed the faculty of divining, which was a divine gift and a natural quality, to explain the meaning of this mysterious new thing" (History 461). The histories of these two colonial wars, 150 years and thousands of miles apart, followed common emplotments, but Durán included dramatic scenes of the native leaders that Anglo-American authors would not develop until the 1820s.

In Durán's history, the Indian tragic hero's response to the dread omens is complex enough to compare to Oedipus or Lear: "Motecuhzoma cried out to the gods asking that his days end soon so he would not have to see what had been foretold—all those calamities that were to happen in his time" (History 452). Moctezuma nonetheless tests Nezahualpilli's prophecy by launching an attack on Tlaxcala, which, sure enough, is soundly defeated. But another try the following year is more successful, so Moctezuma is uncertain about the prophecies' reliability. As for the eight omens listed by Sahagun, Durán repeats most of them, but in a different order and only in the context of Moctezuma's responses. The warning from Nezahualpilli comes well before the appearance of the comet, and when it does appear, the Tezcoco leader reiterates that this sign "comes out of the east and is directed toward Mexico-Tenochtitlán and this whole region. It is an ill omen for our kingdoms" (462). Moctezuma curses his fate: " 'Alas, if only I could turn into stone, wood, or some other earthly matter rather than suffer that which I so dread! But what can I do, O powerful monarch, but await that which you have predicted? For this reason I kiss your hands and thank you. Alas, I cannot at this moment become a bird in order to fly into the woods and hide in their depths!' With these words, says our chronicle, the two kings said farewell to each other with great sadness" (462).

In following chapters, Moctezuma's apostrophes are brought to fruition. Concerned about his legacy, he decides to order a new *temalacatl* (sacrifice stone) for the Feast of the Flayed Man (*Tlacaxipehualitl*). On this platform, the sacrifice victim was commanded to engage in single combat with a series of four Aztec foes, and if victorious over all of them, he might be released (see Clendennin 94–97). A new stone would be a lasting monument to Moctezuma's rule. But the stone itself becomes an oracle and antagonist for Moctezuma. After it is cut from the quarry, it refuses to move. Moctezuma orders death to the messengers who bring this astonishing news, yet the stone repeats its message: "Have I not told you I shall never reach Tenochtitlán? Go, tell Moctezuma that it is too late. He should have thought of this before, it occurred to him too late. Now he no longer will need me; a terrible event, brought on by fate, is about to take place. Since it comes from a divine will, he cannot fight it" (Durán, History 479). When the workers finally do move the stone toward Tenochtitlán, Moctezuma greets it with propitiatory sacrifices, but then a bridge on one of the causeways into the city suddenly collapses, sending the stone to the bottom of the lake. Divers cannot locate it, and it is later found back in the quarry from which it was carved, "all covered with paper and with signs of the sacrifices it had been offered" (480). Moctezuma goes to see it there, to pray and make more offerings, but his melancholy persists:

> "I am determined to allow death to come just as my brave ancestors did. Let the will of the Lord of All Created Things be done!" He called his stonecutters and ordered that his statue be carved on a rock in Chapultepec, in the place where portraits of his forefathers had been carved. . . . When the work was finished, he wept to see his image and, observing it, moaned, "If our bodies were as durable in this life as this carved effigy is upon the rock, who would be afraid of death? But I know that I must perish and this is the only memorial that will remain of me!" (481)

In a moment of despair, Moctezuma wished that he might be turned to stone rather than endure his fate. Now, in a moment of hubris, he seems to be taking his revenge on the earthly substance that refuses to heed his will. But of course the statue only fulfills the dark omens of his defeat. Stone wins by turning Moctezuma into a stone effigy. The carvers he pays for their handiwork are the same ones who had hewn the stone of *temalacatl* and attempted to drag it to Tenochtitlán. And the new carving might not obey his will any better than the first. Moctezuma returns to his palace and asks his lords or ministers about his anxiety: "O my brothers! How can I find consolation when I am surrounded by worries and anguish? Am I greater than Nezahualpilli, who was a prophet and who could tell of things to come and who died in spite of all his knowledge?" (481).

Moctezuma orders a memorial to himself, such as the elaborate relief carvings of Quetzalcoatl that supported his status as Mexica cultural hero or, further east in Mesoamerica, those on the great temples of the Yucatan that until the decipherment of Mayan script were the only historical record of the region's other great despotic rulers. For modern Anglophone readers familiar with *Hamlet*, *Don Juan*, and gothic novels, the scene may seem hackneyed, but in sixteenth-century and colonial contexts it is powerful indeed. Remember that the Mexica ruler maintained such an extreme isolation from his subjects that such a sculpture might have been the first chance his subjects would have had to see his likeness. And as we will see in the histories of Pontiac and Metacom, Indian leaders often inspired their warriors to valor in battle by invoking the memory of their fathers, and this imperative to match the bravery of the ancestors is echoed by Moctezuma's anxiety over how he compares to his predecessors. Yet ironically, since North American tribes had no traditions of monumental stone carving, the only stone memorials raised to those heroes were erected by Euro-Americans, such as the obelisk inscribed with Logan's name at Auburn, New York, or Ziolkowski's enormous relief sculpture of Crazy Horse.

Moctezuma confronted by the stone likeness of himself should be read not as a set piece of gothic melancholia but as a scene of tragic recognition or anagnorisis, a stony figuration of the literary device first theorized by Aristotle. Furthermore, the myth identifying Cortés as the return of Quetzalcoatl and the entire exchange between the two rulers leading up to the moment when Cortés takes his rival captive constitute a series of scenes of recognition. The word recurs many times, if allowance may be made for the varying translations from Greek, Nahuatl, and Spanish. In Sahagun's second chapter, immediately following the enumeration of the eight omens, the first ship of Spaniards to arrive at the Gulf Coast (presumably the Grijalva expedition) is met by emissaries who already "thought that it was Quetzalcoatl's Topiltzin who had arrived" (Schwartz 92), and the Spaniards evidently already knew that the Mexica came from the land's most powerful city, returning the natives' gifts by saying "here is what you are to give the ruler Moteucçoma, whereby he will recognize us" (92–93). When Cortés arrives in the following year, he receives "the appurtenances of Quetzalcoatl: a serpent mask, made of turquoise; a quetzal-feather head fan" (94) along with other valuables pertaining to Tezcatlipoca.

Everything hinges on the problem of recognizing who or what the Spaniards are. The natives' ultimate failure to resist the invasion can be attributed to their mistaken belief that the Spaniards were *teules* (gods) and that Cortés was the returning Quetzalcoatl. Historians still dispute the question of this recognition: Did Moctezuma really believe when Cortés landed that he was Quetzalcoatl, or did this recognition come about only later, after the conquest? Did Spanish ships' earlier explorations of the Yucatan alert the Mexica to the presence of these strangers and prepare the ground for the auspicious event in the year 1 Reed (1519)? These questions are important, but to frame them as arising from confrontation between two opposing cultures with no knowledge of one another is to misunderstand the nature of the recognition. Lafaye (150) and others conclude that the Mexica quickly rejected any initial belief in the divinity of the Spaniards when their hostile intentions became clear. Yet the ambiguity of the Quetzalcoatl recognition problem does not go away so easily, as Moctezuma's continued civil treatment of Cortés shows. Moctezuma may have identified Cortés with Quetzalcoatl only briefly or may have continued to do so right until he defeated the Mexica, but either way Moctezuma certainly saw much of himself both in his semidivine predecessor and in his strange adversary. Across his many manifestations, Quetzalcoatl is always a projection of the self that sees him. Cortés, in suggesting that he is the long-lost chieftain returned to claim his throne, casts the figure of Quetzalcoatl as exactly what Cortés wants him to be—an imperial despot. Other sixteenth-century historians who wrote about the myth in much more detail than Cortés also projected themselves into it.

In the first chapter of the *Book of the Gods and Rites*, Durán recounted the legend of Quetzalcoatl as he had heard it from a native who possessed a painted manuscript of the story. Topiltzin Quetzalcoatl, the human form of the god, had been a *papa* (Mexican priest), "an old man with a long red beard turning white" (57) who "fasted and abstained" and attracted "disciples known as Toltecs" (58). Topiltzin possessed the virtues we might expect a Dominican monk to admire most. Durán then endorses a theory shared by many missionaries in sixteenth-century Mexico, that St. Thomas the apostle had visited Mexico in the time of Christ. Durán stops just short of identifying Topiltzin Quetzalcoatl as St. Thomas, instead saying only that God "cannot have left [the Indians] without a preacher of the Gospel. And if this is true, that preacher was Topiltzin" (59). The persecution that Topiltzin suffered at the hands of the followers of Tezcatlipoca Durán verifies by reference to his own difficulties in preaching the faith to "these natives—rude, inconsistent, rough, and slow in understanding the things of their salvation" (59). Where Cortés cast himself as Quetzalcoatl, the exiled monarch, Durán casts himself in the persona of Topiltzin, the persecuted apostle of Christ. Topiltzin Quetzalcoatl's prophetic return becomes a jeremiad sermon: "He prophesied the arrival of strangers who would come to this land from the east. . . .

This was the punishment which God was to send them in return for the ill-treatment which Topiltzin had received" (61). The strangers "would be seen by the fourth or fifth generation, 'These will be your master! These you will serve. They will mistreat you and take your lands away, just as you have done to me!'" (62). Durán's Topiltzin is a missionary much like Durán: Topiltzin's ancient visit ensures that the Indians were part of God's creation and recipients of the message of the Gospels, while his persecution by retrograde idolaters resembles the difficulties that the church was facing, both from the natives and from greedy secular colonists, in the 1570s, when Durán was writing. As if aware of how self-serving his story might sound, Durán insists that he writes only what he has learned from indigenous painted documents.

Father Olmos, the likely author of the *Cronica X* and a member of the first generation of missionaries, the famous Twelve Franciscans who imagined themselves as a variant on the Twelve Apostles, wrote of how, after Quetzal-coatl's death, "his servitors burnt his body and . . . from the smoke of this fire was created the star Hesperus," the evening star (Thevet 214). Motolinia (the nickname of Father Toribio de Benevente, another of the twelve) also explicitly connected Quetzalcoatl to the Spanish myth of King Hesper, writing, "Spain at one time was called Hesperia" (qtd. in Lafaye 141) and suggesting that the natives' reverence for the Spaniards in general was a result of the cult of Quetzalcoatl and his association with that star. I believe Cortés was also alluding to it in the speeches he ascribed to Moctezuma. Because Venus is both the morning and the evening star, because Mayan and Mexican astronomers followed it very closely, the symbolic recognition works in both directions. The Aztec belief that Quetzalcoatl would reappear from out of the east answers to the Spanish legend that its own ancient king and culture hero, Hesper, had voyaged into the west. The twin manifestations of Venus capture succinctly the mimetic rivalry between Moctezuma and Cortés and the bidirectional *translatio empiri* encoded in the myths that each invoked for the other.

Sahagun, for his part, did not mention the identification of Quetzalcoatl with Venus and remained doubtful of any ancient visit by St. Thomas. But Sahagun offered evidence of how the Mexica ruling elite and their literate priests regarded the deity as their own. "The nobles made many sacrifices and offerings in honor of this god," Sahagun wrote (book 4, chap. 8, qtd. in Lafaye 143). As the high priest of Tula or Tollan, Topiltzin Quetzalcoatl embodied the Aztecs' identification with the Toltecs, the high civilization that they had displaced and appropriated when their Chichimec ancestors migrated from the north toward the valley of Mexico. A document titled *Origen de los Mexicanos*, attributed to Juan Cano, husband of Moctezuma's daughter, Isabella, asserts that the Mexican ruler was a direct descendant of Topiltzin (and hence that Cano himself, through his wife, was as well). According to another early source, the *Leyenda de Soles*, Quetzalcoatl's successor as ruler of the Tulas was Huemac, who was finally defeated by the Mexica and was forced to marry his daughter to them, much as Isabella became the wife of Cano (see Mackenthun 119–20).

In the epic myth-histories of imperial Tenochtitlán and New Spain, Topiltzin Quetzalcoatl was alternately self and Other, inside and outside. This is the liminal status held also by the sacrificial victim, the prisoner of war whose heart and blood are offered to the gods and whose flesh is incorporated into the bodies of the faithful sacrificers. Much like other Native American societies that engaged in the ritual torture and cannibalism of captured prisoners, the Aztecs' victim was perforce an enemy, yet the rituals implied his symbolic adoption and incorporation. Oddly, however, the lurid sacrifices that the Aztecs practiced atop their pyramidal *cues* are believed to have been a relatively recent development, beginning within a century and a half before 1519. Topiltzin Quetzalcoatl, whose death Clavigero has dated to 1052, is portrayed in nearly all sources as an opponent of human sacrifice (Schwartz 10), and this was part of the reason for his persecution by followers of Tezcatlipoca. Fernando de Alva Ixtlilchochitl, a native historian from Texcoco, made a similar claim that Nezahualpilli had attempted to put an end to human sacrifice. Brasseur de Bourbourg wrote in his lengthy biography of Quetzalcoatl that he was honored "as a hero and a martyr" (qtd. in Keen 341–44), a sacrificial victim whose Christlike attributes made him ripe for reappropriation by creole priests such as Durán and later by Servando Teresa y Mier, whose famous sermon of 1794 attributed the apparition of the Virgin of Guadalupe to the preaching of St. Thomas–Quetzalcoatl. Cortés proudly reports that after telling his people to obey "this great King," Charles V, Moctezuma also ordered a stop to human sacrifice (Cortés 99, 107). In the terms coined by Girard, Topiltzin Quetzalcoatl functions in the mythology as the surrogate victim who resolved the sacrificial crisis. Persecuted and driven into exile by the primitive ancestors of the Aztecs, his deity was later associated with wealth and cultivation by the elite. His demise made possible the rise of a modern civil society with a system of justice. But the Aztecs then betrayed his legacy by again taking up the practice of human sacrifice, and Cortés then arrived to repeat the process by sacrificing Moctezuma, Quetzalcoatl's descendant.

Girard's work also inspires the final move in my interpretation of the Cortés-Moctezuma-Quetzalcoatl story—reading it alongside the tragedy of Oedipus. Moctezuma's defeat is a drama that, like Sophocles', begins with omens delivered by messengers and proceeds through a series of recognition scenes. In the first scenes as recounted by Sahagun, Moctezuma "thought and believed that Topiltzin Quetzalcoatl had landed," that a foreigner had come to claim a vacant seat. Moctezuma ordered his messengers to deliver to Cortés the appurtenances of that god, symbols that served as the tokens of identity Aristotle describes in his first definition of the recognition scene. Oedipus, initially identified as the son of Polybus, the ruler of Corinth, comes to be recognized by recognizing himself as the son of the murdered king, Laius of Thebes. Likewise, final recognition of Cortés's identity as Quetzalcoatl can only come from his ultimate success in murdering Moctezuma and replacing him as ruler of Tenochtitlán. The improbable conquest of a great empire by a crew of five hundred Spanish soldiers is imbued with the suspense of Greek tragedy. It is a narrative not of Christians triumphing over infidels but of a battle between mimetic rivals. As Aristotle wrote, "Of all recognitions, the best is that which arises from the incidents themselves, where the startling discovery is made by natural means. Such is that in the *Oedipus* of Sophocles" (58), and such is the tragedy of Cortés, Quetzalcoatl, and Moctezuma.

Furthermore, the tragedy of Moctezuma's melancholic temerity and self-absorption, particularly in Durán's version, respects the dramatic unities of time and place as demanded by Aristotle. Prevented by royal custom from appearing before his people, he communicates only through messengers, whom, like Creon and Tieresias, he deeply mistrusts. Even as he rules over Tenochtitlán, Moctezuma remains invisible to his people and blind to their interests. "The king must never appear in public except when the occasion is extremely important and unavoidable," Durán writes in a list of laws decreed for Tenochtitlán by Moctezuma I (*History* 208). Describing the final scene of Moctezuma II's life, the disputed events on the rooftop where Cortés trotted out the captive in the hope that he might order his people to cease their attacks on the Spaniards, Durán writes, "The Aztecs, then, no longer recognized Motecuhzoma as king; he and his children and wives, his whole lineage, were to be killed, erased from the face of the earth! With them would die the wicked Spaniards who had perpetrated such evil among them!" (540). This may have been the first time that many in the violent mob had seen their ruler, yet it is also the moment when they cease to recognize him as ruler and identify him instead with the Spaniards and Cortés.[6] Durán first writes that a stone thrown by an Aztec killed Moctezuma, but in the next chapter he cautiously challenges this official Spanish version of events, reporting instead, based on his indigenous written sources, that Moctezuma and his lords had been stabbed to death as the Spaniards fled the building, "the *Historia* states all these things and a certain painted document verifies them. . . . I am obliged to record what the authors tell, write, or paint" (545).

It is difficult to determine exactly how the people of Tenochtitlán felt about their fallen ruler. Moctezuma's melancholic and cowardly behavior as portrayed in both Durán's and Sahagun's accounts can be read as a resentful ex post facto condemnation by the descendants of his subjects or, since most of the native or mestizo sources come from rival states such as Tlatelolco and Tlaxcala, as their historians' vengeance against a hated despot who had reduced their cities to tributary status. Because of the controversy over who killed Moctezuma and how, the final recognition scene in this tragedy is equivalent to the one that in *Oedipus Tyrannus* precedes the action of the play. Laius's murderer was either a highway robber or his son and successor. Moctezuma's murderer was either his subjects throwing stones at him or the foreign robbers who will be his successors. Yet from the point of view of either the Spanish or the Mexicans, his sacrifice was necessary. The ominous curse foretold in eight ways and then visited on Tenochtitlán, as on Thebes, can end only with the sacrifice of the man who interpreted the omens and articulated the curse—Moctezuma himself. Oedipus was his own monstrous double, while Moctezuma finds his in Quetzalcoatl and in Cortés. To cite Girard again, "To say that the monstrous double is a god or that he is purely imaginary is to say the same thing in different terms" (*Violence* 161).

The reasons for these parallels between the tragedies of Oedipus and of Moctezuma are as hard to pin down as the truth of the myth of Quetzalcoatl. They may be historical, coincidental, or mythopoeic. In contemporary U.S. academia, beliefs about cultural difference and the ongoing critique of Euro-centrism make it difficult to claim that the genre of tragedy is indigenous to non-Western cultures. After all, the same Aristotle who theorized the genre around its greatest exemplar, *Oedipus Tyrannus*, also theorized that barbarous peoples were natural slaves who had no rights to equality or humane treatment from those who, like the Spanish, conquered in the name of civilizing.[7] The texts about Moctezuma are of course a product of this conquest; thus, it is possible that the tragedy of his fall is an imperial form imposed by Durán. Or Durán may have been an unwitting tool of his informants. The students at the Colegio de Tlatelolco, who worked for Sahagun on his *General History*, were taught Latin and the classics, and many learned it so well that Sahagun praised them to his church superiors, who responded by closing down the academy. If Durán also worked with some of these students, who may have read Aristotle or Sophocles, or if they worked with the author of the *Cronica X*, then the version of Moctezuma's story that emerged from this collaboration may be a subversive mimicry of one of the colonizers' most cherished literary genres. The process of mimicry would be similar to what Durán says he encountered when piecing together the myth of Topiltzin Quetzalcoatl:

When I asked another aged Indian what he knew about the departure of Topiltzin, he narrated to me Chapter Fourteen of Exodus, stating that the Papa had reached the sea with a number of followers and that he had stricken the water with his staff. The waters then dried up, and a road appeared. . . . When I realized that [the Indian] had been reading what I know and I recognized the path that he was following, I ceased interrogating him in order to stop this repetition of Exodus. I suspected that he was acquainted with this book. (Book 62)

Durán writes his own scene of recognition here. The native informant tells Durán what he believes Durán wants to hear—evidence of his knowledge of the Bible. But Durán does not want to be led down that path. The path through the Red Sea might make Topiltzin Quetzalcoatl another Moses, but for Durán this type is a travesty.

This ironic encounter from the sixteenth century can be seen as paradigmatic of the cross-purposes of ethnographic encounters in the postmodern era. The colonized subject practices what Homi Bhabha has called mimicry, the replication of cultural forms inculcated by the colonizers. By the double standard endemic to colonization, the Spanish missionaries forced the Indians to practice Christian faith and learn Christian scriptures but rarely accepted the converts as full and true believers and always remained suspicious of syncretic "pagan" beliefs that persisted beneath the practice of Christian rites. Durán was particularly schizoid in this manner: his three-volume work is entirely devoted to recording Aztec culture, yet he frequently lashes out in denunciations of idolatry and the demonic Aztec deities. The second prong of the double standard comes when ethnographers seek out informants and ask for "authentic" native cultural materials, only to find the European beliefs that others had worked so hard to teach and enforce. Durán as missionary and as ethnographer thus experiences both prongs of frustration. The legacy and cultural memory of Moctezuma and Cuauhtémoc enact another version of this double standard. Moctezuma's mimetic rivalry with Cortés, his possible identification of Cortés with Quetzalcoatl, and his tragic drama can all be seen as mimicries of European forms. For these efforts, those who claim to regret the conquest have denounced Moctezuma as a traitor and a coward. Just as unsympathetically, skeptics of the myth of Quetzalcoatl such as Gesa Mackenthun have dismissed much of Moctezuma's story as inauthentic.

An alternative point of view, more popular among Latin American than among U.S. scholars, regards the tragic drama of the Aztec leader as perfectly authentic and the universality of the genre of tragedy as perfectly plausible.

To compare Native American civilizations to those of ancient Greece was a commonplace among colonial authors, a trite reflex among many such as Colden or Volney, a deep intellectual obsession among a few such as Lafitau. The commonalities are indeed striking. And from a perspective that takes seriously the cultural similarities between Native America and classical Greece, to claim Greek tragedy as unique to Western literature and therefore alien to Native Americans is just another form of the colonization of the past. Tragedy from this perspective is not an imperial literary form—or at least not one limited to Mediterranean empires. Uruguayan historian and liberation theologian Enrique Dussel asserts that the "cultured Toltecs were to the Aztecs what the Greeks were to the Romans" (192 n. 72) and takes quite seriously "the Aztecs' tragic vision of existence [in which] everything was predetermined according to the old rule of life (*Huehuetlamanitiliztli*)" (99). Dussel's *Invention of the Americas* blends Aztec eschatology with European teleology to interpret the fall of Tenochtitlán from within a native perspective or at least within what I would call a creole compromise. Aztec cosmology placed its own society in the "fifth sun," or fifth age of history. Four previous ages were identified, each associated with a color, a direction, and a particular god. According to Dussel, Moctezuma identified Cortés with Quetzalcoatl only after considering the still more ominous possibility that "this apparent Quetzalcoatl only masked the actual presence of the divine presence Ometeótl. This truly ominous event would have spelled the end of the fifth sun" (105). Moctezuma attempted to stave off this apocalyptic event first by yielding to the putative Quetzalcoatl and then by fighting him, but it occurred nonetheless: "The Spaniards installed modernity by emancipating those oppressed by the Aztecs and by denying their bloodthirsty gods any more victims. The sixth sun had dawned" (105). Dussel's rejection of Hegelian Eurocentrism barely conceals his own millenarian, pan-American teleology. He derides the analyses of Todorov, Léon-Portilla, Lafaye, Octavio Paz, and Nathan Wachtel for failing to recognize the rationality of Moctezuma's response and thus labeling him as weak or indecisive. Dussel's Latin American response to Eurocentric modernity, like that of Paz and some other Mexican academics, celebrates the mestizo identity and its "double origin, as the peripheral, colonized, victimized other face of modernity and as the modern ego which lords it over the land invaded by Cortés" (125). Although it endorses a romantic colonial appropriation of the subaltern Mexican identity, Dussel's attitude holds some advantages compared to the characteristic Anglo–North American critical posture, which lacks any term for mestizo identity and which too often insists on the strict separation of native from colonized and authentic from inauthentic. The Anglo-American perspective insists that the question of the Quetzalcoatl myth is its authenticity and fails to recognize how the myth has always involved a projection of those who defined it. Dussel's rebuttal is to embrace the myth of Quetzalcoatl and then connect it to a millenarian vision of the Spanish conquest as a kind of second coming.

For my part, I cannot confirm that the genre of tragedy has any cultural universality, and I will not attempt to pass judgment on the authenticity of the myth of Quetzalcoatl and his return as Cortés. The more important critical project, I believe, is to trace how postcolonial dreams of nationalism and millennial revival such as Cortés's, and Indian (or mestizo) plans for resistance to colonization like Moctezuma's have each appropriated political, rhetorical, and historiographic assistance from the other and from their common history of colonial conflict. For example, Gesa Mackenthun has identified how the accounts of Topiltzin Quetzalcoatl by mestizo historians Ixtlilxochitl and Chimalpahin suggest that the myth of Quetzalcoatl's return was not completed by Cortés's conquest but survived "among the inhabitants of Mexico, who appear to have nourished a nativistic and revivalist hope that their ancient leader-god would come and liberate them from Spanish bondage" (125). Mackenthun also quotes from the presentation of Quetzalcoatl in the *Codex Rios*: "Today, after the year 1550, when the Zapotecs rose up they explained it with their belief that this god has come, as was expected, to redeem them" (125). The Zapotec uprising of that year decoupled the figure of Quetzalcoatl from Cortés and restored its millennial promise and was regarded with hope by other Indians who did not participate but of course shared an interest in its success. In later chapters we shall see how subsequent episodes of Native American resistance formed a tradition of nativist revivals, from Neolin to Tenskwatawa to the Ghost Dance, that owes equal parts to Christian millennialism and to Native American mythologies.

Xicoténcatl

In the legacy of Mexico-Tenochtitlán, this process of creole and mestizo reversals of the conquest has been greatly abetted by the contrast between Moctezuma's tragic demise and the heroic resistance of Cuauhtémoc, who rallied the city's forces to fight the siege against the Spaniards in the summer of 1521. If Moctezuma surrendered his throne to Cortés, Cuauhtémoc reclaimed it. If Moctezuma's tragic drama turns on inward self-recognition and respects the Aristotelean unities by keeping the violence offstage, Cuauhtémoc's follows a more melodramatic style like that used in the nineteenth-century Indian dramas. Cuauhtémoc ordered that Spanish captives be tortured to death on rooftops in plain sight of the Spanish soldiers, including Bernal Díaz, and the Spaniards retaliated by torturing Cuauhté-moc to try to reveal the location of treasures of gold. After Cuauhtémoc was captured on 12 August, Cortés reports that the Mexica leader "came to me, and, speaking in his language, said that he had done all that he was bound to do to defend his own person and his people, so that now they were reduced to this sad state, and I might do with him as I pleased. Then he placed his hand upon a dagger of mine and asked me to kill him with it" (264–65). Of this scene, Alexander Von Humboldt remarked, "This trait is worthy of the highest glory of Greece and Rome. Under all climates, whatever be the color of men, the language of strong souls is always the same when they struggle against misfortune" (qtd. in Fuentes 234; my translation). The same indeed, since these lines result only from Cortés, who also claimed that Moctezuma freely resigned his title. Yet in the popular imagination, the courageous resistance of Cuauhtémoc compensates for the cowardice and tragic flaws of Moctezuma. In the *Dance of the Great Conquest*, a mission play recorded by ethnologist Bodil Christensen in 1894, Cuautemoc addresses Moctezuma:

> They come to mock you. All those who come here are second rate or Spaniards who lost out, who come telling you that in their country there are great cities, talking of another king at the head of the empire of Castile by the name of Charles the Fifth, of a Catholic religion.
>
> These are only stories, lies. . . . You will likewise lose your kingdom, your crown, and your scepter. You will lose all the esteem that I main-tained for you because you gave yourself up. (Léon-Portilla 164)

Cuauhtémoc articulates the Indians', mestizos', and creoles' resentment toward the Spanish and champions these peoples' pride in Mexico. How-ever, shortly after giving this speech in the play, he is killed. Cortés in fact hanged Cuauhtémoc in 1525, accusing him of conspiring with other leaders to kill Cortés and his company and then "to incite people to kill all the Spaniards wherever they might be. This done, they would place strong gar-risons in all the seaports so that no ship which arrived could escape them and return to Castille with the news. In this way they would be lords as they were before" (366). The plot had been revealed to Cortés, he claims, by a traitorous convert named Mexicalcingo.

In 1813, at the Congress of Chilpancingo, José María Morelos, a mixed-blood priest, champion of Indians and creoles, and leader of the Mexican insurgency, rose to declare Mexico independent of Spanish rule. The name of his land had been taken from that of the empire centered at Tenochtitlán and led by the ill-fated Moctezuma. Morelos unabashedly linked the new nation to that of the Indians before the Spanish invasion:

We are about to re-establish the Mexican empire. . . . Spirits of Moc-
tehuzoma, Cacamatzin, Cuauhtimotzin (Cuautémoc), Xicotencalt (Xicoténcatl) and of Catzonzi, as once you celebrated the feast in which you
were slaughtered by the treacherous sword of Alvarado, now celebrate
this happy moment in which your sons have united to avenge the crimes
and outrages committed against you, and to free themselves from the
claws of tyranny and fanaticism that were going to grasp them forever. To
the 12th of August 1521 there succeeds the 14th of September 1813. (qtd.
in Brading 580–81)

Another insurgent, Vicente Guerrero, even claimed to be descended from the
kings of Texcoco. Because the insurgencies of the 1810s and 1820s never fully
succeeded and because Mexico suffered foreign domination by France during
the Napoleonic era and then an invasion by the United States in 1846–48,
nationalists' compulsion to identify with the Aztecs of Cuauhtémoc remained
strong through the rest of the nineteenth century.

The most interesting period for our purposes, however, is the 1810s and
1820s, the era of radical mestizo insurgencies in Mexico and of revisionist
histories of the Indian wars in the United States and the start of the craze for
Indian dramas and romantic poems. The history of the conquest of Mexico
briefly converged with the U.S. literature of Indian rebels and republican
virtues with the appearance in Philadelphia in 1826 of a curious novel entitled *Jicoténcal*. Philadelphia may seem an unlikely site for the publication of
a work that Hispanist scholars identify as the first historical novel in Spanish
America. However, when Latin American independence movements erupted
in the 1810s, many revolutionaries and literati gathered there as exiles. Fray
Servando Teresa de Mier, a leading theorist and propagandist of Mexican
independence, was in Philadelphia in 1821–22. Poet José Maria Heredia
passed through as well, and many other Spanish-language books were published in Philadelphia and New York in this era. Precisely which exiled patriot wrote this novel about the leaders of Tlascala during the conquest three
centuries earlier is uncertain. Luis Leal, who coedited with Rodolfo J. Cortina a 1995 edition as part of the Recovering the U.S. Hispanic Literary
Heritage Project, presents a detailed historical and philological argument in
support of the Cuban priest and political thinker Felix Varela as author of
Jicoténcal. Guillermo I. Castillo-Feliú, who translated the text for a 1999 edition from the University of Texas Press, acknowledges Leal's work but also
cites other scholars who hold out the possibility that the author may have
been Mexican. A Mexican origin would be much more satisfying, given the
novel's historiographic interpretation of the conquest as a type or cautionary

antitype for Mexico's struggle to escape Spanish colonial domination in the creole insurgencies of 1808–21 and its attempt to appropriate an image of the native Tlascalans as virtuous republicans.

The plot for this historical novel was taken from the chronicles of the conquest of New Spain, particularly that written by Bernal Díaz del Castillo. When Cortés and his men first approached Tlascala, a city-state some forty miles east of Tenochtitlán, in the first days of September 1519, it was one of the few polities in the region that had resisted the expansion of the Mexica empire and did not pay tribute to it. The Tlascalans initially believed the Spaniards to be allies of the hated Moctezuma, and a fierce battle ensued: "Over forty thousand warriors and their captain general, named Xicotenga, were lying in ambush, all wearing a red and white device for that was the badge and livery of Xicotenga. . . . We were certainly in the greatest danger in which we had ever found ourselves" (Díaz 126–27). Xicotenga the Younger, as Díaz writes later in his history, "was tall, broad shouldered, and well made . . . about thirty-five years old and of a dignified deportment" (145). This man, whose name Cortés spelled "Sintengal" and "Sicuntengal," surpassed even Cuauhtémoc as the most defiant native leader in the conquest of Mexico and consequently became the noble chief of the anonymous novel. His initial success in September 1519 did not last long: as Díaz reports, two captains refused to join him in the next battle, where Cortés won a partial victory and sent messengers to ask for terms of surrender. Xicotenga then launched another attack, inflicting many casualties, but when Cortés again sent his messengers, all four of Xicotenga's subordinate captains defied the Tlascalan leader by surrendering. The Tlascalans soon became the Spaniards' most important native allies in the battles for Tenochtitlán.

The younger Xicotenga, however, continued to resist even after his father, Xicotenga the Elder, went over to the Spanish. Later, when Cortés was fleeing to the coast after the *noche triste*, Díaz writes that Mase Escasi (the Tlascalan political leader, spelled "Magiscatzin" in the novel) made an obsequious tribute to the Spanish and, just like Moctezuma, alluded to the myth of Quetzalcoatl for ideological support: "Their ancestors had said to them many years ago, that from where the sun rises there would come men who would rule over them" (325). Xicotenga the Younger protests this proclamation, only to have Mase Escasi and Xicotenga the Elder tear his mantle, shove him down some steps, and give him to Cortés as a prisoner. Then, when Mase Escasi dies of smallpox and needs to be replaced as leader, "Cortés ordered and decreed that it should go to a legitimate son of Mase Escasi" (336) rather than allowing the Tlascalans to choose a successor. The fact that the Tlascalas wished to choose hints at the city's republican tradition of government. During the final assault on Mexico, Xicotenga the Younger is still leading an army of Tlascalans, but according to Díaz he slyly returned to his city to stage a coup and was apprehended and hanged by Cortés. His father supposedly turned him in (397).

A complete tragic plot was thus made available to the author of *Xicoténcatl* (I have Nahuatlized the name, in accord with Castillo-Feliú), enhanced by the hero's conflict with his father and by the peculiar fact that Xicotenga the Younger retained command of an army allied with the Spaniards even after he vociferously protested such an alliance. The conflicts among military duty, filiopietism, and passionate patriotism, between loyalty to Spain and to Tlascala, made for a perfect allegory to Mexican politics in the early nineteenth century. And where Moctezuma and his Mexica empire had nearly always been recognized as a feudal despotism, Tlascala could be seen as a republic. Bernal Díaz portrayed the battlefield courage of Xicoténcatl and the Tlascalans in accord with the chivalric codes he knew best, as an army in which "each company had its device and uniform, for each Cacique had a different one, as do our dukes and counts in our own Castile" (129). The postconquest Tlascala Codex, drawn by Tlascalans who survived the 1520s and wished to lobby for preferments and tax abatements from the Spanish, also conformed to feudal style, showing Xicoténcatl (presumably the Elder) and Magiscatzin coming to give tribute to Cortés and Malinche (figure 2.4), in the precise iconographic form seen earlier (see figure 2.2) in the image of Moctezuma. But the author of *Xicoténcatl* rejects such feudal associations. Supported by accounts by Clavigero and others, he writes, "The Republic of Tlaxcala . . . was a confederated republic; sovereign power dwelt in a congress or senate, composed of members elected one for each party" (8)—that is, for each of the city's four independent districts.

The novelist also seems to have been well aware of the ethical and literary conventions of republican tragedy. He (or she?) may have attended productions of some of the early Indian dramas during his stay in Philadelphia, and he certainly knew of some of the major British dramas that established the genre. The style of the novel resembles a stage drama, for much of it is given over to long dramatic speeches by the Indian characters, extended versions of the sort that Cortés wrote on behalf of Moctezuma and Díaz wrote on behalf of Mase Escasi and others. As Castillo-Feliú reveals, the author copied several passages out of a lesser-known seventeenth-century work, the *Historia de la conquista de México* (1684), by Antonio de Solís. This was an odd choice: Solís was an energetic apologist for the conquistadors. His *Historia* justifies the infamous massacre at Cholula and attacks Las Casas and other historians who denounced such atrocities. But Solís's ideological slant evi-

FIGURE 2.4. Cortés receiving Xicoténcatl, from the Tlascala Codex, an expanded version of the *Lienzo de Tlascala* that was presented to Philip II of Spain in 1585 as part of the city's case in a legal dispute. Courtesy of Special Collections, Glasgow University Library.

dently did not dissuade the author from copying him. As we shall see again in the next chapter, such were the methods of historical revisionists in the service of heroic Indian rebels.

Xicoténcatl is a thorough republican deist. In him the values of Thomas Paine are projected onto Native America three centuries before, and the triumphalist historiography of earlier authors (including Solís) is rejected. When Magiscatzin describes the Spaniards' guns and ships and recalls prophecies about rulers returning from the east, Xicoténcatl replies, "Human frailty has always received such prophesies with a timid credulity, but woe to those people that allow themselves to be deluded by those that try to profit from them! Their firearms, their floating palaces are nothing more than works of man's ingenuity" (12). He later asserts that "government by one does not seem to me to be bearable except among peoples whose ignorance makes them incapable of finding out for themselves or whose vices and degradation make them insensitive to oppression" (56–57). He finds a friend and kindred spirit on the Spanish side in Diego de Ordaz, the lone positive character among the conquistadors. Cortés sends Ordaz to try to climb Popocatapetl, and Xicoténcatl is impressed by this act of scientific skepticism: "More than once, I have wished to climb the mountain and my father has stopped me . . . because for such an enterprise it was necessary to demonstrate that one shows disdain for the worry that one has for what is sacred" (61). Ordaz, however, does it in part to impress an Indian girl, Teutila, for whom he harbors an irrational passion.

The key plot element that the historical sources could not provide was, of course, the love interest, and the dilemma that virtuous men faced between loyalty to love and to country was essential to Indian tragedy. But the novel updates this device by applying it to women as well. Doña Marina in *Xicoténcatl* transcends her stereotype as fallen woman and is perhaps the book's most complex character. She falls in love with Diego Ordaz, the only Spaniard who shares the hero's republican virtues, and after he resists her attempts to seduce him, she calls him "a ridiculous Cato." When Malinche gets pregnant, either by Ordaz or Cortés, she repents of her treachery and her Christian conversion and reaffirms her Indian roots. She expresses an instant affinity for Teutila, the daughter of a cacique of Zocotlan who had been allied with Tlascala until Magiscatzin double-crossed her father and delivered him into subjugation by Moctezuma. Teutila is captured by Cortés, who lusts after her. A love quadrangle develops connecting Doña Marina, who loves Ordaz, who loves Teutila, who loves Xicoténcatl, who develops a brief crush on Doña Marina. But love remains a weak force indeed among these noble republican Tlascalans. When Cortés departs for Mexico and Xicoténcatl is in command of one of the Tlascalan detachments, Teutila rushes to her lover's side and begs to join him, but Xicoténcatl insists that she return to her captor because the "voice of the nation is the only one that the republic's soldier ought to hear" (76–77).

The hero's rigid attention to his military duty over his sentimental love is a virtue, but like Juba in Addison's *Cato*, the tragic pathos is derived less from the lost love than from the fact that these very republican virtues seem to doom his cause. Xicoténcatl fights alongside Cortés because the city's ambitious and craven ruler commands Xicoténcatl to do so and in spite of the fact that he knows it will lead to ruin. Not until Xicoténcatl is arrested by Tlascalan authorities for meeting with an ambassador from the rebel forces led by Guatamotzin (Cuauhtémoc) does the hero finally turn against Cortés and devise a plan to assassinate him. Yet he still intends to resign his commission first so that his act will not be punished by a massacre of his people. Cortés becomes suspicious and orders Xicoténcatl arrested and tortured. Under these torments, Xicoténcatl sheds a manly tear for Teutila and delivers his death song. This is not a curse on the colonizers, as Metamora delivers, but a political prophecy aimed at the Mexican creole insurgents: "Tlaxcala will be the victim of a tyrant, and the fiery Tlaxcalans will prostrate themselves," but "the torments that I am suffering, are going to awaken your former valor, and undoubtedly you, oh valiant Tlaxcalans, you will avenge America, punishing the monsters that are tormenting me! A thousand times happy am I if my sacrifice makes you return to your former heroism!" (142).

North American audiences read or heard the death songs of Indian heroes with a cathartic ambivalence. Because they did not fully identify with the colonizers who had defeated the chief, they sometimes, as we will see in the next chapter, transformed the curse into a blessing for their own revolt against colonial rule. But for Mexicans, as for the author of this novel, the anxiety of self-recognition when they read, watched, or contemplated the tragedy of the conquest was even more acute. The tension between Mexican creoles and Spanish *peninsulares*, "which emerges whenever one attempts to grasp the meaning of a political episode in New Spain" (Lafaye 7), left the former in a liminal position that could be identified either with Moctezuma, the victim of the *peninsulares*' invasion, or with Cortés, who was removed from his office as governor of New Spain in 1526 by an envoy from the peninsula, or with Cuauhtémoc and Xicoténcatl, who rose up against Cortés. The myth of Quetzalcoatl offered one solution to the problem of self-recognition faced by all postconquest Mexicans—native, mestizo, creole, and Spanish. Seravando Teresa de Mier's famous 1813 dissertation, in which he expanded on Durán's hint that Quetzalcoatl was St. Thomas and attributed to this latent Christian influence the apparition of the Virgin of Guadalupe, was one important contribution to the myth in the early nineteenth century. But I believe that the problem of recognition was already operating within the Quetzalcoatl myth in 1520 and that it affected not only Moctezuma and the Aztecs but Cortés, Durán, and other Spanish historians as well. For before struggling to create a myth of nationhood, Mexicans struggled to emplot the history of their land's violent past. Its genre was tragedy, and the difficulties of recognition, the ambivalent reversals in character and ethos, formed part of this literary structure.

CHAPTER 3 / METACOM

> It is not now a time to talk of aught
> But chains, or conquest, liberty, or death.
> —Cato, in Joseph Addison, *Cato* (1712)

> Is life so dear, or peace so sweet, as to be purchased at the price of chains
> and slavery? Forbid it, Almighty God! I know not what course others may
> take, but as for me, give me liberty, or give me death.
> —Patrick Henry to the Virginia Convention, 23 March 1775

> Death! Death! Or my nation's freedom!
> —Metamora, in John Augustus Stone, *Metamora; or,*
> *The Last of the Wampanoags* (1829)

Metamora; or, The Last of the Wampanoags marked the height of the
craze for Indian chiefs as tragic heroes on the American stage. Although
it had many precursors in the genre and many followers, no other play
achieved the same degree of success. "*Metamora* was the Indian drama of
the nineteenth-century American theatre," wrote theater historian Richard
Moody ("Lost" 354), and Metacom, the actual name of the Wampanoag
leader, became around 1830 the Indian hero. In fact, eight separate plays
were written about Metacom between 1822 and 1894 (Eugene Jones 66), but
only the text of *Metamora* survives. John Augustus Stone's drama won a prize
competition sponsored by twenty-three-year-old actor Edwin Forrest, who
became exclusive owner of the work and played the lead in hundreds of
performances during a superstar career that continued into the 1860s. Metamora thus became the most popular role for the most popular actor in the
nineteenth-century United States.

A series of recent studies of *Metamora* and of Forrest have emphasized
how this play about King Philip's War in 1675–76 reflected contemporary
political concerns about Indian relations. The play premiered in New York
on 15 December 1829, exactly one week after President Andrew Jackson, in
his first annual address to Congress, articulated his policy of Indian removal.
Jill Lepore asks rhetorically, "Did the same forces that brought thousands of

Americans to see *Metamora* also lead them to support sending thousands of Cherokees to Oklahoma?" (193). Her answer is yes, and Scott C. Martin, Teresa Strouth Gaul, Jeffrey Mason, and B. Donald Grose ("Edwin Forrest"), in separate articles on the play, all agree that the stereotype of the vanishing Indian, personified in *Metamora*, helped to justify what many white Americans believed to be an inevitable process of terminating the sovereignty of native peoples. But these readings gloss over the fact that substantial opposition to Indian removal existed at the time and that the relationship between the play's politics and the nation's Indian policy was and is far from obvious.[1] I propose a different interpretation of the play that takes seriously the figure of Metacom/Metamora as a heroic political leader whose rebellion was justified by the same ideologies articulated in histories of the U.S. revolution against England. The context for a historicist reading of Metamora is not simply the removal controversy of 1829–30 but the historiography of sovereignty and revolution in both England and America. The play's plot closely follows that of several historical romances published in the 1820s that linked the cause of Indian sovereignty to the fate of a melodramatic heroine and to England's revolutionary strife during the seventeenth century.

Metacom, whom the English called King Philip, had the fortune to schedule his uprising with portentous coincidence. As James Fenimore Cooper wrote, "The first blow was struck in June, 1675 . . . just a century before blood was drawn in the contest that separated the colonies from the mother country" (xi). In the historiographic style of Puritan New England and of the 1820s, King Philip's War became an analogue or typological figure for the war of American independence. And as the epigraphs to this chapter indicate, the rhetoric of Metamora and of republican tragedy in general both contributed to and was influenced by the most stirring oratory of the American Revolution.[2] Such an analogy between native resistance to colonization and the war of independence in the thirteen colonies seems fairly obvious today, for we have inherited the politics of heroic Indian chiefs. But as Americans set out to write and interpret the history of their young nation's origins in the early 1800s, such an analogy was risky and unstable, because Metacom and his warriors could be equated with the British foes or with the American patriots. Samuel Gardner Drake, the author/compiler of fifteen editions of *Indian Biography*, was certainly no Indian hater. But he wrote in his first book, an annotated edition of Benjamin and Thomas Church's *Entertaining Passages Relating to Philip's War*, that on 20 August 1676, when Benjamin Church crossed Bristol Bay in pursuit of Metacom's head warrior, Annawon, at the bitter end of the war, the event occurred "but a few days more than one hundred years before the celebrated passage of Washington over the Delaware to attack the Hessians at Trenton, which has been so beautifully described by [Joel] Barlow" (Church and Church, *History* 128). Benjamin Church, the war's rugged military hero, secured New England for religious freedom and English hegemony; hence, he stood for Washington, while Metacom stood for an enemy Hessian mercenary. Drake was acutely aware that such an historical typology must be expressed in literature if it was to take hold, for he then exhorted "that another Barlow may arise and sing over the events of these days of yore. A vast theme for a poet!" (128).

However, the epic poems and historical novels written in the 1820s more often made King Philip their hero than Benjamin Church. These works' authors held that Metacom was the true patriot, the man who embodied the spirit of '76. Lydia Maria Child called Metacom a "heroic chief [who] displayed the most undaunted determination to preserve his independence, and guard the rights of his country against a foreign power who usurped dominion over them" (*First Settlers* 157). In his "Eulogy on King Philip" Pequot Indian activist William Apess reversed Drake's analogy by proclaiming that Philip's escape across the Connecticut River in July 1675 was "equal, if not superior, to that of Washington crossing the Delaware" (297). These revisionists very carefully studied the seventeenth-century sources but read them against the grain. Washington Irving, in his famous sketch, "Philip of Pokanoket," explained that as he read Puritan historian William Hubbard, "the homely pen of the chronicler is unwarily enlisting the reader in favour of the hapless warrior whom he reviles" (514). Benjamin Thatcher declared in his *Indian Biography* that if Hubbard called the Narragansett sachem Canonchet "a 'damned wretch,' enlarge[d] upon his cruelty and blasphemy, and exult[ed] over his final destruction . . . this furnishes, as a modern writer has aptly remarked, irresistible evidence of his heroic character" (1:304).

So who embodied the spirit of Washington, appearing ghostlike in New England a century before his time—Metacom or Benjamin Church? Were the English settlers who fought the Indians to be equated with British oppressors or with American patriots? In the 1820s and 1830s, poems and plays, novels and histories, orations and reviews all debated the proper interpretation of King Philip's War with regard to the American Revolution and grappled with principles of political sovereignty and the just rebellion of subjects against monarchs. This literature was part of a broader trend of New England writers reevaluating their Puritan forebears from amid the young republic. As Michael Davit Bell wrote in 1971, "They were torn between the patriotic impulse to idolize the founders as heroes and the romantic impulse to criticize them as enemies to independence and individual liberty" (14). But Bell did not discuss the role that King Philip and other Indian rebels played in this process, and other critics writing about Cooper, Child, and Catharine

Maria Sedgwick have likewise failed to appreciate how carefully these writers placed the histories of Metacom and other native leaders into their novels.

If Metacom was a hereditary king, the legitimate sachem of Mount Hope (in Bristol, Rhode Island), on what basis could English colonists justify killing him and installing their own polity in his place? The inescapable precedent for English Puritans was their own uprising and regicide of King Charles Stuart in 1649. Thus Cooper's *The Wept of Wish-ton-Wish*, Stone's *Metamora*, and James W. Eastburn and Robert C. Sands's *Yamoyden* (as well as Robert Southey's unfinished *Oliver Newman*, which I will not discuss) all give prominent roles to the regicides of Charles I who found exile in New England after 1660. These works assessed New England's treatment of its Indian leaders in King Philip's War against the background of Englishmen's assassination of their king. These works engaged most profoundly this historical typology, not just the contemporary issue of Indian removal.

Rebels and Sovereigns of Seventeenth-Century New England

In the chapters that follow, on Pontiac, Logan, and the Natchez, we shall see how the transformation of these Indian resistance leaders from enemy into hero began almost immediately after the uprisings were quelled, in the first writings about the wars by Euro-Americans. Metacom's rebellion was perhaps the best documented of all—Lepore lists twenty-nine contemporary reports of King Philip's War (241–44)—yet notwithstanding Benjamin Church, this war lacks a figure such as Joseph Doddridge, Robert Rogers, or Antoine-Simon Le Page du Pratz, whose published texts about wars they knew firsthand expressed the spirit of the heroic Indian chief. The heroic image of Metacom had to wait nearly 150 years before it finally matured in the revisionist histories of 1814–36. This delay occurred for several reasons.[3]

First, seventeenth-century New England's theocratic society stifled the kinds of publicity and expression that were used elsewhere to develop the heroism of Indian rebels—the theater, nonsermonic oratory, and the self-promoting campaigns of war heroes such as Cortés, Rogers, and William Henry Harrison. And even if the theater had been permitted in Boston in the 1680s, the subgenre of Indian tragedy had only begun to emerge in England. There was thus no stage on which the defiant words of Metacom, authentic or imagined, might be spoken.

Second, accounts of the war written from 1675 to 1685, such as those by Mary Rowlandson and Increase Mather, strongly resisted any heroic portrayal of Metacom. The Indians were called devils, wolves, lions (qtd. in

Slotkin 88), tigers, monsters (Church and Church, "Entertaining" 223), and "roaring Lions and Savage Bears" (Rowlandson 361); Metacom was termed a "greasy lout" (Tompson 218). Even Benjamin Church, in other respects so different from previous Puritan historians of the war, described the captured Philip as "a doleful, great, naked, dirty beast" (Church and Church "Entertaining" 451). These epithets express not simply racist contempt but the providential, evangelical hermeneutic of the Puritan patriarchate, which saw the Indians as beasts controlled by the devil or at best as human specters sent by the hand of God to punish the sins of the recalcitrant. The histories of the Mathers and of Hubbard, Benjamin Tompson's poem, and to a large degree Rowlandson's captivity narrative denied human agency to Metacom and other Indians. Without conscious, rational action, Metacom could not be a proper tragic figure or even a conspirator. The eschatology of the patriarchs often even denied such agency to their own warriors. Cotton Mather wrote that he was grateful that an Indian, not an Englishman, had killed Philip, for this showed that God was really responsible and prevented the capturer from becoming proud of his valor (2:449).

Metacom was shot by an Indian named Alderman who "offered Capt. Church to Pilot him to Philip, and to help to kill him, that he might revenge [Alderman's] Brothers death" (Church and Church "Entertaining" 449). Nineteenth-century writers made much of the treason of this man and of Metacom's tragic flaw of having earlier killed Alderman's brother, but Metacom's ignominious end was almost too gruesome to represent. "Philip's" body was drawn and quartered. Alderman received as a prize the chief's hand, the head was displayed on a post at Plymouth, and Cotton Mather reputedly stole the jaw from his skull. This treatment was consistent with seventeenth-century European criminal justice, of course, but it is nonetheless disturbing because it also fits a pattern of desecration of Indian graves and bodies, a "war trophy complex" (see Lepore 174–78) that still today fosters a morbid fetish for the corpses and artifacts of Indian chiefs such as Osceola (see Wickman). These actions by Church and the Plymouth colonists appear to have succeeded at ridiculing Metacom and disgracing his memory. He did not commit suicide like a tragic stage hero, nor did he escape capture to die years later in more mysterious, if anticlimactic circumstances, as Pontiac and Logan did. By comparison, the fate of the Narragansett sachems Miantonomo and Canonchet, father and son, was much more tragic than Metacom's. Both were apprehended and interrogated by the English before being assassinated by Mohegan mercenaries on orders from English authorities. This may be why Cooper chose to make Canonchet rather than Metacom the Indian hero of The Wept of Wish-ton-Wish.

A final barrier to the heroic image of Metacom in his own time was the lack of English interpreters who could speak Algonquian and move between native and English communities. Unlike New France and the colonial Southeast, New England did not foster a class of traders working across commercial, cultural, and linguistic frontiers. The fact that Roger Williams, leader of Rhode Island, a colony of accused heretics expelled from Plymouth and Massachusetts Bay, was asked in 1645 to interpret between the Narragansetts and the United Colonies (Jennings 275) suggests the absence in New England of the cross-cultural mediators that the French called *truchements*. Williams's stature and his controversial opinions would otherwise have rendered him too suspect for the job. Also instructive is the fate of Joshua Tift, who was taken captive by Narragansetts just before the Great Swamp Fight in December 1675 and married a Wampanoag woman. When the English recaptured him in January 1676, they did not employ him as a translator or spy but instead executed him (Lepore 132–36; Hutchinson 1:259).

Without good interpreters, we lack access to the spoken works of Metacom. Lepore writes, "Not a few historians and writers have dearly wished that Philip had left a speech. . . . But no such speech survives" (219). James Fenimore Cooper satisfied his wish for an authentic speech of Metacom by supposing the existence of a document in Algonquian, which he coyly declined to produce in "the precise words in which it has been transmitted to us" because he assumed none of his readers would understand it (314). We do have words imposed on Metacom, however, for the Plymouth Colony recorded its negotiations with him, such as the 1671 Taunton Treaty in which he agreed to surrender weapons and pay tribute.[4] But for modern readers, such language lacks the authenticity and the eloquence that are part of the figure of the heroic Indian chief. The New England Puritans made no attempt to mimic the style of Indian eloquence, as William Henry Harrison and many others did in the eighteenth and nineteenth centuries.

Philip's amanuensis for written communication with Plymouth was John Sassamon, whose mysterious drowning in January 1675 nearly all histories identify as the key event precipitating the war. Sassamon "lived like a heathen in the quality of secretary to King Philip," wrote Cotton Mather (Samuel Drake, *History* 49). In today's parlance, Sassamon was "a cultural mediator, a man who was neither English nor Indian but who negotiated with both peoples" (Lepore 25). Yet unlike the career mediators in other colonies, such as Logan's father, Shickellemus, Sassamon's skills seemed to attract only resentment from both sides. Lepore's fine chapter on Sassamon traces his long relationship with John Eliot, the Puritan "apostle to the Indians" who with the assistance of Sassamon and others translated the Bible into the Massachusetts language, yet she concludes that Sassamon's literacy made him suspect to Metacom and his tribe and may have led to his death. Sassamon attended Harvard College for a term and in 1673 became minister to the converts, or "praying Indians," of Nemasket. As relations between Metacom and Plymouth deteriorated, Sassamon's value to each side might have increased, but instead he became less trusted. In 1671, when Plymouth ordered Sassamon to go again to Philip and try to convert him to Christianity, it is likely that the Wampanoags perceived Sassamon as a spy.

The motive for Sassamon's murder remains the great mystery of King Philip's War and therefore constitutes a fertile ground for revisionist interpretations. His body was found under the ice in Assawompset Pond near Nemasket. Less than a week earlier, he had paid a visit to Plymouth Governor Josiah Winslow to warn him that "Philip . . . was Indeavouring to engage all the Sachems round about in a warr" (qtd. in Lepore 21). Three Indians were apprehended, convicted of the murder, and hanged in Plymouth. It was widely assumed that they were assassins directed by Philip. The rope suspending one, Wampapaquan, broke, and in apparent hope of a reprieve he supposedly turned and condemned the other two, Tobias and Mattashunnamo (Jennings 296). In this act of betrayal, Sassamon fills a role played in the history of other uprisings by invidious females exposing the plans of male chiefs. The actual importance of Sassamon's betrayal is uncertain, for it neither foiled nor directly caused the uprising. War did not break out, after all, for another five months. Nonetheless, historians have given Sassamon a key role, and some have blamed him for spoiling what might otherwise have been a more successful Indian uprising. Lydia Maria Child quotes from Hutchinson's *History of Massachusetts*, "The war was hurried on by a piece of revenge which Philip caused to be taken upon John Sausaman"; by this act, "Philip precipitated his own nation and his allies into a war before they were prepared" (*First Settlers* 140–41; Hutchinson 1:242). Apess concurred that "this murder of the preacher brought on the war a year sooner than it was anticipated by Philip" ("Eulogy" 294). Eastburn and Sands's *Yamoyden* echoes this account concisely: "But SAUSAMAN untimely slain, / Kindled too soon the fatal train" (13). Daniel Gookin, whose two books on the conflict were greatly sympathetic to the praying Indians and denounced their internment and persecution during the war, believed "this John Sasamand was the first Christian martyr of the Indians" (qtd. in Lepore 41).

The words of John Sassamon's final message to Governor Winslow—that "Philip . . . was Indeavouring to engage all the Sachems round about in a warr"—may not be verbatim and may not even be true. If fabricated, it would not have been the first time that New Englanders had imagined a widespread Indian conspiracy against them. In August 1642 informants came to Connecticut leaders claiming that "the Indians all over the country had combined themselves to cut off all the English" (Winthrop, *History of New England*

2:78–79 qtd. in Jennings 260), but a court interrogation of detainees concluded that the story was false. Philip had been interrogated in another false
alarm around the time of his brother Wamsutta's death in 1662. The 1671
Taunton agreement effectively put Philip's signature on an admission that he
had plotted a revolt, convenient justification for a war that Plymouth may
have already intended. The belief in a conspiracy of many tribes, even in the
absence of evidence, was, as Lepore writes, part of a paranoid misconception
that all Indians would unite in common cause, even as some like the Mohegan Uncas consistently aided the English in both military and intelligence
actions. The perception of a "confederacy of the Indians . . . larger than yet
we see" (Massachusetts Council to John Winthrop Jr., 28 July 1675, qtd. in
Lepore 165) was also consistent with the Puritans' epistemology, with their
belief in a world busy with demonic spirits, many taking the form of Indians,
and a God so concerned with the colonists' punishment and restoration that
he allowed Philip's escape from their pursuit and later carefully guided their
bullets into the bodies of Indian foes (Increase Mather 91, 114). Studying
this paranoid discourse of religious and historical providentialism, Francis
Jennings wrote, "Puritans had long known the power of propaganda presented as history," concluding that in spite of English representations, King
Philip's War was not "a racial showdown" and that "the Indians never for a
moment aspired to drive out all the English or hoped for mastery over them"
(298–300).

This misconception about King Philip's War began with the Puritans, but
it also appealed to the early-nineteenth-century revisionists. A hyperbolic
passage in Benjamin Thatcher's *Indian Biography* described Metacom in the
early 1670s as "maturing one of the grandest plans ever conceived by any
savage;—that of utterly exterminating the English of the northern provinces. . . . Nothing less, than a general union of the New England tribes . . .
would furnish a safe guarantee for the complete success of such a war"
(1:151–52). Apess explained the failure of Philip's rebellion only by asserting
that all the natives should have fought together and condemning traitors and
"Indians who were hired to fight against Indians" ("Eulogy" 297). Later
pan-Indian nativist movements promoted the ideal of a unified resistance to
colonial dispossession. But to appreciate the fatal decisions that both natives
and colonists had to make in the 1670s requires recognizing, as Jennings
has, the dissensions within the ranks on each side. For as in Pontiac's
Rebellion, King Philip's War forced both colonizers and colonized peoples
to reform around new political motives. New England was slow to make a
military alliance against Metacom's uprising because its separate colonies
had for years been squabbling over land along their boundaries. The United
Colonies of New England, founded in 1643 by Massachusetts, Connecticut,

Plymouth, and New Haven, only slowly came together to mount a common force for combat against native adversaries and even then had difficulty in recruiting soldiers. Rhode Island was excluded from that group and tried to remain neutral in King Philip's War, a neutrality that was possible in the summer and fall of 1675 only because the local Narragansetts did not fully support Metacom in the uprising until colonial fighters slaughtered hundreds of their people in the Pettyquamscott Swamp Fight in December.

Like many historical romances, the story of Metacom's uprising is a multigenerational saga, beginning in the 1620s when his father, Massassoit, allied with the first Plymouth colonists and in the 1640s when Canonchet's father, Miantonomo, battled with Uncas in the wake of the Pequot War. Most modern histories of King Philip's War begin with the Pequot conflict, and William Hubbard appended "A Supplement concerning the Warr with the Pequods" to his 1677 history of King Philip's War. The slaughter of the Pequot village at Mystic in May 1637, where between three and seven hundred men, women, and children were burned alive, became a flashpoint for revisionists from the 1820s onward. Plymouth historian William Bradford wrote of Pequots "frying in the fire and the streams of blood quenching the same, and horrible was the stink and scent thereof; but the victory seemed a sweet sacrifice, and [the English] gave praise thereof to God, who had wrought so wonderfully for them" (331). Catharine Sedgwick quoted these words as well as similar ones from Hubbard in *Hope Leslie* (54) as a way to turn her readers' sentiments against the Puritans.

The revisionists also knew that the key to English victory in the Pequot War was assistance not from God but from the Narragansett and Mohegan Indians. Roger Williams secured the help of the Narragansetts, led by Miantonomo, who allowed Connecticut soldiers to approach Mystic from the east across his tribe's lands. And the English received direct assistance from Uncas, the sachem of the Mohegan villages west of Mystic, ethnic kin but political rivals to the Pequots led by Sassacus. Uncas's services to the English enabled him to emerge as the leader of surviving Pequots and Mohegans after the war, and he then turned against the Narragansetts. Connecticut and Massachusetts resented the Narragansetts' hospitality toward the radical dissenters in Rhode Island, Roger Williams and Samuel Gorton, and feared what might happen if the Narragansetts defeated Uncas and his Mohegans. In 1643 Uncas captured Miantonomo after a fierce battle and delivered him to the colonists at Hartford. The newly formed United Colonies told Uncas to take Miantonomo "into the next part of his own government, and there put him to death: provided that some discreet and faithful persons of the English accompany them, and see the execution, for our more full satisfaction" (Records of the United Colonies qtd. in Samuel Drake, *Aboriginal Races*

129). The clandestine style of this murder suggests that the English sensed that, as Drake put it, they would "stand condemned in the trial of time at the bar of history" (129). Even in the seventeenth century, portrayals of Mian- tonomo and his martyrdom carried the ambivalence characteristic of the heroic Indian chief, whose defiance was both admired and feared. Lion Gardener, an early colonist at Saybrook, Connecticut, recorded in a 1660 "Relation" a speech Miantonomo delivered to Long Island Indians at Man- tacut (Montauk) in 1642:

> He gave them gifts, calling them brethren and friends, for so are we all Indians as the English are, and say brother to one another; so must we be one as they are, otherwise we shall all be gone shortly, for you know our fathers had plenty of deer and skins, our plains were full of deer, as also our woods, and of turkies, and our coves full of fish and fowl. But these English having gotten our land, they with scythes cut down the grass, and with axes fell the trees; their cows and horses eat the grass, and their hogs spoil our clam banks, and we shall all be starved; therefore it is best for you to do as we, for we are all the Sachems from east to west, both Moquakues and Mohauks joining with us, and we are all resolved to fall upon them all, at one appointed day. . . . When you see the three fires that will be made forty days hence, in a clear night, then do as we, and the next day fall on and kill men, women and children, but no cows, for they will serve to eat until our deer be increased again. (154–55)

Notwithstanding the opposition of the Mohegans, Miantonomo came to Long Island to speak to the village led by Waiandance, a sachem who held a close alliance with Gardener, and appealed for pan-Indian unity in an upris- ing against the English. This plot fits some of the features of the "surprise attack betrayed" as outlined in chapter 7. Just after this passage, Gardener writes that Waiandance was not at home to hear the speech, but some of the village elders were persuaded to take part in the conspiracy. Waiandance quickly came and informed Gardener, and he spread the word among the English. Then "the old men when they saw how I and the Sachem had beguiled them, and that he was come over to me, they sent secretly a canoe over, in a moon-shine night, to Narragansett to tell them all was discovered" (155). Hence, Gardener gives himself credit for foiling a conspiracy for which there is little evidence apart from his own "Relation." When pub- lished in 1833, this text would only have enhanced Miantonomo's prestige as a resistance leader, for it suggested that thirty years before Metacom's upris- ing, at a time when Metacom's father, Massassoit, was honoring an alliance with the Plymouth colony, Miantonomo saw the need for a pan-Indian de- fense of New England.

Thus at midcentury the Narragansetts and Wampanoags and their chiefs represented contrasting responses to colonization—Miantonomo's tragic resistance and Massassoit's steadfast loyalty. As the only one of the five New England colonies that in 1675 still did not have a royal charter, Plymouth relied on an indirect legal claim to Wampanoag lands by virtue of its long-standing alliance with Massassoit, whom it regarded as a tributary leader. Plymouth counted on him to offer the colony the option to purchase any additional parcels before offering them to Massachusetts Bay or Rhode Island. Upon Massassoit's death, Plymouth tried to maintain the Wampa-noags' tributary status by anointing his sons and heirs: "Att the ernest request of Wamsitta, desring that in regard his father is lately deceased, and hee being desirouse, according to the custome of the natives, to change his name . . . for the future hee shalbee called by the name Allexander Poka-nokett; and desireing the same in the behalfe of his brother, they have named him Phillip" (Plymouth Colony Records 3:192 qtd. in Lepore 251–52 n. 26).

As Lepore points out, the names Alexander and Philip were also alluded to in the Massachusetts Bay Colony seal, which depicts a man holding bow and arrow, his crotch concealed in Adamic fashion by a tree's leaves, speaking words from Acts 16:9, "Come over and help us" (figure 3.1). In Acts, the apostles wrote of their successful proselytizing of Philip, king of Macedon, and the Pilgrims saw themselves as apostles, though they lacked the missionary zeal of the twelve Franciscans in sixteenth-century Mexico. The allusion remained merely an allusion, a fine example of the historiographic use of biblical typology, through which Puritans in New England interpreted their world. Much as the Old Testament prefigured the New, events in either part of the Bible were used to interpret even the minor events of King Philip's War. The revisionist historical fiction of the 1820s engaged in a secular version of this historical typology, interpreting the events of 1675–76 as prefiguring those of a century or century and a half later. Jennings suggests that the names and biblical allusions behind them were "derisive" in the minds of the English (290). Later Anglo-Americans made a popular habit of giving black slaves the names of such classical leaders as Pompey, Caesar, and Scipio, as if to suggest by travesty their lack of power or the antique obsolescence of that power. But for the New Englanders, the derision was not so mean-spirited. As the apostles had converted Philip, so too would the Plymouth Colony convert Metacom and his people, or so Plymouth believed at the time. This biblical type, however, was miscast.

Even as religious exiles, most New England colonists considered themselves English subjects and conceived of civil government in monarchical terms. As James Fenimore Cooper wrote in the preface to *The Wept of Wish-ton-Wish*, "The Europeans, accustomed to despotic governments, very natu-

FIGURE 3.1. The seal of the Massachusetts Bay Colony, founded in 1630. Courtesy of the American Antiquarian Society.

rally supposed that the chiefs, found in possession of power, were monarchs to whom authority had been transmitted in virtue of their birthrights. They consequently gave them the name of kings. How far this opinion . . . was true remains a question, though there is certainly reason to think it less erroneous in respect to the tribes of the Atlantic States, than to those who have since been found farther west" (viii). Cooper was correct insofar as the more western Indian nations such as the Ojibwa generally had no hereditary succession for their chiefs, whereas the sachemships of the Wampanoags and Narragansetts were embodied in a "royal" line that continued even into the eighteenth century. These lineages not only connected the stories of the Pequot and King Philip's War but also offered a sense of nobility that even republican revisionists such as Lydia Maria Child invoked in defense of Indian sovereignty. Child writes in her portrait of the Narragansetts that "their great qualities were, like their royal state, hereditary" (First Settlers 82) and charges the English with hypocrisy in accusing Philip of "pride and ambition, in aspiring to the sovereignty of a country which he would have enjoyed as his inheritance if they had not prevented" his succession (139). Irving described Philip still more romantically as "a true-born prince, gallantly fighting at the head of his subjects to avenge the wrongs of his family, to retrieve the tottering power of his line, and to deliver his native land from the oppressions of usurping strangers" (508).

The cliché last of the Wampanoags/last of the Mohicans/last of his race has recently been read as expressing the ideological bad faith of the vanishing Indian, wishfully and falsely declaring that these nations would be exterminated in a natural, inevitable process (see, for example, Dippie; Lepore 210–11). However, during the 1820s, "race" was often used to signify lineage or family, and such lines should be interpreted in light of this meaning. "Wampanoag" or "Pokanoket," like "Stuart" or "Windsor," was not so much a distinct tribe or culture as a name for a native band taken from the "house of" its leaders. Hence the title of Irving's sketch, "Philip of Pokanoket." This was a trope widely used in gothic tales as well. At the end of the play, Metamora learns of his only son's death and then kills his wife, to leave himself as the last of the line. Hubbard's account of Canonchet's death cast him as a stoic captured monarch, for he requested that he be executed by Oneco, the son of the Mohegan who had, by order of Uncas and of Massachusetts authorities, assassinated his uncle, Miantonomo, in 1643.[5] Consequently, Cooper in *Wept* portrayed the execution of "the last sachem of the broken and dispersed tribe of the Narragansetts" (407) in tragic style, effectively snuffing out the mixed-blood progeny that might have continued the royal line. So although recent ethnohistory has been at pains to point out that tribes such as the Pequots that have been presumed extinct in fact still survive today (see, for example, O'Connell, introduction to Apess, "Eulogy" xxvi), the literary "last" Mohican or Wampanoag really referred only to the tribe's hereditary leader, ignoring the commoners around him. Still, if colonials eliminated every heir to the throne, as it were, then the political sovereignty of a tribe could be challenged and its lands stolen. If Indian sachems were like kings, then the commoner Indians, like European peasants, had no right to choose or depose them.

This royal representation of native New England becomes even more significant in light of the fact that the Pokanoket and Narragansett houses became linked through the marriage of Wetamoo, the widow of Alexander/ Wamsutta, to Quanopin, the son of Cachanaquant, who was the brother of Miantonomo, making Quanopin a cousin of Canonchet (figure 3.2). In *Metamora*, as we will see, the connection is more direct—the hero's wife, Nahmeokee, is the daughter of "Miantinemo." Mary Rowlandson was intimately acquainted with this alliance. After she was captured at Lancaster in February 1676, Quanopin purchased her for the price of a gun. Her narrative expresses some respect for Quanopin but much disdain for Wetamoo, the most prominent of Quanopin's three wives: "A severe and proud Dame she was; bestowing every day in dressing herself neat as much time as any of the Gentry of the land; powdering her hair and painting her face" (96–97). Laura Arnold has explained that "Rowlandson appears to be unaware of how women obtained status in Wampanoag and Narragansett communities. . . .

Weetamoo was a sachem and a military commander, yet Rowlandson never makes any mention of this fact" (9, 11). The Puritan captive took for granted the existence of a patriarchal aristocracy, or "gentry," among the Indians as among the English. Faced with a wealthy and powerful native female, Rowlandson not only mocked the idea of an Indian gentlewoman but also chastised the vanity and ornament of wealthy and vain women, vices that Puritan ministers had reproached among Englishwomen. Rowlandson wrote of meeting Philip three times, and the absence of vitriol in these scenes suggests that she accepted his status even as she challenged Wetamoo's. She nowhere questions his authority, and her familiarity toward him implies that she was conscious of her own high status as the wife of a minister.

Benjamin Church offered a more direct acknowledgement of King Philip's royal status, at least after his death. When Church captured Metacom's lieutenant, Annawon, Annawon gave his captor "Philips Royalties which he was wont to adorn himself with when he sat in State," consisting of two wampum belts, "two horns of glazed Powder, and a red cloth Blanket." Annawon declared Church to be the just inheritor of these "royalties" because "Great Captain, you have killed Philip, and conquered his Country, for I believe that I & my company are the last that War against the English" (460). Like Cortés, Church implied that he should have sovereignty over the kingdom he had conquered and included in his narrative a symbolic transfer of power. Yet Church also complained frequently that his successes were not recognized by the Plymouth governor. Indeed (according to Bourne 205), Josiah Winslow sent the objects to Charles II in England instead of giving them back to Church. If Metacom really said to Winslow's messengers during the exchanges that followed Sassamon's death, "Your governor is but a subject of King Charles of England; I shall not treat with a subject; I shall treat of peace only with a king" (Hutchinson 1:294), then Metacom eventually did treat a king, but not in the manner he wished. Instead, the English monarch claimed Metacom's "royal" wealth as tribute.

The status of Metacom, Canonchet, and other sachems as "kings" of nations bearing a subordinate relationship to the New England colonies bears a disturbing resemblance to the U.S. legal concept of Indian tribes as "domestic, dependent nations" elaborated by Chief Justice John Marshall in his 1831 decision in *Cherokee Nation v. Georgia*. Thomas Hutchinson wrote that "the Indians have acknowledged themselves subjects to the Kings of England, yet they still retained, in their idea of subjection, a degree of independency which the English subjects have no pretence to. The Six Nations go no farther than to call the great King their father. They never call themselves subjects" (1:239). This anticipates Marshall's analogy of the relation of tribes to the U.S. government as one of "a ward to his guardian," and we shall see

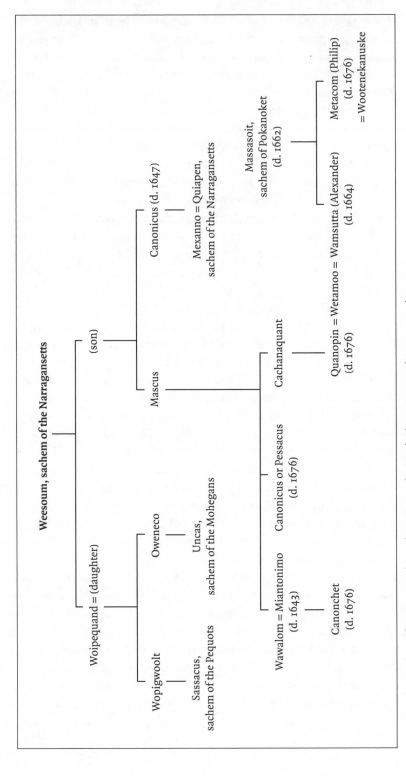

FIGURE 3.2. Genealogy of Metacom, Miantonimo, Canonchet, and other seventeenth-century sachems. Not all siblings are included. Based on Howard M. Chapin, *Sachems of the Narragansetts* (1931).

in the chapter on Pontiac how the forms of address toward imperial power—as "father" or "brother"—became a key issue in that uprising. Hutchinson explained in a note that the Massachusetts colony preferred not to see Philip in such subjection, for such a relationship to Plymouth preempted the colony's ability to negotiate with him. Thus, Philip's words are recorded in a Massachusetts Bay Colony document saying that although "his predecessors had been friendly with Plimouth governors . . . they were only agreements, for amity and not for subjection. . . . He knew not that they were subjects. Praying Indians were subjects to Massachusets and had officers and magistrates appointed, [Plymouth] had not such thing with them, and therefore were not subject" (1:239). Because Hutchinson was the last colonial governor of Massachusetts, both lines provoke interesting comparisons with the law and rhetoric of the American Revolution as a rejection of paternalism and assertion of independence. And in a larger context, the status of Metacom is paradigmatic for that of other postcolonial sovereignties, including the United States. King Philip's War could be called Metacom's "rebellion"—with that word's archaic meaning—only if his status as a subject to the king of England were accepted, and in the light of their own revolution, few American writers would accept it. So Samuel Drake commented, "This war was called a rebellion, because the English fancied them under the King of England, but that did not make them so. As well might emigrants from the United States land on the coast of France, and because they were disputed by the inhabitants, of their right so to do, call them rebels; yet, when the country was neither claimed nor improved, certainly, to take possession and improve was not wrong" (*History* 26). Drake insisted on Philip's political independence even while denying his title to his tribe's lands, according to the doctrines of "improvement" theorized by John Locke.

Metacom's Types and Revisions

William Apess's "Eulogy on King Philip, as Pronounced at the Odeon, in Federal Street, Boston" was delivered there twice, on 8 and 25 January 1836, and was published as a pamphlet in two editions, in that and the following year. As editor Barry O'Connell has noted (lxix), the eulogy mimicked and subverted a genre that had become very popular in the 1820s—public orations delivered on 4 July and, in New England, on 22 December, the anniversary of the Pilgrim landing at Plymouth Rock in 1620. With brilliant Indian irony, Apess rebuts and deconstructs the consecration of such dates: "Say to the sons of the Pilgrims (as Job said about his birthday), let the day be dark, the 22nd day of December 1622 [*sic*]; let it be forgotten in your celebration, in your speeches, and by the burying of the rock that your fathers first put their foot upon" (286). Apess may have known that Plymouth Rock itself was an invented tradition (see Seelye, *Memory's Nation*; Shields), but even if he did not, his prescription for willful forgetting skewers the typological historiography that these holiday orations were dedicated to establishing. His speech attempts to perform the act for which this passage calls, to "bury the rock," but he knows that like a grave its site will still be recognized, that the only way to rebut a historiography is to offer a revision of it, to enshrine King Philip in place of the heroes consecrated by white New Englanders and their holidays, and his rock at Mount Hope in place of theirs at Plymouth. The eulogy hence promotes a complex series of substitutions—or, to use the term coined by Joseph Roach, "surrogations"—between Metacom and King Philip of Macedon, Metacom and King Charles, Metacom and George Washington, Metacom and Napoleon. That these four men can all be brought together as possible analogues suggests just how conflicted are the politics of monarchy, republic, and empire in the figure of the heroic Indian chief.

Apess opens with a disclaimer: "I do not arise to spread before you the fame of a noted warrior, whose natural abilities shone like those of the great and mighty Philip of Greece, or of Alexander the Great, or like those of Washington" (277). Yet Apess knew that these were the names bestowed on Metacom and his brother, and a few lines later he makes an initial analogy between Metacom and Washington:

> Those few remaining descendants who now remain as the monument of the cruelty of those who came to improve our race and correct our errors— and as the immortal Washington lives endeared and engraven in the hearts of every white in America, never to be forgotten in time—even such is the immortal Philip honored, as held in memory by the degraded but yet grateful descendants who appreciate his character; so will every patriot, especially in this enlightened age, respect the rude yet all-accomplished son of the forest, that died a martyr to his cause, though unsuccessful, yet as glorious as the *American* Revolution. (277)

The syntax is a bit confused here, as at other spots in the eulogy, but in spoken delivery such errors may have passed unnoticed. Apess here includes himself among the descendants of King Philip, just as in his autobiography, "A Son of the Forest" he claimed that "My grandfather was a white man and married a female attached to the royal family of Philip, king of the Pequot tribe of Indians" (3). He presents himself as a living monument, answering to the countless stone ones erected to Washington in the previous decade. Apess knew full well that Philip of Pokanoket was a Wampanoag, not a Pequot. The reason for the error was to mirror white historiography with one of his own.[6] If white New Englanders referred to themselves as "sons of

the Pilgrims" without producing genealogical proof, Apess would produce a father to answer to "your fathers." If George Washington is the father of the United States, a figure revered as patriarch and promoted by some as king
and by many others as a virtuous republican, King Philip will be the father of his country, of all Indians, whether Wampanoag or not. The pantribal, post-colonial goals of Metacom's uprising shall have their influence not only in the subsequent rebellions discussed in this book but in Apess's own identity. The eulogy fails to make much of the mestizo nature of this legacy, however, of the fact that his genealogy resembled that of the offspring of crossblood unions evoked, only to be suppressed or assimilated, in Hobomok, Hope Leslie, Yamoyden, and The Wept of Wish-ton-Wish.

In many respects, Apess's treatment of the history of King Philip's War and his promotion of King Philip as royalty share much with Irving, Child, and other texts. Where it stands out is in the analogies to Washington and to Napoleon, for Apess challenged the platitudes equating republican rebels with freedom. On the opening page of the eulogy, Apess establishes the historical typology linking Metacom's rebellion to the American Revolution. Near the end of his speech, Apess compares King Philip instead to imperial conquerors such as his namesake: "He outdid the well-disciplined forces of Greece, under the command of Philip, the Grecian emperor; for he never was enabled to lay such plans of allying the tribes of the earth together, as Philip of Mount Hope did. And even Napoleon patterned after him, in col-lecting his forces and surprising the enemy. Washington, too, pursued many of his plans in attacking the enemy and thereby enabled him to defeat his antagonists and conquer them" (305–6).

The suggestion that the use of particular military tactics connects Meta-com to his republican heirs may have a shred of truth, but I do not think that is the point. The real purpose of these lines is to make Apess's audience hear the word "enemy" refer to the Pilgrim fathers as well as to the foes of Washington and Napoleon. Apess asks us to consider both English and natives as suffering, wartime victims. The heroic image of Metacom as conqueror, imperial or republican, must be tempered, in a careful reading of the eulogy, by Apess's concern for the victims, the losers, because in pro-nouncing King Philip "the greatest man that was ever in America" (308), Apess provoked an audience that saw its ancestors as the victims of King Philip, and he also could not fully conceal an awareness that Philip's re-bellion was not as successful as the one led by Washington. Napoleon is just as significant a type as Washington in the historiography of the eulogy.

In the 1810s and 1820s, an image of Napoleon as a self-made military hero had captivated many Americans. Napoleon and Andrew Jackson had been allies against the British during the wars of 1812–14, and the two men employed similar political styles of populist demagoguery. "Metamora" himself, Edwin Forrest, spoke of Napoleon in terms that echoed Apess's description of King Philip, with its figures of elegy and monumentality: "Wherever [Napoleon] passed he has left traces of his greatness stamped in indelible characters. A thousand imperishable monuments attest to the magnificence of his genius" (William Alger qtd. in McConachie 86). Napoleon was not only a victor but a vanquished hero. His defeat and exile to St. Helena added a romantic martyrdom to the image, which was, of course, shared by many heroic Indian chiefs. After his narration of the Swamp Fight, Apess concludes, "It appears that God did not prosper them much, after all. It is believed that the sufferings of the Pilgrims were without a parallel in history; and it is supposed that the horrors and burning elements of Moscow will bear but a faint resemblance to that scene" ("Eulogy" 299). Napoleon's invasion of Russia was a recent epic winter battle that raised the stature of the Swamp Fight. But is the analogy here between the Muscovites and the English who died in the Swamp Fight, while the retreating Philip stands for Napoleon? Or, since the Russians ultimately defeated Napoleon, is Apess linking the Muscovites to the Narragansetts in hopes that his people too might one day be victorious in defending their land? As Cheryl Walker has observed, the instability or obscurity of Apess's historical typology may have been intended as a kind of satire of the technique.

Apess's concern in "Eulogy" for the war's dispossessed also found expression in references to slavery, where his rhetoric matched closely that of Lydia Maria Child. The timeworn cliché that death is better than slavery, used by Patrick Henry and in stage speeches by defiant Indian chiefs, represented more than just rhetoric during King Philip's War, because the English sold many captured Indians into slavery in the West Indies. Benjamin Church denounced the policy (411) but did so only because he felt Indians faced with such a threat would be too fearful for him to persuade them to switch sides and fight for the English. As Neil Schmitz has shown, white advocates for American Indians later in the nineteenth century patterned their movement after that of earlier abolitionists. And in Apess's and Child's texts, the dilemma between death and slavery takes on the sentimental pathos that would be so effective in abolitionist writing, notably Uncle Tom's Cabin. Child later became a prominent abolitionist and edited the slave narrative of Harriet Jacobs. In First Settlers of New England, she wrote in the "familiar format," adopting the persona of a mother responding to questions from two daughters about New England history and Indian policy. The mother declares, "Nothing appears to have operated so powerfully on the natives, as their extreme fear of being transported and sold for slaves" (156) and later asks, "Can the torments of a few hours be compared with the anguish and despair of those who were forced to linger out a protracted and miserable existence in the basest servitude?" (163).

Sarah Savage's *Life of Philip, the Indian Chief* (1827) was another text written in the familiar format, in this case a dialogue between "Mrs. Edgerley" and her son, Charles. The ironically named Savage may have been writing for a juvenile audience, but she echoed the political theories of sovereignty and independence articulated by Hutchinson and Apess. The text begins with a portrait of Massassoit as a "sovereign" who "could yet with real greatness lay aside the state" and show hospitality to the colonists. He "even carried his politeness so far as to acknowledge himself subject to the King of England," although "Massassoit lost none of his independence by his acknowledgement of subjection" (9–10). Describing the Taunton Treaty of 1671, Savage says that Philip did not want to attend the signing, which was "galling to a mind natively independent" (30). And Philip's death at the foot of Mt. Hope evokes the same death-before-bondage stoicism as Child used: "a willing sacrifice at the altar of freedom, choosing rather to die than yield his own liberty or the rights of his nation—freedom and his country, were dearer than existence" (50).

Apess concurs that "the most horrid act was in taking Philip's son, about ten years of age, and selling him to be a slave away from his father and mother" ("Eulogy" 301). On 2 August 1676, ten days before Metacom was killed, Benjamin Church and his warriors captured Philip's wife, Wootonekanuske, and their nine-year old son. Eight months later, the son was shipped to the West Indies to be sold (Lepore 150–54). This fact made both Apess's rhetoric and the ending of *Metamora* seem palpably real. Apess's audience would likely have been familiar with this scene in the play, where the young son is shot by English troops as Nahmeokee tries to carry him across a river to safety, and then Metamora stabs his wife just before he is shot. Metamora says, "She felt no white man's bondage—free as the air she lived—pure as the snow she died!" (98). Metamora wished to save his family from the fate that Metacom's family had endured.

Melodramas of Rebellion: *Yamoyden* and *The Wept of Wish-ton-Wish*

A dictum circulates in anthropology that when two unfamiliar peoples meet, they first fight and then intermarry. This is the phenomenon explored by literary works of the 1820s that contributed so much to the revisionist image of Metacom: *Yamoyden, Hobomok, Hope Leslie, The Wept of Wish-ton-Wish*, and *Metamora*. A verse romance, three novels, and a stage drama, these works share elements of a common plot involving Indian leaders, sympathetic English heroines, and the stern patriarchs of Puritan New England.

Child's and Sedgwick's novels have recently seen a resurgence in popularity as part of revisions of the nineteenth-century canon of American literature.

But although critics have called Cooper's *Wept* a rewriting of Child's *Hobomok* (Dekker 64–72) and his *Last of the Mohicans* a response to both *Yamoyden* and *Hobomok* (Baym), and although Child admitted that she was inspired to write *Hobomok* by reading *Yamoyden*, no scholar I have found has continued to trace the thematic thread to *Metamora*. The play does not precisely fit the plot of the other four works, but bringing it into the group not only accentuates the importance of the figure of the regicides from the English Civil War but also inspires a reading of the other four texts as melodramas. Melodrama, as David Grimsted has explained, was the great democratizing genre of nineteenth-century America. It was the solution to the problem of creating high art for a democratic nation. Whereas tragedy from Aristotle to Racine had been concerned with the virtues and flaws of the great, melodrama endowed common people with that same dignity and power of feeling (Grimsted 204–6). Casting Metamora and other Indian chiefs as tragic heroes offered an ideal transition from traditional tragedy to popular melodrama, for they were noble monarchs in their own societies yet also vulgar primitives in the eyes of many whites. They carried the Aristotelean virtues of antiquity into a modern age. "Early in the century, drama was the most respected form of literature," Grimsted has written (170), and of course it could reach the illiterate masses at a time when the novel was still often seen as frivolous and feminized. Furthermore, tragic melodrama brought artistic edification to the widest possible audience. The proliferation of touring companies and local venues in nineteenth-century America meant that plays might have a much wider distribution than novels. Plays often were more successful than prose versions of the same story. *The Wept of Wish-ton-Wish* was not a strong seller for Cooper, but it inspired four separate stage versions from 1830 to 1850, none of which remains extant (Eugene Jones 60). Robert Montgomery Bird's *Nick of the Woods* had three separate dramatic productions in 1838–39, in New York, New Orleans, and London (Eugene Jones 75). Yet because so many of these plays are lost (and perhaps because the competing versions frustrate literary canonicity), nineteenth-century novels receive much more attention today than do nineteenth-century plays.

Reading the literature of Metacom as melodrama thus fosters a rapprochement between genres long segregated in American literature: drama and the novel, the tragic and the sentimental. The first step in this process is to displace the central role in the plot, at least briefly, from the tragic hero to the heroine. As Grimsted has written, "virtue and the heroine stood almost indistinguishable at the center of the melodrama, one a personification of the other" (172). The other three essential roles in his taxonomy of melodrama are the villain, the hero, and the figure of the heroine's father. By starting from the heroine and the Indian hero and proceeding to secondary characters reflecting the seventeenth-century colonial and intercultural set- ting of these stories, we can analyze the plots of the five works and reveal their common design (figure 3.3).

Child and Sedgwick, by setting their novels in the late 1620s and early 1640s, respectively, avoided the direct representation of King Philip's War or of the English Revolution. But their novels are nonetheless invested in the history of those conflicts as well as of the Pequot War. In chapter 4 of *Hobomok*, Child portrayed the politics of native New England as it would shape the wars to come. Hobomok defies the provocations of Corbitant, a Wampanoag sachem subordinate to Massassoit and "a stubborn enemy to the Europeans" (30) who accuses Hobomok of wearing "the war belt of Owanux" (an Algonquian term for English) and of turning the other cheek to threats by a powerful Pequot leader, Sassacus. In the next chapter, Hobomok informs Plymouth Governor Endicott that Corbitant may be planning an ambush. Hobomok's story in chapter 12 about Tatobam, a Pequot who resists his tribe's calls for war, seems designed to justify his apparent betrayal of the Wampanoags by making it a sign of pacifist virtue: " 'But Indian can love' " he says (86).

Many critics have applauded Sedgwick's revisionist interpretation of the Pequot War in *Hope Leslie*. Magawisca narrates the Mystic massacre from the Pequot point of view, "putting the chisel into the hands of truth" (53) and refuting the accounts of William Bradford and William Hubbard that I quoted earlier. Hubbard may have constituted Sedgwick's source for the names of Magawisca's parents, Monoca and Mononotto, whose children were placed in John Winthrop's custody following the war (356–57 nn. 4, 5). And while Hope is also living in the Winthrop household, she refuses a marriage proposal from Hubbard (154), an episode no doubt motivated by Sedgwick's historiographic preferences.

Sedgwick's ingenious solution for accommodating both melodramatic and revisionist plots in the same novel was to create three heroines, each of whom lives out different elements of a common plot outlined in my chart. In plotline b, Faith Leslie becomes the mate of the Indian Oneco, whom she marries in a Catholic ceremony. But Sedgwick avoided some of the controversy that Child incurred because, unlike Mary Conant (and Ruth Heathcote Jr.), Faith is not the main heroine and no offspring result; furthermore, like those two, she surrenders a large part of her identity and sanity at the moment of her marriage. When Hope arranges a brief meeting with her sister, Faith fails to recognize her and has even forgotten how to speak English (228). Magawisca is both the heroine of a parallel plotline, which I

	Yamoyden (1820)	Hobomok (1824)	Hope Leslie (1827)	Wept of Wish-ton-Wish (1829)	Metamora (1829)
Time period	1676	ca. 1629	Early 1640s	1662, 1675	1676
Heroine	Nora Fitzgerald	Mary Conant	Hope Leslie, Faith Leslie, Magawisca	Ruth Heathcote Jr./Narra-mattah	Oceana
Heroine's father	Fitzgerald	Roger Conant	John Winthrop Sr., Mononotto	Mark Heathcote Sr., Content Heathcote	Mordaunt
Heroine's lover/hero	Yamoyden	Charles Brown	Everell Fletcher	Conanchet	Walter
Crossracial lover	Yamoyden	Hobomok	Oneco	Conanchet	None
Crossblood child	Unnamed (raised by Fitzgerald)	Charles Hobomok Conant	None	Unnamed	[United States?]
Villain	Philip/Metacom	Corbitant	Philip Gardiner	Uncas, Philip	Lord Fitzarnold
English history infects	Fitzgerald		Philip Gardiner	Submission	Mordaunt/Hammond of Harrington
Tragic Indian hero	Philip/Metacom	Hobomok	Magawisca	Conanchet	Metamora

FIGURE 3.3: Key literary works published in the 1820s about seventeenth-century New England.

have labeled c, and a female version of the Indian mates Hobomok, Yamoyden, and Canonchet, for she nurtures a crossracial love for the hero, Everell, whom she saves from execution in a mimicry of the Pocahontas myth. The main thread of the novel features heroine a, Hope Leslie, who defies the dictates of her foster father, the ultimate Puritan patriarch John Winthrop Sr., and eludes the machinations of the crypto-Catholic villain, Sir Philip Gardiner, to find happiness and finally marriage with the hero, her cousin, Everell. This plot is very close to what Stone later created among Oceana, Mordaunt, Fitzarnold, and Walter in Metamora.

By contrast with Hope Leslie's proliferation of characters and subplots, Yamoyden reduces the cast to an essential core while still combining elements of tragedy and melodrama. And because this work, unlike Hope Leslie and Hobomok, has received very little critical attention, I shall discuss it in greater detail. When he wrote the poem in 1817–18, James Eastburn was barely twenty years old and was studying for the ministry under the Reverend A. V. Griswold in Bristol, Rhode Island. According to Charles Robert Sands, who revised and published the work in 1820 after his friend's untimely death, Eastburn "was constantly in the habit of amusing his hours of relaxation, with poetical composition; and the local traditions connected with the scenery, in his immediate vicinity, suggested to him a fit subject for his favourite employment. He often mentioned, in the course of his correspondence with the Editor, his intention of making some of the adventures of King Philip, the well known Sachem of Pokanoket, the theme of a poetical romance" (preface to Yamoyden n.p.). Sands then says, as if to deflect challenges to the work's historical verisimilitude, that Eastburn outlined it with some help from Hubbard's History and then wrote the poem very quickly. Although most literary histories attribute the work to Eastburn, John McWilliams believes that "the published poem is largely the work of Robert Sands" (132). The hero, Yamoyden, has no apparent historical original, but an eighty-five-page appendix to the poem contains lengthy notes and quotations referencing not only William Hubbard but also Heckewelder, Charlevoix, Jefferson, Mather, Mackenzie, Trumbull, Colden, Carver, Lahontan, and others. Yamoyden's mediocre verse, epic histrionics, and romantic excesses have left it inaccessible and seldom read today, but the notes suggest that its authors took themselves seriously as ethnographers of American Indians. They got many of the details wrong, but their effort should be judged by its attempt at tragic gravity, ethnohistorical accuracy, and sympathy for the hero, Yamoyden.

Metacom's tragic flaw in Yamoyden lies in his suspicion of his warriors' loyalty. He refuses to forget old dynastic enmities and thus fails to forge a successful pantribal alliance. In the opening scene, he recalls the betrayals of the Pequot War, which had made a martyr of the Narragansett sachem:

MIANTONOMO'S honoured head
Our laggard vengeance will upbraid;
CANONCHET and PANOQUIN, slain
By coward hands, look forth in vain,
From their eternal towers, to spy
Mohegan ghosts go wandering by;
For blood a thousand heroes cry,
Whose bones, untombed, dishonoured lie. (35)

Because the killers of the Narragansett sachems were Mohegans led by Uncas, Metacom distrusts Agamoun and Ahauton, two Mohegan warriors who are now members of his camp. Agamoun expresses his commitment to the cause and warns of the fate that awaits them if they do not resist colonization in language that echoes Gardener's speech of Miantonomo:

ye've known me long,
Ye saw me when your cause was strong
Ye proved me when your hopes were weak,
If ye have found me wanting, speak!
Here if we linger, what remains?
Inglorious death, accursed chains! (40)

Yet Metacom still distrusts the two men, and, denouncing the traitorous Uncas, he kills Agamoun. His loyal henchman, Annawon, then declares that a Nipmet warrior in his camp, Yamoyden, is also under suspicion. Yamoyden lacks republican martial virtues: he

Lists in Aquetnet's woods to hear
A bird, whose music is more dear
Than vengeance or than liberty.
A turtle dove he nurses there,
And shelters with a parent's care.
That nest must be despoiled! (50)

Yamoyden is a Christian convert and the husband of the "turtle dove," the heroine, Nora. They live in secluded domestic bliss until in the second canto Yamoyden leaves to go on the warpath, and Nora and her infant are kidnapped by Wampanoags following orders from Metacom. Ahauton, evidently based on Alderman but named for praying Indians Anthony and William Nahauton (Lepore 40), turns against Metacom after his brother, Agamoun, is killed, and when he learns of the kidnapping he sets out to rescue Nora, successfully freeing her but not her infant son.

The third canto presents the background and the sentiments of the two sides in King Philip's War, which mirror one another. First a "War Hymn" that the Indians address to their god asks that their enemies "shall fade like the smoke which is lost in the air, / They shall melt from thy wrath when its fury shall glare" (92). Then a minister tells a narrative of England's colonial settlers, recalling the omens of the present war (111). Third on the scene is Nora's father, Fitzgerald, whose story echoes elements of Ahauton's and Metacom's:

> I had a brother whom I loved,
> The only kindred death had left;
> And wo our mutual friendship proved,
>
> .   .   .   .
>
> We parted, when a venturous band
> In quest of wealth, to foreign land,
> The aspiring Edward drew;
> 'Twas with a deep, foreboding gloom
> Beside our parents' sacred tomb,
> We spoke our last adieu.
> And tidings rare and far between,
> Told where the wanderer's steps had been;
> Till silence o'er his fate was spread,
> And when long years had come and fled,
> I deemed him numbered with the dead.
> But now, to blast the realm's repose,
> The banner dark of discord rose,
> And friends became each other's foes
> In that unnatural war. (117–18)

Fitzgerald had fought with Cromwell's men at Naseby Plain, where he attacked a courser, and

> as my descending sword
> Through the reft mail his bosom gored,
> Then sunk, his fleeting vigour gone;
> The staggering steed rushed blindly on;
> O God! as round my victim gazed,
> His eye with death's dull amel glazed,
> I saw my brother in my foe!
> And he his murderer seemed to know
> For pardon lingered in his eye,
> As death's drear shadow flitted by. (122)

This is a tragic recognition scene as defined by Aristotle in the drama of Sophocles. And Fitzgerald's traumatic memory of it mirrors Metacom's tragic flaw and fate. Failing to recognize his Mohegan allies as brothers in a common cause, Metacom has killed Agamoun and consequently incurred the vengeful wrath of Ahauton.

In the wake of this scene, Fitzgerald marries and has a daughter, but when his wife dies he leaves for America. In Massachusetts, his daughter is soon visited by Yamoyden, and although Fitzgerald tries to forestall their courtship by promoting an English suitor in Yamoyden's place, "I trod too rudely on the shoot / Of that young passion's embryo root" (128), and Nora runs off with the Nipmet. Fitzgerald plays the role of the blocking father in this frontier melodrama. As Fitzgerald finishes his narrative, Ahauton carries in the unconscious Nora, who has fainted in the midst of her deliverance. The Puritan patriarch lashes out at his daughter—"Polluted outcast of the wild / I cannot brook to see my child!" (137)—but grudgingly accepts her return and is informed that her son was not recaptured with her. At the end of the third canto, he and Ahauton set out to look for the child.

Yamoyden's fourth canto is a gothic masterpiece, the most preposterous yet creative part of the work. Eastburn and Sands deploy a wealth of ethnographic sources to create a scene for which there is no basis in the histories of Metacom's uprising. A prophet, doubtless inspired by the Shawnee Prophet whose fame spread so widely during the War of 1812, delivers a long harangue detailing the history of the Indian tribes and of the grievances that motivated the war. The importance of native spiritual leaders in anticolonial uprisings dates back to Nemattenow and Neolin, as we have seen, but appears to have gained popular currency only after Tecumseh and Tenskwatawa, and Eastburn's contribution to the trope is much stronger than *Metamora*'s Kaneshine. However, consistent with Werner Sollors's diagnosis that such defiant curses are actually oblique blessings of white colonization, this prophet's message is finally comforting to white readers. For if his vision of the past motivates him to invoke the spirits of slain warriors in the name of the uprising, his clairvoyance reveals an image of the self-satisfied Americans of 1820:

> the white sails gleam thick o'er the bosom of ocean;
> As the foam of their furrows is lost in the sea,—
> So they melt in one nation, united and free!
> Mourn, land of my fathers! the red men have past,
> Like the strown leaves of Autumn, dispersed by the blast!
> Mourn, land of the victor! a curse shall remain,
> Till appeased in their clime are the ghosts of the slain! (158)

The prophet then yields the platform to a wicked priestess, who begins a "Song of the Pow-wahs," invoking a spirit of evil and "Hobomaqui, power of night."[7] She picks up Nora's infant, who has been drugged with opium, and is about to hurl him into a tree when Yohoweh appears and with a thunderbolt strikes down the priestess, saving the child. Yohoweh is actually Fitzgerald and his gun. Eastburn, like Cooper and Child, uses the Indians' supposed faith in superstitions and prophetic visions as colonialist shorthand for their weakness in the face of Anglo-Saxon progress but also as a key plot device in what are not so much historical as historiographical fictions.[8] Philip, like the reader, knows the outcome of his war, and this anachronism is consistent with heroic Indian chiefs such as Moctezuma. Just before the scene of his final stand on "Mount Haup" (Mount Hope), Metacom dreams of his tribe's happy past, of Sausamon's death, and Wetamoo's flight. This is based on a report by Increase Mather, echoed by Hubbard and Cotton Mather, that Eastburn and Sands included in their notes: "Increase Mather says,—'It seemeth that night Philip (like the man in the Host of Midian) dreamed that he was fallen into the hands of the English'" (330–31). Who knows what Increase Mather's source was? In the poem the dream employs the figure of the tiger or panther, which as we shall see is important in *Metamora* as well.

> Now in a gloomy glade he stood;
> Along the sward, the tracks of blood
> Led, where in death a cougar lay;
> Fast ebbed the crimson stream away;
> But fiercely rolled his balls of fire,
> And flashed their unextinguished ire
> Toward the forest; where the chief
> An armed Indian could descry,
> Who, less in anger than in grief,
> Seemed to behold his victim die,
> Though lost his features were in gloom.
> But Philip knew his hour was come,
> And death from Indian hand was nigh.
> For that red tiger oft had been,
> In earlier dreams prophetic, seen.
> It was the emblem of his soul,
> The shade that still his life attended. (203)

For the final canto, the narrative point of view shifts to Nora, who learns from Ahauton that he had saved her and that her son may still be alive. She paddles with him to Mount Hope and witnesses the final combat and death of Philip, as Benjamin Church had told it. But as the battle continues, she hears the death song of her beloved Yamoyden. His demise occurs in a manner that anticipates Magawisca's sacrifice for Everell in *Hope Leslie*:

> A well-known form she marked among
> That haggard, fierce and desperate throng,
> Round, howling for their prey;
> And, o'er her father's white hairs swung,
> As high a murderous axe was hung,
> She saw YAMOYDEN stay
> The lifted arm; alas! too late
> To break the blow; impelled by fate!,
> Averted from the old man's head,
> On his own faithful breast it fell! (248)

She rushes to his side, and the scene of her *liebestod* is as lush and erotic as in Chateaubriand's *Atala*, though the father is now a Calvinist patriarch rather than a Catholic priest:

> She strove, with her long locks unbound,
> To stanch the grim and ghastly wound;
> Her husband's arms, with dying grasp,
> Her lovely, wasted form enclasp;
> Her constant bosom to his breast
> Closer and closer still he prest;
> Her gaze met his, where every ray
> Of earthly passion past away;
> The glance of love, that conquers time,
> Was blent with confidence sublime;
> As if on their departing view,
> With heaven, love was opening too
> FITZGERALD, bending o'er them, brushed
> Aside the tears that freely gushed.
> "Farewell, misguided one!" he said,
> "Dim light along thy path was shed;
> There may be mercy, even for thee!
> Thy child is safe; may heaven to me
> Be kind as I to him shall be!" (250)

As in *Hobomok*, the child is liberated from his miscegenating parents to be assimilated as an Englishman, and as in *The Wept of Wish-ton-Wish*, the scandalous behavior of a woman who mated with an Indian is exorcised by her death at the end of the tale.

The Wept of Wish-ton-Wish is the only one of Cooper's novels set in seventeenth-century New England and is the most prominent work of prose fiction about King Philip's War. That it offers a typological historiography akin to other romances of the period is easy to recognize, but there has been little agreement as to its proper interpretation.[9] Although several critics, including George Dekker and Warren Motley, have recognized the importance of the character of the regicide, Submission, I have found no full exploration of the complexity of Cooper's portrait of the Indian hero, Canonchet.

Because, as we have seen, Canonchet inherited his title from the martyred leader, Miantonimo, and was captured and assassinated by Mohegans loyal to Massachusetts and Connecticut Puritans, the choices Canonchet faced between obedience and rebellion, between an alliance with the English or with Metacom, reflect the New England colonists' ambivalence toward the English Revolution and the later American one. Cooper's novel argues that the Puritans' apparent antimonarchist ideology, on which a typological kinship to the American Revolution's Founding Fathers might be predicated, was false. It was belied by their reverence for patriarchal authority, by their reactions to the Restoration of 1660, and most of all by their fear and persecution of Conanchet (as Cooper spells the name) as a potential rival monarch.

Because it is set not in Boston or Plymouth but in the Connecticut River Valley, the novel takes a different perspective on King Philip's War than Metamora and Yamoyden. The revised 1833 London edition of the novel was titled The Borderers; or, The Wept of Wish-ton-Wish, emphasizing how the setting distances the action from Boston-area political conflicts. But it does not ensure any autonomy from English politics. As the Heathcote family and farm are introduced in the first two chapters, the frontier they inhabit is an idealized space. Although they had "heard of travellers massacred, and of families separated by captivity . . . the apprehension of danger was greatly weakened in the breasts of those so remote as the individuals who composed the family of our emigrant" (10–11). On the banks of Wish-ton-Wish Creek, a tributary of the Connecticut, Mark Heathcote has built a fortress "on and around a natural elevation in the land, which arose so suddenly on the very bank of the stream as to give it the appearance of a work of art" (14). While numerous tree stumps prove that the farm is a recent establishment, other aspects of Cooper's description suggest that it is much older. The "primeval edifices atop the mound were so disposed as to form, as far as they went, the different sides of a hollow square," and the central hexagonal stone keep "stood on a low, artificial mound, in the center of the quadrangle" (15). This description endows the settlement with a sense of archeological antiquity, and readers in 1829 would likely have recognized the resemblance to accounts of the Mound Builder sites recently discovered in the Ohio Valley and

described in works such as Caleb Atwater's "Description of Antiquities Discovered in the State of Ohio." Cooper also evoked the Mound Builders in *The
Prairies*. Many interpreters of the mounds ascribed them to an ancient civilization distinct from the contemporary Native Americans, and some had
proposed that the culture's demise resulted from an invasion by these red
men (as in the Connecticut Wits' *Anarchiad*; see Gordon Sayre, "Mound
Builders"). The allusion both suggests that the Heathcotes have a "native"
sovereignty over their land equal or superior to that of the Indians and fore-
shadows the attacks to come. As Mark Heathcote welcomes the "stranger"
who turns out to be the exiled regicide, he introduces himself as "the master
of what thou seest" (21), a possible allusion to the famous opening line of
William Cowper's poem, "The Solitude of Alexander Selkirk": "I am the
monarch of all I survey."

The Connecticut setting is thus simultaneously a state of nature in which
sovereignty is established according to Locke's principles from the *Second
Treatise* and a nervous colony subordinate to metropolitan political rule.
When Heathcote greets the "stranger," each man is wary of the other as a
potential enemy, depending on his position with regard to the English Civil
War and Restoration. Mark's first question for the visitor concerns the distant king's authority over this remote colony, whether "he that now sitteth
on the throne of England hath listened to the petitions of his people in this
province" (25). Since the first half of the novel is set in 1662, Heathcote is
eager for news about the journey of Connecticut Governor John Winthrop Jr.
to London the previous year in quest of a royal charter legitimating the
colony's title to land seized from native Pequots, Mohegans, and Narragansetts and in part challenged by neighboring Rhode Island (see Jennings 279–
80). The stranger reports that Winthrop had met with success, but his
explanation of precisely how the charter had been secured departs from the
historical sources and provides Cooper's first hint at the Puritans' bad faith:

> The grandfather of him the good people of these settlements have com-
> missioned to bear their wants over sea, lived in favor of the man who last
> sat upon the throne of England; and a rumor goeth forth, that the Stuart,
> in a moment of princely condescension, once decked the finger of his
> subject with a ring wrought in curious fashion. It was a token of the love
> which a monarch may bear a man. . . . It is said in secret that this ring
> hath returned to the finger of a Stuart, and it is openly proclaimed that
> Connecticut hath a charter. (27)

Hence, the charter was obtained by repudiating the Puritan colonists' support for the Roundhead revolutionaries and affirming in its place a dynastic
alliance between the Winthrop family, including John Winthrop Sr., New

England's leading founding father, and the Stuarts. The Stuarts' persecution of religious dissent was thus easily forgotten in favor of the hunger for land. The ring seems to symbolize a marriage of political expedience between ancient enemies, as if the Winthrops had sold their daughter's virtue to an enemy chief. Moreover, a family of hirelings or vassals who live on the Heathcote farm is named Ring, though the precise reason for this is not clear.

The stranger departs, and Mark, alarmed by fears of an Indian attack, sends his son, Content, on a reconnaissance mission. Content captures an Indian boy. Cooper, as usual, declines to give the boy's name for many pages after he first appears, but it is finally revealed when farmhand Eben Dudley says that "he beareth the look of a chief that was slain by the Pequots, at the wish of us Christians, after an affair in which, whether it was well done or ill done, I did some part of the work myself" (62). This "affair" was the Mystic Massacre of 1637. He gives the chief's name as Leaping Panther, or "My Anthony Mow." Dudley does not speak Algonquian, nor does the boy understand English, but the latter repeats the name "Miantonimoh!" and Ruth Heathcote recognizes that "the Child mourneth for its parent. The hand that slew the warrior may have done an evil deed" (63). The captive is Conanchet.

Any further inquiry into the captive's identity is interrupted by the arrival of new visitors, four men whom Cooper based on the inspectors sent from England by Charles II in the early 1660s to find and apprehend the exiled regicides. The men confirm the stranger's report about the charter and the Restoration, saying, "power now resteth in the hands of a race long set apart for its privileges . . . a merry prince! And one but little given to the study and exercises of his martyred father" (66). In this scene, Cooper sets up two historiographic analogies. The first links the captive Conanchet to Charles II, for both are young princes succeeding martyred fathers. The second links Conanchet to the fugitive regicide, for when the inspectors search the Heathcote "citadel" for him, they instead find the Indian. "By the dark visage of the Stuart!" they exclaim, "here is naught but an unarmed savage boy!" (75). The investigators who expected to find Mark Heathcote harboring a fugitive regicide instead accuse him of posing as a monarch himself and of holding another monarch captive: "Why is this dark-skinned boy a prisoner? Dost dare to constitute thyself a sovereign over the natives of this continent, and affect to have shackles and dungeons for such as meet thy displeasure?" (75). The clash between the frontier patriarch and the young Indian leader portends not just a frontier conflict but a civil war.

Some months after this scene, the mysterious stranger returns. He meets Conanchet outside the fort, and when they enter, the two warn of imminent danger. The Narragansetts indeed soon attack, and after a siege they succeed at recapturing Conanchet, still called Miantonimoh at this point, and take captive the young Ruth Heathcote. The citadel is burned to the ground, but the besieged settlers survive by hiding in a well beneath it.

Chapter 17 begins the second half or, in some editions, the second volume of the novel, set thirteen years later, during King Philip's War. The second generation of settlers, led by Content Heathcote and Reuben Ring Jr., consider reoccupying the ruins of the settlement at Wish-ton-Wish, as if hoping that the patriarchal seat and its natural sovereignty might be restored. Cooper emphasizes the hereditary nature of authority among both English and natives by giving the same names to characters in two or more generations: Mark Heathcote and his grandson, Reuben Ring and his son, Ruth Heathcote and her daughter all share the same name, as do Charles I and Charles II, John Winthrop Jr. and Sr., and Conanchet, who goes by his father's name, Miantonimoh, for much of the novel. Readers can easily be confused by these repetitions, but the thematic point may be that assumptions about heredity can obscure the differences among generations, specifically the declension of the younger away from the elder's purity. Content bears not his father's name but a moniker that suggests his arrogant complacency. He fails to defend Wish-ton-Wish during the first attack; is later involved in the barbaric Swamp Fight, or Pettyquamscott Massacre (263); and then accepts a commission for another military expedition against Conanchet, the man whom his father had sheltered. Reverend Meek Wolfe's name is likewise significant, and like Content he rides on his ancestors' coattails: "The descendant of a line of priests," he holds "one set of opinions so steadily" that his mind repels doctrinal challenges as if "closed by a wall blank as indomitable obstinacy could oppose" (276). His sermons are Cooper's parody of the providential propaganda of Puritans such as Increase Mather: "The army of Mahomet itself was scarcely less influenced by fanaticism than these blinded zealots" (339).

The first sermon, on the English settlers as chosen people of God, is interrupted by the regicide and the former captive Whittal Ring, who rush into the church to warn of an Indian attack. This scene is based on the legend of the Angel of Hadley, according to which that town in central Massachusetts was saved from an Indian attack on 1 September 1675 by the spectral appearance of an elderly man in church. Oral histories collected by eighteenth-century historians Thomas Hutchinson and Ezra Stiles maintained that the figure was William Goffe, one of the four regicides who had fled to New England after the Restoration. The Angel of Hadley is an English Protestant Santiago, a myth consolidating wartime propaganda of a divine dispensation to slaughter a heathen enemy. For Nathaniel Hawthorne in his modified version of the legend in "The Grey Champion," the story's gothic-romantic interest lay in the uncertainty about whether it was a supernatural or a real event. Cooper seems to satirize the Angel of Hadley. But he may also have been inspired by stories around New Haven that another exile, Edward Whalley, Goffe's father-in-law and a first cousin of Oliver Cromwell, had taken refuge for a time with the Narragansetts in Rhode Island (see Welles; Dunn).

In the second attack on Wish-ton-Wish, the Narragansetts take more captives: Content Heathcote; his son, Mark, and daughter, Martha; as well as the regicide, Submission. The captives engage Metacom and Conanchet in a spirited debate over the justice of the Puritan conquest. Content declares that his God "hath led his servants hither, that the incense of praise may arise from this wilderness," to which Metacom replies, "Your Spirit is a wicked Spirit. Your ears have been cheated. The counsel that told your young men to come so far was not spoken in the voice of the Manitou" (311–12). But Conanchet does not second Metacom's defiance; his support for the war is weaker because he has not received the spiritual inspiration that, according to one of the most consistent tropes in the literature about native uprisings, comes from the fathers of its leaders. When Metacom asks if Conanchet "beholds the spirit of the brave Miantonimoh, who died like a dog beneath the blows of cowardly Pequots and false-tongued Yengeese," an Algonquian word for English (314), Conanchet answers, "I do not see the spirit of my father" (315). Metacom tries again by invoking the memory of the Petty-quamscott Massacre, asking if "he sees the warriors of the Yengeese coming into his village, murdering his old women, and slaying the Narragansett girls" (315). But again Conanchet demurs; he would rather forget that trau-matic scene, and he even questions his own courage: "Can he fight with the God of the Yengeese? He is too weak" (316). Conanchet, speaking of himself as usual in the third person, explains that he last spoke with the spirit of his father "ten snows" ago, when he told Miantonimo's spirit of his captivity at Wish-ton-Wish. "They shut him in a cage like a tamed panther!" (317), and "the boy felt the power of the God of the Yengeese! His mind began to grow weak; he thought less of revenge; the spirit of his father came no more at night" (317). In spite of the elder Mark Heathcote's remarks about how the young captive refused to learn English or yield to their attempts at conver-sion, the Christian influence apparently did take hold. Doctrines of for-bearance and justice were instilled in him: "Though their skins were so white, they had not slain his father" (317), he says. Cooper thus oddly reverses the images of the two native sachems and their fathers. "Metacom has no soul but the spirit of his fathers" (316), and this spirit impels him

toward vengeance, even though this father was Massassoit, an ally of Plymouth. Conanchet, for his part, does not hear his father impelling him

toward vengeance, even though Miantonimo had been barbarically murdered by Uncas on the orders of Massachusetts colonial authorities.

The real cause of Conanchet's peaceful forbearance is probably not his
acquaintance with the Christian God, however, but his mating with Ruth
Heathcote, the lily-white Cooper heroine who has been rechristened "Narra-
mattah," supposedly Narragansett for "driven snow." Her "classic beauty"
is introduced in a erotic physiognomy in the following chapter. The trauma
of her transculturation has erased all memory of her life as Ruth Heathcote,
and critics of the novel have argued that this is because Cooper was so
skittish of miscegenation that he refused to represent any conscious adaptation to Indian life (Opferman 37–38; James Wallace 205; Fiedler 203–5). Yet
the scene should be read in the context of Conanchet's remarks in the
previous chapter. Her amnesia may be more complete, but he too finds
himself cut off from his memory of his parent. Cooper was too skittish
perhaps to represent their love and marriage as directly as Child does Mary
Conant's to Hobomok, but seen through the critical lens of the melodramatic plot formula, the amnesiac rejection of the father's will is the manner
in which Narra-mattah and Conanchet express their romantic individualism.
And, in good melodramatic fashion, the tides of war will doom the two
lovers to death. She says, speaking in Narragansett and in the third person
like Conanchet, "Why should she look back in dreams, when a great chief is
her husband?" (329). And he is melted by her expression of devotion: "The
eye of the warrior, as he looked upon the ingenuous and confiding face of
the speaker, was kind to fondness. The firmness had passed away, and in its
place was left the winning softness of affection, which, as it belongs to
nature, is seen, at times, in the expression of an Indian's eye, as strongly as it
is ever known to sweeten the intercourse of a more polished condition of
life" (329).

Philip Gould has argued in regard to this scene that "Conanchet shows an
inability to execute what must be a politics of retribution. . . . Conanchet's
political shortcomings result from his earlier exposure to the domestic ethos
of Christian love. The Narragansett sachem internalizes a feminized ideology" (Covenant 167). If we judge Conanchet by the ethos of eighteenth-
century republican tragedy, Gould is right: Conanchet chooses love over war
and therefore loses the war. But if judged by the ethos of nineteenth-century
sentimental melodrama, Conanchet's actions are perfectly comprehensible,
and in the context of nineteenth-century racism, Cooper's assertion that he
felt affective emotion as strongly as a "civilized" person is a strongly sympa-

thetic line. Let us withhold judgment of Conanchet, however, because the novel is not yet over. The direct cause of his being captured and ultimately killed like his father lies in his affection not for Ruth but for Submission, the regicide.

Sometime after the second attack, Conanchet goes to meet Submission in his hideout in a cave above the Connecticut River. His errand is to deliver his infant son by Ruth into the hands of Mark Heathcote and its other white relatives. But since, as many critics have observed, the son is never named and its fate not explained at the end of the novel, this cannot be the scene's purpose. Cooper's description of Submission's hideout resembles his introduction of the Heathcote citadel in chapter 3. Erosion has created a site tailor-made for human habitation, implying that the regicide's residence there has a native sovereignty: "Time and the constant action of water, aided by the driving storms of winter and autumn, had converted many of the different faces of this ravine into wild-looking pictures of the residences of men" (340; see also Hutchinson 1:186–87). The regicide has become a hermit, and Conanchet believes that the white man has a special relationship with his God: "The Manitou of the pale-men should be pleased with my father. His words are often in the ears of the Great Spirit!" (344). Coming immediately after Cooper's parodic paraphrase of Meek Wolfe's self-justifying sermon, this line suggests that Submission carries the true Puritan religious and political spirit. But the fact that Conanchet calls Submission "my father" is still more significant. The regicide has symbolically replaced Miantonimoh in Conanchet's heart and mind. Conanchet is thrilled to learn that "my father has taken the scalp of a great chief!" and he has consequently been "debarred from the councils of this valley" (348). Conanchet accepts as foster father a man who has proven his defiance of the English. But Conanchet misreads this political rebellion; the enemy of his enemies will not be his friend, for race trumps any political typology in Cooper's novel, and Submission's act of regicide links him to the Puritans who ordered the assassination of Miantonimoh. Conanchet beseeches Submission to join with the Narragansetts: "Let him change the color of his skin, and be a grey-head at the council fire of my nation" (348). Submission declines with words that sound very much like those spoken by his hermit/renegade kin, Natty Bumppo, in The Last of the Mohicans: "It may not be . . . it would be 'easier for the blackamoor to become white, or for the leopard to change his spots,' than for one who hath felt the power of the Lord to cast aside his gifts" (348). Submission's counteroffer is that Conanchet should "break, then, this league with the evil-minded and turbulent Philip" (348).

Cooper's account of Conanchet's capture makes a significant alteration to his historical source, Hubbard. Canonchet was apprehended near the Pawtucket River by two captains of the Connecticut militia. He fled across the river but slipped in midstream and soaked the powder in his musket, "upon which Accident, he confessed soon after, that his Heart and his Bowels turned within him, so much as he became like a rotten Stick, void of Strength" (Hubbard 2:59), as if linking his power to gun and phallus. In Cooper's account, a traitor named Mohtucket leads Meek Wolfe and other Puritans to Canonchet's hideout. Metacom says of Mohtucket that "Metacom hath never looked on this young man like a friend since the brother of Mohtucket was killed," suggesting a motive of fraternal vengeance, as in the case of Agamoun and Ahauton in *Yamoyden*. At the hideout, Canonchet and Submission finally pledge alliance to one another. Canonchet promises to stay by the older man at his slower pace, and in gratitude Submission replies as they are crossing the river, "Though of white blood and of Christian origin, I can almost say that my heart is Indian" (387). At that moment a pursuer shoots at him. Conanchet drops his musket when he sees Submission fall in the water, but the latter had not been hit but had just slipped. Conanchet then helps Submission hide in a tree and makes himself a decoy, sacrificing his freedom to save the white man's life. The Indian rebellion is forestalled by the preservation of the English rebel.

The book's final two pages list the inscriptions on the gravestones of its characters, culminating with "the Narragansett" and, by his side his mate, Ruth Jr., or "The Wept of Wish-ton-Wish." The mood is elegiac. As Leslie Fiedler writes, "Cooper asks of his reader not sympathy for the Indian people in general but for the Indian chief, the aristocrat at the end of his line" (184). Cooper's contribution to the political typology of King Philip's War and the early republic is indeed nostalgic and conservative. In the late 1820s, when he published the novel, Cooper was a Jacksonian democrat with a diplomatic appointment, and he recoiled from the more progressive republicanism that we find in Sedgwick and Child. *The Wept* includes no character such as Hope Leslie whose instincts and aspirations clearly reflect that revisionist New England historiography or who might be interpreted as advancing an antiremoval position sympathetic toward the Indians. In the absence of such a figure, Conanchet's role is all the more significant, for it is he who would challenge the repressive Puritan oligarchy. But his furtive alliance with the man who took the scalp of the English sachem does not lead to another revolution but only delivers Conanchet to a martyr's fate like that of his father and of Charles I. If Conanchet learned from Submission and/or Miantonimo a legacy of revolutionary resistance, it did him no good. His lapsed memory of his father doomed him to repeat his father's fate.

Conanchet's weakness arose out of a need for the guidance of his late father. Like the younger Heathcote, Conanchet lacks not only the bravery but also the political savvy of his patriarch. Metamora also weighs in on the issue of patriarchal authority and political self-determination, but its Indian hero has the perspective of the father rather than the son. Metamora answers the accusations of Errington, the "chief of the council" in New England, with this speech: "Then would you pay back that which fifty snows ago you received from the hands of my father, Massassoit. Ye had been tossed about like small things upon the face of the great waters, and there was no earth for your feet to rest on; your backs were turned upon the land of your fathers. The red man took you as a little child and opened the door of his wigwam" (74).

In the conventional diplomatic language of Indian relations in Anglo America, natives were supposed to address colonial officials, metropolitan kings, and the U.S. president as "father." This passage inverts that tradition. Metamora refers to the Pilgrim settlers as children, orphaned from their father-king and adopted by Metamora's tribe under the leadership of his father, Massassoit, friend of the Pilgrims during nearly fifty years of peace between the Wampanoags and the Plymouth colonists. In Metamora, the heroic chief's rebellion is not that of an ambitious son: it carries the weight of the parents. Metamora, based on the rebellious Metacom, successfully embodies his father even while reversing his policies, whereas Cooper's Conanchet failed utterly to revive the spirit of Miantonomo even in continuing his policy of resistance to English colonization and repeating his unfortunate end. And in contrast to Cooper's critique of declension, Stone's play sanctions a reconciliation between generations—not only the generations of the colonizers, represented by the emigrant, Mordaunt, and his daughter, Oceana, but also those in the contemporary audience, where the elders belonged to the generation of the revolutionary founders and their children and grandchildren to the Jacksonian era. William Apess's political typology identified Metacom with George Washington, and although Washington is never mentioned in Metamora, this is Stone's message as well.

The play opens as Mordaunt regards the setting sun and bemoans his exile: "England, my home! When will thy parent arms again enfold me? Oh! When for me will dawn a day of hope? Will not sincere repentance from my scathed brow efface the brand of regicide?" (60). Unlike Submission, Mordaunt regrets his revolutionary act, and his mordant moniker reflects his grief and nostalgia. It is his late wife's birthday, but he grieves only for himself, and by a typical melodramatic plot structure, intends to sacrifice his daughter's virtue for his own selfish cause: "Yet must she wed Fitzarnold. His alliance can with oblivion shroud the past, clear from my scutcheon every rebel stain, and give my franchised spirit liberty" (61). As Grimsted has written, "The moral flaw of the melodramatic father was often some crime or indiscretion committed as a young man, with which the villain blackmailed him for his daughter's hand" (182). The contrast between father and daughter is replete with nationalistic and, as we shall see, utopian revolutionary overtones. Where he cannot escape the pull of England, she is "born on the heaving deep, the child of storms, and reared in savage wilds" (61). She is in love with Walter, an orphan "ship boy who could trace existence no further than the wreck" from which he had been saved by Wolfe, his guardian. The lovers thus both have the autochthonous innocence of the American Adam, severed from ties to patriarchal England.

Metamora alludes to many historical elements of King Philip's War but revises and alters them to emphasize a theme of the relationship between the revolutions of 1640 and 1776. In act 2, scene 1, a minor character named Church comes to Metamora to summon him before the colonial council, much like the summons that led to Miantonomo's interrogation and death. Stone enhances the relationship by linking the Wampanoag and Narragansett sachems through marriage. Metamora tells his wife, "Daughter of Miantinemo, peace! I will go. . . . Bring me . . . the spear that was thy father's when Uncas slew him for the white man's favor" (69). The council accuses Metamora of a "plot with the Narragansetts," of harboring "a banished man, whose deeds unchristian met our just reproof " (73; no doubt referring to Samuel Gorton or Roger Williams), and of conspiracy in the murder of Sassamond, which has been revealed by the traitorous Annawandah. Metamora does not flatly deny that indictment, for according to the play's most repeated line, "Metamora cannot lie" (69). But the most interesting part of his response echoes the defiant speech of the historical Miantonimo, while adding to it a greater knowledge of English politics: "Why do you that have just plucked the red knife from your own wounded sides, strive to stab your brother?" (73) he says, alluding to the religious and civil strife in which *Yamoyden's* Fitzgerald also stabbed his brother. Although the play contains allusions to the treachery of the Mohegans under Uncas, dissension among the Indians is less significant than among the English, who are divided by faction, sect, and generation. When Metamora stabs Annawandah and delivers another defiant threat, an English soldier fires at him as he flees but instead wounds Mordaunt, as if to symbolize that the consequences of the English Civil War prevented a coordinated response to the 1675 Indian uprising.

Metamora then summons his warriors and invokes his father's spirit in support of the cause, claiming that Massassoit had said to him years earlier, "O son of my old age, arise like the tiger in great wrath and snatch thy people from the devourer's jaws" (77). His wife, Nahmeokee, departs to carry the hatchet to her Narragansett tribe. The warriors attack just as Fitzarnold threatens Oceana's virtue. They burn his ship and Mordaunt's house, but as Metamora is about to kill Mordaunt, Oceana saves him by showing an eagle feather that Metamora had given her in the play's first scene. Since "the Wampanoag cannot lie" (81) and must respect the feather's calumet-like power, he instead takes Oceana, Walter, and Wolfe captive while fleeing the English troops. The English capture Nahmeokee and her son. In act 4, Oceana comes to the villainous Errington and Goodenough to beg for the prisoners' release, and when Metamora learns that his wife is not dead but held captive, he relents from the torture of Wolfe and Walter and goes to negotiate an exchange. The deceitful English instead take him as an additional hostage.

The climax of *Metamora* brings together the melodramatic and historiographic plots and the paternalistic symbolism in each. As act 5 opens, Oceana is at her mother's tomb, lamenting also the lost Walter. Fitzarnold enters and makes a melodrama villain's threat: "Thy father willed thee mine, and with his latest breath bequeathed thee to me. . . . I deem as nothing thy unnatural hate, and only see thy fair and lovely form" (90). Oceana is saved by the arrival of Metamora, emerging through the door of her mother's tomb. Invoking again " 'Revenge!' cried the shadow of my father" (91), he attacks Fitzarnold, who in spite of warning, "This sword a royal hand bestowed! This arm can wield it still." is quickly disarmed and killed. Metamora spares the regicide but has no mercy for the royalist.

The following scene explains Metamora's escape: "The ruined pile which now serves as our prison was, years since . . . the residence of Mordaunt" (92). Mordaunt had dug a secret passage, evidently for his own use to evade royal inspectors, and the chief quickly found and used it. The repressed history of the English regicide facilitates the Indian rebellion. Stone's play repudiates the historical typology implied by the Angel of Hadley episode, which links the heroism of the regicide to the English cause in King Philip's War and promotes instead a revisionist view that makes the Roundhead rebellion against King Charles a mandate for Native American rebellion against Puritan patriarchy in New England. Both Mordaunt's effort to deny his daughter's will and his disrespect for the memory of his late wife are undone by the revolutionary past that he has repressed and is trying to absolve by marrying Oceana to Fitzarnold. He has less in common with Cooper's Submission than with his John Winthrop Jr., who had given up antimonarchist principles by giving his ring back to Charles II. By emerging from the tomb, Metamora also symbolically inhabits the position of Oceana's mother, who, as he tells it in the opening scene, saved the life of his father, Massassoit, during an illness years earlier. And although Oceana is for a time held captive by Metamora, she faces no sexual threat: his maternal role sanctions the long-standing Pilgrim-Wampanoag alliance and the freedom that Oceana will enjoy as an enfranchised republican citizen and native of New England.

The news of Mordaunt's secret passage comes along with the revelation of his true identity as "Hammond of Harrington . . . the outlawed regicide" (92). This was not the name of any of the four regicides known to have fled to New England in the 1660s. Stone's choice of the name is an allusion that clearly signals that Metamora is no vanishing Indian but rather a republican political hero. James Harrington was the author of The Commonwealth of Oceana (1656), a utopia written during the protectorate of Oliver Cromwell and dedicated to him. Harrington was born in 1611 into an aristocratic family and in the 1630s rose to a prominent position in Charles's Privy Chamber Extraordinary. Harrington sought unsuccessfully to mediate between Roundheads and royalists and was present at the king's execution. Oceana takes the form of a lengthy constitutional blueprint for a republican society secured by the redistribution of property in England, or "Oceana," into five thousand equal parcels. The utopia is led by Lord Archon Olphaus Megaletor, clearly based on Oliver Cromwell, to whom Harrington offered the work in hopes of influencing policies and securing a stable republican government in England. Olphaus claims inspiration from the Spartan lawgiver Lycurgus, and I believe that the link to Lycurgus inspired Stone in writing Metamora. For according to Plutarch, Lycurgus was a democratic founding father: "Viewing with joy and satisfaction the greatness and beauty of his political structure" in Sparta, he sought to "deliver it down unchangeable to posterity" (73). Having secured confirmation from the Oracle at Delphi that "the laws were excellent, and that the people, while it observed them, should live in the height of renown" (74), he committed suicide by starvation, a political self-sacrifice "to make his very death, if possible, an act of service to the state" (74). Because Harrington is addressing Cromwell, the ending of his Oceana is less morbid and offers the dictator an attractive retirement, more like Cincinnatus than Lycurgus. Olphaus, "having spoken of his government as Lycurgus did when he assembled the people, abdicated the magistracy of Archon" (245) and "left the senate with the tears in the eyes of children that had lost their father" (246), retreating to a remote country house to enjoy the devotion of his subjects and a pension of 350,000 pounds per annum. The idealized response of the Oceanans to their founder resembles that of Americans to George Washington and his retirement.

Plutarch's *Parallel Lives* offers biography as exemplary life, as edifying political lessons for his readers. By pairing great men of Greece with those of his own Rome, Plutarch engages in a pre-Christian form of historical typology that strongly influenced Cotton Mather in his *Magnalia Christi Americana*. Sarah Savage had commented in her *Life of Philip* that the hero's father, Wamsutta/Alexander, had "a strength of passion, and loftiness of spirit, that, graced by the genius of Plutarch, would have harmonized well with Grecian greatness" (19). Stone's allusion to *Oceana* and through it to Lycurgus and Plutarch makes perfect sense within the logic of historical typology and the reconsideration of New England's past that was ongoing in the 1820s. Ezra Stiles, James Otis, and the two John Adamses had written of their great admiration for Harrington, and at least one scholar has perceived influences of his system on the constitutions of Pennsylvania and the Carolinas (see Russell Smith). Many theatergoers therefore must have caught the allusion, but I have found no critic who mentions it. In this light, Metamora's death takes on new significance.

The fate of Metamora's family also fits with the model from Plutarch. Lycurgus "left an only son, Antiorus, on whose death without issue his family became extinct" (77), like Logan's and like George Washington's. In this manner, the tragic Indian chief asserts his kinship to republican heroes and lawgivers. The apparent racial difference was unimportant to men who had already appropriated Tammany, the legendary Delaware chief, as the titular head of political clubs formed in New York and Philadelphia in the 1790s–1820s (see Deloria 45–58). In *Metamora*, the neoclassical values of republican tragedy enter the age of melodrama and sentimentality. And while this is good for Oceana, it is bad for Nahmeokee. Inspired by the most severe of all republics, the Lacedemonian, Metamora, who had granted mercy to Oceana and Mordaunt, condemns the feminine weakness of Nahmeokee when she intercedes to prevent him from killing the shaman, Kaneshine, who had warned that the rebellion might fail. After she explains how their son died, shot by the English as they fled across a river, much like Conanchet's death, Metamora reminds her of the strict law of virtuous republics and radical abolitionists: "Better to die by the stranger's hand than live his slave" (97). He then takes her weapon, which had belonged to her brother, "Coanchett," and stabs her with it. Moments later, the English shoot Metamora to death.

If, as Grimsted asserts, the most important character in a melodrama is the heroine, then *Metamora* is the story of Oceana, the utopian republic, spawned by a repentant veteran of the English Civil War and born(e) across the sea into the New World. Her freedom and virtue are threatened by the villainous monarchist, Fitzarnold, who also represents the threat posed by

Britain during the American War of Independence. She is saved by the heroic Indian chief, who slays Fitzarnold and makes her his adopted daughter and sole heir. The play makes Metamora an immortal lawgiver, an avatar of republican virtue to be appropriated by Anglo America. In contrast to Cooper's pessimistic vision of Indian and English rebels in a failed alliance against English kings and New English patriarchs, Stone's drama, which far exceeded Cooper's novel in popularity, anoints the younger generation as legitimate heirs to a progressive American sovereignty.

Edwin Forrest thrived in such roles, as stubborn idealists doomed to be defeated by a corrupt oligarchy (McConachie 97–110). The Jacksonian populism of *Metamora* and of Forrest's other starring roles as Jack Cade and Spartacus endorse the values of what Bruce McConachie calls the traditionalist workingmen, who admired Andrew Jackson and distrusted big government.[10] Nonetheless, *Metamora* should not be interpreted as a straightforward endorsement of Jackson's Indian removal policy. A story recounted by nineteenth-century actor James Murdock about an 1831 performance by Forrest in Augusta, Georgia, shows the ambivalence of contemporary political reactions to *Metamora*. The hit play premiered in front of a packed house, but when "Metamora upbraids the elders for their unjust and cruel treatment of his tribe, and denounces war and vengeance upon them until the land they had stolen from his people should blaze with their burning dwellings and reek with the blood of their wives and children," the curse elicited "a perfect storm of hisses from the excited audience, who seemed ready in their fury to tear everything to pieces. Order was with difficulty restored, and the performance continued till the curtain fell upon the dying chief amid unqualified evidences of disapprobation. . . . The next day the public mind was highly excited, and Mr. Forrest openly charged with insulting the people of Augusta by appearing in a character which condemned the course of the State in dealing with the land-claims of the Cherokee Indians" (298–300). Augustans boycotted the following performances, and the play closed early. Georgians clearly interpreted the play as a critique of Jackson's Indian removal policy, yet Grose, Scott C. Martin, and Lepore all insist that the work represented an endorsement of that policy. As Grose sums up, "The Stone script was generally received as a pro-removal vehicle" ("Edwin Forrest" 192). If Georgians interpreted the play as pro-Indian and antiremoval, why would northeasterners, who generally were more sympathetic toward the Cherokee, see it as proremoval? To resolve this contradiction we must look beyond a facile historicism that reads *Metamora* strictly in the context of the political events at the time of its premiere and decode a political allegory that was not topical but typological. The death of Metamora is not that of a vanishing Indian who is forced to abandon his sovereignty and remove beyond the western horizon but that of a revolutionary stoic and lawgiver bestowing his sovereignty on a republic that he has nurtured in the body of his foster daughter, the heroine, Oceana. In *Hobomok* and *Yamoyden*, the mixed-blood offspring of the heroines are raised by the English, so although the children's paternal legacy implies an incorporation of native sovereignty into colonial rule, their native culture is extinguished. Both *Yamoyden* and *The Wept of Wish-ton-Wish* construct an analogy between the English Revolution and Native American resistance only to reject it when familial and racial loyalties prove stronger than political ideologies. Only *Metamora* unambiguously supports the regicide and Parliamentary republican rule, yet even here the heroic Indian leader does not survive. He adopts the role of a legendary lawgiver such as Lycurgus, who in death bestows his sovereignty on young virtuous republicans whose English heritage is dissolved in favor of a new American polity.

Politically, Metamora is an immortal lawgiver. Only in the play's minor symbolic register does he assume the status of vanishing American. In the play's first scene, Oceana tells Walter how the day before, Metamora had saved her life: "When I was lingering on the eastern beach, all heedless of the coming night, a panther growling from the thicket rushed and marked me for his prey" (62). Fortunately, Metamora shot an arrow "swift as the lightning's flash . . . and felled the monster as he crouched to spring" (62). Metamora then enters, still nursing a wound from the panther, who "turned on me—brave beast; he died like a red man" (62). The veiled omen of that simile becomes explicit in act 5, when as Metamora rouses his warriors, he receives a warning from Kaneshine—"an Indian prophet," as the dramatis personae lists him. Kaneshine has "sought the ear of Manito in the sacred places" and "beheld gasping under a hemlock, the lightning had sometime torn, a panther wounded and dying in his thick red gore" (94). In killing the panther to save the life of Oceana, Metamora has sacrificed his avatar of untamed wildness. When in his final lines Metamora delivers a curse on the whites—"May the wolf and the panther howl o'er your fleshless bones" (98)—he has already lost his power over the big cat. Conanchet, too, is likened to a panther in *The Wept of Wish-ton-Wish*. He is called "crouching panther" before his captivity and then "tamed panther" when he remembers his time with the Heathcotes (317). Such language recalls the derisive epithets employed by the Puritans, but in the works of the 1820s it figures the pursuit of the Indian chiefs as a hunt. In *Yamoyden*, Metacom figures himself as a hare hiding in the elderberry bushes from his pursuers (20). As Richard Slotkin has shown, the mythopoeic plot of this pursuit turns the hunter-gatherer natives into the game, as the colonists, educated in the frontier skills of hunting, pursue their prey.

Inspired by *Metamora*, I have analyzed the literature of Metacom's rebellion, published in the 1820s, as melodrama. But however similar these works of verse, prose, and drama may be in plot structure, the stage role of Metamora and the man who commissioned the play and rode it to stardom, Edwin Forrest, functioned in a fundamentally different manner than printed literature and represented a transformation in the way that white men cashed in on the cultural capital of the heroic Indian rebel. My discussions of Pontiac, Logan, and the Natchez in the following chapters will show how the tragic and heroic stature of native leaders was promoted by colonists who had experienced the war firsthand and then wrote historical and/or literary works about their adversaries. In the case of King Philip's War, no contemporary author, not even Benjamin Church, fully realized the potential for a literary and political appropriation of Metacom. The development of his literary figure had to wait nearly 150 years. It was finally realized by Edwin Forrest. Rather than merely collect a reflected glory from the heroic native leader, Forrest could become Metacom by portraying him on stage.

In conceiving the play, Forrest may have consciously built on the tradition of exploiting defeated Indian leaders for political advantage. In 1822, when he was only sixteen years old and beginning his stage career, Forrest traveled with the Jones and Collins troupe to Cincinnati; Lexington, Kentucky; and smaller towns in the Ohio Valley. He performed a range of minor roles, including at least once in blackface. In Cincinnati, "Forrest was taken in by William Henry Harrison. . . . The 'hero' of Tippecanoe believed Forrest was 'exceptional' and regaled the struggling actor with tales about Tecumseh. [Biographer Montrose J.] Moses suggests Harrison was the initial source of inspiration for *Metamora*" (Walsh 463). Six years later, in November 1828, when Forrest announced his competition, with a prize of five hundred dollars "to the author of the best Tragedy, in five acts, of which the hero or principal character shall be an aboriginal of this country" (qtd. in Scott Martin 77), he may have had in mind a play about Tecumseh.[11] Forrest could have also followed the example of William Henry Harrison. The actor was invited to run for the House of Representatives from New York on the Democratic ticket in 1838, but he declined (Scott Martin 95–96). The rewards he enjoyed as the nation's foremost theatrical star were greater than he could hope to achieve in politics. Instead of exploiting King Philip politically, Forrest commodified and owned *Metamora* outright. As sponsor of the prize competition, he claimed copyright of the winning play. John Augustus Stone got the five hundred dollars, but subsequently gave up playwriting, and in 1834 committed suicide by drowning himself in the Schuylkill River. Playing the starring role in the play that he owned (and never allowed to be printed during his lifetime), Edwin Forrest earned as much as thirty-three thousand dollars in one season (1837), a sum that for its time was as astronomical as those enjoyed by Hollywood stars today. McConachie identifies Forrest as one of a few nineteenth-century actors who initiated the star system in American drama and film. The star became a hero and the hero a star, as audiences began to "confuse the personality of the actor with the type of role he or she usually performed, a confusion that continues to this day" (77); in the case of Forrest/Metamora, "his admiring public painted him as a self-made success, a child of nature" (84). Seventeenth-century New Englanders may have seen Metacom as King Philip, the last of the house of Pokanoket, but Americans in the Jacksonian era could imagine the Indian leader's authority and charisma on a different register, one suitable for an age of populist democracy.

Forrest's appropriation of the heroic figure of Metacom was so complete that it seemed to obscure racial and class differences. At least two critics (Scott C. Martin and Gaul) have discussed *Metamora* and other Indian dramas in light of the equally popular nineteenth-century dramatic genre of black-face minstrelsy. Forrest in redface, like the blackface minstrel tradition as analyzed by Eric Lott in *Love and Theft*, contributed to the formation of a white proletarian identity. Scott Martin accordingly emphasizes that "*Metamora* exploited the market in mass entertainment by providing Jacksonian audiences with a commodified patriotism that affirmed (and to some extent linked) nationalism and working class pride" (101). Forrest's working-class appeal helped inspire the Astor Place Riots, which were touched off after Forrest tacitly encouraged some of his fans, New York's rough and tumble Bowery Boys, to taunt the more upper-class audience of visiting British actor James McCready. Forrest's populist image fits with America's myth of itself as a classless society. The American star enjoyed the prerogatives of *Oceana*'s Olphaus Megaletor, with his "golden parachute" severance package of 350,000 pounds sterling. Metacom was not as fortunate. In *Hobomok* and *Yamoyden*, the native leaders' offspring, and by implication their hereditary sovereignty over New England's lands, are absorbed into Anglo culture and raised without any recognition of their Indian heritage. In *Metamora*, the legitimacy of the hero is passed on to the heroine, Oceana, through her symbolic adoption. But Forrest's appropriation of Metacom was even more decisive and effective. By acting his role on stage, Forrest embraced and contained the revolutionary native rebellion of 1675–76 and turned it to the interests of nineteenth-century American patriotism.

CHAPTER 4 / PONTIAC

Pontiac is not as well remembered today as Metacom and Tecumseh—perhaps not even as well known as Black Hawk and Osceola, the adversaries of U.S. military expeditions during the 1830s, when the cult of heroic Indian chiefs was at its height. He never had an audience with a sitting or future president. Relatively few dramas and epic poems were written about him, aside from that singular landmark in the literary history of Indian tragedy, Robert Rogers's *Ponteach*. While nine towns and counties in midwestern and southern states were named for Osceola, Pontiac's name was bestowed only on a suburb of Detroit, a small town in Illinois, and on one other major memorial. Although it is a moving memorial, I would guess that fewer than one in ten of those who drive the automobiles that bear his name could identify the historical Pontiac. Yet the figure of the tragic/heroic Indian chief in Anglo-American culture coheres with a special intensity around Pontiac. His uprising began a series of geopolitical contests in which North American native people tried to preserve their lands and interests by playing the French, British, and American colonizers against one another. Logan's role in Lord Dunmore's War, native strategy in the frontier battles of the American Revolution, and Tecumseh's resistance in the War of 1812 all cannot be understood without reference to Pontiac's rebellion, a fact that nineteenth-century historians fully recognized.

Pontiac's origins are uncertain and the circumstances of his death mysterious. He was probably born between 1720 and 1725 in the Ottawa nation, somewhere around the west end of Lake Erie, although one of his parents may have been Ojibwa. He died in 1769 near Cahokia, Illinois, murdered by a Peoria man. Although his rebellion succeeded only briefly and he lived his last four years in disrepute, Francis Parkman endowed his death with epic significance: "Over the grave of Pontiac more blood was poured out in atonement, than flowed from the veins of the slaughtered heroes on the corpse of Patroclus" (845). Parkman's *The Conspiracy of Pontiac and the Indian War after the Conquest of Canada*, the first of his eight volumes of colonial history, was published in 1851, and so whereas readers of the 1820s and 1830s were treated to a plethora of works about King Philip's War and about the American Revolution, works about Pontiac did not reach a wide popular audience until more than a decade later.

The war of Parkman's epic was Pontiac's rebellion, and its Troy was the now prosaic city of Detroit. It occurred in the aftermath of the Seven Years' War, a war that many argue initiated the global, imperial conflicts of modern history. Fought in Europe and in North America, the Seven Years' War matched France and Britain as imperial superpowers, squaring off against each other in Prussia, in Austria-Hungary, and in the Hudson Valley and among the Iroquois, the Ottawas, and other native peoples from the Great Lakes to the Mississippi. With their defeat of French forces on the Plains of Abraham near Quebec City in September 1759, the British won the war in North America and began to claim the frontier forts of their rival. In December 1760, the French flag was lowered at Detroit, sixty years after the post had been established by Antoine Laumet de la Mothe, Sieur de Cadillac (who of course also got a make of automobile named after him—a more upscale brand than the Pontiac). Not until February 1763, however, did the Treaty of Paris formally transfer French possessions to the English, and because news of such things traveled by sail, canoe, and horseback, months more passed before this imperial transfer could be implemented.

The British were eager to assume control of the French posts on the Great Lakes because of the valuable fur trade. They were less comfortable with taking over the relationships and responsibilities toward native peoples that the French had maintained and that made this trade work smoothly. The friction in these new relationships fostered Pontiac's rebellion and was sustained by recurring rumors among the Indians that the news of the treaty was false or that France would continue to support them against the English (see, for example, Rutherfurd 250). In part by exploiting these rumors and even by producing forged letters of support from French officials, Pontiac organized an alliance among many native tribes of the Great Lakes region. Under his leadership, they besieged Detroit from May to October 1763, and his allies captured thirteen other English forts from Pittsburgh to Mackinac and raided dozens of frontier settlements west of the Alleghenies, forcing many colonials to retreat eastward. Although the rebellion may seem like frontier war of red versus white, it was in fact part of an imperial contest between England and France. So why did Pontiac favor the French?

For Parkman, the reasons lay in an essential, almost racial contrast between French and English colonists. He and others saw an aptitude for Indian relations as part of the French national character. Parkman took the fact that so many French traders had married into native communities—the origin of Canada's métis community—as evidence that the "French became savages. . . . The wandering Frenchman chose a wife or a concubine among his Indian friends; and in a few generations, scarcely a tribe of the west was free from an infusion of Celtic blood" (411). Conversely, "the English fur-traders, though they became barbarians, they did not become Indians" (412). Like early-nineteenth-century writers of historical novels, notably Sir Walter Scott and James Fenimore Cooper, Parkman explained the contest of nations or races by the purity or corruption of blood and evoked racial nationalism by reference to medieval identities, Celtic for French and Saxon for English. Throughout Parkman's seven-part magnum opus, *France and England in North America*, the French are assimilated to the Indians as common victims "destined to melt and vanish before the advancing waves of Anglo-American power" (347), as he wrote in the preface to *Conspiracy of Pontiac*.

Most twentieth-century scholars understandably do not share Parkman's racialism. Richard White, one of the most highly respected historians of native and early America, has examined Pontiac's rebellion in *The Middle Ground* (1991), his influential study of Native American communities and French and English colonists in the Great Lakes region from 1650 to 1815. His title refers not to the mixture of races but to "a place in between: in between cultures, peoples, and in between empires and the non-state world of villages" (x). White's concept of middle ground is built on practices established between the natives and the French and only sporadically adopted later by the British and Americans. Although articulated in a cultural rather than racial paradigm, his analysis of the causes of Pontiac's rebellion is really not very far from Parkman's, as it turns on the assimilation of or resistance to native symbolic and material exchange by colonial traders and soldiers. For example, White explains how English officials often refused to compensate the native families of victims murdered by Europeans or by people from other villages, a judicial practice that helped prevent cycles of vengeance and maintain alliances and trading relationships and that the French had carefully cultivated since the early 1600s. White also explains that Jeffrey Amherst, the British general who led the administration of Indian affairs in the western territories from 1761 to November 1763, refused to honor the native customs of diplomatic gift giving as the French had done. Amherst "blustered into Indian affairs with the moral vision of a shopkeeper and the arrogance of a victorious soldier" (257); he insisted on a petty capitalist doctrine that Indians must be paid only for services rendered, not honored or conciliated with presents. The British indulged in an imperial fantasy that native people should play by the rules that governed subaltern classes in British society. Amherst's subordinate, Major Henry Gladwin, who as commandant at the besieged fort of Detroit was Pontiac's primary adversary, wrongly believed that he had no need for the Indians. And for a year, in 1763–64, British forces paid dearly for this mistake.

The uprising of 1763 included coordinated attacks by warriors of many Indian nations: the Seneca in western New York, the Shawnee and Miami of Ohio, the Ojibway and Ottawa of northern Michigan, the Illinois of the land later named for them. Of course the region had seen large-scale conflicts and multiethnic fighting forces before—large French-organized attacks on the Iroquois had occurred in the late seventeenth century, for example—but this may have been the first time that so many tribes acted in concert without the direct instigation of a colonial power. The precise importance of Pontiac's leadership in this process is uncertain. Parkman gave him a central role as Indian leader while suggesting that the French encouraged the revolt. Howard Peckham in his 1947 history of Pontiac's war downgraded his importance and presented evidence of some French leadership, while in his 2002 book and in a 1990 article Gregory Dowd restores much of Pontiac's stature and contends that the Indians acted independently of the French.[1]

The question of Pontiac's leadership elicits various answers from modern historians, but the answers of eighteenth- and nineteenth-century writers were colored by a pattern of anxiety about native conspiracies. The genesis of the conspiracy was presumed to be either the French or Pontiac, as if mere self-interest were not enough to motivate concerted attacks by "savages" on more than a dozen widely separated forts during the summer of 1763. British officers' letters were filled with anxious conspiracy theories and rumors of red wampum belts passing among the tribes. Because the tribal identity of native warriors and the dynamics of their allegiances were difficult for the average white observer to ascertain, any band of Indians might appear to be conspiratorial. (In a like manner today, the ignorance of U.S. soldiers and leaders regarding Middle Eastern languages and Muslim sects makes it difficult for the Americans to distinguish terrorists from innocent civilians.) Moreover, many natives saw an advantage in frightening frontier traders by warning of an impending revolt by all the Indians. For example, James Kenny wrote in his journal in January 1763, "We hear that Bill Hickman a Delaware Indian has Informed Paterson and the Inhabitants about Juniata that the Indians intends to break out in a War against us Next Spring; but as we know him to be a Roague and a Horse thief, we judge his report to be more for Self Ends than Truth or Good Will to us, not but what the Mingoes I believe would set on the Western Nations to Strike us if they Could" (184).[2]

Pontiac's Republican Rhetoric

Given the work of historians Peckham, White, and Dowd, I cannot hope to reach a more definitive answer than they have to the question of Pontiac's leadership role. My goal in this section is to analyze Pontiac's speeches and the rhetoric of his political thinking. Contemporary sources included many orations recorded firsthand by bilingual witnesses whose veracity is quite strong (compared, for example, to Seattle's speech or the orations of Moctezuma contained in Cortés's letters). Pontiac's use of figural and sentimental language in these speeches was not mere "savage eloquence." It engaged the highest levels of political discourse of the time. And because his rebellion happened in the ten- to fifteen-year period after the imperial war between France and Britain and before the revolutionary war between the American colonies and Britain, Pontiac and his rebellion reflected key questions about the legitimacy of power and rebellion. Many modern historians regard his uprising through the lens of the U.S. rebellion. Both Peckham and Wilbur Jacobs called it the "Indian war of independence." Pontiac's orations and the portrayals of him from contemporaries on down to Parkman, engaged in three discourses that were foundational to the American Revolution and to late-eighteenth-century politics generally: first, classical history, especially the Roman republic; second, theories of monarchy and of republican government; and third, the language of paternalism and metaphors of the nuclear family.

The heroic portrait of Pontiac, as of other Indian leaders, draws heavily on literary epics and classicism. "In generous thought and deed, he rivalled the heroes of ancient story" (517), wrote Parkman, who elsewhere compared him to Patroclus, as we have seen, and to Alexander the Great (537) and even alluded to Milton to call Pontiac the "Satan of this forest paradise" (508). We saw in chapter 1 that Rogers's *Ponteach* did not simply emulate Shakespeare and Racine but looked through them toward Aeschylus, Herodotus, and Homer, Greek writers who established a tradition of representing enemy leaders as honorable and dignified. The only specific contemporary comparison I have found between Pontiac and a classical ruler is more obscure but even more apt. One William Smith wrote of the rebellion in a letter to Horatio Gates in November 1763, "The besiegers are led on by an enterprising fellow called Pondiac. He is a genius [who] has had the address to get himself not only at the head of his conquerors, but elected generalissimo of all the confederate forces now acting against us. Perhaps he may deserve to be called the Methridates of the West" (qtd. in Peckham 109). Mithradates VI Eupator, king of Pontus in Anatolia, ruled from 120 to 63 B.C.. He aided the Greeks of the Crimea in wars against the Scythians and then sought their alliance for an effort to drive the Romans out of Asia Minor. As an eastern, "barbarian" leader, he resembled Xerxes, and in allying with one European empire, the Greeks, against another, the Romans, Mithradates' position resembled that of Pontiac between the French and English. He even massacred thousands of Romans in an effort to force the Greeks to align with him by making them his accessories in Roman eyes. Roman Republican leader Pompey finally defeated Mithradates in 66 B.C., but as one of the few foes to mount a serious military challenge to Rome, he acquired a stature that offered an obvious classical analogue to Pontiac. He promoted a vision of a Greco-Asiatic empire analogous to the French-Indian middle ground. A myth arose that he inoculated himself with poison so that he would be immune to such attempts to assassinate him and that he ordered all his concubines killed so that no conqueror would be able to enjoy them as spoils. The fact that the Romans defeated him only made this historical typology more attractive for an Anglo-American such as Smith, and the honor that Pompey accorded his vanquished foe, burying him in the royal tomb at Sinope, also fits the pattern of the Indian tragic hero.

These classical analogies emphasize the contradictory images of Pontiac's leadership. He was variously seen as a despotic king with grand imperial designs, as the sovereign of all native peoples of the region, and as a self-made upstart, a radical republican with the audacious courage to challenge the empires of England and France. For nineteenth-century observers, an analogue seemed obvious: Edwin L. Sabin's *Boys Book of Indian Warriors* includes an illustration of Pontiac (based on no authentic source) with the caption, "Pontiac, the Red Napoleon." But for those in the 1760s, the nature of Pontiac's leadership was more obscure. On first meeting him, Robert Rogers wrote, "The Indians on the lakes . . . are formed into a sort of empire, and the emperor is elected from the eldest tribe, which is the Ottawawas. . . . Ponteack is their present king or emperor, who has certainly the largest empire and greatest authority of any Indian chief that has appeared on the continent since our acquaintance with it. He puts on an air of majesty and princely grandeur, and is greatly honored and revered by his subjects" (*Concise Account* 240). Accordingly, a dispatch from Detroit printed in August 1763 in Benjamin Franklin's *Pennsylvania Gazette* referred to "Pondiac, who is the Indian Chief, and calls himself King from the Rising of the Sun to the setting." Yet Rogers in his ethnographic "Manners and Customs of the Indians" section of the *Concise Account* described native military authority as noncoercive and meritocratic. In military expeditions, "a general is appointed over the others, not properly to command, but to give his opinion and advice, which they make no scruple to disregard" (228–29). Among the rank-and-file warriors, "every private man has a right to return home when he pleases" (230), for "every man is naturally free and independent" (233). This reflected to some degree the situation of Rogers's Rangers, an independent fighting force apart from the British army with Rogers as popular commander. Rogers also obscured distinctions between civil chiefs, who governed by consent and consensus, and war chiefs, who held a stronger power but only in wartime, as well as between soldiers, who are obliged to fight by national and military law, and warriors, who fight at their own discretion (see Richard White, *Middle Ground* 378).

A better-informed source on Native American political structures was James Smith, a captive of the Caughnawaga Iroquois for several years during the Seven Years' War who wrote in a narrative first published in 1799: "How any term used by the Indians in their own tongue, for the chief man of a nation, could be rendered King, I know not. The chief of a nation is neither a supreme ruler, monarch or potentate—He can neither make war or peace, leagues or treaties—He cannot impress soldiers, or dispose of magazines.... With them there is no such thing as hereditary succession, title of nobility, or royal blood, even talked of" (Gordon Sayre, ed., *American Captivity Narratives* 339). Smith ironically applied the concepts of European government to native America to show the absurdity of such ethnocentrism, and he astutely recognized the question as one less of political theory per se than of a translation between European and Indian languages and societies. Pontiac exposed and exploited this irony and the problems of translation. In leading a rebellion against the British empire in support of the French, he brought himself into European politics and demanded just the sort of comparisons Smith rejected. He did "make war or peace, leagues or treaties," he upset the Treaty of Paris and the policies of the most powerful states in the world at the time. Euro-Americans often mistranslated Pontiac's power into terms that they understood, but these mistranslations did not reduce the reality of his power. And while colonizers may have projected their political sentiments onto Pontiac, Pontiac also projected his ideas of power onto colonial politics.

The difficulties of interpreting political leadership in a cross-cultural context have not become much easier even with the ethnohistorical methods of recent scholarship. Richard White's *Middle Ground* rejects Parkman's vision of the rebellion as a "racial struggle" and of Pontiac as master conspirator. He dismisses the idealized image of Pontiac as heroic Indian chief by emphasizing his short temper, drunkenness, and cruelty—for example, in ordering the killing of a seven-year-old captive English girl, Betty Fisher, in 1764 (see also Dowd, *War* 255–58). We might expect White to reject "great man" historiography as outmoded, but the language he uses to describe Indian politics is just as provocative as Rogers's "king or emperor." One of the key characteristics of White's middle ground is that traditional indigenous communities were disrupted by flows of refugees from colonial wars and replaced by multitribal villages led by opportunistic self-fashioned leaders, some of them métis, who could not have been chiefs under traditional kinship structures—the clan lineages led by hereditary chiefs whom French writers often termed kings (see 217). James Smith's comments well describe this topsy-turvy world. According to White, "These multiethnic villages were the first republics" (188) outside French or British control, and the leaders were "rebels," and he must have been conscious of what he implied by these terms. Pontiac and other native leaders of the middle ground anticipated the politics of the American Revolution. Pontiac's political syncretism likewise posed a peculiar challenge for Parkman because it embodied republican virtues that he wished to applaud, that he saw as distinctly American, yet came from what he believed to be a doomed race. He acknowledged that Pontiac had been "born the son of a chief" yet noted that "many a chief's son sinks back into insignificance" in meritocratic Indian societies. "Courage, resolution, address, and eloquence are sure passports to distinction. With all these Pontiac was pre-eminently endowed. . . . Though capable of acts of magnanimity, he was a thorough savage. . . . His faults were the faults of his race; and they cannot eclipse his nobler qualities" (483).

Pontiac's leadership arose at a key moment of imperial transition, a post-colonial turn in North American history.[3] Twentieth-century history has demonstrated that the greatest challenges facing postcolonial states are forging a national identity and political legitimacy that meet the standards established by the European nation-states, within geographic boundaries that have often been established by European colonialism, without surrendering the local forms of power that produce many of the best leaders. The best solutions lie in adapting the political structures of one culture for use in another, and this adaptation works in both directions. We have already seen how Mexican insurgents adopted the indigenous sovereignty of Moctezuma and of Xicoténcatl's Tlaxcala as an ideological weapon against Spanish colonial rule and how historians of the United States appropriated Metacom's allied defense of Indian lands a century and a half later. Pontiac offers our best opportunity to examine how a Native American leader adopted the rhetoric and ideology of European and colonial politics. Pontiac was savvy enough to employ imperial ideology against itself.

Pontiac had to develop an intercultural political discourse for his communications with the local civilians. During the siege of Detroit, he had to maintain the support of French habitants of the settlement, who were regarded as noncombatants but who were essential allies because they were a source of food and supplies. According to well-traveled British agent George Croghan, these settlers "consist of three or four hundred French families, an idle, lazy people. . . . They scarcely raise as much as will supply their wants, in imitation of the Indians whose manners and customs they have entirely adopted, and cannot subsist without them. The men, women, and children speak the Indian tongue perfectly well" (152). The British in the fort offered amnesty and appealed to a sense of racial loyalty in an effort to make the French turn against Pontiac, yet simultaneously destroyed some of the habitants' buildings and crops around the fort for fear that they would provide cover to the besiegers. The habitants thus became frustrated with both sides in the siege and at one point employed the language of revolution, complaining to Pontiac, "You do not speak to us any more like brothers, but like masters, and you treat us as we treat our slaves" (Robert Navarre in Quaife 96). Pontiac responded, "I am French, and want to die French" (100). In July, after two months of siege had yielded no success, Pontiac spoke again to the French settlers, appealing to them to take up arms, to "either remain French as we are, or altogether English as they are. If you are French, accept this war-belt for yourselves, or your young men, and join us; if you are English we declare war upon you" (161). How can a Native American say to French colonists that he is more French than they are? For Pontiac, unlike Parkman, "French" refers not to any racial or ethnic identity but only to an imagined community held together by the tenuous thread of allegiance to a king he has never seen but whose authority Pontiac invokes and tries to imitate. And "English" refers to the enemies of that community. He goes on to say, "We know you to be children of our Great Father [the king of France] as well as we" (161). To call the king "Great Father" captures the dual significance of the king as the guarantor of political identity in the empire and of ethnic French identity in the nation. Pontiac cannot be included in the latter, yet he still rejects the demand that he transfer his loyalty to a new father, the king of England. The result is a theory of power and identity that refers only to the absent presence of a specular kingship, a French power that Pontiac represents in both the transitive and intransitive forms of the word.

The situation becomes still more complex as Pontiac makes an ultimate appeal for assistance in a final desperate attack on the English in the fort, speaking to "you," the French habitants: "To make war upon our brothers for the sake of such dogs pains us, and it will cost us an effort to attack you inasmuch as we are all French together; and if we should attack we should no longer be French. But since we are French it is wholly the interests of our Father, yours and ours, that we defend. Therefore answer, my brothers, that we may come to an understanding; and behold this belt which makes its appeal to you or your young men" (Quaife 161–62). Being "French" means allying with Pontiac to attack the English, as imperial alliance trumps birthplace or even language in the definition of national identity. But then, "one of the principal Frenchmen"—in fact, the likely author of the *Journal of the Siege* in which these speeches are recorded, Robert Navarre, who "had brought with him to the council a copy of the Capitulation of Montreal and Detroit" (162) and who writes of himself anonymously and in the third person—announces that the habitants would like to stand and "with you defend the interests of our Father" but that their hands are tied because "the King of France . . . commanded us not to fight against the English, but to regard them as our brothers and the English father and king as our father and king" (162–63). This scene pits two forms of diplomatic writing against one another: on the one hand, the capitulation that ended the Seven Years' War and made the English into "our brothers"; on the other hand, the war belt, which reiterates the alliance between French and Indians and puts the habitants into the same position as Pontiac, warrior-subjects of the French Great Father. Like many revolutionary situations, this one also involves a generation gap, for the text of the *Journal of the Siege* (which I will discuss in more detail later in this chapter) then explains that the older Frenchmen, who had families, refused to join Pontiac in an attack while the younger "renegade" French did so. One of the latter says, "I and my young men break away from our bonds; we all accept the war belt which you offer us" (165), but the narrator, Navarre, is hostile toward these younger men and toward Pontiac. The next day, one of these "renegades" rejects his decision, takes the belt accepted from Pontiac, and deserts, giving the belt to his father, who takes it to Pontiac and chastises the Indian leader, warning that even if he succeeds, even if "our Father" comes back, the French king will give credit for defeating the English to the French habitants rather than to Pontiac and his warriors.

With these scenes, we have already reached the third type of republican rhetoric, the figures of paternalism. Pontiac always referred to the king of France as "father" but did not so honor the English, using "brother" or occasionally "uncle" instead. The habitants challenged him when they defined the king of England as the new father and when a literal father applied his paternal power over the young renegade who had taken up the war belt with Pontiac. Even some British negotiators employed the native uses of the terms "father" and "brother," as when Thomas Morris explained to Pontiac that "their father the King of France had ceded those countries to their brother the king of England" (306). Pontiac's use of paternal metaphors echoes in some ways that used in the rhetoric of the American Revolution. But it even more powerfully critiques the notion of Anglo-American paternalistic control over Native Americans.

Beginning in the seventeenth century, the metaphor of the white colonial father and his Indian children passed from diplomatic courtesy to ideological cliché. Michael Paul Rogin's *Fathers and Children: Andrew Jackson and the Subjugation of the American Indian* and Francis Paul Prucha's *The Great Father: The United States Government and the American Indians* make this patriarchal relationship their title and theme. Rogin plays the figure for all its Freudian potential, associating infantile Indians with a sense of maternal plenitude and oral dependence, which oedipally arrested men such as Jackson sought both to escape and to dominate. But other scholars have tried to deconstruct this metaphor. Many have recognized that under the kinship systems of the Iroquois and many other tribes, fathers had no power to command children. Eric Cheyfitz contends that for natives, this use of kinship terms was not patriarchal at all but nonhierarchical, characteristic of a society outside of the European imperialist order (53). I would discount Cheyfitz's statement as overly utopian, but it is true that in most Native American languages and kinship structures, "father" would not have the same connotations of power or even the same referent as in English. It might include maternal uncles as well, whereas "brother" might include in-laws or cousins. We will see in the next chapter that this has important consequences for Logan's kinship relations.

Richard White emphasizes the symbolic values behind the paternal figure. Indians imputed to the French king certain responsibilities that were part of the mutuality of native kinship and of the middle ground. The French "fathers" were expected to "provide the *bon marché*" for trade goods at fixed prices and to defuse traditional tribal revenge by "covering" for murders with presents. In an essay on "The Fictions of Patriarchy," White shows how after Pontiac's rebellion, Anglo-Americans and natives engaged in "a diplomacy of mirrors" (71), repeating the conventional familial terms even as they came to have less real meaning beyond each side's hopeful imagination. But for Pontiac and his allies in 1763, the most important feature of the French paternal role was that it did not imply an ownership of American lands, lands that would continue to pass to younger generations of Indians. As Charlot Kaské, a Shawnee who was poised to assume Pontiac's leadership role in the aftermath of the rebellion, said to French Governor Jean Jacques-Blaise d'Abbadie,

> I ask you, my father, to help your children, the Shawnee, who have always held the Frenchman's hand. Our warriors, our old men, our wives, and our children are sad because they see the French no more at my house. The English come here and say that the land is theirs and that the French have sold it to them. You know well our fathers have always told us the land was ours, that we were free there, that the French came to settle there only to protect us and defend us as a good father protects and defends his children. You put the tomahawk in our hands to strike the English, which we did; and we shall preserve it forever; and we shall recall ceaselessly to our children that they should preserve it likewise. (Alvord and Carter 445)

Charlot Kaské had traveled from Illinois to New Orleans in 1764–65 to plead with French officials to again provide military support to their native allies.

They refused, but he, like Pontiac, nonetheless told his followers that help was on the way.

Fictions of patriarchy were just as important to Thomas Jefferson, who similarly argues in the *Summary View of the Rights of British America*—that the British king's sovereignty did not extend to American lands. Garry Wills and others have argued that Jefferson's Declaration of Independence casts the king of England as a father so as to naturalize revolt by suggesting that his colonial children have reached their maturity and earned their rights of autonomy. We should likewise read the Indians' diplomatic use of "father" as inclined toward rights and responsibilities, not servility. Even in Euro-American usage, the father/child metaphor figured the relationship between God and humans, lord and vassal, as well as king and subject, carrying rights and duties for both sides. Pontiac in his use of the fraternal and paternal figures was able to float ambiguously between these metaphors of rights and of obligations.

In his play, *Ponteach*, Rogers gives his hero a speech that clarifies these political and patriarchal definitions:

> The French familiarized themselves with us, . . .
> Call'd us their Friends, nay, what is more, their Children
> And seem'd like Fathers anxious for our welfare.
> Whom see we now? their haughty Conquerors [the English]
> . . . .
> With Pleasure I would call their King my Friend
> Yea, honor and obey him as my Father;
> I'd be content, would he keep his own Sea,
> And leave these distant Lakes and Streams to us;
> Nay I would pay him homage, if requested,
> And furnish Warriors to support his Cause.
> But thus to lose my Country and my Empire,
> To be a Vassal to his low Commanders . . .
> Can this become a King like *Ponteach*,
> Whose Empire's measured only by the Sun? (201–2)

Here, "father" explicitly does not mean political subordination for the children. As Ponteach understands the outcome of the Seven Years' War, the English victory does not render the Indians subject peoples to their king, for Ponteach regards himself as an independent king with his own empire. "Think you, because you have subdu'd the French / That Indians too are now become your slaves?" (188–89). Or, as Rogers put it in his *Concise Account*, Pontiac "was far from considering himself as a conquered Prince" and would address the king of England as "his uncle" (242–43). A subsequent speech in *Ponteach* reads like a propaganda poem from the American Revolution, turning the duties of filiopiety away from obeisance to the king and toward revolt:

> Better to die than see my Country ruin'd,
> Myself, my Sons, my Friends reduc'd to Famine,
>
> . . . .
>
> Oh! could our Fathers from their Country see
> Their antient Rights encroach'd upon and ravag'd,
> And we their Children slow, supine, and careless
> To keep the Liberty and Land they left us,
> And tamely fall a Sacrifice to Knaves!
> How would their Bosoms glow with patriot Shame,
> To see their Offspring so unlike themselves? (220)

Of course, the actual Pontiac never spoke these words, but since Rogers likely knew Pontiac and some of his men, the words can illuminate the translation of patriarchal power and paternalistic figures across the cultural divide. Ponteach invokes Indian tradition through the grandfathers, much as contemporary Native American literature often does. He must show fealty to his ancestors, not to the diplomatic fiction of the French (or English) king as a father. And his tradition has a martial spirit. He continues,

> Rouse, then, ye Sons of Ancient Heroes, rouse,
> Put on your Arms, and let us act a Part
> Worthy of the Sons of such renowned Chiefs. (220)

The primary sources confirm this rhetoric of revolution. In speaking of William Johnson, the longtime agent to the Iroquois who solidified the "covenant chain" alliance of the English with that confederacy, Pontiac said, "There is the chain of our brothers which united us during some time, but we have broke it and trod it under foot; we are free" (Thomas Gage Papers qtd. in Peckham 247) and announced that his men at Detroit "would rather die with their tomahawks in their hands than live in slavery" (246). Like the lines put in Metamora's mouth by John Augustus Stone, these words recall the rhetoric of the American Revolution, yet they were set down a decade before it. Rogers also conveys well how the English had failed to fulfill the obligations of their status as symbolic father and thus provoked their "sons" to rebel. An English governor named Sharp tells Ponteach that the king of England "like a Father loves you as his Children" (192), yet Sharp steals the ritual presents that Ponteach gives to him for the king, saying, "What would the king of England do with Wampum?" (196).

The Delaware Prophet

The political rhetoric of Pontiac's rebellion is thoroughly intercultural.
Both his speeches and the writings of his adversaries, notably Robert Rogers, reveal a cross-projection of terms and strategies. I wish to turn now to
the spiritual side of the rebellion and to show how here also, Pontiac drew on
the ideas of his foes as well as on native strategies of resistance that go far
beyond the evocation of the tribal fathers. No discussion of the rebellion is
complete without accounting for the spiritual prophecy that helped to inspire it. Just as the Sioux uprising at Wounded Knee in 1890 was inspired in
part by the Ghost Dance religion and much as Opechancanough's attack on
the Jamestown settlement in 1622 drew on the spiritual leadership of Nemattenow, Pontiac's rebellion had a spiritual prophecy behind it. And Rogers
even represented it in *Ponteach*.

As Gregory Dowd's fine study, *A Spirited Resistance*, has shown, the nativist
phenomenon behind Pontiac's rebellion began in the 1730s, flourished with
the rise of the Delaware Prophet, Neolin, just before Pontiac's rebellion, and
was sustained by many minor prophets across the eastern part of North
America well into the nineteenth century. Their common appeal was to
restore spiritual power by rejecting the growing dependency on European
colonists' trade goods, credit, and especially alcohol. "Nativist" does not
imply a retrograde traditionalism. These prophets often espoused a rejection
of European goods such as firearms or even of fire made from flint and steel,
but the pantribal consciousness that spread with the movement, as with
Pontiac's alliance, was highly innovative. As Dowd has put it, these prophets
set in motion an "intertribal movement that shook the local foundations of
Indian government while spreading the truly radical message that Indians
were one people" and that "the late eighteenth-century was, until very recently, the period of North America's most widespread intertribal activity"
(xix). Not until the American Indian movement in the early 1970s would pan-
Indian consciousness reach a similar level. Like Richard White, Dowd's
language at times echoes the language of U.S. politics, as when he writes of
"the nativist conviction that Indians were one people under God, at least
equal to but quite different from the Anglo-Americans" (42).

Like the American Indian movement, the nativist ideas espoused by Neolin and Pontiac were not only spiritual but political and intercultural. Neolin's was not a spiritual movement that Pontiac "altered" and "twisted," as
Peckham writes, in an "ingenious trick, by which he gained divine sanction
for his own scheme" (116). The doctrines of the Delaware Prophet, particularly as expressed by Pontiac, were thoroughly political in their own right

and were fully cognizant of the imperialist power struggles of the day. The power of the "Master of Life," a term used by Tenskwatawa, Pontiac, Neolin, and earlier nativists and by the Frenchman Lahontan as early as 1703 (434), is not actually the Great Spirit or any native deity but a manifestation of a distinct version of power, an absent presence of political influence akin to European kings or to the forces that might, to Indian eyes, explain the invasion itself. Another scholar of the nativist movements, Charles E. Hunter, has argued that they "may be interpreted not as an outgrowth of indigenous tradition, but rather as a basically European innovation . . . adapted from contemporary white missionary activities" (40). Ample evidence shows Christian influence in the prophet's message. But the religious syncretism of Neolin's message is less significant, I believe, than its political syncretism. The spiritual side of Pontiac's rebellion reveals a blending of native and European forms of political awareness manifest in the speeches attributed to Pontiac and the writings of participants in the war. In the histories of Moctezuma and Metacom, the role of shamans and oracles arises mainly in the stage plays and in secondary sources such as Diego Durán. But in the history of Pontiac's rebellion, the role of the Delaware Prophet was acknowledged by eyewitnesses.

The words of the Delaware Prophet come to us from a few fragmentary but independent sources among the journals of captives, traders, soldiers, and missionaries in the Old Northwest. Although Dowd and Hunter draw on a few others, the five most important sources are the following.

- Charles Beatty, a Presbyterian minister, kept a journal of his journey into the Ohio country in 1766 to preach to the Indian nations and "the Distressed Frontier Inhabitants" in the aftermath of Pontiac's rebellion. It was published only in 1962. He is the only one of the five who reported meeting Neolin face to face, and, aside from a passing reference by Colonel Henry Bouquet (Hunter 48 n. 2), is the only one to refer to him by that name. Beatty paraphrased Neolin's vision of God judging sinners and welcomed the prophet as a convert, but all this is contained in only a few lines of Beatty's journal. He did not directly quote any of Neolin's words.
- James Kenny, a Quaker trader at a post near Pittsburgh in the early 1760s, spoke some of the Delaware tongue and kept a journal that was first published in 1913. On 12 December 1762, he wrote of the "new Religion raised amongst the Indians" by an "Imposter" who "tells them he had a Vission of Heaven where there was no White people but all Indians, & wants a total separation from us, and for that purpose advisses the Indians to Impose upon the Traders" (175). In other entries

written during the preceding months, Kenny described a book circulated by the prophet and reported that local Indians were performing daily devotions according to this plan.

- John Heckewelder, a Moravian missionary to the Delaware Indians and author of two volumes of history and ethnography, outlined in a chapter on "Preachers and Prophets" the Delaware Prophet's message alongside that of the Shawnee Prophet and Tecumseh and described what this "famous preacher of the Delaware" called his "great Book of Writing" (*History* 291).
- John McCullough was a boy of eight when captured near Conococheague, Pennsylvania, in July 1756. In 1808, he published a narrative of his eight years with the Indians, offering a brief account of the nativist movement from an insider's point of view. His is also the only text to include an illustration of Neolin's hieroglyphic book or text.
- Finally and most importantly for my purposes here, Robert Navarre, the apparent author of the manuscript *Journal or Narrative of Pontiac's Conspiracy*, reported Pontiac's version of the prophet's message from God as delivered in a famous speech just before his warriors laid siege to Detroit.

All five of these men were in the Old Northwest in the 1760s, and all evidently wrote of the same man, Neolin, yet all except Beatty place us at one or more removes from the prophet. A skeptical historian might ask if all five accounts truly refer to the same prophet (see, for example, McConnell 222). One should neither demand nor expect certainty on this matter. In the case of a social/religious movement such as this, a nativist revival that Dowd terms "The Indians' Great Awakening" (the title of his chapter 2), the diffusion of the prophetic message, with its transitions between oral and written forms, is not just a mediation or complication of the sources but is a theme of the prophetic message itself. Of the five sources, only Pontiac's speech (as transcribed by Navarre) thematizes the question of the revelation and its communication; hence, this source is of greatest interest here.

Pontiac invoked the Master of Life and the nativist message in his first major speech to the assembled natives and French habitants at Detroit, delivered on 27 April 1763, just ten days before the beginning of the siege. This oration, the genesis of his "conspiracy," if such it was, was recorded in the *Journal ou Dictation d'une Conspiration*, a manuscript journal of the siege written in French and, according to legend, found hidden in the walls of a French settler's house when territorial Governor Lewis Cass acquired it in 1832 (Quaife xiii). Cass's friend, Henry Rowe Schoolcraft, had Pontiac's speech translated and published it as "Paradise Opened to the Indians" in

Algic Researches (1839), his anthology of "Indian Tales and Legends." Francis Parkman relied heavily on the journal, which he referred to simply as the "Pontiac manuscript," for his *Conspiracy of Pontiac*. Internal evidence clearly shows that the journal was penned by a resident of Detroit who spoke French and who was sufficiently trusted by both sides that he was able to move in and out of the besieged fort. By comparing the handwriting in the manuscript with that on signed documents that survived the siege, Detroit historian C. M. Burton identified the author as Robert Navarre. Burton's name is now connected with the manuscript held at the Detroit Public Library in a collection that bears his name, and he commissioned the first complete translation and published it in 1912.[4] Like Rogers and Parkman, Navarre portrayed Pontiac as the mastermind of the rebellion. The opening lines of the text introduce "Pontiac, great chief of all the Ottawas, Chippewas, Potawatomies, and all the nations of the lakes and rivers of the North, . . . a proud, vindictive, war-like, and easily offended man" (3) who "resolved within himself to wrest the lands away from the English and French people" (5). Within the first five pages, Navarre sets the scene for Pontiac's momentous speech and prophetic tale, delivered at the Rivière des Écorces just outside Detroit.

Unlike other instances of native eloquence in support of an anticolonial uprising, this oration was not delivered to colonizers at a diplomatic conference. It is not clear if Pontiac used a native language or French, and he does not speak directly of his or his tribe's situation at that moment. The speech instead offers a parable about "an Indian of the Wolf nation," who, "eager to make the acquaintance of the Master of Life . . . resolved to undertake the journey to Paradise" (Quaife 8–9), guided by a dream. He "equipped himself for a hunting journey, not forgetting to take provisions and ammunition, and a big kettle." Thus far this journey to the afterlife resembles widespread Algonquian beliefs in a "happy hunting ground," located in the West, for which the dead were prepared by being buried with their possessions. After a week's travel, the Wolf sees from his camp three roads, illuminated in the night. The next day he follows each of the first two until his progress is halted by "a great fire coming out of the earth" (11). The third road leads to a "mountain of marvellous whiteness" (11), where a woman "of radiant beauty" tells him he shall ascend the mountain but "must forsake all thou hast with thee" (12), referring presumably to the kettle and ammunition, European trade goods that the Delaware Prophet renounced. Naked, the Wolf climbs the mountain to three villages on top, where a handsome man clothed all in white leads him to the Master of Life, who offers him a hat to sit on. (The hat was a common symbol for white men in native hieroglyphics.) The threefold roads and villages and the general resemblance to a vision of the Judeo-Christian God (Anthony Wallace has likened it to the story of Moses and the Ten Commandments; see *Death* 117), all present for the narrative's white readers a familiar flavor, which helps to explain why Schoolcraft printed the tale under the misleading title "Paradise Opened to the Indians" sixty years before any published translation of the entire manuscript.

Finally, the Master of Life delivers his message to the man of the Wolf tribe, and it includes several moral proscriptions characteristic of nativist movements, with their syncretic blend of Christian and traditional ethics: "I do not love that ye should drink to the point of madness, as ye do; and I do not like that ye should fight one another. Ye take two wives, or run after the wives of others, ye do not well, and I hate that. Ye ought to have but one wife, and keep her till death. When ye wish to go to war, ye conjure and resort to the medicine dance, believing that ye speak to me; ye are mistaken,—it is to Manitou that ye speak, an evil spirit" (14).[5] "Manitou" is of course the Algonquian term for spirit, both singular and pantheist. Yet this puritanical message, which appears to have been influenced by missionary teachings, shifts to a separatist message: "Whence comes it that ye permit the Whites upon your lands? Can ye not live without them?" All this is consistent with other accounts of Neolin's message. But Pontiac then alludes to the Master of Life's support for the French over the English by again evoking the paternal figure: "I do not forbid you to permit among you the children of your Father; I love them. They know me and pray to me, and I supply their wants and all they give you. But as to those who come to trouble your lands,—drive them out, make war upon them. I do not love them at all; they know me not, and are my enemies, and the enemies of your brothers. Send them back to the lands which I have created for them and let them stay there" (15). In spite of the idiom of the tale and its consistency with other nativist prophecies, the Master of Life is not an Indian "Great Spirit" (Matchimanitou), is not the creator of the Indians' America who is equal to but separate from the European Christian God.[6] This Master of Life created England and supplied the "wants" of the French, and the French pray to him. And most important, by instructing the Wolf to "drive out" the British, the Master of Life becomes a partisan, a political as well as a spiritual power. He in fact resembles a king more than a God. James Kenny in his diary wrote similarly about an "Old Indian" who told him of his dream of traveling to a "Spacious Building" suspended in the sky where he met the "Great Creator of all things, sitting an a Glorious Seat & appeared like a Man (as he Immagined like ye King of the White People" (176).

To explain this idolatrous heresy, we must consider the natives' perspective on the power of writing—specifically, the writing emanating from the sources of European power. Pontiac had of course never met the king of France, but the French had frequently reminded him of the king's influence over affairs in America and may have described the king in such grand terms as to suggest a godlike being, in spite of the weak rule of Louis XV. The king's will was delivered in the form of writing, of letters bearing orders to his officers. Since the time of the early Jesuit missions to the Hurons of the Great Lakes in the 1630s, the French had used the apparently miraculous power of writing to impress the Indians and occasionally to secure their submission (see Axtell; see also Wogan). Secular officers and traders, for their part, spoke to the natives of being obliged to follow the will of the distant king, delivered in the form of written messages. For example, at a treaty negotiation, the Iroquois Decanosora reported a French official's message that "it is not in my power to make Peace, this can only be done by my Master, who lives over the Great Water" (Colden 155). By 1763, the novelty of writing may have worn off, but the perception of a link between writing and the dynamics of power among the colonists remained. Pontiac and other Indians saw the king as a graphocentric force, an absent origin of writing.

Moreover, the specific techniques of symbolic communication on the middle ground would also reinforce the notion that writing and power were connected in ways that literary theory has not really addressed. Indians of the northeast woodlands used wampum belts to symbolize and warrant the speeches of chiefs and diplomats at intertribal and intercultural councils. He who carried the belts was empowered with a national mission, and belts were conserved as the record of a treaty. Yet wampum was also a trade currency, exchanged for pelts or trade goods, and its value increased with the distance from its sources on the Atlantic coast. Negotiators often found it hard to collect enough beads to sew a belt for an upcoming meeting. Similarly, Anglo colonists developed a custom of handing out medals to friendly native leaders, often coins bearing the image of the king of England, which the recipient wore about his neck. In 1781 Thomas Jefferson gave Jean-Baptiste Ducoigne, a chief from Kaskaskia, in Illinois, a silver medal and received in return painted buffalo hides. Thus, the two cultures exchanged symbols that represented the language of diplomacy but also represented exchange value or money. Furthermore, the medals given by the colonists often bore an image of the king or president who secured the systems of monetary value and imperial power. Pontiac learned how European currency worked, for "in the course of the war, he appointed an Indian Commissary, and began to issue bills of credit. These, which are said to have been punctually redeemed, are described as having the figures of whatever he wanted in exchange for them, drawn upon them, with the addition of his own stamp in the shape of an otter" (Thatcher, *Indian Biography* 2:114).

Pontiac's rebellion took place as written news arrived in the Old North-west of the French surrender to the English in the 1763 Treaty of Paris. The veracity of these texts was all-important, and their authenticity had to derive from Louis XV. Yet how could Pontiac or another native verify this news and thereby reject the persistent and hopeful rumors of a renewed French offensive? James Kenny wrote in February 1762 of news from trader and negotiator Frederick Post about the Delaware "King Neetotwhelemy, i.e. New-comer," who "hearing of Peace being made & the French to quit this side of the Missisipi . . . was Struck dumb for a considerable time and at last said he did no know whether the News was true but if they could hear it from their fathers i.e. the French he would believe it. . . . He said the English was grown too powerfull & seemed as if they would be too Strong for God himself" (187). Newcomer did not like the news, was suspicious of its messenger, and therefore chose to doubt its veracity. He wanted to hear it straight from the French "fathers." Similarly, Thomas Morris reports that in 1764 Pontiac said " 'that Ononteeo (the French king) was not crushed as the English had reported, but had got upon his legs again,' and presented me with a letter from New Orleans, directed to him, written in French, full of the most improbable falsehoods" (305).[7] When Morris tries to correct these misconceptions, he is taken captive, and, as he reports it, is saved from torture and execution only by Pontiac's insistence that " 'we must not . . . kill ambassadors.' " Morris reflected that this "shews that [Pondiac] was acquainted with the law of nations" (307).

For my quasi-deconstructionist reading of the Master of Life, it is important that Pontiac says that the man of the Wolf tribe received the prayer in writing: "The Wolf replied that he did not know how to read. He was told that when he should have returned to earth he would only have to give the prayer to the chief of his village who would read it" (Quaife 15). Upon his return from paradise, the man takes it directly to the unnamed chief of his tribe.[8] This extra layer of mediation suggests, I believe, Pontiac's position as the authenticating herald for the Master of Life's message. The Wolf is the messenger to whom the master's will has been revealed, and by the Wolf Pontiac was probably referring to the Delaware prophet Neolin, but the way Pontiac delivers the Wolf's message in his speech insists that only a chief can give a prophet's message its full influence. Pontiac coordinated the spiritual and political sides of native resistance even better than Tecumseh and Tenskwatawa, and one reason Pontiac could do so was that the divine message was a written one. After all, no text can verify itself except, for pious Christians, the Bible. Navarre wrote that those assembled to hear Pontiac "listened to him as to an oracle" (17). Furthermore, it is a telling coincidence that the story was told at the Rivière des Écorces, or Bark River, since Indians of the northern forests used birch bark for paper.

Pontiac was not a despot like Moctezuma; his followers did not cringe and grovel before his august presence. He was more modern in his sensibility than Moctezuma and learned perhaps from Oedipus the lesson not to be controlled by oracles. Pontiac's skills lay in wedding the power of oracular speech to that of distant, "divine" writing. He delivered the nativist prophecy directly to the warriors whose loyalty he sought; he did not, like Moctezuma, attempt to find a shaman who would deliver the prophecy that he wanted to hear. Parkman seemed to sense this because although he at first declared that Pontiac's "authority was almost despotic" (482), he later emphasized the importance of the story of the Wolf by reminding readers that Pontiac "had no other control" over the assembled warriors "than that derived from his personal character and influence" (502)—that in effect, his virtues were those of a charismatic republican leader. Pontiac's republican skills likewise included the manipulation of written language, even though he could not read or write French or English. Thomas Gage wrote that his French counterpart, Governor Abbadie, "says, that Pondiac keeps two Secretarys, one to write for Him, and the other to read the Letters He receives; and He manages them so, as to keep each of them ignorant, of what is transacted by the other" (Alvord and Carter 241). John Rutherfurd, in his captivity narrative, recalled being taken before Pontiac and instructed to read some French letters found on the body of his commander, Captain Campbell, who had just been killed. Pontiac threatened Rutherfurd with death if he concealed anything that was in the text and appointed another prisoner who knew French to look over his shoulder to make sure (249).

Pontiac's genius thus lay in recognizing the forms of distant authority and power among the Europeans and the dynamics of its mediation through writing. After his siege of Detroit had been broken, Pontiac met the French commander, Pierre Joseph Neyon de Villiers, at Fort Chartres near St. Louis in April 1764. Villiers of course knew of the Treaty of Paris and was eager to retreat down the Mississippi and return to France. But Pontiac still hoped to rouse the French troops and the local Illinois warriors to continue the struggle, and so he lied to them by saying that his warriors still besieged Detroit. He invoked again "the Master of Life that made us red" and said to Villiers, "What made me come here was that I might charge thee to carry to the king the words of all the red men. It is I, my father, that loved thee without seeing thee. I see thee and I still love thee more. I know that thou knowest the red men. It is me, my father, that ought to speak to thee for them; therefore I pray thee harken to me" (Thomas Gage Papers qtd. in Peckham

248). The "Father" here seems triply overdetermined: it refers to Villiers but also points beyond him to the king of France and to the Master of Life, or God. Yet Pontiac's filial loyalty is deceptive because the three fathers do not

line up. Pontiac as son reproaches Villiers for abandoning his red allies and claims for himself the power of kingmaker: "My father, if thou hadst come at my first demand, the red men would have made thee the greatest man in the world. Thou art a great chief, thou art a father, thou knowest the Master of Life; it is He who had put arms in our hands and it is He who has ordered us to fight against this bad meat that would come to infect our lands" (249).

Having established that the figure of the father is the origin of the power of writing in both political and religious discourse and that these two discourses are intertwined, we can now turn again to the written message of the Delaware Prophet. The illustration that McCullough includes in his captivity narrative (figure 4.1) is the only surviving graphic representation of it. McCullough writes that in 1761 or 1762, his adopted Indian brother went "to Tus-ca-la-ways, about forty or fifty miles off, to see and hear a prophet that had just made his appearance amongst them; he was of the Delaware nation. I never saw nor heard him. . . . I saw a copy of his hieroglyphics, as numbers of them had got them copied and undertook to preach, or instruct others" (272–73; I date this from the fact that McCullough later refers to "the memorable battle at Brushy Run" [281], which occurred during the summer of 1763). The doctrines he attributes to this prophet, such as abstinence from sex and from the use of steel and flint to start fire, are consistent with other accounts. And because McCullough was a young boy when captured, because he claimed to have forgotten how to speak English during his eight years captivity and to have "wept bitterly" (276) and run back to his Indian family when his birth father first came to redeem him, his account of the prophet comes the closest to the Indian point of view. Yet McCullough offers only inexact corroboration for Pontiac's account of the vision of the man of the Wolf tribe and seems to have been influenced by Christian doctrines to a degree to which he may not have been conscious. McCullough explains the engraving as follows:

> They taught that all those on the right hand of the square surface, or the world, went immediately after death to heaven—and part of those on the uppermost square, to the left; those on the lowest square to the left, are those who are abandonedly wicked; they go immediately on the road that leads to hell.—The places marked A, B, C are where the wicked have to undergo a certain degree of punishment, before they are admitted into heaven—and that each of those places are a flame of fire—the place on the right hand line, or road to heaven, marked D, denotes a pure spring of

water, where those who have been punished at the aforesaid places, stop to quench their thirsts, after they had undergone a purgation by fire.—It must be observed, that the places marked A, B, C, differed, (as they taught) in degree of heat, still as the mark, or hieroglyphic decreases in size, it increases about one third more in heat—the first is not as hot as the second by one-third, nor the second as the third, in the same proportion. (275–76)

The tripartite arrangement of the roads and the fires is the strongest evidence that McCullough was exposed to the same prophecy that Pontiac's Wolf obtained on his journey to meet the Master of Life. The ladder-shaped design of McCullough's map does not precisely the match the "trois chemins, Bien large et Bien frayé [three roads, wide and plainly marked]" (Quaife 10) that the Wolf saw from his campsite. Still, as the first two of the three paths that appeared to the Wolf Indian led to a large fire while the third led to the woman in dazzling white who directed him to the master's mountain, we might suppose him to have endured the purgation of the B and C fires before passing over to the right-side trail and on to heaven.

McCullough's editor/publisher, Alexander Loudon, appended a footnote to this passage: "It would appear, by the above recital, as if they had some idea of the Popish tenet of purgatory." And if in Pontiac's account the Master of Life favors the French over the English or even is a mask for Louis XV himself, then he would presumably be Catholic. But the other three sources were written by men from different sects of Protestantism, and the presence of the "Book" in these reports of his revelation may bear the mark of their doctrines or of other Protestant missionary activity among the Indians. Heckewelder's account of the revelation to the "famous preacher of the Delaware nation" reports that "he had drawn, as he pretended, by the direction of the great Spirit, a kind of map . . . which he called 'the great Book or Writing' " (History 291). Indeed, it must be more map than alphabetic text, for the prophet, like Pontiac's Wolf, cannot read English, although like an itinerant evangelist he asks his listeners to buy a copy from him, price one buckskin. Kenny, a Quaker, also described the map and critiqued the news of the "Imposter's" revival according to the terms of Protestantism. When in the tenth and eleventh months of 1762 one "Indian Simon" showed Kenny the "Book containing their new Religion" and explained that he said his prayers by the book, Kenny "told him it offended the Good Spirit to make any likeness of him" such as the "Image of the Son or Little God at the top" of the book (173). Kenny's description of the layout of the book closely matches McCullough's engraving except that the engraving lacks any pictured icon of the "Son or Little God" and depicts only the devil. Heckewelder's account in

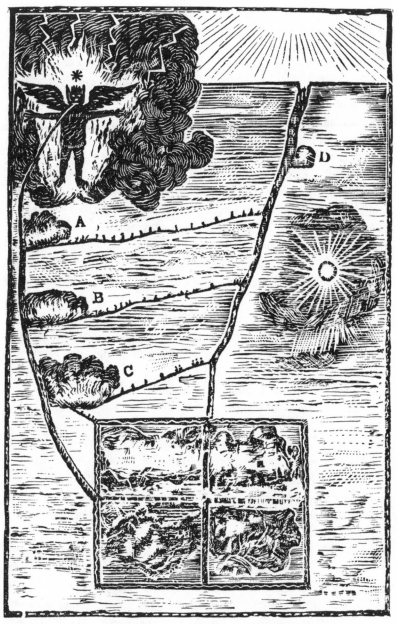

FIGURE 4.1. Neolin's map of the paths to the afterlife. From John McCullough, "A Narrative of the Captivity of John McCullough, Esq.," in *A Selection of Some of the More Interesting Narratives of Outrages Committed by the Indians in their Wars with the White People*, edited by Archibald Loudon (1808).

turn resembles Kenny's, a map of a path from earthly life, at the bottom of the page or parchment, past several tests or torments to a heaven at the top. The narrative by Heckewelder's Moravian mentor, David Zeisberger, also contains a good description of the "Book" but does not attribute it to Neolin or any prophet and, like Kenny, says that it represented both God and the Son of God.

So although McCullough's engraving is the only surviving copy, the prophetic book must have circulated widely and acquired an authority independent of any individual's revelation. In this regard, it deserves to be considered as an "Indian Bible" with all the implications that follow. In Kenny's eyes, praying from written texts is ineffective, and a religious book or hieroglyph cannot graphically represent the God whose will it claims to convey. If it does, its claims are invalid. In the Protestant tradition—indeed, in the general Jewish, Christian, and Islamic prohibitions on idolatry—this problem is resolved by a distinction between textual and visual representations of divinity. Sacred texts contain the Word of God, but they never include a picture of God. For Native Americans, however, whose written languages combined hieroglyphic, ideographic, and (at least in the case of the Maya) phonetic methods, this distinction between word and image would have been incomprehensible. Hence the confusion of terminology in the five sources: Heckewelder and Kenny call the prophetic document a "Book" because the Indians endow it with sacred power like the Bible, even though it is clear from their descriptions that it is just one leaf of paper or skin and includes no alphabetic words. Beatty, the Presbyterian missionary, receives Neolin's account of his vision of heaven and hell as a promising sign for his evangelical project: "There is an appearance of a Door opening here it if be not neglected & considerable thoughtfullness about the great matters of religion seemes to prevail" (65). The natives ignored warnings such as Kenny's against idolatry because the concept made no sense to them, but they may well have learned from Protestant missionaries, around the time of the Great Awakening, valuable lessons about how to spread a spiritual message of revival. A document—we might properly call it a codex like the hieroglyphic texts of Mesoamerica—that was spread by copies from one person to another could represent and authenticate the power of such a prophecy, and spreading it widely might help bring about its own promise of "a Heaven where there was no White people but all Indians." It does not matter whether Kenny's "Imposter" is the same man as Beatty's "Neolin"; in fact, the power of the prophecy is all the greater if they are not. Pontiac perceived that if this spiritual movement was to take effect, it must also have a war chief, and he took this role for himself. As a result, I believe, Pontiac made the curious innovation of separating into three parts what the other sources combined as one: the visionary quest that the Wolf Indian experiences, the prophetic message that he hears from the Master of Life, and the written prayer that the Master of Life gives to him:

> "Here is a prayer which I give thee in writing to learn by heart and to teach to the Indians and their children."
>
> The Wolf replied that he did not know how to read. He was told that when he should have returned to earth he would have only to give the prayer to the chief of his village who would read it and teach him and all the Indians to know it by heart. (Quaife 15)

The text that follows includes a prohibition on "making medicine," or shamanism, and the command to "drive off your lands these dogs clothed in red who will do you nothing but harm," a clear reference to the English. It continues, "And when ye shall have need of anything address yourselves to me" (16). Pontiac's speech turns the spiritual message of the Delaware Prophet to political ends by reasserting the power of the chief, to whom the Wolf must take the prayer bestowed by the Master of Life, which the Wolf cannot read. If the Master of Life were truly the Indian God or Great Spirit, it would make no sense for him to transmit a prayer in alphabetic English or French that the Wolf could not read, and as we have seen, the actual prophetic codex was not alphabetic. But Pontiac's ingenious innovation was to make the Master of Life not a god but a king and his prophetic message a political one supporting Pontiac's rebellion against English colonization. To do so, the illiterate Pontiac employed all that he knew about the power of alphabetic writing as he had seen it used by European soldiers, settlers, and missionaries.

The Navarre manuscript lay hidden until the 1830s, but others who heard Pontiac's speech at the Rivière des Écorces must have spread the message, for Rogers's *Ponteach* includes a character named the Wolf, identified in the dramatis personae as an "Indian King who sides with Ponteach." His only lines are one speech in act 3, scene 3, set in "an Indian Senate House," urging an attack on the English by evoking one of the common tropes of Indian tragedy, a golden age of "our great Forefathers, ere these Strangers came" and put to shame "we their soften'd Sons, a puny Race, [who] Are weak in Youth, fear Dangers where they're not." "Dare to be like your Fathers," he says, by attacking the European invaders: "Destroy their Forts and Bulwarks, burn their Towns" (224). Interestingly, the same scene includes a French priest who seconds the Wolf's call for war, describing the foe as

Enemies of God;
Rebels and Traitors to the King of Kings;
Nay those who once betray'd and kill'd his Son,
Who came to save you *Indians* from Damnation. (225)

He tries to blame the English for crucifying Christ, one of a few instances in the Indian dramas where the tragic sacrifice of the Indian hero is compared to that of Christ. But the priest's motives are entirely selfish. In an earlier scene, he says that if he can help regain this land for the French, he might be chosen as Pope. Rogers was expressing an anti-Catholic and anti-French perspective, but his play nevertheless explores the more subtle meanings of "Father" in the 27 April speech. The hero's lines in *Ponteach* bring out the overdetermination of the paternal figure. And Pontiac himself seems to have invoked the Holy Father, the ancestral fathers, and the French father or king as a trinity of powers behind his epochal rebellion.

Robert Rogers

I argued in chapter 2 that Cortés formed his conception of the power he could wield in Mexico by studying and usurping the status of Moctezuma, and I have contended elsewhere that John Smith modeled his vision of his authority in America on his understanding of the power of his foe Powhatan (Gordon Sayre, "*Sauvages*" 49–78). The same sort of relationship developed between Robert Rogers and Pontiac. Rogers's image of "Ponteach" not only resonated with the rhetoric of republican tragedy and broke with the conventions of Indian tragedy established by Dryden (Slotkin 238) but also eerily foretold the course of Rogers's career. The paths of the two men reflect and intersect each other like a contrapuntal dance across the frontier of the Old Northwest, and because each attempted to forge a power base independent of French and English colonial domination, each man's heroism has been interpreted variously as patriotic and as treasonous.

Rogers was born in 1731 in Methuen, Massachusetts, and was living in New Hampshire in 1755 at the start of the Seven Years' War. He joined the New Hampshire regiment of the British colonial army, probably as a means to escape prosecution on a charge of counterfeiting the province's currency. As he showed a potential for military command, William Johnson, the prominent British Indian agent in New York, assisted Rogers in organizing a corps of volunteers that came to be called Rogers's Rangers. The Rangers' exploits in the Lake George area in 1758–59 were among the British side's few successes in that theater of the war, and press reports both in America and England celebrated Rogers. In heroic nationalist accounts, such as Kenneth Lewis Roberts's 1937 novel, *Northwest Passage*, and the film version starring Spencer Tracy, the fortitude, woodcraft, and independence of the Rangers anticipates the revolution's minutemen and contrasts with the stuffy, ignorant British Redcoats. This is also the main thesis of the second play based on the rebellion, Alexander Macomb's *Pontiac; or, The Siege of Detroit* (1835).

Because Rogers never received a formal commission, the British army refused to pay many of the debts he incurred in organizing the Rangers, and Governor Thomas Gage even refused Rogers back pay on the rationale that he was merely a volunteer. In January 1764 he was thrown into debtors' prison in New York City, where he remained until some of his former troops broke in to set him free. So in 1765 Rogers sailed to London to seek a reward for his services in the war. Given the publicity his wartime exploits had received in the London press, he had some reason to expect success. When Rogers's initial petitions in London did not bear fruit, he prepared a proposal for an expedition to find the Northwest Passage, which he expected lay between the headwaters of the Mississippi and "the river called by the Indians Ouragon." He requested thirty-two thousand pounds. Dismayed by the cost, the Lords Committee of Council denied the grant, but King George III ordered that he be made commandant of Fort Michilimackinac, and on 17 October 1765, Rogers met the king to receive the royal blessing and his new commission.

While in London, the soldier and backwoodsman also became an author. He published two books under his own name. *Journals of Major Robert Rogers* is a narrative of his war exploits up to 1761, including copies of correspondence and a list of twenty-eight points of instruction to his Rangers on backwoods battle strategy. The narrative ends just as the account of Pontiac and his rebellion begins. The second book, *A Concise Account of North America*, provides a description of the colonies from Newfoundland to Florida supplemented by additional chapters on the "Interior Country" of the Great Lakes, a thirty-page "Customs, Manners, &c. of the Indians," and a brief narrative about Pontiac. Both of these publications were well received and established him as such an authority on American matters that the *Monthly Review* called his *Concise Account* "the most satisfactory account we have yet been favored with, of the interior parts of that immense continent which victory hath so lately added to the British empire" (Cuneo 175). In truth, the two-hundred-page text is superficial compared to other colonial histories of the 1750s and 1760s such as the one by Le Page du Pratz, but Rogers's book came at the right time and from the right source. Because Britain had just acquired some of this territory from France, it was necessary to put this knowledge at the disposal of English readers as an instrument for imperial power, and in the postwar climate they would not be inclined to trust information from the French.[9] As the opening lines put it, "The British Empire in North America is become so extensive and considerable, that it is presumed any attempts to transmit a just notion of it to the public will be favourably received by any Englishman who wishes well to his country." Rogers feared that without such publicity, a land so "new and unsettled [and] so distant from the seat of empire" would not attract attention and investment. By combining all the colonies in one brief book, Rogers rhetorically united what would soon be politically divided. He dreamed an imperial dream of an Anglo North America that the later revolutionaries, failing to conquer Canada, never managed to create.

Rogers's third work was *Ponteach; or, The Savages of America: A Tragedy*. It appeared anonymously from the same publisher as the other two, J. Millan, in 1766 some months after he left to sail back to America. It apparently was never produced on stage and did not meet with the critical acclaim that his other two publications had received. The few scholars who have written about the play agree that Rogers probably did not write the entire text. Biographer John Cuneo believes the genesis for the play may have come from the *Critical Review*'s remarks on *Concise Account*: "The picture which Mr. Rogers has exhibited of the emperor Ponteack, is new and curious, and his character would appear to vast advantage in the hands of a great dramatic genius" (181). Perhaps Rogers seized on this suggestion and came up with an outline or plot and then a ghostwriter with a greater fluency in iambic pentameter penned the speeches of Ponteach and the other characters (see Ellison 90). But contemporary readers believed Rogers to be the author, and so I have proceeded under this assumption.

Most commentators, including Parkman, have concentrated on the play's first act, which presents a critique of the British exploitation of the Indian trade in the form of a comic farce. The first four scenes introduce pairs of villainous Englishmen, first the traders McDole and Murphey; then the settlers/hunters Orsbourn and Honnyman (Orsbourn says he "could eat an Indian's Heart with Pleasure" [184]); then officers at the Detroit fort, Colonel Cockum and Captain Frisk; and finally the Governors Sharp, Gripe, and Catchum (likely based on Sir William Johnson or Jeffrey Amherst), who talk about embezzling the presents sent for the Indians. Cuneo believes that this is the only part of the play Rogers actually helped to write. Although comic in presentation, the account of British abuses of the customs of the middle ground were quite accurate. Parkman reprinted the first two scenes in appendix B to his *Conspiracy of Pontiac*, "The Causes of the Indian War," and commented, "The rest of the play is of a different character. The plot is sufficiently extravagant, and has little or no historical foundation" (853).

Although more modest in scale and less pretentious in style than John

Smith's *General Historie of Virginia, New England, and the Summer Isles*, Rogers's two volumes of colonial history and one of drama made a similar bid to raise his stature into the genteel trinity of courtier, soldier, and poet and to win him appointment to a position of prominence in a subsequent colonial venture. Rogers retells the story of Smith and Pocahontas in the chapter on Virginia in *Concise Account*. And like Smith's three books about the Jamestown colony, Rogers's three books contain a curious discrepancy. Smith's account of his rescue by Pocahontas appeared in the *General Historie* in 1624, but, as many have noted, the 1608 and 1612 narratives of his captivity under Powhatan do not mention Pocahontas rescuing him. Some have speculated that the notoriety aroused by Pocahontas's visit to England with her husband, John Rolfe, prompted Smith to include the story of his dramatic involvement with this Indian princess. Rogers supposedly first met Pontiac in 1760, when traveling along the south shore of Lake Erie on the way to take control of the fort at Detroit. *Concise Account* tells of "an embassy" from "Ponteack, the King and Lord of the country I was in" (240) and of meeting with him to smoke the calumet. Pontiac even "expressed a great desire to see England, and offered me a part of his country if I would conduct him there" (242–43). But the *Journal*, in its account of this journey to Detroit, mentions no Indians by name, and in that text not Pontiac but the French commandant, Bellestre, is Rogers's adversary. George Croghan, who was with Rogers on this journey, wrote in his journals only of meeting with the "principal Man of the Ottawas" (105), which may or may not have been Pontiac. If the *Journal* entries truly were written in 1761 and earlier, while the *Concise Account* was penned after Rogers arrived in London, it appears that he may have invented the 1760 meeting with Pontiac to make some of the prestige of the Indian tragic hero rub off on himself.

And the parallels between Smith and Rogers go even further. Whereas John Smith had implied an imperial translation of power from Powhatan to himself via Pocahontas, Rogers hinted that in the aftermath of Pontiac's rebellion, he might start his own empire. When he arrived at Michilimackinac with his wife, Elizabeth, in August 1766, Rogers assumed control of a ramshackle fort at the remote limits of British influence in North America. Since Rogers had left the region three years earlier, Jeffrey Amherst, whose ungenerous policies had so angered Pontiac, had been replaced by Sir Thomas Gage. Although Gage's Indian policy more resembled that of the French, a partial victory perhaps for Pontiac's rebellion, the new governor was much less friendly toward Rogers than Amherst had been. Gage was angry that Rogers had gone to London to seek preferment, bypassing the military chain of command. Sir William Johnson also now disliked Rogers. And Rogers did in fact have designs to usurp his superiors. While at Michilimackinac he penned a lengthy memorandum, addressed to his majesty but never sent, in which he declares his plans "to erect Michilimackinac into a Civil Government independent of any other Post" (Rogers, "Michilimackinac Journal" 270). Rogers saw himself as the head of this government, and he requested funds adequate to garrison "two three, or more Companies" of Rangers and for presents to ensure the allegiance of "more than one third of the Indians on the Continent," who would be trading at the fort (272). Rogers envisioned that he might attract the allegiance of as many natives as Pontiac had, and he even appealed to the lessons of "the last Indian War of 1763" (273) to support his plan for a single fort under his command rather than a network of local posts that might be more easily pillaged, as had occurred in that year. In his frontier fantasy, Rogers would outflank the Hudson's Bay Company to control the interior of North America, and he did not forget his plan for an expedition to the Northwest Passage, for he wrote that his influence would extend all the way to the Pacific.

This document was not published until 1918, but it is clear that Rogers attempted to follow through on it. On 2 September 1766 a party left Michilimackinac, commanded by Captain James Tute and including Jonathan Carver, who like Rogers had fought out of Fort William Henry in 1757. Carver made Rogers's scheme famous. His narrative of this expedition, *Travels in the Interior Parts of America*, which was first published in London in 1778, achieved a lasting success and was reprinted in America, which Rogers's works were not. Among its attractions was a romantic account of the attack on the fort at Detroit at the beginning of the siege. According to Carver, on the evening before a 7 May council between Pontiac and the British, "an Indian woman who had been employed by Major Gladwin, to make him a pair of Indian shoes, out of curious elk-skins, brought them home" (78). The major was pleased with them, paid her, and ordered another pair for a friend. She lingered at the door on her way out, and when pressed to explain herself, said that "she was unwilling to take away the remainder of the skin, because he put so great a value upon it" and that "she should never be able to bring them back" (79). The double entendre of the valuable elk-skin shoes hints at what was confirmed by other Detroit witnesses interviewed in the 1820s by Lewis Cass, governor of the Michigan Territory (Parkman 510, 866–68). The girl, known as Catherine, had been Gladwin's mistress and wished to save her lover's life. John Mix Stanley portrayed this meeting in his painting *Unveiling the Conspiracy* (figure 4.2), a mural in the Detroit Public Library (where the Navarre manuscript is held). Catherine, wearing a cross, gestures toward the elk hides while Gladwin, his finished moccasins on the table in front of him, intuits her meaning. The scene is interpretable only to a viewer aware of the legend recorded by Carver and was painted for the library on the

FIGURE 4.2. John Mix Stanley, *Unveiling the Conspiracy* (1863).
This mural is on the wall of Adam Strohm Hall in the Detroit Public Library.
Courtesy of the Detroit Public Library.

hundredth anniversary of the siege, so important for the city's history. (The Navarre manuscript reports the less romantic story that Gladwin was tipped off by a disaffected Ottawa man named Mahiganne.) Unlike the French commandant, Chepar, who was killed in the Natchez Massacre (see chapter 6), Gladwin heeded this warning. The next day the Indians entered the fort concealing under their blankets their muskets with the barrels sawn off. Gladwin had all his troops armed and ready on the parade ground, and therefore Pontiac called off his plans and did not deliver the signal to launch the surprise attack. Instead of a quick victory at Detroit, Pontiac was forced into a lengthy siege. This trope of the "surprise attack betrayed" in the literature of Indian rebellions will be the focus of chapter 7.

In addition to such entertaining tales as this, Carver's *Travels*, like Rogers's *Concise Account*, asserted a textual mastery over the extensive lands claimed from France by plagiarizing from earlier French texts. As John Parker demonstrated in his edition of Carver's manuscript journals (which are preserved in the British Museum), the 1778 *Travels* was edited by Alexander Bicknell, who rearranged manuscript material and added lengthy commentaries on questions such as the origins of the Indians, drawn from books by Adair, Charlevoix, Hennepin, Lahontan, and others. But to the time of his death, Carver was celebrated as an intrepid explorer.

Rogers was not as fortunate. In his attempt to realize the empire that had eluded Pontiac, he imitated the Indian leader all too well, becoming both agent and victim of conspiracy. In the summer of 1766 Rogers assumed control of the fort at Michilimackinac, and in the winter of 1767–68 he left it in shackles, bound for a court-martial in Montreal. The turn in his fortunes has left a long paper trail but remains susceptible to varying interpretations. General Gage claimed to have received in April 1766 in New York a letter from Joseph Hopkins, a Marylander who, like Rogers, had commanded a company of Rangers at Detroit and who, when his trip to England in 1764–65 did not result in the kind of recognition or preferment offered to Rogers, apparently plotted with him to defect to the French. At Rogers's court-martial in October 1768, an affidavit from his secretary, Nathaniel Potter, corroborated the mysterious letter by asserting that Rogers had confided to Potter that if his proposal for a "separate government" was refused, he planned to go "to the French towards the Mississippi and to enter the Service of the French" (qtd. in Cuneo 222). Potter claimed that Rogers had threatened to kill him if he revealed knowledge of the plan. Yet Potter had died on a ship bound for England before the court-martial began. Other witnesses who had earlier supported Gage failed to produce damning testimony against Rogers, who was acquitted. But this did not clear his name, for the scandal was played out in the periodical press that just a few years earlier had celebrated Rogers's exploits. On 18 August 1768, the *Virginia Gazette* printed a letter from Niagara claiming that "Rogers's design was, after having taken and plundered Detroit and the Illinois, and carried the spoils to his accomplice Captain Hopkins, at New-Orleans, to have returned himself, and fallen upon New-England and Carolina, which he looked upon to be two of our richest provinces." The stratagem for this rebellion is roughly what Pontiac may have had in mind when he implored Villiers for assistance at Fort Chartres in 1764. A letter from Michilimackinac in the 13 June 1768 *Boston Chronicle* reported the failure of Rogers's rebellion in the style of the playbill for a stage melodrama: "Joyful news of Michilimackinac preserved, or the plot discovered, a dismal treachery carried on by its late commandant to massacre the garrison . . . and march against Detroit afterwards, make the best of his way to Capt. Hopkins, on the Mississippi." The 29 August issue of the same paper bore the comforting news of Rogers's arrival in prison in Montreal.

After his acquittal, Rogers did not give up on a military career, but his fortunes continued to decline. According to written comments by the powerful men to whom he subsequently petitioned during a period of heightened suspicion during the Revolutionary War, Rogers was regarded as a potential traitor and conspirator. When he visited Eleazar Wheelock in November

1775, the founder of Dartmouth College wrote to George Washington that a French captive had informed him that "Major Rogers was second in command under [British] General Carleton; and that he had lately been in Indian habit through our encampment at St. John's, and had given a plan of them to the General" (qtd. in Cuneo 259). Traveling on to his hometown of Portsmouth, New Hampshire, he was examined by General John Sullivan, who also suspected him of supporting the British. The British, for their part, suspected he would side with the rebels.[10] In the summer of 1776, George Washington ordered Rogers's arrest, and just two days after voting on the Declaration of Independence, the Continental Congress voted to return him to New Hampshire. Their fears apparently were justified: Rogers escaped from prison, joined with the British, and organized a new corps of Queen's American Rangers. Although he scored some successful raids, the British officers were not pleased with his assortment of "Negroes, Indians, Mulattos, Sailors, and Rebel prisoners" (Cuneo 275), a multiethnic force akin to Pontiac's bands of warriors. General William Howe persuaded Rogers to resign his commission. Like Pontiac, Rogers's denouement was inglorious: drink, poverty, and poor health until his death in London in 1795.

In his 1832 novel, *Wacousta; or, The Prophecy*, John Richardson dramatized Pontiac's rebellion from the perspective of the Anglo-Canadians besieged at Detroit. According to some accounts, Richardson's grandmother, an Indian, was at Detroit at that time. In one brief speech with the British commandant, de Haldimar, Ponteac alludes to Robert Rogers, without naming him, as an Englishman he respected. But since Rogers was not at the fort during the siege, he has no role in the novel. Ponteac boasts of having taken all but two of the British forts in the region and conceives a plan to take Detroit as well, a plan that Richardson adopted not from Carver or other more relevant sources but from Alexander Henry's account of the Indians' successful attack on Michilimackinac in the summer of 1763. During a lacrosse game, the Indians will throw the ball over the wall of the fort and then request permission to come in and fetch it. When the door opens, they shall rush in to attack. De Haldimar's son spies on the Indians and is tipped off to the plan by a sympathetic woman, Oucanasta, and so the troops in the fort are prepared for Ponteac and his warriors. As in the actual events of 7 May 1763, the British allow the Indians whose surprise attack has been foiled to retreat from the fort unharmed rather than risk a bloody fight with them.

Alexander Macomb, a hero of the War of 1812 and an army general stationed at Detroit in the 1820s and 1830s, published in 1835 an Indian tragedy based on Pontiac's rebellion that Macomb had written and staged as a diversion for his troops (Eugene Jones 33). *Pontiac; or, The Siege of Detroit* is dated 1826 and dedicated to Lewis Cass. The most engaging part of its plot turns on an Indian woman, Ultina, who considers whether she should "disclose to the white man the plots which Pontiac meditates for his destruction" (13). Although unlike Carver's Catherine, Ultina admits to no romantic involvement with the British leader, she does recall that Gladwin has been kind to her and says, "A woman's heart leads her to save, not to destroy" (13). Confronting Pontiac with his foiled conspiracy, Gladwin conceals his informant and instead claims divine protection: "The Great Spirit watches over his white children, and sends guardian angels to advise them of the evil intentions of their enemies" (20). Macomb's play thus reproduces part of the common formula of the Indian tragedies, but neither his talent nor his sentiment was up to the task of creating stirring, defiant speeches for Pontiac, who speaks in bland prose. Macomb explains in a preface that he altered history to have Pontiac captured by Major Gladwin and then killed by an Indian henchman named Agushaway in a climactic scene that is utterly flat and lifeless.

Thus, aside from Robert Rogers's works, Pontiac scarcely received any heroic literary treatment. His reputation seems to have become bound up in the geopolitical conflicts that followed his rebellion, not only in North America but back in Europe. Thomas Morris, the envoy sent by Colonel Bradstreet in 1764 to try to conclude a peaceful ending to the rebellion, was held captive and narrowly escaped death at the hands of rebel leaders. In perhaps the most charming and quixotic scene in all the records of Pontiac's rebellion, Morris writes that he had been saved by his taste for stage drama. After he was first apprehended, "an Indian called the little chief, told Godefroi [Morris's interpreter] that he would send his son with me, and made me a present of a volume of Shakespear's plays; a singular gift from a savage" (308). A few days later, Morris avoids being seized by the Miamis because "I had the good fortune to stay in the canoe, reading the tragedy of Anthony and Cleopatra, in the volume of Shakespear which the little chief had given me, when the rest went on shore" (312). Although England's greatest dramatist had saved his skin in that instance, Morris nonetheless makes clear his taste for French tragedy. He published his journal in a little volume of *Miscellanies in Prose and Verse* (1791) that included an ode in honor of the National Assembly of France and a "Letter to a Friend on the Poetical Elocution of the Theatre and the Manner of Acting Tragedy." The latter text expressed scorn for David Garrick, the greatest English actor of the time, and his preference for Mademoiselle du Ménil, whom he had seen in Racine's *Phèdre*, a work he had translated and hoped to stage in London. Such Francophile sentiments in politics and art, expressed in the midst of the French Revolution, were unlikely to earn Morris many friends in London, and he had failed in his earlier efforts to use his wartime exploits to attract patronage from the crown, as Rogers had done. But it is tempting to imagine that his fluent spoken French and even his French cultural tastes might have won over Pontiac and saved his life. In any case, from our point of view today, Morris's success lies in his contributions to the documentary drama of Pontiac's rebellion. His journal, along with the writings by Robert Navarre and a few other little-known eyewitnesses, convey the speeches of Pontiac, the dramatic lines of a rebel leader acting in a tragedy of historic dimensions.

CHAPTER 5 / LOGAN

"I appeal to any white man to say, if ever he entered Logan's cabin hungry, and he gave him not meat; if ever he came cold and naked, and he clothed him not. During the course of the last long and bloody war, Logan remained idle in his cabin, an advocate for peace. Such was my love for the whites, that my countrymen pointed as they passed, and said, 'Logan is the friend of the white men.' I had even thought to have lived with you, but for the injuries of one man. Col. Cresap, the last spring, in cold blood, and unprovoked, murdered all the relations of Logan, not sparing even my women and children. There runs not a drop of my blood in the veins of any living creature. This called on me for revenge. I have sought it: I have killed many: I have fully glutted my vengeance. For my country, I rejoice at the beams of peace. But do not harbour a thought that mine is the joy of fear. Logan never felt fear. He will not turn on his heel to save his life. Who is there to mourn for Logan?—Not one."

—Logan, qtd. in Thomas Jefferson, *Notes on the State of Virginia* (1785)

What better proof might one want of the power of literature? This lament of scarcely two hundred words, spoken by a solitary outlaw to an audience of one, in remote Ohio, generated an elaborate legend and has remained in print for more than 225 years. Perhaps no other orator or poet in American history can claim to have risen to fame on the basis of a single performance of such brevity. Next to Pontiac or Metacom, Logan may appear undeserving of such renown. He was not truly a chief (though of course he was later called one), and he never organized a concerted war of resistance against colonial invaders. He acted alone as a vigilante. Nevertheless, in continuing defiance of Logan's assertion that no one would mourn for him, his legend influenced several early-nineteenth-century novels, has been honored by memorial sites and monuments, and even briefly inspired its own historical society and journal.

Indian oratory had of course been praised before. Speeches by native leaders at eighteenth-century treaty councils had been collected and celebrated and compared to the words of Roman statesmen, notably by Cadwallader Colden and Ben Franklin.[1] But with Logan's speech, the craze for Indian oratory reached a singular extreme: the oration became the most frequently reprinted, most hackneyed text of the genre. Perhaps its most important reprinting was in *McGuffey's Eclectic Reader*, a successful series of nineteenth-century school texts.[2] Through this means, Logan's speech was used to educate and form the character of young Americans. As the *American Pioneer*, the journal of the Logan Historical Society of Cincinnati, declared in its 1842 editorial prospectus, "It has truly been stated that no piece of composition ever did more, if so much as, the speech of Logan, the Mingo Chief, to form the mind and develop the latent energies of the youthful American orator. Its influence has extended even into the halls of Congress, and has been felt upon the bench and in the bar of this nation; nay more, the American pulpit has been graced by energies which that speech has, in its warm simplicity called forth" (1:7).

The speech seems an odd choice for training a nation's future leaders. Logan did not lead his people politically or culturally. Instead, he expressed an extreme autonomy, speaking for no one but himself. Far from presenting the demands of his tribe to a colonial adversary, he delivered his speech after refusing to attend a peace council with Lord Dunmore, the leader of the army that had defeated Logan's allied Shawnee. Nor was his stoic appeal designed to arouse fellow warriors to the defense of an intertribal republic such as Pontiac and later Tecumseh envisioned. He spoke of his "countrymen" only to say that he did not follow or lead them. When they went to war, he stayed home; when they proclaimed peace, he went back on the warpath. Logan's words and actions were those of radical individualism and vigilante justice and came from a man apparently bereft of all human sympathies and obligations. In an age that treasured sympathy, Logan invoked it all the more powerfully by claiming to be beyond its reach. The speech defies its audience to sympathize with his tragic fate. So perhaps we should not be surprised if his appeal, and the sympathetic identification it inspired, did little or nothing to protect the land and future of Native Americans, even after it captured the attention of Thomas Jefferson, who recalled that it "used to be given . . . as a school exercise" (234).

When young American boys (and girls?) memorized and recited Logan's words out of *McGuffey's Reader*, they repeated what thousands were saying in other schoolrooms around the nation. Subjected to a forced conformity with American individualism, some of these young students must have mouthed the words in a monotone, while others, better coached by their teachers, embellished it with histrionic tones and gestures. Either way, few were concerned with Logan's plight or history. Logan's words were not so often listened to as ventriloquized, addressed to no one in particular, and spoken without engaging the agency or identity of the speaker. In this manner, the speech continued to invoke a mourning without mourners, a kinship without kin, the memorable paradoxes of Logan's conclusion.

The real reason that schoolboys trained to become ministers or lawyers by learning Logan's speech was not so much that it inculcated leadership skills as that so many powerful American political leaders had either championed or derided it. The lament first appeared in a letter from future president James Madison to the *Pennsylvania Journal*, printed by William Bradford in the issue for 1 February 1775 and again three days later in the *Virginia Gazette*. It was quickly reprinted in several colonial newspapers (for a list, see Seeber, "Critical Views" 146). Its importance was firmly established when another future president, Thomas Jefferson, included it in his *Notes on the State of Virginia* (1785), and it is for this reason that I have quoted Jefferson's text of the speech at the outset of this chapter. Jefferson offered the speech as proof of the American talent for eloquence: "I may challenge the whole orations of Demosthenes and Cicero, and of any more eminent orator, if Europe has furnished more eminent, to produce a single passage, superior to the speech of Logan" (67). This boast set Logan up as a target for Jefferson's political foes. The authenticity of the speech became a red herring. Those who wished to defend Logan's nemesis, Michael Cresap, and the other Maryland and Virginia "long knives" who fought against Logan or who wished simply to damage Jefferson marshaled evidence to clear Cresap's name from Logan's accusations or argued that the entire speech was a fraud. The exchange began when a well-known British actor, or "elocutionist," named James Fennel gave a public recitation of the speech in 1797. The effect must have been powerful, for Jefferson's opponents quickly responded. Maryland Attorney General Luther Martin, a Federalist who was also the son-in-law of Michael Cresap, published a letter to Fennel in the *Pennsylvania Gazette* on 30 March 1797 defending Cresap and attacking the speech's authenticity: "No such specimen of Indian oratory was ever exhibited" (Sandefur 289; Peterson 581).[3] Jefferson responded by soliciting depositions in the form of letters from eyewitnesses to the killings of Logan's family members and from John Gibson, the lone auditor of the speech. Jefferson published this brief as an appendix to the 1800 edition of *Notes on the State of Virginia*. Detractors of Jefferson and Logan continued the polemic in an 1826 biography of Cresap by John J. Jacob (who married Cresap's widow) and a 1851 book by Brantz Mayer. The quarrel was fought across the Mason-Dixon Line, pitting Maryland and Virginia against Pennsylvania and its Philadelphia elite, with Jefferson now identified with the Pennsylvania home of Logan rather than with his native Virginia.

Curiously, no one chose to defend in print the brilliance of Demosthenes and Cicero from their American challenger. It seems that Jefferson's desire to promote "native" American oratory and intellect was widely shared even among his political foes. Jefferson even began his appendix by attempting to sidestep the issue of the speech's authenticity in favor of affirming its nationalism: "Whether Logan's or mine, it would still have been American" (237). After thousands of schoolchildren had recited the speech as a model of American eloquence, to challenge its brilliance was to impugn the national intellect. Another president, Theodore Roosevelt, in his The Winning of the West, devoted two chapters to Dunmore's War and revived Logan as a nationalist touchstone by once again reprinting the speech, calling it "perhaps the finest outburst of savage eloquence of which we have any authentic record" (1:237). Into the 1960s and 1970s, scholarly articles about Logan's speech were primarily concerned with establishing its authenticity (see, for example, Sandefur; O'Donnell).

The recent controversy over Rigoberta Menchu's autobiography, set off by David Stoll's examination of its authenticity, offers an instructive context for considering Logan's speech. The study of testimony (testimonio) in literary studies, which has concentrated on the Holocaust and on the human rights abuses of civil wars in Latin America, has championed the intersubjective appeal of such voices (see, for example, Felman and Laub; Montejo). Curiously, this critical concept has rarely been applied to frontier wars and genocide in North America. Yet in the Menchu controversy as in that over Logan's speech, the question of the authenticity of the autobiographical subject became a foil for well-entrenched political conflicts. The speech set Logan up as a victim or martyr figure, and his foes assailed the authenticity of his text in part because they were reluctant to attack the political and sentimental power of his persona. But if we step back from the ideological quarrel, Logan, Jefferson, and their rivals are really not so different after all. I believe that Logan's lament and the legend around it developed in response to the social polarities of the frontier society where it took place. It problematized the separation of vengeance from justice, savagism from civility, white from native, frontier from metropole, and even Logan from Cresap. Accordingly, after a synopsis of the events alluded to in Logan's speech, this chapter will examine a series of oppositions between these concepts so important to the pervasive nineteenth-century doctrines of a progressive social development from barbarism to civilization. First, I will turn to the concepts of vengeance and justice, referring again to René Girard's studies of primitive practices of violence and sacrifice. Second, I will look at kinship and sentiment, for Logan not only demanded sentimental identification with his grief for his slain kin but also had kinship relations across racial lines. Third, I will examine the nineteenth-century historical image of Logan's or Dunmore's

War, particularly in the writings of Joseph Doddridge, to show how mourning by and for Logan was appropriated as the basis for a historiography of the settlement of western Pennsylvania. Finally, I wish to show how the racial, moral, and social reversals that the Logan legend thematizes were worked out in Gothic frontier novels by Charles Brockden Brown, John Neal, and Robert Montgomery Bird.

Frontier Vengeance, Frontier Justice

Logan's or Dunmore's War can be seen as a continuation of the Seven Years' War and of Pontiac's rebellion, which was no doubt the "last long and bloody war" to which Logan refers in the speech. Following a few years of anxious calm after the Seven Years' War was concluded in 1759, warriors inspired by Pontiac rose up in June 1763 and captured Fort Venango, Fort Le Boeuf, and Fort Presque Isle in western Pennsylvania and killed or threatened many settlers in the region. Soldiers and local militiamen responded with both military and guerrilla reprisals. On the military side was the expedition led by a Swiss mercenary, Colonel Henry Bouquet, against the Ohio Indians and chronicled by William Smith and Thomas Hutchins in a book published in 1765. The guerrilla aspect consisted of a series of vicious backsettler attacks on Indians, attacks goaded by the peculiar politics of Pennsylvania. As Ben Franklin explains in his autobiography, the Quaker elite in the eastern part of the province, whose influence dated to the colony's founder, William Penn, refused to fight in the Seven Years' War and only reluctantly approved financing for it. The settlers in central and western Pennsylvania were largely Scots-Irish Presbyterians, and this ethnic and religious contrast exacerbated resentments aroused by the Quakers' perceived favoritism toward the Indians, by Philadelphia merchants who continued to trade with the Indians during the conflict, and by an unequal franchise that kept the Provincial Assembly under Anglican and Quaker control. As Francis Parkman has written, "Two thousand persons had been killed, or carried off, and nearly an equal number of families driven from their homes. The frontier people . . . were divided between rage against the Indians, and resentment against the Quakers" (701). On 14 December 1763, a group of men from the town of Paxton, on the Susquehanna River, attacked and burned the Indian village of Conestoga, just to the south. Six Indians were killed, among them, according to some sources, relatives of Logan. Other locals sympathetic to the Indians escorted fourteen survivors to a refuge in the jail at Lancaster, only to then watch the so-called Paxton Boys break into the jail and lynch the survivors. Moravian missionaries horrified by these vigilantes evacuated Christian Indians from the towns of Wequetank and Nain and took them under a strong guard to Philadelphia, where they remained in an army barracks until December 1764. The Paxton Boys gathered a force of about 250 and marched toward Philadelphia in February with the goal of attacking these refugees. Philadelphia nearly erupted in riots, and Benjamin Franklin took it on himself to help defuse the crisis. A pamphlet war raged throughout 1764, with Franklin's A Narrative of the Late Massacres representing the best-known volley. Franklin invoked a sacred ethic of hospitality to defend his offer of asylum to the Indians and labeled the Paxton Boys and other Scots-Irish who sought to violate this principle "the CHRISTIANS WHITE SAVAGES of Peckstang and Donegall" (743). Parkman recounts this story with relish. Although it was something of a digression from The Conspiracy of Pontiac, in telling it the Boston Brahmin expresses his equal contempt for the ruffian Paxton Boys, the supercilious Quakers, and the pitiful savages. Parkman and Franklin's disdain reflects a perception of the Scots-Irish back settlers as culturally and racially distinct from the elites; in response, as Jane Merritt has argued, the "white [back] settlers drew on a language of 'savagism' to describe and circumscribe Indians, to differentiate themselves from their frontier rivals" (267), and appealed to provincial and British imperial forces to recognize only whites as subjects deserving of military protection.[4] One success of this effort was that Bouquet's expedition against the Ohio Indians made the repatriation of white captives living with Indian tribes one of its primary goals. As is clear from the sentimental scene of separation portrayed in Smith and Hutchins's book (74–80), many of these individuals considered their true family to be among the Indians, regardless of the new racial doctrines. In this manner, Pontiac's rebellion and its aftermath in Pennsylvania helped to establish racialized identity politics as we know it today, where the Irish are "white" and the Indians are not.

The literature of guerrilla wars in our own time (such as Menchu's book) confirms that it is easier to evoke sympathy for pathetic victims than for strident aggressors. Hence, rival propagandists in the Logan controversy sought to portray either the back settlers or the Indians as victims. But it is difficult to determine who struck first in this cycle of vengeance. During the decade following the Paxton riots, Logan's whereabouts amid the festering frontier strife in the Susquehanna and Upper Ohio valleys are uncertain, and his history resumes only in 1774, when he was living in a Shawnee village at the confluence of the Ohio River and Yellow Creek, near modern Wheeling, West Virginia. In April of that year, tension and suspicion between Indians and whites remained high. Michael Cresap, misinterpreting a letter circulated by John Connolly, Lord Dunmore's agent for western Pennsylvania, as a declaration of war, on 30 April murdered two Indian employees of a white trader and then attacked a party of Shawnee that had encamped just downstream near the mouth of Grave Creek. A few days later, on 3 May, another band of white men, reportedly led not by Cresap but by Daniel Greathouse, arrived at Baker's Bottom opposite Logan's village at Yellow Creek. They lured two men and one woman across the river with promises of rum from Joshua Baker's tavern. According to some sources, members of Logan's band had earlier killed members of Baker's family.[5] After the three Indians were drunk, Greathouse and company murdered them as well as several others who came looking for them, including Logan's youngest brother and his sister, who was either pregnant or mother to a young child.

In the wake of these killings, Logan vowed revenge and took to the warpath. Still, as his speech hints, he acted without the support of tribal leaders. Shawnee and Delaware chiefs including George White Eyes tried on 5 May to cover for these deaths and to secure peace, but they "could not control Logan, already a deeply disturbed man who believed himself pursued by evil manitous" (Richard White, Middle Ground 361; Heckewelder, Narrative 131). At this point, Pennsylvania Indian agents, including George Croghan and the mixed-blood Alexander McKee, also tried to prevent the outbreak of a race war. But Virginia leaders, such as Connolly and provincial Governor Lord Dunmore, continued agitating for it. The efforts at peacemaking, Richard White observes, "only served to limit the war to a battle between the Shawnees and the Virginians" (Middle Ground 363). Some evidence indicates that Lord Dunmore's motive may have been to seize for Virginia land to the south or on both sides of the Ohio River, thereby outflanking Pennsylvania's claims in the area both in what is now Ohio and in Pennsylvania downstream of Pittsburgh (Anthony Wallace, Jefferson and the Indians 53). Logan identified Cresap as a Virginian and in his vengeance sought to kill only Virginians and to spare Pennsylvanians.

Lord Dunmore's War climaxed in the battle of Point Pleasant, at the mouth of the Kanawha River, on 10 October. Two armies had marched westward from Virginia, one led by Dunmore, the other by General Michael Lewis. The Shawnee, wishing to prevent these two forces from combining, attacked Lewis's eleven hundred men before they could cross the Ohio. Because other nations had refused Shawnee requests for aid, the Indians were outnumbered, although they still took the lives of seventy-five Virginians, and Point Pleasant was one of the larger battles in the colonial wars of North America to this time.[6] In its aftermath, Dunmore ordered Lewis not to pursue the retreating Shawnee and convened peace talks with war chief Cornstalk at Camp Charlotte on the Scioto River. Dunmore secured a treaty in which the Shawnee promised not to hunt on the south side of the Ohio. Jefferson may have detested Dunmore, but the expedition unquestionably strengthened Virginia's claim to the Kentucky region, which Jefferson accordingly included as part of the state described in his *Notes*.

Logan, however, refused to attend the council between Cornstalk and Dunmore. Dunmore sent a messenger to fetch him. According to the prevailing view of events articulated by Jefferson, this messenger was John Gibson, later a general who treated with Tecumseh in Indiana but at the time only a frontier trader and interpreter. Because Logan was not a chief and he spoke outside of military and diplomatic contexts, he did not address his colonial foes formally, but he did ask that Gibson deliver a message to Dunmore. This meeting, its setting, the message or speech, and the bond created between the two men constitute the genesis of the Logan legend.

Although Logan's captive, William Robinson, later reported that Logan "spoke English well," Jefferson wrote that Gibson heard the speech in Shawnee or perhaps in Oneida or Cayuga, translated it into English, and committed to paper the text later sent to the *Pennsylvania Journal* by Madison. The authenticity of Logan's words therefore hinges on Gibson's translation, transcription, and editing. In this respect, the speech is no different from other more extended works of early Native American autobiography, notably the story of another heroic chief, Black Hawk, which Arnold Krupat has described as "the first of those compositely produced texts I call Indian autobiographies" (*Native American Autobiography* 5). Black Hawk had spoken in his own Sauk language to Antoine LeClair, a government interpreter of métis birth who furnished his translation to Galena, Illinois, newspaper editor John B. Patterson, who published it in 1833 and later proclaimed himself "editor and sole proprietor" of the text. LeClair's manuscripts have been lost, frustrating any modern efforts to recapture a Black Hawk unaltered by Patterson. The original sources of Logan's voice are likewise inaccessible. When in 1800 Vice President Jefferson sought confirmation for the now-famous speech, Gibson simply referred Jefferson back to his own canonical version, testifying that Logan "delivered to him the speech, nearly as related by Mr. Jefferson in his notes on the state of Virginia" (241).

The history of the Logan speech reveals contradictions between the codes for authenticity of textual and of oral sources. In spite of all the insistence on the oratorical force of the speech, its source, Gibson, like its subsequent admirers, could not give up dependence on a textual form. This desire for a greater authenticity led some to propose the existence of an original text written in wampum beads. The stage directions in Doddridge's play say Logan "reads the speech from a belt of wampum" (37). The title page of the *American Pioneer*, the short-lived journal of Cincinnati's Logan Historical Society, shows Logan reciting as Gibson follows his words in a wampum belt that lies across their laps (figure 5.1). They sit on a fallen log beneath the elm tree that legend identified as the setting for their exchange. Attempts to pin down the transitions and differences between oral and written literature lead into a catch-22. For the oration to be canonized, it must take a definitive textual form. But if the speech is prized for its eloquence, for the qualities of its oral performance, then these qualities are not contained in the text and cannot be recaptured. You had to be there, as they say, and only Gibson was. If the English text of the speech does not in fact measure up to Demosthenes or Cicero or if, as others have pointed out (Seeber, "Critical Views" 140–43), it lacks the figural style characteristic of other popular instances of Indian oratory, then the lost power of its original delivery only becomes more significant. This power has to be translated for us, in a separate act from the translation of the text of the speech itself.

John Heckewelder, a Moravian missionary who spoke Lenape (Delaware) fluently and collaborated on dictionaries of that language, attacked "the prejudice that exists against [the Indians'] languages" by defending Logan's eloquence: "I am convinced that [Logan's speech] was delivered precisely as it is related to us, with this only difference, that it possessed a force and expression in the Indian language which it is impossible to transmit into our own" (*History* 132). Indian eloquence for Heckewelder thus became a vanishing point, a platonic ideal for which there was no tangible form. And instead of developing a truly intercultural and multilingual notion of Indian eloquence, admirers fetishized the English words of Logan's oration without troubling themselves with the real problems of its translation. Few other commentators shared Heckewelder's knowledge of native languages, yet this did not stop them from squabbling over minor differences.[7] R. H. Taneyhill, another anti-Jefferson polemicist, claimed that the president "in trying to purify its diction, has lessened its sublimity and force. . . . Mr. Jefferson should have kept in mind what he well knew, that oratory is a native product and cannot be tampered with" (qtd. in Sandefur 295). Yet Taneyhill in fact knew nothing of the original language of Logan's production and had no basis on which to judge how it had been tampered with other than to compare Jefferson's text with that of the first printings in 1775.[8] Heckewelder and Taneyhill nevertheless shared with many in the early republic a notion of natural language as an ideal transparency between word and thought and feeling, an ideal that in practice was as inaccessible as a direct knowledge of another's feelings. Jay Fliegelman has termed this ideal an "elocutionary revolution [that] made the credibility of arguments contingent on the emotional credibility of the speaker" (*Declaring Independence* 2), a definition very close to Heckewelder's opening definition: "The eloquence of the Indians is natural and simple; they speak what their feelings dictate without

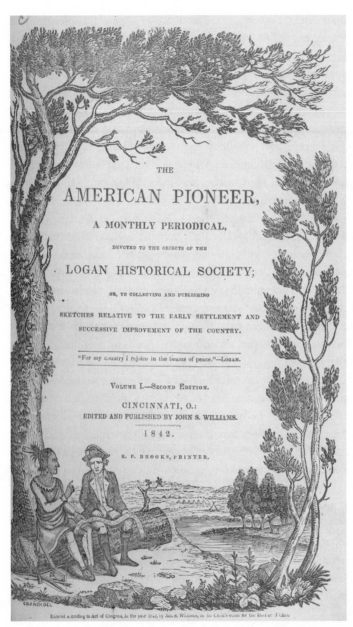

THE

AMERICAN PIONEER,

A MONTHLY PERIODICAL,

DEVOTED TO THE OBJECTS OF THE

LOGAN HISTORICAL SOCIETY;

OR, TO COLLECTING AND PUBLISHING

SKETCHES RELATIVE TO THE EARLY SETTLEMENT AND
SUCCESSIVE IMPROVEMENT OF THE COUNTRY.

"For my country I rejoice in the beams of peace."—LOGAN.

VOLUME I.—SECOND EDITION.

CINCINNATI, O.:
EDITED AND PUBLISHED BY JOHN S. WILLIAMS.

1842.

R. P. BROOKS, PRINTER.

FIGURE 5.1. Title page of the *American Pioneer*, the journal of the Logan Historical Society of Cincinnati, 1842. Beneath the famous elm, Logan lays down his tomahawk and bow and reads the text from the wampum belt to John Gibson, who holds the calumet (peace pipe). Courtesy of the Knight Library, University of Oregon.

art and without rule" (*History* 132). The figure of Logan, the wronged and grieving Indian, epitomizes the contradictions of this elocutionary revolution. Those who admired and ventriloquized his speech could claim to feel the emotional sincerity in it, yet his cultural and linguistic foreignness and the uncertainty about the speech's origins call into question such sympathy and sincerity. The cathartic ambivalence that Anglo-Americans of the early republic felt toward Logan was thus even more acute than that toward other Indian tragic heroes, not only because the regional divisions of the Paxton Riots and of Lord Dunmore's War were still contested but also because Logan's oratorical performance was mediated through several levels of translation and repetition.

In the eyes of French *philosophes* Denis Diderot and Guillaume-Thomas Raynal and French immigrant J. Hector St. John de Crèvecœur, Pennsylvania was a utopian social experiment, a place of religious toleration where poor emigrant peasants could acquire land and become independent farmers. These Frenchmen anticipated the yeoman farmer ideal promoted by Jefferson in his *Notes on the State of Virginia*. Diderot copied into his notebooks a translation of Logan's speech from the *Gazette de France* of 21 April 1775 (see Seeber, "Diderot"), and Raynal published the speech in the third edition of his *Histoire des Deux Indes* (9:76–77). But like other utopias, Pennsylvania had its dystopian side as well. If Logan's speech is an articulation of a natural man, his primitive nature can be defined by its barbaric violence as much as by its simple virtues. So before returning to the expression of grief and feeling, we must examine the issue of vengeance. From Conestoga to Yellow Creek to Point Pleasant, the history of Logan was a cycle of violence and counterviolence. As Parkman wrote, "The chronicles of the American borders are filled with the deeds of men, who, having lost all by the merciless tomahawk, have lived for vengeance alone" (702). He refers to white men such as the Paxton Boys, but replace "tomahawk" with "long rifle," and you have Logan. Ideology of the period held that such violence and savagery was a regrettable but necessary prelude to the advance of civilization. Even the more complex accounts of backwoods violence, such as Crèvecœur's "Distresses of a Frontier Man," still adhered to a stadial theory of history and anthropology that placed Indians, backwoods whites, and civilizing colonists on a temporal and spatial spectrum, thus distinguishing between "barbarian" and "civilized" forms of violence. To understand Logan's vengeance, however, we need to discard this savagist, progressivist doctrine and look for interpretations that will integrate native and colonial, ancient and modern cultural formations.

Girard's *Violence and the Sacred* analyzes the origins of tragedy and mythology as reflections of primitive sacrificial rites that were intended to put a stop to cycles of vengeance. In Cain and Abel and in Romulus and Remus, Girard sees myths of fraternal vengeance suppressed by a law of the father. In Oedipus and Tiresias, he diagnoses "violent reciprocity in action, canceling all distinctions between the two men" (71). Logan's relationship to Michael Cresap (and in some ways to John Gibson) is similar. Richard White calls Logan "a man in many ways very similar to Cresap" (*Middle Ground* 358), and Girard might have added that the two rivals are monstrous doubles, "antagonists, incapable of perceiving that nothing actually stands between them" (161). As frontier vigilantes, their tactics and motives were identical, and the question of which one was a hero and which a monster depended on one's racial, regional, or political sympathies.

Moreover, aside from the rivalry with Cresap, Logan fits Girard's larger theory of the sacrificial victim. He is an iconic figure, at once separate from and similar to both sides in the conflict, whose sacrifice marks a moment of crisis that makes possible a transition from primitive to modern society, from frontier to "civilization" and even from colony to nation. The primitive society in question is not fifth-century B.C.E. Greece, of course, or even native Shawnee or Mingo culture but frontier Pennsylvania, with both its Indian and white populations. Logan's rivalry with Cresap and the vow of vengeance it inspired transformed Logan into a monster who practiced the same violence of which he accused Cresap. But his relationship and kinship to Gibson mark his intimate resemblance to frontier whites. Logan's death, which his speech foretells, is an offer of sacrifice that might bring about unanimity and put an end to frontier vengeance. His speech inspired a mixture of pity and fear, just as the tragic hero did according to Aristotle. Although Logan lacks the chiefly stature of Metacom or Tecumseh, his status as a surrogate victim, his rivalry with Cresap, and his kinship to Gibson all reflect Girard's anthropological theory of tragedy. Logan lifts the sordid details of frontier history to the dignity of high literature. The tragic violence and imminent death recounted in the speech provide a ritual catharsis that enables a primitive society to move out of a cycle of violence into a national myth of sacrifice at the same time that Pennsylvania and the twelve other colonies begin to negotiate their differences and enter into a common nationhood.

I have traced the cycle of revenge on which Logan embarked back to the Paxton riots and could have gone farther. For colonial apologist Teddy Roosevelt, a schoolboy "he hit me first" ethic determined the right and wrong in Lord Dunmore's War: "The war was not only inevitable, but was also in its essence just and righteous on the part of the borderers. Even the unpardonable and hideous atrocity of the murder of Logan's family, was surpassed in horror by many of the massacres committed by the Indians about the same time" (1:241). But balancing the unpardonable against the horrible does not really lead to any moral high ground, and Logan's speech invokes other ethical standards. As John O'Donnell has pointed out, the speech indicts Logan's foes for violating several practices for limiting random violence that were observed by both Native Americans and biblical Hebrews. Logan says that he honored the ethic of hospitality, offering meat and clothing to white strangers who visited his cabin, yet his hospitality was violated. Matthew 25:35–36 says much the same thing, though from the point of view of the guest: "For I was an hungered, and ye gave me meat: I was thirsty, and ye gave me drink: I was a stranger, and ye took me in: Naked, and ye clothed me." Jesus warns that only those who honor this ethic will be welcomed into the kingdom of heaven. Logan's speech tries to invoke the same threat of damnation on his foe Cresap (or Greathouse), who violated this ethic by luring his victims across Yellow Creek to Baker's tavern, offering them drink and then murdering them.

Girard's book builds its authoritative breadth by combining Greek and biblical literature with anthropological sources about how primitive societies prevent (or fail to prevent) cycles of vengeance. He uses only a few North American examples, but he might have found more. The weakness of his theory is that it asserts the existence of an actual, primal scene of sacrificial crisis as foundational in every social order, even though this moment lies beyond the scope of history. In truth, such a single originary moment is unnecessary, for efforts to contain vengeance are as ancient and as recent as vengeance itself. Both the Iroquois condolence ritual and the related practice, essential to the French-Indian middle ground, of "covering" for violent deaths by offering gifts to the relatives of the victims exemplify such efforts. Logan's speech and story occurred against an Indian cultural background not of primitive violence but of diplomatic efforts at containment. According to Richard White's painstaking research, the murders of the ten Indians at Baker's tavern on Yellow Creek led to such efforts. White Eyes, a Delaware leader but also a trader and former tavern keeper like Joshua Baker, went to Pittsburgh and met with agents Croghan, McKee, and Connolly to try to cover for the deaths of Logan's relatives and the others. As we have seen, however, those efforts failed. Logan would be the necessary sacrificial victim, but his death was not a judicial punishment; it brought about a symbolic act of sacrifice conveyed through his speech.

"According to Cicero," whom Logan purportedly surpassed with his speech, "eloquence was the force capable of transforming humanity from barbarism to organised and civilised society" (David Murray 41). Yet Logan's acts of vengeance and the murders he avenged were barbaric acts. To determine if his eloquence did in fact help to transform Pennsylvania into a

civilized society, we must consider both the effect of the speech on its readers (reading it on the page or reading it aloud for elocutionary training) and
the model provided by Logan's behavior. As an elocutionary exercise, his
oration educated and civilized. But by most evidence, the transition that
Logan made after his speech was retrograde. "Logan is the friend of the
white man," his countrymen had said of him when he sat in his cabin and
refused to join Pontiac's rebellion or retaliate for the atrocities of the Paxton
Boys. But that was then: Cresap's murders have transformed him into an
enemy of the white man, a machine of vengeance. Though the speech remains unspecific when he says, "I have sought it. I have killed many,"
historical legend suggests that Logan stopped at thirteen murders, matching
the thirteen killed at Baker's Bottom and in the two previous attacks (Richard White, *Middle Ground* 362; Roosevelt 1:213)

However, other sources suggest that Logan was not transformed into a
savage monster, that he remembered the ethic of sacrifice and forgiveness
even after May 1774. Heckewelder wrote that in 1779 Logan adopted a white
female captive into his family as a sister, replacing the sister killed at Baker's
tavern (Draper 166). Another story told of Logan going to a judge to seek
redress from a trader who had given him bad wheat in exchange for deer-
skins: "When Judge Brown decided in his favor he replied 'Law good, makes
rogues pay.' " (Sawvel 66; Draper 155).

The "declaration of William Robinson" included in Jefferson's appendix
of 1800 is the most notable evidence of Logan's generous temperament.
Robinson told of being captured by Logan on the west fork of the Monongahela on 12 July 1774. According to Robinson, "Logan spoke English well,
and very soon manifested a friendly disposition to this subscriber, and told
him to be of good heart, that he would not be killed, but must go with him to
his town, where he would probably be adopted in some of their families"
(249). Six days later, when Robinson was tied to the stake for torture, Logan
prevailed on the captors to adopt him and took him to an "old squaw" who
became his aunt "and two others his brothers, and that he now stood in the
place of a warrior of the family who had been killed at Yellow creek" (250).
This adoption is exactly the sort of covering or requickening that Algonquian
and Iroquoian peoples used both to restore tribal members lost at war and to
forestall cycles of vengeance. It applies specifically to the murders that, by
other accounts, Logan said could be answered only with blood. Interestingly,
during Pontiac's war Gibson had been captured and saved from death by
being adopted by an Indian woman (Thwaites and Kellogg 11). But was
Robinson in this case the subject of a requickening or merely a prisoner held
in anticipation of an exchange? His deposition continues, "About three days
after this Logan brought him a piece of paper, and told him he must write a

letter for him, which he meant to carry and leave in some house where he should kill somebody." Robinson wrote the message, using gunpowder for ink, and all versions of the legend concur that this note was found tied to a club at the house of some of Logan's victims, a written counterpart to his more famous oral performance.[9] It exists in two versions, both of which appeared in Jefferson's appendix. As Robinson recalled the words he had been forced to write twenty-five years earlier, "Why he had killed his people? That some time before they had killed his people at some place (the name of which the subscriber forgets) which he had forgiven; but since that he had killed his people again at Yellow creek, and taken his cousin, a little girl, prisoner; that therefore he must war against the whites; but that he would exchange the subscriber for his cousin" (250). Robinson's pronoun shift, from first-person to third-person free indirect discourse, destroys here the eloquent verbatim speech that was so important to Logan's other recorded text. However, the other version of the note on the war club does speak in Logan's "voice." It was printed earlier in the appendix in a letter from Judge Harry Innes of Frankfort, Kentucky, who claimed to have copied it into his memorandum book from the original left on Logan's club "at the house of one Robertson, whose family were cut off by the Indians":

> Captain Cresap,
> What did you kill my people on Yellow Creek for? The white people killed my kin, at Conestoga, a great while ago; and I thought nothing of that. But you killed my kin again, on Yellow Creek, and took my cousin prisoner. Then I thought I must kill too; and I have been three times to war since; but the Indians are not angry: only myself.
> Captain John Logan
> July 21, 1774 (Jefferson 239)

Beyond the greater immediacy and eloquence of the second version, the two differ on the facts. Where Innes's version echoes the speech in presenting Logan as a lone vigilante, Robinson's version suggests a prisoner exchange that might quell the cycle of vengeance that Logan was fostering. Yet if Robinson was merely a hostage, then Logan was not acting in accord with the customs of adoption and requickening: Robinson had not been chosen to replace an Indian victim of colonial attacks but served as bait for the return of Logan's kin. This contradiction balances war against family, the family of the warrior Robinson requickened against Logan's cousin or niece. In the European system of war, the soldier fights not for an actual family but for an army and a nation that is only figuratively his *patria*. In the more intimate world of frontier violence, one fights for one's family, as in the

Hatfields versus the McCoys. Logan marks and then crosses the boundary between the two.

Logan's Lament as Gothic and Sentimental Literature

> It is grossly unjust and would falsify human nature to suppose that Logan
> and the Red Men had no feelings of human kindness in their bosoms;
> and it would falsify history to say they had no inhuman wrongs to incite
> them to malicious revenge and that their savagery was cold-blooded
> murder in which they took fiendish delight.
> —Franklin V. Sawvel, *Logan, the Mingo* (1921)

The gothic and the sentimental genres of literature are close kin, related by common appeals to the sanctity or to the violation of family bonds. Logan's famous line, "There runs not a drop of my blood in the veins of any living creature," makes him "the last of his race." Like Poe's Roderick Usher, Logan is doomed to die intestate, with no "collateral issue" (Poe 317). For his readers/listeners, this might elicit antithetical reactions. Those in the 1770s might fear Logan because as a man with nothing or no one left to lose, his quest for vengeance could not be halted by threats of retribution against his family (although Robinson's account suggests that Logan's cousin remained alive in 1779). They might suspect him of incest according to the logic that a family lineage dies out only if it refuses exogamy (see Girard, *Violence* 75). Sentimentality, the ethic of an enlightened Christian era that believed it had sublimated pagan violence, counters these fears by urging the reader/listener to identify with Logan, to become kin with him. I will argue that the Logan legend works as a cathartic purging of frontier violence by refracting and confounding the fear that motivated it.

The relationship between horror and sympathy in the Logan legend hinges on matters of kinship and reproduction. In *Notes on the State of Virginia*, Jefferson cites the Logan speech not merely to support the claim that America had the intellectual potential to equal Europe's Demosthenes or Cicero or to rebut Raynal's slander that "America has not yet produced one good poet" (69; see also Rigal 574–75). Logan's eloquence forms part of Jefferson's ethnographic answer to the Comte de Buffon's attack on American Indians, an attack aimed not at their power of intellection but at their power of procreation. Jefferson moves from his rebuttal of Buffon's attack on America's "brute animals" to answer the French naturalist's lowest blow, that "the savage of the new world . . . is weak and small in the organs of generation; he has neither hair nor beard nor any ardor for his female" (Jefferson 61, 305).

The remainder of Jefferson's long French quotation from Buffon's *Histoire Naturelle* is characteristic of French Enlightenment materialism insofar as it collapses distinctions between genteel and vulgar aspects of relations between the sexes. Translated, it reads in part, "They lack ardor for their females and, by consequence, love for their fellow man; not knowing this attachment, the strongest and tenderest of all, their other feelings are cold and languishing; they love their parents and children weakly; the society the most intimate of all, that of the family itself, has for them only feeble ties" (62, 306). Jefferson's answer shares this view of sexuality and anticipates twentieth-century anthropological doctrines of functionalism and the power of the environment. The Indian male "is neither more defective in ardor, nor more impotent with his female, than the white reduced to the same diet and exercise," Jefferson insists (63). His education is not in the salon but in the chase. The Indian female is stronger than the white woman and has fewer children because she must follow the men on the hunt, and the Indians "experience a famine once in every year" (65). But when married to white traders, Jefferson adds, Indian women "produce and raise as many children as the white women" (65). Logan's lament, therefore, does more than display an Indian male's eloquence in council or his valor and honor in warfare: it attests to the faculty of reproduction and the strength of family bonds among the Indians as equivalent to those of whites living in the same environment. If propriety prevented Jefferson from making explicit claims about male Indians' "ardor for their female," he could nonetheless offer Logan's grief and rage as evidence of his attachment to his lost family, "the society the most intimate of all." Eliciting or appropriating this grief for white readers was a means for Jefferson to assert a cultural and emotional commonality between the natives and colonists who inhabited Virginia. The fact that Logan's family feeling was expressed not only through tender sentiment, as Buffon suggested, but through violent revenge did not by any means destroy this commonality, for both colonists and Indians engaged in these cycles of revenge.

The sentimental appeal becomes still stronger when we take Logan's speech out of the context of Jefferson's *Notes* and put it back under the elm. The circumstances of its delivery to John Gibson invoke more specific bonds of kinship. Gibson's deposition, the key document in Jefferson's appendix, conveys the famous scene with Logan, as I quoted earlier: "They went into a copse of wood, where they sat down, when Logan, after shedding abundance of tears, delivered to him the speech, nearly as related by Mr. Jefferson in his notes on the state of Virginia" (241). Although the word "nearly" suggests a wrinkle of inauthenticity in the famous text, the "abundance of tears" is the real basis on which Gibson stakes his veracity, just as it is the verification of Logan's grief. And Gibson responded all the more sympathetically because he was, in fact, kin to Logan. The victims of the notorious attack at Yellow Creek included Logan's sister, who was also the mother of Gibson's child (Thwaites and Kellogg 15). Hence, Gibson shared with Logan the tragic loss of family to the predations of frontier vigilantes. Logan's lament is also Gibson's.

Gibson was in Anglo-American kinship terms Logan's brother-in-law. The child of Logan's sister would by Iroquois kinship be a member of the same tribal phratry as Logan and therefore as close or closer kin to him than his own child. But his ties to Gibson would have been ambivalent. Among some native North American peoples—for example, the Assiniboines as described by John Tanner (134–35)—men observed taboos against speaking or even looking at their fathers-in-law or sons-in-law. Furthermore, Logan was killed in 1781 by a man named Tod-kah-dos, who may have been Logan's "cousin, or brother in law," according to John Ritenour in an essay published as an appendix to the 1912 edition of Doddridge's Notes on the Settlement (299); Logan's nephew through his wife (Sawvel 101); his brother; or a man with the same name as one of his brothers. Ritenour cites "Dah-gan-on-do, a Seneca, who said he got it himself from Tod-kah-dos" (300), who lived on Cornplanter's Allegheny Seneca reserve until 1844. Although it is difficult to sort out all these accounts, Logan fell at the hands of a kinsman, possibly in fratricide, and in retaliation for an act he committed while drunk. By common Indian custom, such a killing by a close family member precluded any organized process of justice or revenge by the other members of the tribe, so it would not have set off a cycle of vengeance such as Logan pursued. Logan's relationship to these kinsmen nicely captures how he was attacked by his own people yet honored by his enemies, how the usual boundaries and loyalties of race and kinship were disrupted by his provocations.

The Anglo-American sources for the Logan legend do not well understand Iroquois kinship but are concerned with Gibson's child. According to an article published in connection with the dedication of the Logan Elm historical site near Circleville, Ohio, "Collateral relatives deny that Gibson was the husband of Logan's sister" (Galbreath 5), but the author points out that Gibson never denied it in spite of many opportunities to do so. In his deposition to Jefferson, Gibson made no mention of his relations with Logan's sister, but several witnesses to the massacre at Baker's tavern did. Judge Henry Holly recalled that after being shot, the mother "lived long enough however to beg mercy for her babe, telling them that it was a Kin to themselves. . . . I very well recollect my mother, feeding and dressing the Babe, Chirping to the little innocent, and it smiling, however they took it away, and talked of sending it to its supposed father, Col. Geo. [John] Gibson" (Thwaites and Kellogg 10–11). George Edgington confirms that

Gibson was the father of the child (Thwaites and Kellogg 17). John Sappington, in a letter in Jefferson's appendix, states that Gibson "educated the child, and took care of it, as if it had been his own" (264). Curiously, Ritenour claims that the child, a boy, was ten years old at the time his mother was killed. Robinson's letter, however, recalled that Logan and the others among his adopted people believed that "amongst the Indians killed at Yellow Creek, was a sister of Logan very big with child, whom they ripped open, and stuck on a pole" (250). Either way, we have a sentimental melodrama: one is a story of atrocity, a graphic abortion of a fetus conceived in love across the lines of race and frontier; the other is a warmhearted tale of compassion, first by the purported Indian haters, who amid a horrific massacre take pity on a young child, and then by a father who admits his paternity as the result of a cross-blood liaison and raises the child.[10] And even before this Gibson-Logan mating, a long history of interracial relations surrounded the Logan legend. In a superficial reading, the speech seems to convey the demise of one race—the natives—and the victory of the other. But if we look into the names and family histories of Logan, Gibson, and some other participants, we see that such a racial opposition is groundless.

As the title of Doddridge's play indicates, Logan was the son of Shickellamy (or Shickellemus), an Oneida leader who became in the 1730s and 1740s a key ally and negotiator for the province of Pennsylvania. Shickellamy had traveled with Quaker naturalist John Bartram from Shamokin to Onondaga in 1743, taking his son(s) with him, and in introducing Shickellamy in the journal of that trip, published in 1751, Bartram writes, "He was of the six nations, or rather a Frenchman, born at Mont-real, and adopted by the Oneidoes, after being taken prisoner, but his son told me he was of the Cayuga nation, that of his mother, agreeable to the Indian rule" (17). In the numerous records of his speeches and negotiations with colonists, however, Shickellamy never affirmed his French-Canadian origins, and James Merrell, probably the historian most familiar with these records, doubts that he had Euro-American parentage ("Shickellamy" 253). Regardless of parentage, Shickellamy was culturally "between." Conrad Weiser, one of Pennsylvania's most important Indian agents in this period, traveled with Shickellamy on the journey with Bartram and on other trips and built his native counterpart a log house at Shamokin near the forks of the Susquehanna River. This village became a center for Mingoes, Iroquois who had relocated southward into Pennsylvania. The Six Nations of the Iroquois had a long-standing alliance with the English, but the Delaware and Shawnee of Pennsylvania did not always share the interests of the Iroquois, so a mediator such as Shickellamy had a particularly important role. Perhaps because of his exiled position or his alliance with the colonists, he held himself apart from natives around him. One story first told by George Loskiel had it that Shickellamy never drank and that "he built his house on pillars for security against the drunken Indians" (Noyes 557).

Shickellamy's wife, Logan's mother, was a Cayuga, and, as Bartram observed, in the matrilineal Iroquois practice this became Logan's tribal affiliation. Logan was most likely born at Shamokin, notwithstanding the claim of the huge birthplace monument to him at Auburn, New York, in the heart of Cayuga territory. Logan was Cayuga by lineage and Mingo by residence, and if Shickellamy had in fact been a French Canadian taken captive by the Oneida, then Logan was also a mixed-blood (métis), like many other negotiators or go-betweens on the eighteenth-century frontier, including Alexander McKee and Alex Montour. In Iroquois kinship practice, he would not have inherited his father's status as a sachem; thus, the epithet "last of the race of Shickellemus" was misplaced. But Logan did follow in his father's career path. When Shickellamy died in 1748, Weiser asked his son to take over his father's role as a "true correspondent" of the Pennsylvania government (Draper 142). The claim in the speech that Logan was a "friend of the white men" consequently was backed up by years of friendship preceding his storm of vengeance in 1774. His parentage, his acts, and his name all captured the kinds of divided allegiances the speech expresses.

The names of Logan fragment any grasp of his identity. We know that he was named for James Logan, a wealthy Quaker merchant who served as "provincial secretary, Clerk of the Council, the Penn family's man in the province during the first half of the eighteenth century" (Merrell, Into 62). James Logan played a key role in the infamous Walking Purchase of 1734–37, which used a fraudulent treaty with William Penn's name on it to take land in eastern Pennsylvania away from the Delaware Indians (Dowd, War 36). He met frequently with Shickellamy, and the two were on good terms. Logan's name therefore implied kinship with the colonists: he had in James Logan a symbolic father among the colonial "fathers." But the moniker "Logan" was applied to more than one of Shickellamy's five sons, and which one of these became the man who made the famous speech is uncertain. The eldest son was known as John Shickellamy and as Tachnechdorus, and according to James Merrell he succeeded his father as Pennsylvania Indian agent. Merrell asserts that a younger son, Soyechtowa, acquired the nickname James Logan and is the Logan of the speech. But biographer Franklin V. Sawvel says the eldest brother was passed over for Weiser's appointment because he was blind in one eye, and a younger son, Tah-gah-jute, was Logan, serving as an Indian deputy for Pennsylvania until 1762. Brantz Mayer's book also called Logan Tah-gah-jute. Lyman C. Draper's biography, "Logan—The Mingo Chief," is much more scholarly and better documented than Sawvel's book, and this work agrees with Merrell that the second-eldest, Soyechtowa ("Say-ugh-to-wa") (Draper 139) received the name James Logan but maintains that the Logan of the speech was in fact the eldest, Tach-nech-do-rus. Neither Draper nor Merrell mentions Tahgahjute. During the decade following Pontiac's war, during which time Logan moved to Ohio to live among the Shawnee, there are fewer surviving documents about the sons of Shickellamy, so the identities of the brothers merge to the point where it is impossible to identify which one became the notorious rebel of 1774.

Mourning and History in Pennsylvania

In the spring of 1773, John Doddridge lost title to his land in Bedford County, Pennsylvania, and moved his family west to Washington County, near the modern border with the northern panhandle of West Virginia. His eldest son, Joseph, then just four years old, later recalled the hardships of that first summer, as the family was forced to become hunter-gatherers while waiting for their garden of squash and potatoes to mature: "The Indian meal which he brought over the mountain was expended six weeks too soon. . . . The lean venison and the breast of the wild turkey we were taught to call bread. The flesh of the bear was denominated meat." The family survived that year, but the following spring brought a new crisis: "Those most atrocious murders of the peaceable inoffensive Indians at Captina and Yellow Creek brought on the war of Lord Dunmore" (Notes 82). The Doddridge family was forced to flee to Uniontown, east of the Monongahela River. In spite of this traumatic memory, when the Reverend Joseph Doddridge published a history of western Pennsylvania a half century later, in 1824, he expressed a great deal of sympathy for the local Indians and their leader, Logan. As quoted in chapter 1, Doddridge called Lord Dunmore's War "a dishonorable blot in our national history." He was ashamed of the atrocities of his father's generation, yet he held out hope for the potentially edifying lessons of this history, a hope that these events might be a sacrificial crisis that would mark an end to frontier violence: "The injuries inflicted upon the Indians in early times by our forefathers may induce their descendants to show justice and mercy to the diminished posterity of those children of the wilderness whose ancestors perished in cold blood under the tomahawk and scalping knife of the white savages" (Notes 171).

Where most other historians of colonization sensationalize the scalping of white settlers by the Indians, Doddridge reverses those sentiments. The weapons of the Indians, scalping knives and tomahawks, are wielded also by the whites, much as he had eaten the foods of the Indians when a child of the wilderness fifty years earlier. Doddridge is hardly unique in attributing to colonists some traits of the "savages." However, he is unusually self-conscious in the way he not only documents such reversals but uses senti-mental language to dramatize them. His account of the lynching of the Conestoga Indians at Lancaster is illustrative: "The Paxton boys broke open the jail door and murdered the whole of them, in number from fifteen to twenty. It was in vain that these poor defenseless people protested their innocence and begged for mercy on their knees. Blood was the order of the day with those ferocious Paxton boys. The death of the victims of their cruelties did not satisfy their rage for slaughter; they mangled the dead bodies of the Indians with their scalping knives and tomahawks in the most shocking manner, scalping even the children and chopping off the hands and feet of most of them" (168). Parkman also writes of the "outrageous brutality" of this act, but in contrast to Doddridge, Parkman sets his account of it in a passive construction that softened the accountability of the Paxton Boys (707–8). Doddridge represents the violence in its full horror and is unapologetic about his narrative techniques: "Should I be asked why I have presented this unpleasant portrait of the rude manners of our forefathers, I in my turn would ask my reader, why are you pleased with the histories of the blood and carnage of battles? Why are you delighted with the fictions of poetry, the novel and romance? I have related truth, and only truth" (*Notes* 106).

Doddridge did not try his hand at prose fiction, although he did write the play about Logan, which we will examine shortly. His contribution to history writing also deserves to be taken seriously, however. In 1824, as the wealthy New Yorkers Washington Irving and James Fenimore Cooper worked to fashion a literature that would be native to America and consistent with the interests of the landowning class in New York, this poor and obscure fron-tier minister published a history of his rude country that invoked the grand-est forms of the genre in the service of his region and his generation of early settlers there. And the Ohio Valley of which Doddridge wrote was, as Edward Watts has observed, "demographically much more complex than the East" (118), mixing natives and settlers of many nations and languages. Our under-standing of the Ohio Valley and Old Northwest has been dreadfully im-poverished, Watts argues, insofar as "the views of such Eastern tourists as Francis Parkman and Washington Irving [have] garnered more attention and, even today, represent the 'American' view of the frontier" (110).

Doddridge's ultimate goal was not to champion the Indians over the likes of Cresap and the Paxton Boys. In later chapters, Doddridge narrates the exploits of notorious Indian hater Lewis Wetzel with tacit approval and re-counts several captivity stories in the conventional savagist style. Moreover, he frequently expresses his belief in a progressivist historiography, his intent to provide a "correct and detailed view of the origin of societies, and their progress from one condition or point of wealth, science and civilization, to another" (*Notes* 83). The strategy behind Doddridge's inversion of the savage and civilized is not at all to extol the virtues of the primitive but to appropriate Logan and the Indian peoples into a historiography of his region and its settlement. His book, *Notes on the Settlement and Indian Wars Of the Western Parts of Virginia and Pennsylvania from 1763 to 1783, Inclusive, together with a Review of the State of Society and Manners of the First Settlers of the Western Country*, endows the early settlers with the status of natives and impresses on his readers the importance of historical memory, beginning not with Pontiac's rebellion or Logan's but much deeper in antiquity.

Like most of his contemporaries, Doddridge espouses the doctrine of the vanishing Indian: "The Indian nations are now a subjugated people, and every feature of their former state of society must soon pass away." Unlike many Jacksonians, though, he sees this process not as elimination but assimilation: "They will exist only through the medium of their admixtures with the white people. Such has been the fate of many nations. Where are now the Assyrians, Chaldeans, and Romans? They no longer exist; and yet the English, French, and Italians are, in part, descendents of the ancient Romans. Such will be the fate of the aborigines of our country" (*Notes* 9–10). And if other romantic or nationalist historians might challenge that assertion, Doddridge is ready to answer with the special nature of his evidence: "In every region of the world, except our own, the commencement of the period of their history was long posterior to that of their settlement; their early history is therefore buried in impenetrable oblivion" (7). In his region, however, "the present generation are witnesses of both the savage and civilized state of mankind" (9); therefore, the cultural progress and transformation that took thousands of years in Europe and the Mediterranean world could be documented in America in just fifty. The "Indian wars of the Western parts of Virginia and Pennsylvania from 1763 to 1783," almost precisely the period between the end of the last intercolonial war and the end of the War of Independence, provided the epic foundation for his history down to 1824 when he wrote it.

If such a hypercompression of stadial history seemed implausible, Doddridge also has a proper antiquity waiting in reserve. The Upper Ohio Valley that was the scene of Logan's war was also the locale of several major earthworks attributed to the mysterious Mound Builders. Grave Creek Mound at modern Moundsville, West Virginia, one of the largest in the Ohio Valley, is located just a few miles north of Captina (or Capteena), where Cresap killed the two Shawnee on 27 April 1774, the first act of bloodshed that precipitated Logan's revenge. In his history, Doddridge gives the precise dimensions of this mound; compares it to similar "ancient sepulchres of the dead" in Europe, Asia, and Africa; and speculates on the "myriads of human beings" (*Notes* 29, 28) whose remains might be contained within. Doddridge had in 1819 written a letter to Caleb Atwater, the leading authority on the Mound Builders at the time and author of an 1820 treatise on the subject, about the Grave Creek site and the partial excavation of it: "This lofty and venerable tumulus has been so far opened, as to ascertain that it contains many thousands of human skeletons, but no farther" (qtd. in Silverberg 100). Speculations about the Mound Builders imagined grand cities built around the earthworks, and most assumed that such a civilized ancient culture could not be the ancestors of the local Indians. But Doddridge observes that if the builders of the "forts or town walls . . . had left behind them any monuments of arts and sciences, they in like manner would have descended to us" and that in the absence of such artifacts, the Mound Builders must have been barbarians and, therefore, were "unquestionably" the Indians' ancestors (36). For Doddridge, it was not necessary to believe the Mound Builders to be a high civilization equal to the Greeks or Romans to respect them as antique forebears of the settlers of the region. Proper respect and mourning for these sepulchres became part of the civilizing process of the frontier settlements. In 1824, Grave Creek Mound was in the possession of an owner who "has expressed his determination to preserve it in its original state during his life," and Doddridge adds, "May his successors to the title of the estate forever feel the same pious regard for this august mansion of the dead, and preserve the venerable monument of antiquity" (28–29).

When Doddridge wrote, nearly fifty years after Concord and Lexington, Americans were becoming acutely aware of the passing of the revolutionary generation and of the nation's founding fathers. The deaths of John Adams and Thomas Jefferson on 4 July 1826 appeared as the poetic and typological distillation of this sentiment. Doddridge also captures the mood of this period by making mourning an essential aspect of filiopiety and regional pride. And by connecting this mourning to that for native peoples, including Logan, Doddridge introduces a "nativist" or uniquely American angle. Doddridge's historiography employs a North American version of the "patriotic epistemology" that Jorge Canizares-Esguerra has recently identified as an important trend in Mexico around the same time. As a creole, Doddridge celebrated the exploits of men who shared his regional origin and decried the meddling of outsiders, whether from Britain or tidewater Virginia. Most importantly, he assimilated his creole identity with that of the local natives or at least those of the distant past. Canizares-Esguerra has found similar attitudes expressed by Mexican creole historians of the late eighteenth century, such as José Joaquín Granados y Gálvez.

Logan in his speech feared that no one would mourn for him, and Doddridge evidently shared this anxiety, since he so strongly implored his readers to respect the memory of the pioneers of western Pennsylvania, including himself, who quickly acquired the prestige of "ancient" founders.[11] In contemplating sepulchral mounds such as at Grave Creek, Doddridge assumed that at the center of each lay "the sarcophagus of the patriarch, or first monarch of the tribe or nation to which the sepulchre belonged. Thenceforward all his people were deposited in the grave of the founder of the nation. In process of time, the daily increasing mound became the national history" (*Notes* 31) of the place and of its people.

Philip Freneau's "The Indian Burying Ground" (1787) emphasizes the differences between colonists' and natives' funerary customs and elegizes an Indian whose tomb aroused gothic spirits that appeared to the vision of the poet. Doddridge instead imagines a massive tomb containing all the deceased people of the area that not only represented but became the national history of that people. Whites could then regard Grave Creek Mound as a monument to—and of—their ancestors, and Doddridge's views on race and climate support this radical assimilation. He observes that "white people who have been brought up among the Indians from their infancy differ from them but little in point of color" (*Notes* 47) and emphasizes how dress rather than race plays an important role in forming national identity, as when the British prohibited the tartan kilt during the 1745 Highland Rebellion.[12]

How then might Doddridge reply to the already hackneyed question, "Who is there to mourn for Logan?" Not one but thousands, if Logan could assume the status of a founding patriarch at the center of a growing regional tomb. Not one but zero, if the speech's persona of the "last of the race" adheres. The paradox hinges on the definition of "race" as either family or as nation, both of which were common usage at the time. The title of Doddridge's play, *Logan, the Last of the Race of Shikellemus*, exemplifies the former. But Logan's status as a patriarch was tenuous. First, he had no known tomb. His tragic denouement, a decline into drunkenness and a sordid slaying somewhere between Detroit and Sandusky, left no grave and no cult for his remains. Doddridge instead mourns "The Death of Cornstalk" (the title of chapter 28 of his *Notes*), the Shawnee leader of the attack on General Lewis who signed the treaty with Dunmore when Logan refused to appear and who was killed by cowardly officers at Point Pleasant while a prisoner of war in 1777.

A modest stone obelisk stands in a park in Point Pleasant, West Virginia, inscribed with the name of Cornstalk, who might appear to be the noble martyr of Lord Dunmore's War, leaving the drunken, vengeful Logan as the ignoble double. However, a fifty-foot-tall obelisk stands in Auburn, New York, "erected in 1853 to commemorate the greatest of the Cayugas with the simple inscription 'Who is there to mourn for Logan?'" (Noyes 561). This monument, built in Fort Hill cemetery but lacking any remains beneath it, marks not the final resting place but the putative birthplace of Logan, and it deflects any question of its inauthenticity by turning the interrogation on its visitors, hailing them as mourners. A curious 1859 article published in *Knickerbocker* magazine, "Logan and the Home of the Iroquois," opens with an engraving of this obelisk (figure 5.2) and goes on to explain that this site at the north end of Owasco Lake, "according to the traditions of the Cayugas, was the birth-place of Logan" (554), although, as mentioned earlier, historians today believe he was born at Shamokin, Pennsylvania, the home of his father, Shickellemus.

The article tries to reclaim Logan from exiled Mingo to full-blood Cayuga and to create around him an antiquity much like the one Doddridge found at Grave Creek Mound. The author, James O. Noyes, describes "a pentagonal work of earthen ramparts . . . a famous Indian stronghold" at the Auburn site, which Henry Rowe Schoolcraft claimed had a circumference of twelve hundred feet. Then, drawing on myths told by Heckewelder and in the *Walam Olum*, Noyes wrote that "the Mound Builders of the Western world were a people denominated Alleghans" who migrated northward before the overthrow of the Toltec empire. Cayuga traditions supposedly confirm that these invaders from the Southwest built "as far east as the ancient village of Osco, earthen altars for the worship of the sun, mounds for the sepulture of their dead, and embankments for personal defence" before being "forced to acknowledge the rightful sovereignty of the Iroquois" (Noyes 555). The dubious monument of the birthplace of Logan therefore becomes also a memorial for the demise of the mound-building Toltecs, identified as the great ancient civilization of the Americas. And to attract readers to visit Auburn and the monument, the article is illustrated with picturesque scenes of waterfalls and views of the Finger Lakes, a region it dubs the "Scotland of America" (554). All the ingredients for a nineteenth-century touristic spectacle are put into place: a defeated Indian, a great antique civilization, a monument to an edifying history, and various scenic amenities.

Although Doddridge's model of national filiopiety through mourning did not create a heroic role for Logan, Doddridge did well by the Indian in a four-act play, *Logan, the Last of the Race of Shikellemus, Chief of the Cayuga Nation* (1823). American theater historian Richard Moody has called it "probably the most historically accurate of all the Indian plays" (*America* 91). As Rogers does in *Ponteach*, Doddridge opens with a series of scenes documenting how

THE KNICKERBOCKER.

Vol. LIII.   JUNE, 1859.   No. 5.

LOGAN'S MONUMENT.

LOGAN AND THE HOME OF THE IROQUOIS.

EMBOSOMED in Central New-York lies a group of beautiful lakes, varying from ten to forty miles in length, and nearly parallel with each other, which cannot escape the eye glancing ever so casually over a map of the Empire State. The quotations of flour have given the 'Genesee County' almost a world-wide reputation, but the region em-

VOL. LIII.   36

FIGURE 5.2. Illustration of the Logan obelisk in Auburn, New York. From James O. Noyes, "Logan and the Home of the Iroquois," *The Knickerbocker* (June 1859). Courtesy of Special Collections, Knight Library, University of Oregon.

colonial injustice precipitated the Indian revolt led by his hero. Captain Furioso, modeled on Michael Cresap, says that the Indians "are Canaanites, whom Providence has doomed for extermination" (7), and speaks admiringly of the Paxton Boys, a sentiment his first lieutenant echoes. Their opinions are answered by a Captain Pacificus (apparently modeled on Colonel Ebenezer Zane) who, as Doddridge explains in *Notes*, believes that a war would bring great suffering on white settlers: "On you, and your party, be the blame of the widows, and orphans, whose husbands, and fathers, must soon perish by the savages, in revenge for their relations, and friends, whom you are about to slaughter. Their sighs, their tears, and their poverty, will be laid to your account. To the latest posterity your names will be stained with blood" (*Logan* 13).

As in other Indian dramas, in Diego Durán, and in the Mathers' histories of King Philip's War, the characters in Doddridge's play share a preoccupation with omens. The first lieutenant remarks, "Did we not all see the great lights in the north last winter. They looked like ranks of soldiers, and troops of horsemen. . . . A few nights ago I dreamed that I saw a black cloud coming slowly from the westward; when it came over my house it gathered into a bunch, fell down into the yard, and turned into blood" (9). In act 2, Logan and fellow Indian leaders Kuhn, Shahillas, Tawatwees, and Wingemind (the prophet Wangomend) discuss the same aerial phenomena and then learn of the murders at Wheeling and Captina. Shahillas, who resembles Cornstalk, also sees ill omens in the vestiges of the Mound Builders. After the battle of Point Pleasant, he compares the threat to his people with the demise of that ancient culture: "We see the big bones about our licks; where shall we now find the race of beasts to which they belonged? They are all gone. Do we not walk every day over the bones of a race of men who have vanished from the earth? . . . Perhaps they were killed by our forefathers" (23). If the Shawnee and other Indians had killed the Mound Builders, as William Cullen Bryant's "The Prairies" and other texts maintained, then the advancing whites might be avenging the death of the Mound Builders, whom Doddridge assimilated to both the Indians and the white settlers in his history but whom he differentiates from the Indians here.

There is one other significant point where the play complicates Doddridge's history. In *Notes*, he accuses Lord Dunmore of calling a halt to the pursuit of Cornstalk and the Shawnee because of the impending geopolitical shifts of the revolution: "It was the general belief among the officers of our army, at the time, that the Earl of Dunmore, while at Wheeling, received advice from his government of the probability of the approaching war between England and the colonies, and that afterwards all his measures with regard to the Indians had for their ultimate object an alliance with those ferocious warriors for aid of the mother country in her contest with us" (179). Such an alliance never amounted to much in the Ohio Valley during the revolution. In the play, however, Shahillas sounds more like Tecumseh, finding cause for hope in the possibility of aid from the "great father" whom the Shawnee identify as British: "Brother Kuhn has said that the white men will not be long at peace. That their great father is angry with them. . . . We will then join our great father. . . . By the side of our great father, we shall be strong enough for the white men" (19). And in the final scene, Logan observes that the "great chief of the white men is getting very angry with his children here because they dont give him money enough. . . . They will save Logan the trouble of killing any more of them. They will cut each others throats very soon" (34).

Little is known about the performance history of *Logan, the Last of the Race of Shikellemus*. Sawvel claims that the play "was very popular in the thirties and forties" (102) during the craze for Indian tragedy, but modern theater historians have not confirmed this finding. Moody declares that the play's "colorless prose and almost total lack of action made it unfit for stage presentation" (*America* 91). If it was performed, audiences probably waited impatiently for the dramatic oration that they knew was coming: Doddridge withheld it until the end. If Rogers's *Ponteach* suffered from being unable to represent its hero's tragic death, which occurred three years after it was written, Doddridge's *Logan* suffered not only because of the uncertain and unheroic circumstances of its hero's death but also because he was too closely associated with the famous lament and because, as the lament claims, he was without family. No sons or daughters were available for romantic or traitorous subplots or for dramatic dilemmas between love and republican virtue. Logan had two wives, the first a Cayuga who died at Shamokin in 1747 and the second a Shawnee who, in spite of the accusation against Cresap, outlived Logan, though she bore him no children. Yet the wives are virtually absent from the legends about him and hence absent from the play as well. The best opportunity for melodrama in Doddridge's play comes in act 3 in an episode modeled on that of William Robinson. Logan returns from one of his raids with a prisoner, whom the hawkish Kuhn insists must be tortured, just as their forefathers sacrificed captives atop the mounds. But Logan replies that he has promised the prisoner his life, "and must he say with his last breath that Logan has told a lie?" (27). The play's only female character, Queeta, who wants to requicken her dead son, offers the prisoner the chance to "come to life again" through adoption, and Logan gives his assent. To emphasize the greater humanity of the Indians' treatment of prisoners, Queeta asks the prisoner if he has lost a brother: he has.

The sentimental potential that might have been realized from Logan's lost nephew, Gibson's child, is wasted in the play. Perhaps afraid to take a position on the most controversial aspects of the Logan legend, Doddridge has Logan deliver his famous speech, together with its wampum text version, not to Gibson but to an unnamed interpreter. The relationship between Logan and Gibson remains unexplored, and Logan the stage hero remains essentially a dramatic monologue. Although the play is not equal to *Ponteach* or *Metamora*, Doddridge had grand ideas about the literary potential of his

subject and the gravity of its political import, and he acknowledged the great models of stoic heroism. I quoted in chapter 1 the lines from his preface comparing Logan to Ossian. John Burk had a similar reaction in his 1804
History of Virginia: "Nothing can be imagined, more venerable than the strain of tender and lofty sentiment running through this short address. Parts of it rise into the highest order of moral sublimity. It reminds us of Ossian, 'the last of his race'; of Fingal, 'in the last of his fields' " (3:398). The comparison is not merely romantic hyperbole, for Doddridge extols Logan for some of the same purposes as MacPherson created Ossian—to recover the heroism and memory of an indigenous people displaced by an invasion from imperial England. However, Logan as a tragic hero in drama or in verse romances such as Samuel Webber's *Logan: An Indian Tale* idealized him and thereby lost the feature that made the legends about him so compelling, his manic synthesis of sentimental feeling and violent revenge.[13] This character was best represented in another genre, even more popular in the early nineteenth century—gothic prose fiction.

Logan, the Gothic Indian

> "I know that I have two souls, the one good, and the other bad. When the good has the ascendant I am kind and humane. When the bad soul rules I am perfectly savage and delight in nothing but blood and carnage."
> —Logan, speaking to John Dunkin in 1780, *American Pioneer* (1842)

The gothic potential of the Indian in American literature from 1774 to 1824, the period of the early republic and of the development of Logan's literary legends, has been well recognized. As Teresa Goddu writes in her study, *American Gothic*, "The gothicized Indian provided the nation with a distinctive literary asset as well as a politically useful cultural image. Though America did not have crumbling castles and antiquated traditions, it did have in the Indian a symbol of a ruined and conquered past" (55). Doddridge's appropriation of the legacy of the Mound Builders as the basis for national mourning and filiopiety is symptomatic of this move. But few novelists or critics had the talent required to make a mound of earth into a haunting locale for a ghost story. Goddu's book regards both gothic and the foundation of an American national literature primarily as problems of setting. To participate in the prose genre that was most popular in England in the 1790s, America had to offer appropriate substitutes for castles, dungeons, and monasteries. Thus, Charles Brockden Brown, in his famous preface to *Edgar Huntly*, boasts "of calling forth the passions and engaging the sympathy of the reader, by means hitherto unemployed by preceding authors. Puerile superstition and exploded manners; Gothic castles and chimeras, are the materials usually employed for this end. The incidents of Indian hostility, and the perils of the western wilderness, are far more suitable." As John Seelye has shown, Brown's novel fulfilled this promise with the parodic setting of Norwalk, a mountain in the form of a castle, penetrated by dungeonlike caverns and protected by a river flowing, M. C. Escher–style, in an endless circle like a castle's moat (*Beautiful Machine* 165–68).

A full definition of the "Indian gothic," however, must look beyond setting. The gothic addresses the pervasive danger of transgressions between reason and unreason, sanity and insanity, life and death, waking and sleeping, day and night. The Logan legend is highly gothic in the way it violates the closely guarded boundaries between such categories, particularly savage and civilized, vengeance and justice, Indian and white. Just as gothic novels have character doubles who mirror one another across these dichotomies, so the Logan legend has its multiple doublings: Logan and his namesake, James Logan; Logan and Cresap; Logan and Gibson. Jefferson and other promoters and polemicists in the Logan controversy sought to shore up these boundaries by separating good from evil, heroes from villains. But the gothic nature of the Logan legend destabilized these efforts by revealing the doublings, reversals, and fuzzy boundaries between these characters and between the good and evil, civilized and savage values that some would have them represent. Epic and tragedy are imperial literary forms insofar as they insist on the differences between the winners and losers of imperial contests, even if the losers display valor and deserve sympathy. But the gothic, as a product of the eighteenth-century Age of Revolutions in Europe, questions the claims of legitimacy and liberation in which the European imperial powers cloaked their conquests. Gothic novels about the Ohio Valley wars of Logan's time challenge, in a more or less covert manner, the justice of colonial expansion and the moral stability of the white frontiersmen.

Probably the most successful novel about the Indian wars in the Upper Ohio was Robert Montgomery Bird's *Nick of the Woods; or, The Jibbenainosay* (1837). Bird had submitted a script, now lost, titled "King Philip; or, The Sagamore," to the competition won by John Augustus Stone's *Metamora*, and Bird's 1831 play, *The Gladiator*, won another contest sponsored by Edwin Forrest and became the star's second-most-successful vehicle. In 1835 Forrest asked Bird to revise *Metamora* but then declined to use the new version and asked Bird to return the two thousand dollars he had been paid (Grose, "Here Come" 90–91). The dispute may have been what prompted Bird to switch to writing novels. While his works were once valued as equal to James

Fenimore Cooper's in the U.S. literary canon, his stock has declined severely in the critical market, likely as a result of his gory violence and harsh portrayals of Indians. In *Nick of the Woods*, the Indians are crude instruments of violence, so lacking in humanity and agency that even their violent resistance to the Kentucky frontiersmen turns out to be led not by an Indian rebel leader but by two white renegades. Bird uses as the climax of his novel the 1782 attack by George Rogers Clark and bands of Kentucky militiamen on Picqua (Pecaway), a Shawnee village in southwestern Ohio and the childhood home of Tecumseh. This skirmish can be seen as a continuation of Lord Dunmore's War, eight years after Point Pleasant, and stepped up the viciousness of the cycle of vengeance. Clark took prisoners at Picqua, including a woman whom he killed, he wrote, "by ripping up her Belly and otherwise mangling her" (Richard White, *Middle Ground* 388).

Bird's real artistic contribution to the frontier gothic is his title character, Nathan Slaughter, a.k.a. the Jibbenainosay, a spectral figure who, like Logan, has a manic split personality incited by family trauma. Nathan is first introduced to the novel's protagonist, Roland Forrester, a Virginian emigrant, as a loner and misfit, "the only man in all Kentucky that won't fight!" (55). He comes to the aid of Roland and his cousin, Edith, after they set out without arms or guides to cross a stretch of deep woods. A Pennsylvania Quaker, Nathan had moved his family to the Kentucky frontier some years before only to face violence from Indians and suspicion from other settlers. He recalls how his new neighbors, the Ashburns, "held me in disfavor, because of my faith, and ever repelled me from their doors with scorn and ill-will" (148). They refuse to honor the ethic of hospitality that Logan invokes in his speech. When an Indian war party enters the area, Nathan goes to warn the Ashburns, but "they held my story light, and laughed at and derided me . . . because I held it not according to conscience to kill Injuns as they did" (149). He then went to the nearby "station," or fort, to ask for assistance and was again refused, returning to the Ashburns' just in time to witness the slaughter of the family. For two-thirds of the novel, Nathan professes to Roland to be a Quaker pacifist and conceals his alter ego. The Jibbenainosay is therefore presented as a monstrous, mythical creature known for killing Indians and marking the corpses with a cross. The narrator withholds the identity of his two characters until Roland sees Nathan scalp his victims in chapter 24, and then Nathan finally tells of his past. His family had been massacred and he had been scalped by Wenonga, a Shawnee, to whom he had loaned his gun when the Indian asked for it to go hunting. This scene haunts him and creates his monstrous double, a frontier Mr. Hyde. "Jibbenainosay," Bird claims, means "the Dead Man who walks" in Shawnee, confirming the figure's ghostly gothicity. Moreover, Nathan's monstrous double is his racial as well as moral inverse. In the climactic battle scenes, Nathan dons Indian garb and face paint. In one of his drafts for the novel, Bird even refers to Nathan as the "Fighting Quaker—Last of his Line" (xxxiii), an epithet typically applied to Indians. Another sketch included plans to introduce Logan and the notorious renegades Simon Girty and Simon Kenton into the novel. The character of Nathan Slaughter, like the infamous history of the Paxton riots, suggests how the violence of frontier Pennsylvania in Logan's time was not defined simply along racial lines. To be identified as a Quaker or friend of the Indians was to take a risky stance with regard to backwoods Scots-Irish settlers. Among Indians, to be known as Logan says he is, as a "friend of the white man," was to risk attacks by more militant natives. These hostilities, like those between the rebels and loyalists in the war that erupted between 1774 and 1783, were exacerbated by the fact that they often divided brother from brother and father from son, inciting the sort of fratricidal violence that took Logan's life. The kinship relations of the characters in Nick of the Woods allude to this history, for Roland and Edith are children of Virginia brothers, two of whom were killed fighting for the rebel cause in the Revolutionary War while the third, a loyalist, raises the orphaned pair.

The doubling of identities is even more pronounced in the stage version of Nick of the Woods, written and produced by Louisa H. Medina, one of the most popular actresses of the 1830s and 1840s. In the final scene of Medina's drama, Nathan Slaughter is revealed to be the same man as Reginald Ashburn, the first victim of Shawnee attacks who in the novel had scorned Nathan's warnings and derided his Quaker pacifism. The play also enhances the doubling of Nathan and Wenonga, his rival. Bird had written of how Wenonga had been driven mad by the Jibbenainosay, and in the play the Shawnee chief, speaking of himself in the third person, like Logan did, bemoans that "Wenonga is a great chief, he is childless" (29) because the Jibbenainosay has killed all of his children, just as Wenonga and his warriors had killed all of Slaughter/Ashburn's children. This scene, roughly corresponding to chapter 33 in the novel, occurs when Roland and Nathan, disguised as Indians, are captured as they attack the Shawnee village, and Wenonga appeals to the captive Nathan, "My brother is a great medicine man. He knows where to find the Jibbenainosay, and will show him to me" (28). Wenonga may be a racist caricature, but this line reveals something less clearly acknowledged in the novel. The pacifist Quaker, the violent frontiersman, and the Indian are all bound in brotherhood as Gibson and Logan were. Their mimetic rivalry is not simply a projection of white men's consciousness into their racial and moral unconscious. It is a mutual relationship. This brotherhood is sealed by the common traumatic memories of the acts of violence that both are trying to avenge. Nathan is haunted by his memory of the attack on Ashburn's cabin, which in the play is Nathan's own cabin. In the novel, he also at one point imagines the Indian warriors' view of that cabin, where they "glut their eyes with the sight of their ruins, where the blood of nine poor white persons was shed by their brothers in a single night; though, truly, in that case, they must have also thought of the thirteen murderers that bled for the victims; which would prove somewhat a drawback to their satisfaction" (153). The Indian warriors think of the thirteen victims among their kin that motivated their revenge, the same number that Logan sought to avenge by killing an equal number of Virginians. In The Word in Black and White, Dana Nelson has analyzed the ideological power of the novel as one of identification: "Nathan Slaughter's story seeks to implicate its readers in its drive for revenge precisely by absolving them of complicity in political and historical circumstance. Instead, it offers them a reason to hate Indians that arises from a sense of innocent personal loss" (43–44). But the context of Medina's stage version and of the Logan legend reveals how the novel does not so much consolidate racial and imperialist ideology as undermine it, much like testimonio literature encourages those from dominant groups to identify with the victims of imperialism.

The themes of a double life and of blood vengeance found in Bird's Nathan Slaughter are also present in the foundational work of frontier gothic in American literature, Charles Brockden Brown's Edgar Huntly (1798). Although it lacks the specific historical context of Nick of the Woods, it is set in Pennsylvania and like the Logan legend explores the motives of frontier vengeance and the cross-racial confusion that can result from it. Edgar Huntly takes place in 1785 or 1786 in a wilderness of "steeps and precipices" known as Norwalk, "the termination of a sterile and narrow tract, which begins in Indian country" (165). This tract connects the fictional settlement of Solebury, near the forks of the Delaware, to central and western Pennsylvania and further to "the banks of the Wabash and Muskingum" (198) in Ohio, where Delaware Indians had been forced to relocate after losing their lands around the forks in the devious Walking Purchase. So although the western bank of the Delaware was well within the frontier in the 1780s, the novel's gothic wilderness setting evokes the haunting memory of a fraudulent colonial land claim—and the Indian vengeance it might arouse—to make the region a frontier once again. This haunting setting is matched by a traumatic memory of the title character: "During former Indian wars, this rude surface was sometimes traversed by the Red-men. . . . My parents and an infant child were murdered in their beds. . . . I never looked upon, or called up the image of a savage without shuddering" (165–66). After this attack, Edgar and his two sisters are forced to live with an uncle whose "barn yard and orchard" stand on the site of a village formerly home to one clan of the Delaware (198).

The action of *Edgar Huntly* follows Edgar's obsessive pursuit of an Irish farmhand named Clithero, whom he suspects of killing Edgar's close friend, Waldegrave. The suspicion arises when Edgar first sees Clithero digging a pit "beneath the shade of that fatal Elm" (7) where Waldegrave's body had been found some weeks earlier. Edgar hails the man, only to watch him rise and walk right past as if asleep. Memorial and landmark trees were numerous in early America, including the "treaty elm" at Kensington, Pennsylvania, where William Penn signed his first treaty with the Delaware. It is nonetheless possible that the Logan Elm, scene of the legendary meeting with John Gibson, inspired Brown to make an elm the site of this fateful encounter in the novel. On the following night, Edgar again stakes out the elm and follows Clithero from it to the mouth of a cave, which later proves to be a passageway into the castlelike mountain of Norwalk. In the book's most harrowing scene, Edgar wakes up in the darkness of the cave. Like Clithero, he has been sleepwalking and cannot recall how he got there. To survive and escape this wilderness dungeon, Edgar first kills a panther in the cave, consumes its flesh and blood, and then kills one of a band of Indians he finds near one of the cave's entrances. His weapon in both cases is a "Tomhawk," which he wields like an expert. Edgar's protestations about his "aversion to bloodshed" (171) and the "religious scruples" (172) that he must overcome before killing the Indian suggest that, like Nathan Slaughter and Charles Brockden Brown, Edgar is a Quaker. Also like Nathan, Edgar's haunting memory of his slain family overpowers his religious teachings and induces manic bursts of violence in which he adopts the weapons and guise of those he detests. "My abhorrence of bloodshed was not abated" (191), Edgar claims after killing the first Indian, but because he wrongly assumes that these men have just attacked his home and killed his uncle and sisters, he kills the other four in the party too. His vengeance for his family resembles that of Logan, who blamed Michael Cresap for killing his sister and brother although most witnesses believed Greathouse to be responsible. As Edgar learns later, the Indians killed his uncle but not his sisters, and when his uncle's neighbors went in search of him, Edgar mistook them for Indians and shot at them. Racial identity thus becomes confused in the psychosis of vengeance.

The only individuated native character in the novel is Old Deb, whom Edgar nicknames Queen Mab, an elderly woman who refused to join the Delaware as they fled westward. She took up residence in an abandoned hut, which Edgar happens upon and uses as cover when he kills the four Lenni

Lenape who pursue him from the cave. Part of Edgar's description of Old Deb reads like a cruel parody of Logan's stoic eloquence:

> Her tongue was never at rest but when she was asleep; but her conversation was merely addressed to her dogs. Her voice was sharp and shrill, and her gesticulations were vehement and grotesque. . . .
>
> She always disdained to speak English. . . . I had taken some pains to study her jargon, and could make out to discourse with her on the few ideas which she possessed. (199–200)

At the end of the novel, Edgar recounts how Old Deb was "seized in her hut on suspicion of having aided and counselled her countrymen, in their late depredations" (270). Like Logan, she suddenly becomes defiant toward the whites who had until then treated her with patronizing acceptance. She "gloried in the mischief she had done; and accounted for it by enumerating the injuries which she had received from her neighbours" (270). So when one of her tribesmen returned to visit her and "would not depart, without some gratification of his vengeance" (271) against the colonizers, he and other warriors were "councelled and guided, in all their movements, by Queen Mab" (271). Although she is hardly treated heroically, the old woman becomes the source of a small Indian conspiracy to avenge the theft of her tribe's land.

The one gothic novel that explicitly followed the Logan legend is much less known today than Bird's or Brown's. John Neal's Logan: A Family History is, as he put it, "full of darkness, repetition, anachronism and extravagance. Nobody can read it through, deliberately, as novels are to be read" (qtd. in Goddu 175). In this work the transgressions across the boundaries of life and death, civilized and savage, reality and dream are so frequent and so dizzying as to leave readers utterly disoriented. Entire chapters are given over to the main character's delusional ravings. Logan is pronounced dead and buried early in the first volume, but his body goes missing and he reappears as a ghost at the end, a ghost with sufficient corporeality to shoot and kill his son, Harold. Harold's half-brother, Oscar, jumps overboard in the mid-Atlantic only to walk across the water and reappear later. In spite of these gothic excesses, the basis of Logan: A Family History in the historical legend, which was in its heyday in 1821, when Neal was writing, is actually quite thorough. Neal takes as his starting point the idea that Logan's blood did flow on in others' veins after his death.

Like the classics of dark gothic, Neal's novel is rife with incest and oedipal violence. Harold, the hero, nearly kills his blood father, Logan, after Logan threatens Harold's adoptive father, Virginia's colonial governor. Harold later tells the governor that he has killed the assailant and all of his family except the women and the youngest son. But Logan survives Harold's attack and returns to the governor's fort for a council, where he threatens to kill the governor's family in revenge. Harold at this point is madly in love with Elvira, the governor's wife but young enough to be his daughter. She was initially his adopted ward after she was freed from captivity among the Indians. But Harold later falls in love with an Indian woman, Loena, described as "the last of the Logans, directly descended from the Mingo chief, and . . . believed to be the legitimate inheritor of his terrible powers. . . . Her deportment and tread were queen-like, prompt, and resolute" (1:201). As a kinswoman of Harold and Logan, Loena is cursed with two incestuous suitors, for Logan also wants to marry her and according to her explanation had once tried to rape her. Other Indians are horrified at this incestuous union with his daughter.

Incestuous affairs were a commonplace of gothic and romantic novels, yet, as we have seen, Neal's plot has a basis in fact. Through Gibson and his child by Logan's sister (a son, according to most sources), Logan's blood was mingled with the whites. The ephemeral narrator would seem to be Gibson's son, the descendant of Logan who was suppressed in the historical legend only to rise again in Neal's fiction. More significant than this resurrection, however, is the way that the novel portrays the mimetic rivalries between frontier enemies who, like Nathan Slaughter and the Jibbenainosay, turn out to be alter egos of a single family or single psyche. Harold in the opening chapters plays the role of Cresap, an ally of the Virginia governor, who would be Dunmore. Harold boasts of killing Logan's relatives yet soon learns that he is a son of Logan: he believes himself to be the only survivor of the massacre he had carried out against Logan's family. Logan's first Indian mate, Harold's mother, never appears in the novel, just as she is absent from the legend.

In a novel where, as Nelson has described it, the hero, Harold, is driven by a "desire to be repeatedly recognized by the Father" (96), including the Virginia governor and later the governor of New France, Logan is not only his true father but represents king, God, and republican founder. In the novel's only meeting between father and son, Logan with his apparent dying words asks Harold to make war on the whites, to drive them back to England (1:110). A few pages later, Harold, contemplating this burden of responsibility, says he needs "someone, before whom he could fall down on his knees, as he would before his Maker" (1:116). He then asks, "Why meet me . . . in battle, and stand, in thy gigantic self-possession, as courting death, and provoking it, from a parricide" (1:116–17; ellipses in original). The line evokes the ambivalence of revolutionary filiopiety insofar as Harold first attempts to kill his father and then is charged with taking up his father's goal of defeating the fatherland, Britain. This ambivalence not only afflicted U.S. revolutionary founders and their generation's children into the 1820s but also affected the leaders of Native American resistance. Logan seems to have passed on to Harold the mantle of leader of a native revolt, as Pontiac did to Tecumseh and others. But in assuming the powers of the father, or of the Master of Life, the son metaphorically usurps his progenitor. When Harold and Loena travel to Quebec and meet Governor Vaudreuil (who actually ceased to be governor of New France well before the cession to England in 1763), Harold declares his plan "to establish a confederacy among all the tribes of America—wrench back part of our possessions from the English—and prevent all future encroachment" (1:266), a plot that the French governor naturally encourages. Meeting Vaudreuil, Harold thinks he recognizes the governor from childhood. Vaudreuil's wife, the countess, calls Loena "daughter of Logan" and says, "I knew thy mother," who had saved the countess and her child during captivity (279), no doubt alluding to Bartram's story that the historical Logan's father, Shickellemus, was a French boy adopted by the Oneida.

Race is even more confused than kinship in Neal's novel. Logan, whom all his readers would identify as the tragic Mingo chief, turns out to be a British nobleman: "He has not one drop of Indian blood in his veins * * * He is a white man—all over—body and soul" (1:63). He had emigrated to America in flight from a conflict with an English rival over a woman who later encounters Harold. Passages in the novel nonetheless insist on Logan's essential Indian nature. Shickellemus never appears, and the Indian blood of the narrator and of Harold would thus come from the maternal side, just as the real Logan's may have. In his search for Logan early in volume 1, Harold is transformed into an Indian (1:60), say the soldiers at the fort. When he travels to Canada, Vaudreuil remarks that Harold cuts a figure that is noble and commanding, like the undegenerate Indian, while his Indian guide is "like the scorned and derided of white men" (1:265). This Noble Savage evidently derives his sense of honor and his propensity for revolt from his European aristocratic heritage, not from any patrilineage of American Indian chiefs.

In volume 2, Harold returns to the estate in England that he has inherited from Logan and then makes a quick trip back to America to visit all the major tribes except his own tribe of Logans: "He sought for the vestiges of his kindred. There was not a trace left." Seeing "the Indian trampled upon, derided, mocked at, scorned and cheated," Harold asks himself, "Should he build up a coalition, a confederacy? Might he not erect an empire of his own, and roll back, upon the whites, the flood of encroachment?" (2:272). But he declines to become another Pontiac or Tecumseh. In a stark reversal from his behavior in the first volume (a reversal that might be seen as consistent with the historical Logan), Harold declares that "war was no longer a profession worthy of the good man" and instead rushes back to England to address Parliament. Here, at the novel's climax, Neal paraphrases Logan's oration as if it were a ghost's lament from beyond the grave. Harold begins, with a verbosity that evidently necessitates ellipses,

> The petitioner, my lords, with his whole family, is in his grave. But their spirits are here, here, at my side! At this moment, Logan himself is whispering in my ears—my voice flows only at his prompting. . . . He was a monarch. . . .
>
> His dominion was an empire. It was given to him by Almighty God. . . . How have you reverenced his title? You have spoiled him of his inheritance, butchered his family, and banished him beyond the mountains. (2:275–76; ellipses in original)

Harold goes on to claim that the Indians had always respected treaties with the British and to extol "Pocahontas, Alexander, Logan, Philip of Mount Hope, Opechancanough" (2:283). Yet the speech finally does little to promote the Indians' interests. When the speech insists that the Indians have a religion, the example cited is one of a warrior "teaching his naked boy how to feather his arrow and barb his javelin . . . training him in the first lesson of patriotism, and is not patriotism, religion?" (2:282; ellipses in original). Obedience to the father in the cause of violence is the nature of religion, he implies, a creed befitting a primitive people in thrall to vengeance and sacrifice but also perhaps a secular revolutionary state such as the United States. The next paragraph cites as evidence of patriotic heroism the supposed "fact" that one Indian nation, "when their liberties were in peril," was ready to "put all their women and children to death!" (2:282). This might appear as an instance of republican virtue, but it is also just the sort of family massacre that drove Logan to vengeance and that Harold accuses the British of perpetrating. With Old Testament overtones, children are sacrificed by fathers in obedience to the father, a doctrine that Harold should fear rather than affirm because fifty pages later Logan kills him. Harold's voice in this speech, which claims Logan as an ancestor even as it accuses the audience of killing all of Logan's family, is as contradictory as his presence in delivering it: he insists that he defends the Indians yet is complicit in their demise. While the Logan of historical myth refused to address Lord Dunmore and refused to bury the hatchet, Harold abandons hundreds of pages of violence and the promise of leading an Indian revolt to instead renounce war and settle for the honor of speaking to Parliament, a right that as an heir to an estate at Salisbury he might have exercised anyway.

This address is a foretaste of the novel's conclusion, in which the narrator, who proclaimed himself in the first few pages to be "the last of the Mingos" and signs the final page "A Descendant of Logan" yet is distinct from Harold, boasts, "I AM AN AMERICAN" (2:338) and reproaches Englishmen for reviling America. He attacks "your lying witnesses" and "your reviewers," possibly a veiled response to English detractors of American letters, such as Sydney Smith (infamous for the line "Who reads an American book?"), whom Neal took it upon himself to answer. In 1823, the year after *Logan* appeared, Neal traveled to Britain and published in *Blackwood's Magazine* a series of five articles about American writers (appearing from September 1824 to February 1825) that has been called "the first attempt at a history of American literature" (*Oxford Companion* 586). Thus, Neal not only ventriloquized the voice of Logan but used it to one of the same purposes as Jefferson had in raising the speech to prominence some thirty-five years earlier—defending American genius and letters. Neal's novel, though seldom read today and unlikely to ever attract much of an audience, contains all the incestuous relationships and ideological reversals of the Logan legend.

The Logan legend continued to thrive into the twentieth century. On 7 October 1923, Ohio History Day, a ceremony was held to dedicate a state historical monument at the Logan Elm, a huge old tree just north of Chillicothe on the Pickaway Plains. Local tradition held that when Gibson arrived at the Indians' camp, Logan asked him to retire a short distance to this elm and that there the communication of the famous speech occurred. As Sawvel's 1921 biography puts it, "A log in the primeval forest on the Pickaway plans became the throne of justice from which Logan passed sentence on his accusers" (82). The elm had already been associated with this event for nearly a century, for the *American Pioneer* had promoted the project of propagating seedlings of the elm, as if to ensure the survival of a lineage from a man famous precisely for the fact that he was the last of his race. Still today, a small wayside picnic area is preserved as the Logan Elm State Historical Site, with plaques honoring Logan and other Native Americans and early Ohio settlers. The 1923 ceremony featured a poem and address by C. B. Galbreath, who declared that "the central virtue of Logan's famous message is its arraignment of ingratitude. The Logan Elm helps to perpetuate that poignant arraignment" (3). Like other memorials to Indian tragic heroes, this one claims to redress the wrongs that colonials committed against him, to assuage the guilt of these colonial wars not by compensating living Indians but by mourning what is supposed to be a vanished race. Still, Galbreath's archaic use of "arraignment" as a term for a nonjudicial accusation is peculiarly apt. The frontier society in which Logan lived was poised uneasily at a transition between anarchy and law or, more accurately, between two very different systems of justice practiced by native and Anglo-American societies. Sawvel's line about the log as throne of justice and the elm as courtroom blithely erases these differences. But Galbreath suggests that the memorial will not recompense for the wrongs done to Logan. The elm does not return the gratitude or offer the forgiveness that Logan asked for but never got; instead, it repeats the accusation. Unlike the monument at Auburn, New York, the one in Ohio did not address its visitors as melancholy mourners but accused them as ungrateful thieves. The tree, once one of the largest elms in the United States, was struck by lightning and removed in 1965.

> I was still very young when I conceived the idea of composing an
> epic on the man of nature, or delineating the manners of the savages by
> connecting them with some well-known event. Next to the discovery of
> America, I could not find a more interesting subject, especially for the
> French, than the massacre of the colony of the Natchez in Louisiana, in
> 1727. All the Indian tribes conspiring, after two centuries of oppression,
> to restore liberty to the New World, seemed to me to furnish a subject
> nearly as happy as the conquest of Mexico.
> —François-René Chateaubriand, preface to *Atala* (1801)

In introducing the novella that launched him to literary fame,
Chateaubriand declared that the Natchez Massacre offered an epic tableau
that in all the history of America was comparable only to the battle between
Cortés and Moctezuma. The comparison may seem preposterous, a symp-
tom of the author's notoriously melodramatic and self-aggrandizing personality. After all, *Atala* did not fulfill this epic pretension. Although the
novella's hero, Chactas, is a Natchez, it does not portray the Natchez Massacre. Chateaubriand's "epic on the man of nature" was instead *Les Natchez*,
the epic romance that he had begun writing in exile in London in the 1790s
but did not publish until 1826. *Atala* was an immediate success in Europe,
and Caleb Bingham's translation, *Atala; or, The Love and Constancy of Two
Savages in the Desert*, published in Boston in 1802, found wide readership and
influence in the United States (Seelye, *Beautiful Machines* 174). But *Les Natchez*
remains little-read, a lost epic for France's lost colonies in North America.
To appreciate *Les Natchez*, one must recover the literature of French colonial
Louisiana that dramatized the events at Natchez as the tragic outcome of an
alliance between a native nation and a colonial power linked by a common
destiny of loss and regret.

The uprising of the Natchez nation, which actually occurred on 28 November 1729, not 1727, took the lives of about 250 French colonists (out of a
total in the Natchez area of some 700, including African slaves) and destroyed a settlement that had been established barely ten years earlier.[1] It left

unscathed the colonial capital, New Orleans, and the initial French Louisiana forts at Mobile and Biloxi. Thus, the eminent Franco-Americanist Gilbert Chinard wrote in his preface to Les Natchez that Chateaubriand "magnified a banal incident from the French colonial wars and transformed a local rebellion into a war of independence" (30; my translation). The romantic notion of not merely the Natchez but "all the Indian tribes conspiring" to overthrow the European colony was a myth common in colonial history writing, one we shall examine further in the next chapter.[2] But this is no reason to disregard Chateaubriand's work. Epic imperial history has always worked to turn minor battles into major events, and in the words of ethnologist John R. Swanton, probably the foremost expert on the Natchez, the Indians "so strongly appealed to French imaginations . . . that this tribe has been surrounded by a glamour similar to that which until recently enshrouded the Aztec of Mexico and the Quichua of Peru" (2). Because both the Natchez and French Louisiana were defeated in colonial wars, they have been largely forgotten by most in the United States today. It is necessary to imagine an alternative historiography of eighteenth-century colonial North America in which the Natchez uprising and its literary portrayals retain an epic significance. Chateaubriand specified that the Natchez Massacre was epic "above all for the French." If French Louisiana had endured through the nineteenth century or had made the transition to postcolonial nation, the Natchez and their war of resistance might well have been mythologized to the same degree as Moctezuma's confrontation with Cortés and Metacom's uprising in colonial New England. And had this occurred, a literature was available to support the myth, one just as rich as those supporting the U.S. and Mexican traditions.

The study of the Natchez "massacre" in this chapter aims not only to recover some interest in the French colonial literature of Louisiana but also to trace a striking instance of Hayden White's concept of the emplotment of historical events in dramatic narratives. The existence of an Indian "conspiracy" behind the revolt was elaborated by French colonial officials and authors who shared an interest in exaggerating native resistance. What began as a local uprising by the Natchez became by the time of Chateaubriand an epic revolutionary struggle that spoke to an Age of Revolution nearly a century later. Because the uprising was relatively small in scale and the number of historical treatments of it limited, it is possible to fully document the accretion of literary devices beginning with the initial historical accounts. To quote White, "Historical situations are not inherently tragic, comic, or romantic. . . . How a given historical situation is to be configured depends on the historian's subtlety in matching up a specific plot structure with the set historical events that he wishes to endow with meaning" (*Tropics* 85). The eighteenth-century historians of the Natchez uprising added elements of all three genres, as we shall see. But we will need to begin with some historical context—the stage setting for the Natchez tragedy—and an introduction to the two authors who recorded it.

Le Page and Dumont, Historians of French Louisiana

French Louisiana had begun in 1699–1700 with the explorations of Pierre Le Moyne d'Iberville and his brother, Jean-Baptiste Le Moyne de Bienville. They established a post near modern Biloxi, Mississippi, and in 1718 moved the capital of the colony to New Orleans. The French set a goal of connecting their posts on the Great Lakes and in the Illinois country into a trade network that would control the entire Mississippi River basin. The pelt trade was at first the most important, as in Canada, but there were high hopes for other products. The Compagnie de l'Ouest (Company of the West), granted to Antoine Crozat in 1710 and later taken over by John Law and combined with the Company of the Indies, was touting a prosperous future for its concessions on the Mississippi, and there were rumors of rich silver mines upstream. Natchez, with rich agricultural land and a bluff safely above the floods and miasmas of the bayous, became part of a speculative boom, leading to the Mississippi Bubble of 1720 that made Law's name infamous. Law combined the shares of the company with the French central bank and tried to use them to dissolve the nation's debt. After the crash, the potential for settlement at Natchez remained, but the events of 1729 again destroyed French hopes. As Daniel Usner concludes in a recent essay, after 1729, "the commercial potential of Louisiana took a backseat to its geopolitical function . . . and the complex interplay of adaptation and resistance that had characterized this cultural borderland was long forgotten" (32).

For an interesting parallel with English colonial history, the Natchez uprising might be compared to the Jamestown Massacre of 1622. On 22 March of that year, the Algonquians of the Powhatan Confederacy attacked and killed some 350 English, out of a total population in the colony of around 1,250. The leader of the Powhatans' uprising in Virginia was Opechancanough, who had been a heroic foe of John Smith during the founding of the colony in 1607–9. According to some historians, Spanish Jesuits in Virginia had captured Opechancanough during the 1560s, and he had converted to Catholicism and been baptized Don Luis de Velasco.[3] Although the identity of the mastermind of the Natchez rebellion is unclear, there are also hints of a connection to earlier missionary activity. I will reveal the shadowy figure of St. Cosme, the métis son of a French missionary, who according to the most important source on the Natchez rebellion, Le Page du Pratz, may have been its tragically flawed leader.

The consequences of the uprisings for the two colonial projects were also quite similar. Like Natchez, Jamestown was a fledgling settlement less than two decades old that had been established by a private company chartered by the king and promoted by investors (or "adventurers") in the metropolitan capital. Both uprisings constituted a public relations crisis for the companies and prompted a series of bloody retaliations by the colonizers as well as published propaganda that either called the natives "savages" deserving of extermination or offered reassuring visions of Indian subordination. Some read the story of Pocahontas rescuing John Smith, first told in Smith's *Generall Historie of Virginia* (1624), as a soothing response to the fears aroused by the Jamestown Massacre. In both Virginia and Louisiana, the Indian uprising threatened the colony's existence. In 1731, King Louis XV removed colonial Governor Étienne Périer and revoked the charter of the Company of the Indies. In 1624, James I revoked the charter of the London Company and turned Virginia into the first English royal colony.

Whereas the Jamestown "massacre," King Philip's War, and Pontiac's rebellion were quickly documented in periodicals, books, and pamphlets and became important events in Anglo-American historiography, the Natchez Massacre is little known today and was not well publicized in its time. French New Orleans had no printing presses in the 1730s, and while two accounts of the uprising appeared in Paris in 1731, the first full history of the colony to treat the incident did not appear until 1744.[4] By that time, France was fighting England for dominance in North America, and Louisiana's published history was being broken up and sold for parts to English readers. Charlevoix's *Histoire et déscription générale de la Nouvelle France avec le Journal Historique d'un Voyage fait par ordre du Roi dans l'Amérique Septentrionale* (1744), which tells of his brief visit to Natchez in 1722 and devotes a chapter (book 22) to the massacre and its aftermath, appeared during the War of the Austrian Succession. A piece of wartime propaganda published in London in 1746 translated passages from Charlevoix that offered strategic intelligence and claimed that "the French Ministry . . . endeavor all in their Power to prevent copies of it from coming to us." Another writer in Boston in the same year translated from Charlevoix an appendix about Quebec, the target of New England raids.[5] A full translation of the *Journal d'un Voyage*, Charlevoix's narrative of his travels from Quebec across the Great Lakes and down the Mississippi, appeared in London in 1761 to satisfy English readers' desires for a guide to the exploitation of the lands just won in the Seven Years'

War. A similar fate befell the works of the two major Louisiana writers who dramatized the massacre, whom Chateaubriand used as sources and who are the focus of my interpretation here, Antoine-Simon Le Page du Pratz and Jean-François Benjamin Dumont de Montigny.

Le Page du Pratz was in his twenties in 1718 when he joined a group of some eight hundred colonists on a ship from La Rochelle bound for Louisiana. He described himself as an architect with training in mathematics and engineering; while in Louisiana, he also claimed expertise in medicine, collecting specimens of hundreds of native plant remedies ("simples") for transport to Paris. Soon after his arrival, he developed a close relationship with a Chitimacha Indian woman, whose father, the tribe's chief, gave her to Le Page du Pratz as a slave. She later bore him children (Le Page du Pratz, Histoire 1:112–17; Giraud 392). In 1720, he moved upstream to Natchez and acquired three large parcels of land from the natives he called not "sauvages" but "naturels." For eight years he lived alongside the Natchez Indians, learned to speak their language, and conversed with their leaders and tribal historians. In 1728, he returned to New Orleans, where Governor Périer persuaded him to take up management of the company's plantation, which after the 1731 retrocession became the king's plantation ("habitation du Roi") in Louisiana. Le Page du Pratz thus escaped probable death in the rebellion by the tribe he knew so intimately. He returned to France in 1734, because, as he wrote, he was unhappy that Périer had been replaced by Bienville in the wake of the massacre and the largely ineffective series of retaliatory attacks on the tribe.

Dumont was born in Paris on 31 July 1696, a younger son of a prominent magistrate. He was educated at a Jesuit college, or grammar school, and went into the military. He served in Quebec in 1715–17 and then sailed to Louisiana in 1719 with a commission as a lieutenant and the responsibility of guarding five hundred persons being forcibly sent to the colony. Soon after his arrival, Dumont unwittingly insulted Bienville, the popular "father of Louisiana" who was then in his first stint as governor, and thereby began an enmity that Dumont pursued through all his writings. During his time in Louisiana, Dumont revived an old family title and began calling himself "Dumont, dit Montigny" (dit means "called") and finally "Dumont de Montigny," as if he were of the landed gentry. He traveled extensively around Louisiana, from the Red River to the Upper Tombigbee, sometimes serving as a soldier and engineer, sometimes in dereliction of his military orders. As his unpublished manuscript autobiography reveals, he suffered numerous setbacks, including the burning of his home, the capsizing of his pirogue with all his belongings, and a military demotion. He lived in Natchez from

1727 until January 1729 and later participated in an unsuccessful 1736 military expedition led by Bienville against the Chickasaw and the Natchez refugees among them. He sailed back to France in 1737.[6]

The two colonists' books, du Pratz's *Histoire de la Louisiane* (1758) and Dumont's *Mémoires historiques sur la Louisiane* (1753) are the most important published histories of colonial Louisiana (Charlevoix's being devoted to all of New France, including Canada). Even though the books appeared a quarter century later, the events at Natchez in 1729 remained central to their plots of the colony's history. Each devoted several chapters to a detailed, dramatic narrative of the uprising; the events that precipitated it; and the sieges, pursuits, and escapes of the Natchez tribe that continued through 1740. They agree on most circumstantial details but differ in how they cast blame for the revolt and for the French military's hapless efforts at retaliation. As colonists who knew the Natchez well and published accounts of an uprising that could easily have cost them their lives, Dumont and Le Page play a role similar to that of Robert Rogers, Benjamin Church, and Joseph Doddridge with regard to the Indian rebels examined in the previous three chapters. Unfortunately, the two men's books are rarely discussed by scholars in the United States; they have become the losers of imperial and linguistic competitions and neglected classics of colonial American literature. The only available English translation of Le Page du Pratz was published by T. Becket and P. A. de Hondt in London in 1763, the same year that Britain claimed title to Louisiana and Quebec, and reprinted in 1774. *The History of Louisiana, or of the Western Parts of Virginia and Carolina* rhetorically claims Louisiana's history for the English by changing the title of Le Page du Pratz's book, rearranging its chapters, cutting more than half of the text, and adding a long preface asserting the Mississippi Valley's importance to the British: "The countries here treated of, have not only by right always belonged to Great-Britain, but part of them is now acknowledged to it by the former usurpers: and it is to be hoped, that the nation may now reap some advantages from those countries . . . by learning from the experience of others, what they do or are likely to produce, that may turn to account to the nation" (ii–iii). The translation also includes four chapters from Dumont's *Mémoires historiques* concerning tobacco, indigo, and Louisiana's mineral resources. These were the only parts of Dumont's writings to appear in English until the mid–nineteenth century, when Benjamin Franklin French published a translation of the second of Dumont's two volumes in his *Historical Collections of Louisiana*.[7]

The French loss of Louisiana after the Seven Years' War was a blow from which Dumont's and Le Page's books would never recover. But even in the 1750s they faced challenges—from one another. The two authors exchanged accusations of plagiarism and misrepresentation that were all the more bitter because the men were competing for authority over the same material. Le Page du Pratz's first publication was a series of twelve articles in the Parisian *Journal Oeconomique* from September 1751 to February 1753. When Dumont's book appeared later in 1753, it lambasted the "chimerical and imaginary descriptions such as those that we have seen inserted into the *Journal Oeconomique* by a sloppy and misinformed writer" (1:ix). But later in the book, Dumont identified Le Page du Pratz by name in a note and called him "a friend of mine, whom I knew in that land, where he has lived, as I have," and went on to quote several pages of a letter "that he wrote to me, in returning to me my memoirs, that he had asked me to allow him to read" (1:118). It appears that the two authors exchanged ideas and drafts of their books but at some point had a falling out. Dumont had in 1747 composed a manuscript of more than four hundred pages chronicling his adventures since 1715 in Quebec, Louisiana, and back in France, where he was involved in battles at l'Orient during the War of the Austrian Succession. It is today held in the Ayer Collection at the Newberry Library, but it has never been published and differs greatly from the published *Mémoires historiques* of 1753, which was "composed based on the manuscript," as the title page says, by the Abbé le Mascrier, a hack writer and editor of travel texts. Le Mascrier evidently used the manuscript, du Pratz's articles, and other sources to put together the text.[8]

Dumont also wrote, probably prior to his prose manuscript, a 4,962-line epic, "Poème en vers touchant l'établissement de la province de la Loüisiane connüee sous le nom du Missisipy avec tout ce que s'y est passé de depuis 1716 jusqu'à 1741; le massacre des François au poste des Natchez, les mœurs des sauvages, leurs dances, leurs religions, enfin ce qui concerne le pays en général" (Verse poem regarding the establishment of the province of Louisiana, known by the name of Mississippi, with all that has happened there from 1716 to 1741; the massacre of the French at the post at Natchez, the manners and customs of the Indians, their dances, their religions, and finally that which concerns the land in general). This text, held at the Bibliothèque de l'Arsenal in Paris, was first edited and published by Marc Villiers du Terrage in 1931. Another copy is held at the Library of Congress. The first of its four cantos is devoted to the Natchez Massacre, part of the fourth to ethnographic descriptions of the Natchez, and the second and third to military expeditions in 1735–40 against the Chickasaw, who were suspected of collaborating with and sheltering the Natchez rebels. Dumont's versifying was weak, but the poem is more readable than some colonial verse epics about Indian wars. Its ham-fisted use of epic devices, invocation of the muses and use of epithets such as "César" for his heroes, Governor Périer and Louis Juchereau de Saint-Denis, suggest that Dumont saw the Natchez

uprising and his adventures in Louisiana as worthy of a grand literary treatment. But because he was conscious of the failings of the French leadership,
he also brought a mock-epic, even Hudibrastic tone to many scenes. The
poem expresses his contempt for Bienville's command of an expedition
against the Chickasaw with a mock-epic comparison to Moses:

> One might compare, with an open heart
> Our marching army, to those people in the desert
> Led by that great chief, called Moses
> Except, to be totally frank,
> He walked at their head, and ours in mid-rank. (344; my translation)

When the French besiege the Natchez after the uprising, one French soldier
tries to show his contempt for the enemy but suffers horribly for it:

> One morning, at dawn, a sergeant, quite facile
> In the ruses of war, whose name was Brinville
> Was chosen for the job of aiming the cannon
> And met with great misfortune on that one occasion.
> He wanted the enemy to be mocked and harassed
> So he lowered his britches and showed them his ass.
> But in answer, the Natchez, they shot back a ball
> Which lodged between his buttocks, a wound that was fatal. (325)

Publishing *Histoire de la Louisiane* in 1758, Le Page du Pratz had the last
word in the squabble with Dumont. Le Page copied without attribution
passages from Dumont about the retaliatory raids against the Natchez, some
of which took place after he had returned to France (see Carpenter 298). He
also cast doubt on the writings of authors who "write only on hearsay, or
who know nothing of the language of the land for which they are writing the
history" (1:xv), oblique but clear references to Dumont and the Natchez
language.

Compared to Dumont, Le Page shows more sympathy for the Indians and
a greater interest in their culture. Though he did not attempt an epic poem
about the Natchez Massacre, his narrative endows it with the sense of drama
found in the most elegant colonial histories, such as Vega's *La Florida*. The
Natchez leaders are not "savage" antagonists but complex characters whose
actions are motivated by internecine rivalries and expressed in eloquent
speeches. Moreover, by individuating the Natchez leaders and explaining the
tribe's social organization, his book alone provides the evidence to support
my interpretation of the uprising elaborated later in this chapter. The bare
history of the massacre can be traced out of the archival correspondence of
the French officers, who never mention our two authors. But the histories by

Dumont and Le Page du Pratz, published nearly twenty-five years later, build on these official accounts by adding dramatic, epic intensity, and by emplotting and explaining the idea of a pan-Indian conspiracy against the French colony in Louisiana.

Natchez Ethnography

The Gentleman of Elvas, one of the chroniclers of the Hernando De Soto expeditions, wrote that on their descent of the Mississippi in 1543, the Spaniards met at the bluffs near modern Vicksburg a chief named Quigualtanqui, who declared himself, as later Natchez chiefs did, to be a descendant of the sun (Ian Brown 179; Vega, *Florida* 589). La Salle also passed through the area in 1682 on his voyage to the mouth of the Mississippi. But the texts of these encounters recorded little detail about the tribe and in fact never referred to it as "Natchez." So when the early Louisiana explorers reached Natchez, they met a native people quite unlike what the previous hundred years of French colonial experience in North America had prepared them for. In some ways Natchez culture resembled that of Mesoamerican peoples more than it did the Algonquians and Iroquoians of the Northeastern Woodlands, a contrast that Le Page noticed and that shaped his theories about the origins of Native American tribes.

Paul du Ru, who accompanied Iberville on his second voyage to Louisiana, wrote in March 1700 of the Natchez, "The chief's manner impresses me; he has the air of an ancient emperor, a long face, sharp eyes, an imperious aquiline nose, a chestnut complexion, and manners somewhat Spanish. . . . The respect with which the other Savages approach and serve him is astonishing. If he speaks to one of them, that person thanks him before answering. They never pass in front of him if it can be avoided; if they must, it is with elaborate precautions. They call the sky Ouachi or the sun and their Great Chief Ouchilla" (34). The authority of this chief and the European political concepts used to describe it resemble some accounts of the despotic Pontiac. But the Natchez leader's power did not, like Pontiac's, arise out of an innovative scheme for pan-Indian, anticolonial alliance: it was based on his hereditary status at the top of a society stratified into distinct classes. Dumont introduced his account of the Natchez by saying, "In each of the savage nations, as in all the nations of the earth, two kinds of men may be beheld, of which the one seems born to command and to enjoy all the honors, the other to obey and to grovel in obscurity. It is these which we name the great and the people" (*Mémoires historiques* 1:175–76; Swanton 103). Like Old World cultures, the Natchez had a titled aristocracy, the Soleils (Suns) above a mass of commoners. Their elites were literally *Noble Savages*.

Dumont was incorrect in construing the existence of class hierarchies to be universal, but the lines suggest how powerfully the Natchez inspired French colonial authors to do what so many anthropologists would later do—that is, study a Native American culture as an inquiry into the origins and essences of human social structure. The dynamics of the Natchez caste system could be portrayed either as a critique of the French ancien régime or as an homage to it. And because the Natchez had a hereditary ruling class, the political meaning of their revolt was different. French colonial writers such as Dumont, Le Page du Pratz, and Chateaubriand did not invest their projections in a single heroic Natchez chief, and there was no Natchez leader comparable to Pontiac or Metacom, even as the tribe accomplished a major revolt. The dynamic was ethnographic rather than individuated, and the uprising of the Natchez became identified in a historiographic typology not with a revolutionary republican insurgency but with an aristocratic decline, a melancholy tragedy that by the time of *Atala* in 1801 was bound up with that of the French colony and the French monarchy.

Hence we must begin not with the rise of a rebel leader but with the ethnographic literature on the Natchez, which is extensive. John R. Swanton, a prolific early-twentieth-century ethnologist and linguist, devotes more than two hundred pages of his *Indian Tribes of the Lower Mississippi Valley* to the Natchez and barely a hundred pages to twenty-three other tribes. His portrait of the Natchez consists mostly of long quotations from Le Page du Pratz, Dumont, and other French writers, divided into sections on marriage, religion, dress, ornament, and so forth. For non-Francophones, Swanton's translations of ethnographic passages from Le Page du Pratz and Dumont are a valuable complement to the 1763 translation, which omitted much of the ethnographic material about the Natchez. As ethnography, the book's utility cannot be denied. But by chopping up and decontextualizing the sources, Swanton withholds from readers what I will call, following James Clifford, the allegorical dimension of the original sources. "Ethnography itself [is] a performance emplotted by powerful stories," Clifford writes in his contribution to *Writing Culture*, the 1980 essay collection that marked the arrival of poststructuralist textual analysis to ethnographic anthropology. "Ethnographic writing is allegorical both at the level of its content (what it says about cultures and their histories) and of its form (what is implied by its mode of textualization)" (98). If the histories of Moctezuma and Metacom have been emplotted as political allegories, that of the Natchez is in large part an ethnographic allegory. The tribe's class structure mimicked and refracted that of French society, and the intervention of French colonials into the tribe, notably Le Page du Pratz and the missionary St. Cosme, incited a family drama of mimetic rivalry.

Le Page du Pratz stands out among colonial ethnographers of native North American cultures. Not only did he have eight years of fieldwork and language study, but he approached his research with something of the dedication and the methodology of twentieth-century anthropologists. He started by studying Natchez kinship and caste structure, the same issues that have absorbed many important modern ethnographers. He explains, "Most of the Natchez speak the common language," the Mobilien jargon that served as lingua franca in French Louisiana (Swanton 183); however, he "also wanted to learn the language of [the Natchez], so that I could talk to the women who simply don't speak the common language" (Histoire 2:321). Although he printed several Natchez words in the text, he did not include in the Histoire a glossary of the language. In explanation, he claims that such a phrasebook would be useless given that the tribe had become dispersed (2:323). Indeed, it is difficult to seek confirmation for the colonial historians' accounts of the Natchez in the tribe's oral traditions, for the language is now lost. In any case, to attempt a dictionary would have been doubly difficult, since the Natchez "have two languages, that of the Nobles and that of the people; both are very rich" (2:324). This is the first hint at the caste system that Le Page du Pratz explains in volume 2, chapter 26, on marriage ceremonies: "The nobility is divided into Suns, Nobles, and Honored men" (2:394). The common people were called "Puants" (Stinkards), a term of contempt, Le Page explains, but one that he uses frequently nonetheless. The Suns were therefore the Natchez royalty, and their status was enshrined in the tribe's origin myths. Dumont explains that the royal lineage began with "Oüachill-Tamaïll, that is to say, the Female Sun, or White Woman" (Mémoires historiques 1:177), and the Temple Guardian told Le Page that "a great number of years ago there appeared among us a man and his wife, who had descended from the Sun" (2:332). By "descended" he did not mean that the sun itself was parent of one or both of the couple, as in many versions of the Earthdiver creation myth in native America, but only that "when both of them were seen they were still so brilliant that it was not difficult to believe that they had come from the Sun" (2:332), much like the figural association of the French king with the sun. This couple became the ancestral founders of a royal lineage, maintained matrilineally through the succession of female Suns.

Natchez kinship rules therefore combined a patriarchal authority familiar to European observers with a radically unfamiliar matrilineal succession and a strict rule of exogamy. All Suns were obliged to marry Stinkards. And while daughters of a female Sun "are Suns for life without suffering any alteration in their dignity" (Le Page, Histoire 2:396), the male descendants dropped to the next lower caste. The son of the Grande Soleille (female Great Sun), would be anointed as Grand Soleil (male Great Sun) and ruler of the tribe, but his wife would be a Stinkard and his sons and daughters mere Nobles. These children too would marry Stinkards. Their offspring, the Grand Soleil's grandchildren, would be Honoreds, and his great-grandchildren would be Stinkards. Le Page writes that the Soleils were ashamed at seeing "their posterity confounded with the commoners. . . . They never inform Foreigners of this; they do not wish to" (2:396). According to Le Page, only the Scythians, described by Herodotus, shared this peculiar custom (2:394; Herodotus 294). In a bizarre anticipation of the nineteenth-century Louisiana creole elite disowning the illegitimate offspring of their quadroon mistresses, the Natchez Suns concealed the vulgar status of their great-grandchildren. Moreover, in asserting the royal pretensions of the Natchez Suns, Le Page du Pratz made them, by the rules of Aristotle, fit subjects for tragedy.

Although twentieth-century anthropologists might explain the upper castes' exogamy as part of an incest taboo, the way Le Page du Pratz and Dumont describe it exposes the arbitrary nature of social caste and the instability of patriarchy. Their ethnography offers what Homi Bhabha would call an insurgent mimicry of French society. By Natchez kinship rules, the blood of the Suns was carried by the women, by whom alone legitimate descent could be assured, yet the power that blood authorized was exerted by the men. So although several observers wrote of the despotic and absolute power of the male Sun, Dumont explained that the female Sun "has more power as long as she lives than the chief himself, who may be her son or her brother, and never her husband, whom she is able to choose if she wishes from among the Stinkards and who is rather her slave than her master" (Mémoires historiques 1:177; Swanton 104). In one of his rare direct quotations of a native speaker, Dumont gives us a Natchez defense of the logic of matrilineal descent: "Whether the female Sun has children by her husband or by any other person whatever, it matters little to us. They are always Suns on the side of their mother, a fact which is most certain, since the womb cannot lie" (1:179; Swanton 104). If the decadent, adulterous behavior of the French aristocracy threatened to undermine the legitimacy of their hereditary rule, the Natchez had a solution. Dumont also describes the conjunction of inherited and earned status in the Sun caste: "The submission of the Indians to their chief is extreme; he commands them with the most despotic power. . . . But at the death of this chief, his children, sons or daughters, inherit nothing of his power. . . . It is up to the boys to act with the valor that might raise them to the dignity of [the caste of] Honoreds" (1:176). Stinkards could lift themselves into the ranks of the Honored class through exploits in war or service to the religious institutions (such as the post of assistant to the Temple Guardian) or by offering a child's life in sacrifice on the occasion of the death of a Sun.

As Le Page explains, it was not an incest taboo that prevented Suns from intermarrying.

> As the posterity of the two first Suns has become much multiplied, one perceives readily that many of these Suns are no longer related and might ally themselves together, which would preserve their blood in common without any mixture. But another law established at the same time opposes an invincible obstacle to this; it is forbidden for any Sun to be put to a violent death. And it was ordained that when a male or female Sun should pass away, his wife or her husband should be put to death on the day of the funeral, in order to go and keep him company in the country of spirits. (*Histoire* 2:396–97)

Suns had to marry Stinkards because a Stinkard could be put to death following the death of his or her spouse, whereas a Noble could not. This practice of mortuary sacrifice, or, to use a more specific but less euphonious term found in the anthropological literature, retainer death, was not unique to the Natchez. Neighboring tribes such as the Taensas practiced it, as did the Calusa in Florida and various peoples of Africa, as Wole Soyinka's drama demonstrates. However, two features distinguished the Natchez custom from other versions. First, its connection to the caste system, whereby a victim's kin could raise their status by offering a victim for sacrifice or by serving as executioner (Le Page, *Histoire* 3:45). And second, its gender-neutrality, for "the versatile Natchez seem to afford us the only example in culture history of the obligatory immolation of the husband at the death of the wife" (MacLeod, "Natchez Political Evolution" 225). The latter is perhaps the strongest testimony to the power of the female Suns. Their Stinkard husbands lived on borrowed time, predesignated as sacrificial victims, knowing that they would not be allowed to outlive their wives.

Le Page du Pratz's relation to the custom of mortuary sacrifice was more than just ethnographic. Not only did he witness sacrifices in the wake of the death of his friend Serpent Piqué, as we shall see, he also knew intimately the peculiar status of the spouses of the Suns. Just after describing the kinship and caste structure of the Natchez, du Pratz related a curious anecdote: "The Grande Soleille came to see me one morning, early enough that I was still in bed. She was accompanied by her only daughter, about fourteen to fifteen years of age, pretty, and well made" (*Histoire* 2:397). The Grande Soleille pulls a chair up to the side of his bed and launches into a long and flattering speech, calling him "Chief of the Beautiful Head" for his hair and recounting how her brothers praise him because he "knows how to speak our language, he has chased away the big storms that cover the nation and we are starting to see clearly. He has given us knowledge and shown us that our habits destroy our nation, that their customs are more civilized, that the Suns and the Nobles should be allied together" (2:400–401). She thus mocks the belief that sacrificed spouses follow the Suns to the afterlife, and she concludes with a surprising request: "You are like a brother to us and to all of the Suns, and we would like you to be so in fact" (2:398). He must marry her daughter and thereby challenge the customs of exogamy and mortuary sacrifice. For if her daughter, Le Page's new wife, were to die, "You would have the protection of the French, and also the strong mind to put a stop to this law" (2:402), to resist the rule of sacrifice. Le Page gives a disingenuous refusal designed to prevent the Grande Soleille from making the same offer to another Frenchman: "The Great Spirit prohibits us from taking as wives women who do not pray" (2:404). But his initial reaction is more revealing: "Do you take me for a Stinkard?" (2:403). Since Le Page du Pratz is French, it is not obvious what his caste would be among the Natchez or whether such a marriage would violate the rule of exogamy. Does race or class determine his status? Would the possibility of his sacrifice even arise if his young bride died while he was still living at Natchez? The episode ironizes the common American colonialist myth of the man who marries the chief's daughter and thereby legitimates European domination over the tribe. The marriage of Pocahontas and John Rolfe is probably the most famous of these myths, but the pattern repeats in many fictional works, including French ones such as the Abbé Prevost's *Cleveland*.[9] Le Page du Pratz is denied this role because Natchez political structure, although monarchical, is not patriarchal, and the alliance would not accord him chiefly status. He would not become Grand Soleil, although his mixed-blood son might. The Grande Soleille and her daughter therefore cannot be passive objects of a sexual exchange; they are more like mimetic rivals of Le Page du Pratz. If Le Page had married the young Soleille and she had died soon thereafter, he might have preserved his life in defiance of Natchez custom, but he could not have claimed any political power over the tribe.[10]

"Cette Sanglante Tragédie": The Death of Serpent Piqué

The full complexity of the kinship, exogamy, and caste systems among the Natchez was elucidated only by Le Page du Pratz and Dumont.[11] The custom of retainer death, however, was much more obvious and more spectacular and took a central place in the relations of the earliest French visitors to Natchez. About a year prior to Iberville's arrival in 1700, lightning struck the temple of the Taensa tribe, neighbors and close relatives of the Natchez. Horrified villagers threw four or five infants into the fire to appease the forces that had destroyed their sacred building (Iberville 129; Pénicaut 29; du

Ru 41). Father Jacques Gravier reports that the "old man who was [the temple's] Guardian said that the spirit was angry, because no one had been killed in it at the death of the last chief, and that he must be appeased. There were 5 women Cruel enough to throw their Children into the fire, in full view of the french [the missionary de Montigny, no relation to Dumont] who related this to me" (Thwaites 65:137). These reports emphasize the propitiatory, stereotypically barbaric aspect of the human sacrifice, as if it were dedicated to an evil spirit rather than to the soul of the deceased Sun. But Iberville's missionary chaplain, du Ru, also wrote of how the current Sun was gravely ill at the time, stating, "There are so many victims awaiting their fate as soon as he expires. I was distressed and hastened to the village to see him, to persuade him to arrange that he, alone, shall die. I did find him at home. . . . His chief wife, who will rule after him, received me. I presented my arguments to her as well as I could and she promised that no one would be killed when the Ouachilla dies" (37–38). Iberville captures the conflicting motives inherent in retainer death: "At the death of their chief, they observed the custom of killing fifteen or twenty men or women to accompany him, they say, into the other world and serve him. According to what they say, many are enraptured to be of that number. I have strong doubts about that" (129). In André Pénicaut's narrative of a subsequent journey to Natchez with Iberville, "The Grand Noble Female Chief died and we witnessed the funeral ceremonies, which were indeed the most horrifying tragedy that could be seen" (92). Her Stinkard husband was strangled, followed by fourteen infants and young children.

But by far the most important episode of mortuary sacrifice occurred during the first five days of June 1725, following the death of Obalalkabiche, or Serpent Piqué, the head war chief of the Grand Village of the Natchez and the brother of the Grand Soleil. Le Page du Pratz describes Serpent Piqué (whose name translates as "Tattooed Serpent") as "my particular friend and the friend of all the French" (Histoire 3:25). He had aided the French by negotiating an end to a violent clash with the colonizers in 1723, smoking the calumet with Le Page (according to his account, 1:177) and ending a series of attacks by a hostile faction centered in Pomme (Apple) Village. "He was like a Frenchman," a Natchez woman named La Glorieuse said of Serpent Piqué (Dumont, Mémoires historiques 1:215); at the very least, he secured the alliance between French and Natchez.[12]

Because the two published accounts of the death of Serpent Piqué both appeared in the 1750s, at which time the name "Natchez" was associated with the massacre and the failed promise of the concessions and settlements there, the episode needs to be read as a counterpoint to the story of the uprising. Le Page du Pratz alludes to the 1729 events as he introduces the episode by describing the tribe's tombs and funeral customs, "which I am going to relate to satisfy the curiosity of the reader, and on account of the part which I had and the loss which the entire French post, which was near by, has suffered" (Histoire 3:25; Swanton 143–44). His ethnography of the "pompes funèbres" of the Natchez also serves as an elegy for the French and their fort, which the tribe destroyed four years later. For his part, Dumont, who expressed much less sympathy toward the Natchez, wrote that the commandant Brontin feared the Indians might use the funeral as an opportunity to catch the French off guard and strangle them ("prendre les François d'un coup de filet," Mémoires historiques 1:229).[13]

In a more general sense, the "sanglante tragédie" of the sacrificial victims of Serpent Piqué and the epic tragedy of the Natchez Massacre as told by Le Page du Pratz, Dumont, and Chateaubriand form a counterpoint to each other insofar as they illustrate contrasting meanings of nobility and of sacrifice. The heroes of tragedy must be of noble status, wrote Aristotle, and in many stage tragedies of this period, from Addison's Cato to Behn and Sheridan's Oroonoko and Stone's Metamora, heroic individuals from among the colonized racial Other demonstrated nobility by dramatically dying in defense of honor and nation, often in uprisings against the colonizers. The virtuous stoicism that enabled Juba or Ponteach or Xicoténcatl to place military values of duty and nation over sentimental ties of love and family extended the concept of nobility to the "primitives" yet entailed the death of the heroes and of people they led. These subaltern peoples had republican virtues but were usually outnumbered by the opposition; moreover, their renunciation of love prevented the (re)production of the next generation, a problem that both figuratively and practically led to their decline.

The Natchez, however, were not a people of republican government, and the story of their uprising therefore better exposes some of the imperialist ideology that lies behind the republican tragedies. The prerogative of nobility is, in real life, not so often to die honorably as to force others to die on one's behalf. Masses of common soldiers die in battles ordered by a noble leader or officers. And among the Natchez, the Suns also exercised their power to order the death of Stinkards through mortuary sacrifice. Before 1729, while the Natchez of the Grand Village were still close allies of the French, their hierarchical society and custom of retainer death could be seen as evidence of their tractability and subordination. Their Stinkard subjects were willing to give their lives in sacrifice for their leaders not just in war but in mourning. The death of Serpent Piqué plays out like a grotesque parody of the tragedies of republican virtue, and the French who witness it are both inside and outside the proscenium arch. They hold the power to spare Natchez lives or to allow them to perish. Le Page du Pratz and other Frenchmen assumed the prerogatives of a rank above the status of the Suns. The events of 1729 destroyed this fantasy, and the figure of the loyal Serpent Piqué was replaced by that of a mysterious and threatening conspiratorial mastermind.

Le Page du Pratz's friend and informant, the Temple Guardian, came to him in the spring of 1725 to report that "the Tattooed Serpent was very ill, and that if this Sun died, all the Nation, or nearly so, would die also, because the Grand Soleil, brother of the ill one, would kill himself; that they were so close that they had each promised not to survive the other" (Histoire 3:28). Like two lovers in a romance or a tragedy, the death of one will cause the other to die of grief. The Grand Soleil, Yakstalchil, was the elder brother of Serpent Piqué, and both were Suns by virtue of the noble status of their mother, the Femme Blanche and Grande Soleille.[14] As a Sun, Yakstalchil was not obliged to commit suicide, but he evidently wished to do so out of grief and respect for his brother. The Grand Soleil's elegiac self-sacrifice suggests at once nobility and servility. A related contradiction arises in the French response. Le Page du Pratz decides that "the French chiefs would attempt to see to the preservation" of the sacrifice victims but that "in effect, although I loved them, as one has to love men of integrity who do no harm for as long as they are able, we could not flatter ourselves that we could abolish an ancient custom of this Nation" (2:29). Will Le Page express his love by sacrificing his friend or by saving him? Are we reading a republican tragedy or a bourgeois melodrama? His dilemma smacks of both "white man's burden" and a postmodern ethnographer's self-consciousness. Having rejected the marriage that would have secured him a kinship relation to the Grand Soleil but also branded him a Stinkard, he now asserts his superiority over the Grand Soleil and decides to save his life.

Heeding the French requests, Yakstalchil makes an initial promise not to commit suicide, but Le Page disbelieves him and orders a French interpreter, Louis Sorel, to make sure Yakstalchil is watched at all times. Yakstalchil's loués (servants) express their thanks to Le Page: their lives, of course, hinge on that of their master, and "there was not one of them who wished to die" (Histoire 3:38). In a climactic scene, Le Page takes a gun from the suicidal Grand Soleil and gives it to the French commandant, Broutin, who douses the gunpowder with water. Then, in the following chapter and in Dumont's account, are two versions of a long speech by the favorite wife of the Grand

Soleil proclaiming the tribe's thanks, trust, and friendship for the French. She is, of course, a Stinkard, but Le Page du Pratz avoids using that term and emphasizes her nobility: "I have reported these speeches and the bearing of this favorite, who could only be of the common people, being the wife of a Sun, in order to show the skill with which she preserved the friendship of the French for her children, how much intelligence this Nation has [combien cette Nation a d'esprit]" (3:52). The word "esprit" has a wide meaning, including "spirit" as well as "intelligence," but Le Page du Pratz shifts its signification from noble class status and the courage of self-sacrifice, the domain of tragedy, to self-preservation and gratitude toward her colonial saviors, the domain of melodrama. Her sense of self-preservation undercuts the legitimacy of the Natchez caste system and implies that the Frenchmen deserve to supplant the male Natchez leaders. However, readers of Histoire de la Louisiane would have recalled the earlier scene between du Pratz and the Grande Soleille and recognized the sexual overtones in this one. Because the two Suns in question are male, the spouses forced to sacrifice themselves are female, and their gratitude toward the French hints at the bonds of romantic love that in accounts of Indian uprisings such as Pontiac's siege of Detroit betray the conspiracies to the enemy colonizers.

And in fact the only extant source for an indigenous Natchez tribal history of their uprising suggests that sexual alliances between French men and Natchez women were precisely what led both parties toward the fatal clash. George Stiggins, a special agent of the Creek tribe to the United States in the years leading up to their removal to Oklahoma, penned during the 1830s "A Historical Narration of the Genealogy, Traditions and Downfall of the Ispo-caga or Creek Tribe of Indians, Written by One of the Tribe."[15] A few pages in the opening ethnographic section tell of how Natchez refugees were incorporated into the Aubihka branch of the Creeks living in the Talladega Valley of modern Alabama. Stiggins was born at Talladega in 1788, the son of a Scots-Virginian trader, Joseph Stiggins, and a Natchez woman known to Anglophones as Nancy Grey. By the matrilineal kinship systems of both the Creek and Natchez, George Stiggins was fully recognized as a tribal member, and according to an account his son gave to nineteenth-century Alabama scholar William Wyman, Stiggins was even offered the title of Grand Soleil of the remnant Natchez nation (Wyman 18). His account of the 1729 revolt makes no mention of any individual leaders among the French or the Natchez but does describe a process of mutual sexual complicity. After the initial French scouts choose the site for what must be Fort Rosalie, "much against the will of the Indians," they "disguised their chagrin and seemingly were careless and not opposed to the unwelcome encroachment of their unwelcome visitants and neighbors" (Stiggins, "Creek Nativism" 26). Then

the French by their gallantry, pursued the destructive course said to have
been in Sodom of olden times, as tho' danger was not imbruing, nor destruction awfully pending over their ill fated heads[. T]hey made free with
the men and married their women[. T]hey were tolerated in their love to
their women with seeming good will by the natives for they [the Indians]
saw the advantage that would ultimately result through [the French] blind
devotion to love, for it would make them unsuspicious and unguarded
against a design they had in contemplation to effect through that means,
as was expected their lewd practices soon caused a relaxation in their vigi-
lance . . . for they frequented the town at night in a careless manner and
unguardedly admitted the women into the fortress at night. (26)

Stiggins describes the traditional Natchez order as "monarchial. . . . The
throne was hereditary and the King was supreme head of the tribe" (25). The
arrival of the French did not so much disrupt this order as hasten an inevitable decline, for "all earthly institutions tho' made for lasting happiness for
ages, are delusive and visionary" (26). Given this declension, along with the
Frenchmen's "blind devotion to love," the Natchez Massacre was easily
emplotted, as "the Indian men concerted a plan with their women as though
without design for the women to make their appointments with the French
to be and stay within the fortress on such a night. . . . Instead of the expected
women, the fortress was entered by men in disguise and armed who on
entrance instantly fell to work and exterminated the whole garrison of men"
(26–27). Since Stiggins's story includes no names or dates, it neither cor-
roborates nor contradicts the French accounts. But the emphasis on sexuality is consistent with the French versions. Whereas Le Page du Pratz only
once mentions his Chitimacha mate and writes coyly of his invitation to
marry into the Natchez Sun caste and although, as we will see, he and others
only insinuate that the cross-racial love affairs of the French commandant
and the Natchez Grande Soleille may have precipitated the massacre, Stiggins paints with a broad brush the tragic moral flaw of miscegenation—even
though it also represented his family.

Le Page du Pratz's best hint at the extent of the sexual contacts between
the Natchez and the French comes in the context of his account of the death
of Serpent Piqué. Another woman among the intended victims of mortuary
sacrifice is a Noble and close friend of Serpent Piqué's: "The French called
her La Glorieuse, because of her majestic bearing and her proud air and
because she was intimate only with distinguished Frenchmen. I regretted
her so much the more that, possessing a deep knowledge of simples [herbal
remedies], she had saved the lives of many of our sick, and I myself had
drawn good lessons from her" (Histoire 3:36–37). Dumont is less coy about

the nature of her medical knowledge: she "was in any case a very skilled surgeon, above all for venereal diseases; several of our Frenchmen owed to her their lives" (*Mémoires historiques* 1:214).[16] The French Louisianans evidently feel compelled to return her favors by saving her life, but in each case the deadly threat originates among the Indians. Neither Le Page nor Dumont acknowledges the Frenchmen's responsibility for getting infected, and the episode ideologically occludes or compensates for the fact that the French set out to exterminate the tribe in the 1730s.

The melodrama of the sacrificial victims further crystallizes in an anecdote about a male victim called Taotal by Dumont and Ette-Actal by Le Page. Swanton's Natchez-language informant translated the latter term as "skin eater" (144). The man marries a female Sun, who dies soon thereafter. Rather than give up his life in a mortuary sacrifice, he runs away to New Orleans, where Governor Bienville shelters him among his slaves and employs him as a hunter. The Natchez assure Bienville that the exile's death sentence no longer applies after the other sacrifices to his late wife are completed, but after Bienville returns to France, the Grand Soleil declares that Taotal must pay his debt to Serpent Piqué and the royal blood and orders thirty warriors to apprehend the fugitive and bring him back to Natchez (Dumont, *Mémoires historiques* 1:216). His life is finally spared only by the intervention of two women, "who, being extremely aged and wearied of life, offered themselves to pay his debt" (Le Page, *Histoire* 3:48–49), a substitution that lifts Ette-Actal out of the Stinkard caste into the Honoreds, where he will be immune from mortuary sacrifice.[17]

But when he is first brought back to Natchez, his life is still very much in danger. The favorite wife of the Grand Soleil confronts Ette-Actal as he stands before the assembled sacrificial victims. The terms she uses in her speech juxtapose the values of nobility and sacrifice, honor and sympathy, and capture semantically the problems both of balancing between these ethical imperatives and of translating them between native and European cultures.

> Quoi, tu pleures, lui dit-elle? est-ce que tu n'es pas Guerrier? Sans doute je le suis, répondit-il. *Ta vie t'est donc de valeur*, répartit cette femme; & tu en es ingrat? Apparemment, répliqua-t-il; ma vie m'est de valeur: je suis encore jeune, je n'ai point d'enfans; il est bon que je marche encore sur la terre. (Dumont, *Mémoires historiques* 1:216–17)

> "What, you cry?" she said. "Are you not a warrior?" "Without a doubt I am," he replied. "*Your life is therefore of value to you*," the woman replied, "and you are an ingrate." "Clearly," he replied, "my life is of value to me. I am still young, I have no children, it is good that I should still walk upon the earth."

Dumont italicizes the key phrase, which I have translated literally and which Swanton rendered as "Life is then dear to you" (151–52). The line employs a Natchez idiom that Dumont defines some pages earlier, the first time it appears in his text. There he tells how on 2 June, the day after Serpent Piqué's death, he returned from a scene of tears and lamentations among the Natchez mourners to Monsieur Brontin (often spelled "Broutin" in other sources), commandant at Fort Rosalie and director of the concession at White Earth Village, and found there the war chief of the Tioux, another neighboring tribe. This chief, speaking in the Mobilien jargon, explained that the Grand Soleil "would not cry at all, but would kill himself. . . . His women will die along with a great number of warriors, and this is of great value [& *cela est beaucoup de valeur*]" (*Mémoires historiques* 1:213). A note defines the term "valeur": "C'est-à-dire, *c'est dommage* [That is to say, 'It's a shame' or 'It's too bad']." Le Page du Pratz also used the term when the favorite wife of the Grand Soleil says, "You very much miss your husband; it is true that his death is of great value (very unfortunate) [bien de valeur (bien fâcheuse)] as much for the French as for our Nation" (*Histoire* 3:37).[18]

Those who willingly sacrificed their lives might have regarded life as too grievous to continue to live it, whereas those whose caste status would rise by virtue of the death of a relative might regard life as of "great value" to them. For Taotal, who does not want to sacrifice himself, the ambiguous—even oxymoronic—status of "de valeur" captures the incommensurability of his life's value to himself (in living), weighed against its sacrificial value (in dying) to the Suns, to his relatives, and to the tribe as a whole. But in the lines where the two colonial historians define the term, its ambiguity lies in the fact that the value of Natchez life to the Natchez is not commensurable with its value to the French in spite of both authors' humanitarian (or melodramatic) appeals to justify and applaud the French intervention to save the life of the Grand Soleil and his retainers. The favorite wife's line, "of great value (very unfortunate) as much for the French as for our Nation," uses a parallel construction but employs opposite meanings for the same term with respect to the two nations, meanings that reverse themselves depending on one's perspective. Therefore, Le Page had to provide the gloss in parentheses. Similarly, in the scene where the Grand Soleil is threatening to kill himself, an unnamed Frenchman (not identified as Le Page) seizes the gun to stop him, and Dumont accuses Brontin of taking the powder and flint not to keep the man from killing himself but for the mere exchange value of the powder. The Frenchman responds, "Oh chief, listen to me! The commodities are of no value to the Frenchman, you alone are of value to him" (*Mémoires historiques* 1:231). Since the final words mean to the French that the Sun is a valued ally but to the Natchez that the Sun will have to die to honor his brother, the French ambivalence about whether Natchez ritual suicide serves their interests is again expressed in this single word. This is colonial ambivalence at its most obvious yet most unstable. Its poles are defined not only in the subject positions of French and Natchez and their separate interests but in the language they use to communicate with each other, a language that is itself indeterminate—French, Mobilien, or Natchez.

In Le Page du Pratz, this ambivalence emerges powerfully in two pages at the end of the episode that express his bad faith and self-aggrandizing instincts and connect once again the custom of mortuary sacrifice to the epochal Natchez Massacre: "But it was not without some hesitation that we put ourselves to this task with regard to the Grand Soleil, who in his despair would have incited a frightful massacre. Because although religion and humanity determined first of all the course that we took, politics opposed to it some difficulties which were not to be ignored" (Histoire 3:58). These "politics" were of two kinds. On one level, recalling the conflict of 1723 and his role in ending it, Le Page du Pratz claims that only his friendship with these two chiefs and the rule of the chiefs over the masses prevented the simmering resentment of the Natchez from boiling over into a revolt or "massacre" in 1725. The tribe could well have attacked and killed the French to prevent the French from preventing the Natchez from killing themselves, and Le Page therefore was risking his safety to save the Natchez and to save the French. On another level, from the post-1729 perspective, politics dictated that mortuary sacrifice was good for the French: "Therefore we risked nothing. We gained even more in allowing this Nation, if not to destroy itself, at least to considerably weaken itself, by this barbaric custom. The more victims, the fewer enemies" (3:59). Dumont also expressed this view in his "Poème." In the fourth canto, he introduces a brief ethnographic section describing the custom of mortuary sacrifice.

If, since the French had been among the Indians
They had permitted them to follow their old ways
We would not have been forced, perhaps
To destroy all of them, our cruel friends
I refer to the Natchez, for it was their custom,
When a chief died by accident or illness,
His wife and retainers all perished with him
To go wait upon him in the dark beyond. (407–8)

The death of Serpent Piqué constitutes the "sacrificial crisis" of the brief history of Natchez-French interaction, although at the same time, the incident revises some of the metaphysical and ethnocentric weak points of

Girard's seminal theory. Le Page du Pratz offers himself as a "surrogate victim" and ends the primitive practice of human sacrifice. The "monstrous double" of the deceased Grand Soleil is not so much his Stinkard wife (who

is but one among many designated victims) as Le Page du Pratz, who had previously been invited to become the husband of a female Sun, who claims a leadership role in the settlement, and who takes on himself the morbid weight of the Grand Soleil's decision about ending his life. As the Grand Soleil holds a rifle (acquired, of course, from the French), ready to shoot himself, in Le Page du Pratz's account, "I approached the Grand Soleil and extended my hand in the customary manner, so that he might drop the gun and give me his" (Histoire 3:39) in a symbolic passing of the burden of sacrifice. He contends that when he arrived at the tense scene, the "cabin was filled with Suns, Nobles, and Honoreds who were all trembling; our arrival reassured them and made them relax" (3:39). The colonist provides the catharsis that previously only human sacrifice could secure; he civilizes the tribe by taking from the pagan spirits the responsibility for its welfare. Dumont's version does not give Le Page du Pratz the central role and makes the whole scene much more sordid by describing the Grand Soleil as being drunk and whining, "Am I not a chief, am I therefore a Stinkard?" (Mémoires historiques 1:230). But Dumont also lends the scene a hint of Christian symbolism in lines spoken by the wife of Serpent Piqué, who says to the French, "Come dine with me; I have never dined with the French, and now that I am about to go away for ever, let us eat together" (1:225). The allusion to the Last Supper is at once a travesty of Girard's formulation and deeply respectful of it. The reference suggests that the tension was merely ethnographic, that the ritual was merely that—a ritual—and in its representation to French readers will be seen in the way that the favorite wife and the Grande Soleille came to understand it, as absurd and barbaric. Mortuary sacrifice comes to signify not the nobility of the Natchez or their fitness for tragedy but the weakness of nobles such as the Grand Soleil and La Glorieuse, who are ready to kill themselves out of servile respect for Serpent Piqué. Ultimately, on the day of Serpent Piqué's burial, eight of his retainers are killed, including La Glorieuse, and five other lives are offered in executions that raise their relatives and their executioners to the status of Honoreds. Le Page du Pratz includes a crude illustration of the mortuary sacrifice (figure 6.1). The French did prevent the death of the Grand Soleil and thereby postponed the ascendance of the Grand Soleil in waiting, St. Cosme, who may have been a leader of the 1729 revolt, as we shall see.[19]

Two twentieth-century works of literature, both by Nobel laureates, have also dramatized the ritual of retainer sacrifice in ways that connect the customs of the Natchez to those of Africans. Wole Soyinka's tragedy, Death

FIGURE 6.1. Death and procession of Serpent Piqué.
From Antoine-Simon Le Page du Pratz, *Histoire de la Louisiane* (1758).

and the *King's Horseman*, set in Nigeria in the 1940s, follows nearly the same plot as Le Page du Pratz's episode but is told from the perspective of the colonized rather than the colonizers. Elesin, the king's horseman, is obliged to commit suicide upon the death of his master. Simon Pilkings, the British colonial district officer, expresses some of the same callous ambivalence as Le Page du Pratz does in his postscript to the death of Serpent Piqué. Pilkings's wife, Jane, says, "You know this business has to be stopped, Simon. And you are the only man who can do it." Simon replies, "I don't have to stop anything. If they want to throw themselves off the top of a cliff or poison themselves for the sake of some barbaric custom what is that to me?" (31). After further pressure from his wife, however, Simon orders his native police sergeant, Amusa, to prevent the sacrifice by arresting Elesin and imprisoning him in the basement of the colonial residency, a space formerly used as a holding pen for slaves awaiting the Middle Passage. In the final scene, Elesin commits suicide. In Soyinka's Yoruba setting, the dignity of classical tragedy finds modern exemplars in Elesin and his son, Olunde, who concisely picks apart the Europeans' ideological blindness and bad faith. He points out how the English honor the sacrifices of soldiers during World War II (an instance of the prerogative of a noble elite to force the sacrifice of the lower castes) but fail to see the value of his father's sacrifice on behalf of his leader (an instance of the tragic self-sacrifice a nobleman imposes on himself). Soyinka imbues his Yoruba heroes with all the dignity of characters in Sophocles and, like Girard, implies that the social origins of tragedy are found not in a "Western tradition" leading to modern Europe but in "primitive" cultures, in this case in Africa. However, Soyinka's cross-cultural application of Greek tragedy, his suggestion that this most elevated of literary genres is not peculiar to the Greeks but instead is common to many cultures, is possible only because of the patrilineal, endogamous, and patriarchal organization of the Yoruba society it depicts. Only one victim, Elesin, is required, and his son will inherit his status as horseman, an office accorded great respect. Among the Natchez the sacrificial victims are Stinkards, and many are sacrificed in the wake of one Sun. Elesin and Olunde stoically perform noble virtue and suppress sentimentality, a role utterly consistent with traditions of European tragedy. Simon Pilkings clearly lacks these virtues, so in any implied confrontation between African and European ethics and virtues the African emerges as superior. There is no role in the play for such a character as Taotal, not so much because of Soyinka's cultural sympathies as because unlike Olunde, Taotal was a Stinkard spouse of a Sun with an ambivalent investment in the caste system. Dumont writes of another such resistant victim, an old woman who lashes out at Serpent Piqué, calling him a "Chief Stinkard" and claiming that "seven months ago I killed the son of the great chief with a medicine that I gave him" (*Mémoires historiques* 1:224). The French historians may share the bad faith and ill motives of Simon Pilkings, but unlike Soyinka, they also dramatize the tension not just between two cultures but between two castes and two definitions of nobility and of sacrifice.

No stage tragedy was written about the 1729 uprising, but the earliest extant work of theater written and performed by French Louisianans was a tragedy based on a stoic scene of sacrifice involving Indian chiefs. *La Fête du Petit-Blé; ou, L'Héroisme de Poucha-Houmma* (The festival of the young corn; or, The heroism of Poucha-Houmma) premiered on 21 February 1809 at the Theatre de la Rue St. Pierre in New Orleans and was published by subscription in 1814. The playwright was Paul Louis Le Blanc de Villeneufve, a wealthy planter who may have acted in his play (which apparently was performed only that one night) and who in a surviving portrait is shown in full Indian regalia with a tomahawk in hand. He adapted the plot of his tragedy from an episode in Jean-Bernard Bossu's 1768 *Nouveaux Voyages en Louisiane*.[20] A man of the Choctaw nation (spelled "Chactas" in French), close allies of the French, insults the Colapissa tribe by calling them "the dogs of the French," and Tichou Mingo, the son of the Colapissa chief, shoots the Choctaw dead. The Choctaw go to the French commandant at the German coast just upstream of New Orleans and demand that he order the Colapissa to deliver the assailant's head. Tichou Mingo seeks the protection of the French governor, Vaudreuil, but he has to yield to the demands of the Choctaw, the most powerful tribe allied with the French. In Bossu's text, Tichou Mingo's brief stoic speech insists that he does not fear death but worries for his family and implores the French to look after them. Then his father stands up, and in a speech that begins, "C'est de valeur que mon fils meurt [It is of value that my son dies]" offers himself as a sacrificial substitute for his son. Bossu concludes that "all the Frenchmen who witnessed this tragedy were touched to the point of tears, in admiration for the heroic confidence of this venerable elder," comparing him to a Roman orator (105). In a preface, Le Blanc de Villeneufve claims to have arrived in Louisiana just a few days prior to this event, which must have been in 1752, and to have heard Vaudreuil's interpreter bring the first news of it. However, the author changes the tribe in question from the Colapissa to the Houma, another small nation close to New Orleans, whom he claimed were descendants of the Natchez, and he spins out the events into five rather tedious acts of stoic soliloquies by Poucha-Houmma and his son, Cala-be. Le Blanc also claims to have learned the Choctaw language and to have spoken with Cala-be about his father's brave sacrifice. The author sought to dignify the New Orleans theater with an authentic and local instance of the Indian tragic hero and to appropriate that heroism for the French colonial past.

Le Blanc de Villeneufve is a very obscure footnote to southern literary history, but the dramatic and tragic nature of mortuary sacrifice also motivated William Faulkner to write a short story, "Red Leaves," inspired by Natchez retainer sacrifice. Although the story never mentions the Natchez and is set around 1800, the Mississippi author must have been familiar with legends about the tribe, and he satirically diagnoses the process of mimicry between Indians and the French creole planter "nobility." The story opens with two Indians, Three Basket and Louis Berry, walking through a plantation's empty slave quarters and talking about the recent death of "The Man." This refers to Issetibbeha, the chief of an unnamed tribe and the plantation's patriarch. The Man's father was Doom, an anglicized version of "du homme" (the man). Doom had won a large sum of money gambling in New Orleans and married the beautiful young daughter of a Caribbean planter. Doom "had been born merely a subchief, a Mingo, one of three children on the mother's side of the family" (317), but "under the tutelage of his patron [a French creole named Chevalier Soeur Blonde de Vitry], passes himself off as the chief, the Man, the hereditary owner of that land which belonged to the male side of the family" (317–18). Doom and his son slowly adapt to the plantation economy, clearing their land, raising Negro slaves and selling them to buy more land. At Doom's death, the land had passed to Issetibbeha, his son, and "though the title of Man rested with him, there was a hierarchy of cousins and uncles who ruled the clan" (319), implying that others of the tribe refused to accept the patrilineal descent customary in the Old South, just as the Natchez would have refused to accept that descent. Issetibbeha takes to wife "a comely girl . . . working in her shift in a melon patch"—evidently a black slave—and produces an heir, Moketubbe, who, like the Natchez Sun, is carried around in a litter, although in his case this is necessitated by his great obesity. At Issetibbeha's death, Moketubbe orders the death of his father's horse, his dog, and one of his slaves. In the fourth of the story's six sections, Faulkner switches the narrative to the perspective of this sacrificial victim, the slave who flees into a swamp and hides for several days until he is bitten by a water moccasin and forced to surrender.

Faulkner thus adapts the native custom of retainer death to the southern plantation slave economy. The story parodies the planters' aristocratic pretensions much as the representation of Natchez class system made an implicit parody of French society. Although in 1725 the Natchez loués (spelled "allouez" by Charlevoix and by some ethnologists) were of course separated from the Suns only by caste, not by race, in Faulkner's story African slaves become both the victims of mortuary sacrifice and, consistent with their status as "stinkards" at the bottom of the caste system, eligible mates for the Man (or Sun). And as we know that many slaves escaped and lived with local tribes, it is quite likely that the custom of exogamy among the Natchez nobility encouraged the intermarriage of Native and African Americans. In the uprising, the Natchez spared the lives of French women and children and

BUREAU OF AMERICAN ETHNOLOGY   BULLETIN 43 PLATE 8

FIGURE 6.2. Photograph of Wat Sam, one of the last speakers of the Natchez language. From John R. Swanton, *Indian Tribes of the Lower Mississippi Valley* (1911).

black slaves, holding them as hostages. During the siege in early 1730, surviving women and children escaped or were ransomed to the French, but some of the slaves remained and fought with the Natchez. "The blacks' role was decisive in preventing the total defeat of the Natchez," writes Gwendolyn Midlo Hall (102). She calls Louisiana "a colony of deserters" (131) and recognizes the common fate of the blacks and the Indians. After the massacre, more than two hundred Natchez were captured and shipped as slaves to Hispaniola (Barnett 36), while the more fortunate fled to refuge among the Chickasaw, Creek, and Cherokee tribes, much as some escaped slaves, or maroons, fled to join native peoples in the South. The mixture of Natchez and Africans across nearly three centuries is difficult to trace, but a powerful image of it arises in the person of Wat Sam, one of John R. Swanton's informants for his study of the Natchez history and language and tragically the last living speaker of that language before his death in 1965 (figure 6.2). Wat Sam appears in two photos in *Indian Tribes of the Lower Mississippi Valley*, a thin, dark-skinned man with a dark moustache, holding a bow and arrow. American observers would immediately identify him as black.

Thomas N. Ingersoll cites the Natchez Massacre as the only time in southern history that blacks and Indians united against the colonists. This may be inaccurate, but it reflects the anxiety that the revolt aroused among the French, who began to perceive conspiracy in both races. Such suspicions spread quickly after the shocking news of the massacre arrived in New Orleans. Jadart de Beauchamp, the city's adjutant major, wrote in a letter to Minister Jérôme Phélypeaux Maurepas on 5 November 1731, "It seems that everything is conspiring for the destruction of the country. . . . We were menaced not only by the Indians; the negroes had plotted at New Orleans to massacre all the French who are settled on the river. The plot was to be executed on the twenty-fourth of June" (Rowland, Sanders, and Galloway 4:81–82). In volume 3, chapter 17, immediately following his narrative of the Natchez uprising, Le Page du Pratz tells of this "Conspiracy of the Negroes against the French." He went with a friendly slave to the "Camp des Nègres" and hid there during the night, listening to the plans for the revolt, which was to involve all the tribes along the Mississippi and had been inspired by the blacks who had fought with the Natchez for a year and a half following the uprising. They were to kill all the French and take on their positions of authority; one woman was to become "Madame Périer." The leader of the conspiracy was a Bambara named Samba who "had attacked Fort d'Arguin of the French" in Africa before negotiating a surrender with Antoine-Alexis Périer de Salvert, Governor Périer's brother, who had been in Senegal and later was sent to Louisiana with extra troops following the Natchez uprising. Samba was punished by being shipped to America as a slave (Giraud 419; Gwendolyn Hall 107–10). According to Le Page du Pratz's account, he organized an elaborate, panoptic scheme for arresting all eight conspirators without letting any of them suspect the fate of the others. It went off flawlessly. The conspirators were imprisoned and tortured, but none revealed any accomplices, and French authorities were reluctant to seize more slaves. Hall acknowledges that Le Page du Pratz's account of the foiled revolt "is a bit flattering to him and his role in uncovering it" and that other documents do not mention him, but she nonetheless follows it as "not too much less authentic" than the official reports (107). Hall documents how much French officials feared an alliance between the Africans and the Indians and tried hard to persuade their Indian allies to deliver up any and all escaped slaves who took refuge among the tribes. Surely it is significant that Le Page put his story of the 1731 slave conspiracy immediately after his much longer narrative of the Natchez uprising and gave himself a key role in negotiations and espionage among both groups. After he is captured, Samba says, in creole, "Ah! M. le Page le diable li sabai tout [Monsieur Le Page is a devil who knows everything]" (Histoire 3:317). And as we will examine in greater detail in the next chapter, the historiographic "plotting" of slave rebellions follows some of the same patterns as the accounts of Indian rebellions.

When Pierre Le Moyne d'Iberville, the hero of France's battles with the English for control of Hudson's Bay, founded French Louisiana in 1699, the second place that he chose to build a fort was on an island at the mouth of Mobile Bay. In his journals, he wrote, "I am naming [the island] Massacre because we found on it, at the southwest end, a spot where more than sixty men or women had been slain. . . . As none of these have yet rotted, it appears that this occurred no more than three or four years ago" (38). The fort on this island remained an important post until the founding of New Orleans in 1718, but in 1711 it was renamed Ile Dauphine by Bienville, Iberville's younger brother and the most prominent leader of Louisiana in its first half century. Bienville wrote that he and others "consider the name of Massacre as harsh" (qtd. in Iberville 38 n. 45). French Louisiana was thus founded next to an ossuary, "such a prodigious number of human skeletons that they formed a mountain" (Pénicaut 11), gathered by surviving relatives for mourning, much as the Natchez and other southeastern tribes preserved the bones of dead chiefs inside their temples, possibly following a large mortuary sacrifice. Pénicaut wrote, "This nation was called Mobila . . . a numerous nation who, being pursued and having withdrawn to this region, had almost all died here of sickness" (11; see also Dumont, "Poème" 291). Bienville tried to dispel the gothic haunting of the place by renaming it for his nation's young regents rather than after another nation's dead ancestors. La Dauphine was the title of the French royal princesses, daughters of the Kings Louis for whom the colony was named. But by the end of the century, that name too would be associated with a "massacre," the French Revolution. The word itself—as in Wounded Knee Massacre, Sand Creek Massacre, Jamestown Massacre, Natchez Massacre—is an unstable signifier, a noun sometimes paired with the name of the aggressors, sometimes with that of the victims. The island's name therefore begs the question: Would the French become the perpetrators or the victims? In truth they were both, for as in the other three "massacres," the Natchez uprising led to a French retaliatory campaign against the tribe that, though not especially successful, did drive the tribe away from its homeland at the site of the city that now bears its name.

In December 1729, when the news of the massacre reached New Orleans, panic seized the colony. Although Natchez was located more than a hundred miles north, one-tenth of the entire colony's white population had been killed there (Gwendolyn Hall 8). Governor Périer's initial response, all too typical of the treatment of native peoples in colonial history, was to take vengeance on a convenient, vulnerable, and innocent party: "At the first news that Mr. Périer received of this disaster and on learning that there was a general conspiracy of all the nations . . . this made him decide to send a force to destroy the Chaouachas, a nation of thirty men below New Orleans. He used for this purpose only the negroes of the Company. . . . He has not dared to use all the negro volunteers to destroy the other small nations on the banks of the river for fear of rendering these same negroes too bold and of inclining them perhaps to revolt after the example of those who joined the Natchez" (Périer to Marepas, 18 March 1730, in Rowland and Sanders 1:71). Périer as much as admitted that he ordered the killing for the purpose of intimidation and to assuage French fears of a biracial uprising. For this atrocious act, which might deserve the appellation "Chaouacha Massacre," the governor was chastised by the Paris ministry, and the incident no doubt represented one factor in his dismissal. Philibert Ory, the comptroller of finances in Paris, wrote in reply to Périer, "I absolutely cannot approve that upon a suspicion lightly conceived you were led to cause the destruction of the nation of the Chaouachas, which was composed of only thirty war-riors. . . . That is a thing which I absolutely cannot consent, for that is to act against all the rules of statecraft and humanity" (Rowland, Sanders, and Galloway 4:47–48). Ory also questioned Périer's claim of an Indian conspir-acy: "You give no proof at all of the general conspiracy that you assert was formed by all the nations at the solicitation of the English" (46). Périer also wrote back to Paris about a broad conspiracy behind the narrowly averted slave revolt of 1731, only to later admit that he had no solid evidence of such a conspiracy (Gwendolyn Hall 107). In reading Périer's correspondence, one quickly becomes convinced of his nefarious motives or at least his bureau-cratic instinct to cover his ass. He pleaded with the ministry to send more troops and boasted of the efficacy of his retaliations in the winter of 1730, notably the siege of the Natchez forts in February that was abandoned after most of the rebel Indians and Africans escaped across the Mississippi. He wrote that without his quick response, "the general conspiracy would have had its full effect" (Rowland, Sanders, and Galloway 4:31), virtually admit-ting that these effects were not evident. He also wrote that when he learned of the conspiracy from the first refugees to arrive in New Orleans on 2 De-cember, he "treated this conspiracy as a wild idea in order to reassure our colonists" (39). Périer doth protest too much and writes too self-consciously of his desire to protect his reputation. Early historians who studied the event, Jean Delanglez and Marc Villiers, believed that Périer invented the conspiracy (see Delanglez, "Natchez Massacre" 635; Villiers, introduction to Dumont, "Poème").

But Périer was a hero, a "César," in the estimation of Dumont, and his "Poème" and *Mémoires historiques* as well as Le Page du Pratz's *Histoire* all lay blame for provoking the Natchez uprising on the commandant at Fort Rosalie, Chépar.[21] When Chépar took over the post, he supplanted the authority of Dumont, who claimed that he "had commanded the post under the supervision of M. Brontin," the previous commandant (*Mémoires historiques* 2:127). Dumont had complained to Governor Périer of Chépar's injustices, and Chépar was called to New Orleans to answer the charges but was cleared and returned to Fort Rosalie. In the spring of 1729, Chépar summoned the Sun of the Natchez village of White Apple to demand that he give up lands along St. Catharine's Creek. Chépar claimed to have acted on orders from New Orleans, another clue that Périer might have been ultimately responsible: in any case, Chépar's plans resembled what other concessionaires had been doing under the Company of the West, planting tobacco and corn to "make a quick fortune" (2:128). The Sun replied that "it has been a very long time that our nation has been in possession of this village, and lived here, that the ashes of our ancestors have lain here, in the Temple that they had built" (2:131). The temple in each village was built atop a small mound, which many archaeologists believe is related to the Mississippian mound complexes of a thousand years earlier, and the temple held the bones (not ashes, as Dumont suggests here) of deceased chiefs (see Patricia Galloway 292). Despite showing much less sympathy for the Natchez than did Le Page, Dumont unequivocally condemned Chépar for greed and arrogance. Chépar ignored the protocol that the French had observed at Natchez to settle only on vacant land and even threatened to capture the Sun and send him "down the river" to New Orleans as a galley slave. The Sun finally agreed to remove his village after the harvest and to pay a tribute until that time, but he was already, according to our authors, plotting to make Chépar pay dearly.

The existence of a Natchez "terrorist" plot was necessary for the historical emplotment of the massacre for both political and literary reasons. If the uprising had been a spontaneous act by a Natchez mob, not only might it portend more such acts of resistance to the colony, but it would be impossible to know whom to blame. Likewise today, Euro-American leaders are eager to identify terrorist conspiracies and to demonize their leaders yet are highly reluctant to suppose the existence of a diffuse anti-imperial movement from which violent resistance might erupt without planning or warning. If the Natchez Massacre had been such a spontaneous act, neither (tragic) hubris nor (poetic) justice would be available. And our two authors give us both. In the midst of the uprising, the Natchez get their revenge on Chépar: "Regarding him as a dog, unworthy of being killed like a brave man, they summoned the chief Stinkard, who clobbered him with one blow of a club" (Dumont, *Mémoires historiques* 2:146). Chépar's hubris was having ignored warnings of the revolt. He had "put in irons seven colonists who had asked to assemble to forestall the disaster with which they were menaced" (Rowland and Sanders 1:62). Dumont added in his "Poème" that the previous night, Chépar had gone drinking with the Natchez and

> Demanded from the chief to spend the night with
> several Native girls; he was given them,
> and they slept together. (315)

The existence of a Natchez plot is again supported only by negative evidence—Chépar's foolish refusal to believe in it.

Dumont, motivated by his own grievances, gives us the most detail about Chépar, but only Le Page du Pratz quotes at length the speeches of the Natchez as they plan their response. As Le Page puts it, "This enterprise being of the greatest consequence, it demanded total secrecy, solid planning and careful politics" (Histoire 3:237). The Sun of the White Apple Village goes to the Grand Soleil, who convenes a meeting of vieillards (elders), and after six days they reach a consensus that the only solution is the total destruction of the French. The oldest rises and makes a speech that echoes those in Ponteach and in Metamora as well as the revivalism of the nativist prophets. He denounces Natchez dependence on "the wares of the French," which "debauch the young women, and taint the blood of the nation" (3:238). He likens dependence on the colonists to slavery: "The French . . . will whip us as they whip their slaves; have they not already done so to one of our young men, and is not death preferable to slavery?" (3:239). The first line may allude to intermarriage between the French and the royal blood of the Suns, while the second is not only a cliché of Indian and republican tragedies but recalls how in conflicts during 1722–23, the Natchez had surrendered up the dead body of Vieux Poil, a previous Sun of the Apple Village, who had been accused of killing a Frenchman.[22] After a pause, the vieillard goes on to lay out the plan for the uprising, as it was later reported in the correspondence of the French officials. The Natchez will on the appointed day carry the payment of corn to Chépar and then ask local Frenchman to borrow powder and shot to go hunting. A shot fired at the commandant's house will be the signal to attack.

The vieillard's speech fits closely the rhetoric of defiance to colonization by heroes of eighteenth-century drama and prose works but is unusual insofar as the man who delivers it makes no other appearance in the story. In this regard, it anticipates the "Adieu du Vieillard" in Denis Diderot's Supplément au voyage de Bougainville (1772), which also decries how Europeans have "infected our blood" in Tahiti (149).[23] This speech arouses Natchez defiance by reproaching their temerity as much as by appealing to their political self-interest. But the vieillard is neither the conspirator nor the military leader of the ensuing revolt. His role is closer to that of the nativist prophets such as Nemattenow or Tenskwatawa, who assisted Opechancanough and Tecumseh in planning major wars of resistance against colonization. But we never learn his name. The principles that justify the uprising are generalized by his anonymity, perhaps making his noble qualities more appealing to the contemporary audience. But the *vieillard* precludes any heroic Natchez leader who might articulate principles of liberty and independence with the full rhetorical and political power that would soon be immortalized by Indian tragic heroes such as Ponteach, Metamora, and Tecumseh. Likewise, in Chateaubriand's *Les Natchez* (419–20), it is not one of the three Natchez leaders who delivers a rousing speech to the assembled tribes but an unnamed shaman, "le jongleur des Natchez." Le Page du Pratz does however explain the leadership vacuum, which is linked to the Natchez's matrilinear kinship structures. Yakstalchil, the Grand Soleil whom du Pratz had saved from sacrifice in 1725, had died in 1728, and the "Grand Soleil then reigning was a young man without experience" (*Histoire* 3:242). The Sun of White Apple, one of the pro-English villages, had only local authority but apparently convinced the young Sun of the Grand Village to approve plans for an attack on Chépar and the French. Brontin, the previous commander of Fort Rosalie, had maintained good relations with Yakstalchil and presumably would not have dared to make the demands that Chépar had issued. Hence, in Le Page du Pratz's text, the most detailed account of the Natchez uprising, there is a Natchez chief behind the conspiracy, and he is possessed of tragic hubris. Yet his fatal flaw lies not in his heroic ambitions for freedom but rather in his lack of authority: "Being still young, they held him in contempt, and finally the only way to maintain his authority was to attack the French in the manner and with the precautions that the elders had plotted" (3:243). Among Indian tribes where "republican" or egalitarian social structures obtained—that is, among most of the native peoples of North America—leaders maintained their power through persuasion and charisma, and such a scenario would have been impossible. But because the Grand Soleil held a hereditary title atop a strictly hierarchical order, he misjudged his true influence, and this tragic flaw led to a different sort of plot than applied in the revolts of Metacom, Pontiac, or Tecumseh.

The conclusion of the *vieillard*'s speech introduces the most important trope in the emplotment of the Natchez Massacre, one that afforded Le Page, Dumont, and Chateaubriand the greatest potential for dramatizing and romanticizing the story of the uprising and that had important precursors in the history of Indian rebellions in North America: "After having communicated to several Nations the necessity of taking this violent action, we shall send to them each a packet of sticks, equal in number to our own, which will mark the number of days that are to come before the one on which all must attack at once. So as there may be no mistake, it is necessary to take each day one of the sticks from the packet, to break it and throw it away, and a wise man will be charged with this duty" (Le Page, Histoire 3:241).

As we will examine in more detail in the next chapter, the natives' use of tokens for counting the number of days until the planned attack has a long history in colonial America and reflects a belief in "savage innumeracy"—the supposed incapacity of primitive peoples to think abstractly or even to have words in their languages for numbers above ten. The absurdity of this preju-dice should be obvious. If the Natchez and their allies could count out the bundles of sticks, then they could certainly count the number of days the sticks represented. Le Petit, Charlevoix, and the correspondence of Périer and other officials all fail to mention the use of token sticks for planning the uprising. Dumont or Le Page may have in fact used this trope to explain why there was no coordinated uprising among many tribes. For this primitive method of representation had a tragic flaw, as Dumont explains in his poem:

> The chief of the Natchez, when he went to burn the stick
> Took with him to the temple his young Sun-in-waiting,
> Who, believing that his father found burning sticks amusing
> Threw some in himself, which his father failed to notice. (324)

In Le Petit's 1731 account, the Natchez "strike their blow sooner than they had agreed with the other confederate tribes" (Le Petit in Jesuit Relations 68:165)—two days early—because they wish to plunder some French supply canoes that are preparing to depart upstream. But the buchettes and their theft is a better-motivated plot, and Le Page du Pratz and Chateaubriand build on Dumont's version, replacing the mischievous youngster with romantic femmes fatales.

In Le Page's Histoire, the vieillard insists that none of the Natchez women be informed of the plan. The council of war likewise declares that "it was forbidden under pain of death to speak of what they had done," but the prohibition did not hold, for "it was nothing new, in this as in other parts of the world, to see subjects strive to penetrate the secrets of the court" (3:244). Given the importance of the female Suns in the Natchez royal "court," it is no surprise that the "female Suns (or Princesses) had alone in this nation a right to demand why they were kept in the dark in this affair" (3:244). The Grande Soleille, Bras Piqué, mother of the untested young Grand Soleil, perceives an uneasiness in her son and grills him about what is brewing. The dialogue that ensues, to which Le Page du Pratz devotes four pages, is the climax of his dramatization of the uprising.[24] She prevails on her son by first reminding him that in their matrilineal system, he owes his power to her:

"Are you not from my own loins? . . . Would you be Sun if you were not my son? Have you already forgotten that without my care you would have been dead a long time ago? Everyone tells you, and I do as well, that you are the son of a Frenchman, but my own blood is more dear to me than that of strangers. . . . Have you ever seen in our nation a son denounce his mother?" (3:247). Bras Piqué tells her son that his father was a Frenchman, and the Grand Soleil confirms it in his defensive reply: "Although they know that I am the son of a Frenchman, they do not defy me" (3:248). These lines offer a valuable clue to the identity of the unnamed and tragically weak young Grand Soleil. A document at the Bibliothèque Nationale in Paris, dated 1728, asserts that the Grand Soleil of the Natchez was the son of St. Cosme, a missionary sent to the Tamaroa tribe in Illinois in 1699, who went downstream to Natchez in 1703 and was killed by the Chitimachas in 1705 (Surrey 1:417; Pénicaut 70–72). The unknown author of this text was knowledgeable about the Natchez political structure: "When the son of M. de Saint Cosme came into the world he had 15 Suns ahead of him. They all died one after the other in the 24 years following, and then he became Great Sun in 1728." The document recounts an exchange between St. Cosme and the Grande Soleille over their religious beliefs in which she admits that mortuary sacrifice and the Natchez beliefs about an afterlife were simply a means of enforcing the obedience of the commoners, and "she wanted to extract from this missionary the same avowal with regard to the ceremonies and discourses that he held about his religion, which he did not wish to do."[25]

Although Le Page du Pratz does not identify the young regent by the name St. Cosme, it is possible that Le Page had heard the story or read this document. All the details of his text are consistent with it, and he alludes in a backhanded way to Bras Piqué's liaison: "I am persuaded the colony owes its preservation to the vexation of this woman rather than to any remains of affection she entertained for the French, as she was now far advanced in years, and her gallant dead some time" (3:245). Because under Natchez kinship rules, her legitimate mate would perforce be a Stinkard, a "gallant" (amant in French) surely refers to a Frenchman, who if it were St. Cosme would put their children in their twenties in 1729. Dumont's account of the death of Serpent Piqué mentions "St. Côme" as the presumptive Grand Soleil (Mémoires historiques 1:229). The paternity of St. Cosme may have been an open secret among Frenchmen in Louisiana but one that no writer, least of all a priest such as Charlevoix, wished to declare openly. Likewise, no historian of Louisiana that I have found has made that suggestion in print with the exception of the author of the entry for St. Cosme in the Dictionary of Canadian Biography. St. Cosme's words only deepen suspicions that he may have had a Natchez mistress. His published missionary relations cover only the period before he moved downstream to Natchez, but according to the Jesuit Father Gravier, who wrote a relation about the tribe in 1700, "Monsieur de St. Cosme informed me that the Natches were far from being as docile as the Tounika. They are polygamous, thievish, and Very depraved—the girls and woman being even more so than the men and boys, among whom a great reformation must be effected before anything can be expected from them" (Thwaites 65:135). Father François Le Maire, a brother in St. Cosme's order who arrived in Louisiana around the time of the latter's death, wrote in a memoir of "the scandal given by our Frenchmen in our young missions" and stated that missionaries in the country must be "mortified, in order to be chaste; for without this last virtue, nothing else can be expected but the fatal loss of their souls, since they must necessarily deal with peoples, whose women are weak and impudent, where occasions are always present, and where the isolation warrants silence and impunity" (Delanglez, "M. Le Maire" 153–54).

Le Page du Pratz's dramatic dialogue between Bras Piqué and her son, St. Cosme, invokes ethical and sentimental conflicts familiar from the Indian tragedies but inverts the kinship alliances in such a way as to render them almost unrecognizable unless one understands Natchez kinship. Xicoténcatl the Younger and Ponteach's son, Chekitan, face the prototypical dilemma of the eighteenth-century republican hero, loyalty to *patria* versus love for a woman among the enemy. Villeneufve's Poucha-Houmma sacrifices himself for his son, as does Soyinka's Elesin, but the Natchez Grand Soleil cannot set *patria* against love because his title comes from his mother, not his father. His mother had failed the test of republican virtue by giving in to her love for a Frenchman. Le Page du Pratz insists that "the vexation of this woman rather than to any remains of affection she entertained for the French" led her both "to alert several young women who were in love with Frenchmen" (*Histoire* 3:251) about the planned uprising and to steal a few of the token sticks. Le Page develops a misogynistic view of Bras Piqué as spiteful and jealous of her son's power. "Are you afraid that I will betray you, and that I will make you a slave of the Frenchmen against whom you are acting?" (3:248), she says, hinting at a knowledge of the planned uprising: "The son of this female Sun was paralyzed by the words that she had just told him, with tears in her eyes" (3:248). He avoids referring to the conspiracy but indirectly confirms her hints: "Since you have divined everything . . . you know as much as I do; keep your mouth closed" (3:249). Finally, Bras Piqué warns her son that the French are numerous and powerful, that if he were planning an attack against Indians, she would not worry, but the "Frenchmen have resources that the Red Men do not" (3:249).

Bras Piqué was captured after the French besieged the occupied Fort

Rosalie and was held as a prisoner in New Orleans. There, Le Page du Pratz writes at the very end of his account of the uprising, he learned from her "all the doings of the Natchez before the day of the massacre" (*Histoire* 3:260). As a prisoner, she would have had good reasons to fabricate a story in which she had favored the French. We might also be reminded of the incident when the Grande Soleille came to offer him her daughter in marriage. Le Page du Pratz does not confirm that this Soleille was the same woman as Bras Piqué, and it is possible that she was the female Sun of another village close to his concession rather than of the Grand Village or of the entire tribe. However, if it was Bras Piqué, the daughter who had sought his hand in marriage would now be the princess whom the Natchez called "the White Sun, because she was more white and more delicate than the others" (3:261), whose whiteness may have been literal as well as titular because she was the daughter of a Frenchman, and who, like her mother, may have helped betray the conspiracy to the French. Bras Piqué's theft of the sticks would then be the repetition of the sexual betrayals that have already occurred, and the young Sun St. Cosme would be another offspring of this affair, the brother of the princess. He would be the "tragic mestizo," if you will.

The climax of du Pratz's account of the massacre is in the conspiracy rather than in the uprising itself, and the tragic flaws of Chépar and of Bras Piqué effectively negate one another. Bras Piqué tips off "M. Massé, Sub-Lieutenant" (*Histoire* 3:254) at Fort Rosalie, and he informs Chépar, but Chépar does not heed this or other warnings.[26] She then "took from the fatal bundle several sticks" (3:253), but her theft is ultimately inconsequential: "The massacre was supposed to take place two or three days before it did, but the Natchez having learned that a small galley of merchandise was going to arrive, put off their plan until the arrival of the boat" (3:253–54). Reversing Le Petit's account, which claims that the supply boat prompted the Natchez to attack two days early, Le Page's narrative hastens the attack and then postpones it again. Since the two events cancel each other out, their veracity can scarcely be ascertained.

Chateaubriand's *Les Natchez*

As a plot device, the token sticks are undermined by being overdetermined. In a parallel fashion, the epic historical grandeur of the Natchez Massacre was undercut by the fact that the entire French colony was lost not to the Natchez but to the English and later the Spanish and the United States. The Natchez drama had to wait for the French Revolution and for Chateaubriand to find its full epic treatment. Because Chateaubriand's attitudes toward the revolution changed markedly during his life and because as a

romantic afflicted with a Wertherian "mal du siècle" he relished the anguish of being on the losing side, of being dispossessed, the political meaning of the revolt in Les Natchez is ambivalent. When Robert Rogers arrived in London
in 1765 as the hero of the war against Pontiac, his motives for celebrating his foe were clear—the tragic valor of his nemesis could enhance his status as a soldier, a playwright, and an expert on the American Northwest. But when Chateaubriand arrived in London in 1793, nursing his quixotic memories of his 1791 adventures in the United States and his wounds from his 1792 battles against French revolutionaries, his motives in writing Atala and Les Natchez were more tortuous. As a recovering Rousseauian, an aristocrat and defender of the French ancien régime, Chateaubriand found reasons to identify with the heroic resistance and tragic demise of the Natchez as well as reasons to sympathize with the French colonists sent by that regime. His hero René is, like Chateaubriand, a refugee and renegade, in flight from and in opposition to his nation. In his chapter "Government among the Indians," in Travels in America, Chateaubriand classifies the Natchez polity as "despotism in the state of nature" (155) and denounces their practice of mortuary sacrifice: "The people still obeyed a dead body, so much were they bent on slavery" (160). He recounts from Pénicaut the sacrifice of fourteen people after the death of a Sun in 1700. But then he imagines that a "simple, natural, almost effortless revolution delivered the Natchez in part from their chains." A "reasonable prince" abolishes mortuary sacrifice, and the tribe finds the happy medium between the twin evils of private and communal property. Yet the only possible basis in Chateaubriand's sources for this peaceful revolution would be Le Page du Pratz's tale of how he had intervened to prevent the suicide of the Grand Soleil after the death of Serpent Piqué. Thus, the "reasonable prince" would not be a Natchez at all but the inventive concessionaire and historian Le Page du Pratz. Chateaubriand's sacrificial crisis here is the imperial white man's burden itself.

Moreover, Chateaubriand had a recursive habit of confusing texts about heroic sacrifice with actual acts of heroic sacrifice. He wrote in his autobiography, Mémoires d'Outre-Tombe, that Atala, the text named for the Natchez heroine who poisoned herself to preserve her saintly virginity, made a Pocahontas-like sacrifice to save Chateaubriand's life. When fighting in the Army of the Princes against the revolutionaries at the siege of Thionville on the Rhine in 1792, Chateaubriand was carrying a manuscript of his future best-selling novella in his backpack. Referring to himself in the third person, he claims that under heavy enemy fire "in that town of sacrifice Atala placed herself between him and the enemy's lead" (qtd. in Chinard, L'Exotisme 101). Chateaubriand tells his story, like that of Atala, as a melodrama of sacrifice, and wherever we look we can see Chateaubriand reflected in his characters. René, the romantic exile from France who is adopted by the Natchez, bears Chateaubriand's middle name, and his acceptance by the Indians fulfills a fantasy that he articulated in *Voyages en Amérique*, a Rousseauian dream of a return to primitive virtues. René's exile in America was written during the time of Chateaubriand's exile in England, and the character's love for the Natchez princess, Céluta, may reflect Chateaubriand's passion for Charlotte Ives, the daughter of one of his English hosts. The anecdote about the siege of Thionville suggests that we are dealing not simply with a romantic autobiographical novelist but with a melodrama of the adventures and travails of the texts themselves. Chateaubriand claimed that *Atala* was written in America, "beneath the huts of savages" (*Atala* 35) during his brief voyage to America. Then, when *Les Natchez* first appeared in 1826, its preface claimed that its manuscript, also written in large part during his American travels, had been lost in a trunk left in London when he returned from exile in 1800 and recovered a quarter century later. Somewhat like the legend of the *buchettes*, Chateaubriand spins legends about his manuscripts as if they were fetishes, mimetic objects with a power over his life instead of documents of eyewitness testimony about America and the Natchez.

David Quint has written in *Epic and Empire* that "to the victors belongs epic, with its linear teleology; to the losers belongs romance, with its random or circular wandering" (9). *Les Natchez*, which Quint curiously never mentions, complicates his genre definition by attempting to be both. Chateaubriand claims in the preface that he "had also changed the species of the composition, by turning it from a romance to an epic" (1:8).[27] The first half of the text is divided into twelve books and employs a superabundance of epic devices and epithets. Book 4, in which Catherine Tekakwitha, an Iroquois saint, intervenes with the Virgin Mary to protect the Natchez, is the most preposterous. The second half, including the climactic episodes of the conspiracy and massacre, is a continuous narrative titled "Suite des Natchez" and lacking the epic histrionics. While this inconsistent use of epic devices damages its literary coherence, the book's interest finally lies precisely in these contradictions of its genres and its themes. Because it uses the Natchez Massacre for its climax, it is an epic of the tribe's defeat and of the French colony's loss and then vengeful victory. But as a romance about the entire French colonial experience in North America, it follows René's (and Chateaubriand's) exile, wandering, and defeat. *Les Natchez* combines not only epic and romance but also revolutionary and reactionary, Indian and Christian, in an uneasy, sometimes absurd mix. And its plot splits the Natchez uprising into two battles, creating a doubled account of the responsibility for the betrayal, violence, and sacrifice involved.

Chateaubriand read carefully Le Page du Pratz's and Dumont's texts and copied out of them countless ethnographic details. Michel Butor went so far as to call *Les Natchez* the "first example of a literature founded upon ethnography" (237). But as Chinard's careful scholarship proves, Chateaubriand showed a remarkable tendency to get the facts wrong, to misplace and misuse the ethnography he read. The artifice of his documentation, the pseudoheroism of reducing life to text, is exposed in these errors. Chateaubriand never went to Natchez, never experienced Native American life; his manuscripts, not himself, suffered the pain and exile that they dramatized. Chateaubriand had fled revolutionary France in 1791 for America and traveled from Baltimore up to New York and west to Niagara Falls. Like Jonathan Carver, the veteran of Pontiac's rebellion, Chateaubriand claimed that he wished to discover the Northwest Passage: "In 1789 I communicated to M. de Malesherbes the plan which I had formed of going to America. . . . I conceived the design of discovering by land the passage which was so much sought, and respecting which Cook himself had left doubts" (*Atala* 39). But also like Carver, Chateaubriand's accounts of his travels are not to be trusted. His *Voyages en Amérique* extends his itinerary to "the ruins of the Ohio," the great mounds along the Scioto, and all the way to Natchez, though it is unlikely he went any farther than Niagara.

The climax of Le Page du Pratz's account of the massacre comes not on the battlefield but in the formation of the plot and its betrayal by Bras Piqué. Likewise, the epic high point of *Les Natchez* is not the violent uprising but the formation of the plot behind it, culminating in the affair of the token sticks. The conspiracy begins when all the Indian tribes of North America gather for a council of war on a cliff above Lake Superior. An epic review of the armies begins with the Iroquois and proceeds to Algonquins, Hurons, Abenakis, Powhatans, Creeks, Muscogulges, Seminoles, Cherokees, Yamassees, Chickasaw and Illinois, and finally several western tribes culminating in the Sioux.

Perhaps because this enormous pan-Indian conspiracy had no historical basis, Chateaubriand did not create a heroic Natchez chief. Although he appears to have understood the Natchez caste system from his reading of Le Page du Pratz, Chateaubriand did not place the royal family of Suns at the forefront of the tribe. If he learned the rumor about St. Cosme's missionary father, Chateaubriand no doubt refrained from casting him in the Natchez leader's role out of a desire to avoid blackening the reputation of priests such as his own saintly Father Aubry. Instead, Chateaubriand created a cast of characters representing different positions with regard to the conspiracy and to René. The titular Grand Soleil is over a hundred years old, remains unnamed, and plays no part in the uprising. The Grande Soleille or Femme Blanche (though neither term is used for her) is Akansie, and her unnamed son would be the heir to the Sunship except that she favors a usurper, the villain, Ondouré, for whom she has a fatal passion. Ondouré, however, loves Céluta, the heroine and wife of René, whose daughter, Amélie, born in *Les Natchez*, appears in the concluding chapter of *Atala*. Ondouré's love is forbidden not only by René's prerogatives in the novel's plot but presumably also by the Natchez rule of exogamy, for Céluta, the sister of a noble Natchez hero, Outougamiz, is not a Stinkard. Ondouré gets himself named "édile," or guardian of the young regent, a title Chateaubriand admits to having adopted from classical Rome. Ondouré plans to marry an unnamed and presumably Stinkard woman and then take Céluta as his concubine and manipulate the rules of descent in an effort to become Sun. His plans are resisted not only by Outougamiz and René but by the two sage *vieillards*, Chactas and Adario, who represent Natchez sentiment for and against the French. A scene in book 2 resembles the harangue of the *vieillard* in Le Page du Pratz except that it is shared between Chactas and Adario. Adario begins by reminding the Natchez of the deaths suffered in the wake of the invasions by de Soto and La Salle and of the folly of peace with the French: "Imprudent men! Can the smoke of slavery and that of independence proceed from the same pipe? It requires a stronger head than that of the slave not to be confused by the scent of liberty" (*The Natchez* 1:60). That he should conclude with "liberty" rather than "peace," however, hints at Chateaubriand's true agenda, which opposes the uprising and makes the French its victims, dismissing the Natchez who perished in its aftermath. Adario invokes filiopiety to argue for war: "Prove yourselves worthy of your fathers, and this very day Adario will lead you to the bloody conflict" (1:62). On the following pages Chactas articulates the jeremiad part of the rhetoric of the *vieillard*, reproaching his countrymen for their dependence on the French: "I am no stranger to the encroachments of the Whites: my heart is deeply afflicted by them. But are we sure that we have done nothing wherewith to reproach ourselves? Have we done all that we could have done to preserve our independence?" (1:68). The voice of peace carries the day, and the tribe decides to appease the demands of Chépar, as the Natchez in fact did for several months in 1729.

Between this early scene and the decisive council at Lake Superior are more than 250 pages, or two-thirds of *Les Natchez*. Much of this, from the middle of book 5 to book 8, is devoted to Chactas's narrative of his voyages to France, to which I will return shortly. Books 9 and 10 return to Louisiana and feature a preliminary battle between the French and the Natchez that is treated with more epic grandeur than the final uprising of 1729. This, of course, appears in the first, more epic volume of the work, but Chateaubriand may also have wished to employ these devices on a battle in which the Natchez held the moral high ground. The conflict bears little resemblance to actual skirmishes in 1722–23. It is precipitated by an evil Muslim renegade, Febriano, who first plots with Ondouré and arouses a conspiracy among the African slaves and then goes to Chépar and betrays the plan, hinting that Adario, Chactas, and René are all in on it. When Chactas goes to Fort Rosalie with a calumet to try to defuse the conflict, Chépar takes him prisoner. Then Adario is also captured and sold into slavery, as were several actual Natchez leaders captured in the February 1730 siege. In the aftermath of this battle, René is accused of conspiracy, even though he and Outougamiz were actually far away, at war against the Illinois. René turns himself in to the French in exchange for Adario's release. Put on trial in New Orleans, René is sentenced to (re)exile back in France. At this point, he receives a letter informing him of the death of his sister, Amélie, which elicits the narrative of *René*. (The text of *René* and Chactas's narrative of *Atala* were not actually reprinted in *Les Natchez*; their places in the narrative were simply indicated by notes.) After his release from prison, Ondouré denounces René as a collaborator and sends him to the Illinois with the calumet as a means to get him away from Natchez during the uprising. René therefore does not attend the council on Lake Superior, although Outougamiz, his close friend and brother-in-law, does. Outougamiz faces the dilemma between civic duty and personal loyalty endemic to epics and republican dramas. He participates in an oath consecrating the conspiracy, but when Ondouré orders him to kill René, Outougamiz says he cannot do so even if his refusal amounts to betraying his nation. During their fight against the Illinois, Outougamiz had saved René's life, and the two entered into a sacred brotherhood modeled on that of Achilles and Patroclus but holding the extra appeal of giving René's marriage to Céluta, Outougamiz's sister, the overtones of incest essential to high romantic novels. Faced with betraying either his friend or his nation, Outougamiz briefly contemplates suicide but instead races back to Natchez and partly reveals the plot to Céluta. The young, beautiful Céluta replaces Bras Piqué in the romantic role as thief of the token sticks. She dresses up as a ghost, a spirit of a dead ancestor, to gain admittance to the temple where the bones of the ancestors are kept alongside the bundle of sticks and steals eight of them. (Chateaubriand calls them *roseaux* [reeds].) The theft is witnessed, but its interpretation is open to debate. Outougamiz, who opposes the uprising, treats the tokens as sacred and says Céluta's actions are a sign that "Le Grand Esprit le désapprouve" (471) of the planned uprising, while others insist that it go forward. Hence, the theft of the token sticks is self-negating, as in du Pratz's version. Céluta, echoing Pocahontas, betrays her tribe in an attempt to save the French colony. The plot and counterplot echo but also reverse the events in the first volume when René was accused of betraying the colony by plotting with the Natchez to attack the French.

Laura Murray has written of an "aesthetics of dispossession" in early national writings about Native Americans, of how a "romanticization of the ideas of dispossession, homelessness, and loss served to mask historical differences" (212) between the losses of European colonists such as the French in Louisiana and the more profound losses of colonized natives. Though Murray conceived of the idea in relation to Washington Irving, it is germane to Chateaubriand as well. The romantic pathos of René is predicated not so much on his lovelorn exile (as in *René*) but on his being falsely accused by each side of conspiracy with the other: "With the Natchez, the impious René was the secret accomplice of the hostile plans of the French; with the French, René, the traitor, was the enemy of his former country" (*The Natchez* 2:161). This martyrdom is the fount of romantic melancholy and dispossession: "To feel conscious of his innocence, and to be condemned by the law, would be, according to René's ideas, a sort of triumph over the social order" (2:213). René is a scapegoat, a sacrificial victim in Girard's sense. Like Oedipus, René is an outsider who enters a monarchical nation (the Natchez), is adopted into it, and rises to a position of power. He becomes the confidant of a blind seer (Chactas, whose blindness is also emphasized in *Atala*, where he recounts the events of his youth) and the rival of the pretender, Ondouré. René's horrifying crime of incest (with his sister rather than his mother) destroys his marriage to Céluta and symbolizes his political demise. Ondouré kills René in the midst of the massacre, just hours after he had returned from the Illinois, too late to prevent the uprising for which, had he lived, the French might have blamed him. René's oblique affinity to Oedipus was likely part of Chateaubriand's design. René's incest and outcast status also link him to the two St. Cosmes, one a missionary who may have had a child with a Natchez woman and then been martyred, the other his son, the shadowy mixed-blood Sun who may have led the uprising and subsequent flight of the Natchez.

René perhaps is not so much the tragic hero of *Les Natchez* as Chactas is. Yet Chactas, consistent with Chateaubriand's political sentiments, is not a republican rebel. He does not lead the failed uprising against the colonists but instead tries and fails to prevent it. Chactas is named, of course, for the Choctaw tribe that allegedly had agreed to join the Natchez in the revolt but were so angered when the Natchez struck three days early that they then joined with the French in the retaliation. In *Les Natchez*, Chactas dies just before the uprising, without ever being informed of the plot. Yet Chactas in *Les Natchez* is not the same compliant convert we know from *Atala*. Chateaubriand devoted a substantial portion of the text, books 5–8, to Chactas's voyage to France. His nearly twenty-year exile from Natchez begins amid his grief over the death of Atala, and his narrative of it comes just after he finishes the story of *Atala*. " 'On leaving the pious recluse and the ashes of Atala,' continued Chactas, 'I traversed immense regions without knowing whither I went: all ways were alike to my grief, and life itself was of little value to me' " (1:114). He ends up among the Iroquois, where he happens to meet his countryman, Adario, and joins him and the Iroquois in resisting the 1687 French attack on the Seneca, in which the Baron de Lahontan participated and of which he wrote in his 1703 book. Chactas and Adario are among the native warriors captured and sent back to Europe as galley slaves by Denonville. In Marseilles, however, Chactas meets Lopez, foster father of Atala, and is freed by order of the king. Chactas then has the opportunity to visit and comment on Paris and elite French society. The genre is that form of satire familiar from Montesquieu's *Lettres Persanes* and Goldsmith's *Citizen of the World*, but the most direct source is the satiric dialogue in the third volume of Lahontan's work, which he titled *Dialogues Curieux . . . avec un Sauvage qui a voyagé*. This "sauvage" is named Adario. And although Adario's dialogue with "Lahontan" takes place in Canada, he expresses opinions derived from his time in France, as the title indicates.

Chateaubriand's allusion to Lahontan's text from a century earlier becomes interesting, however, only through the reactionary revisions of it. Lahontan's Adario expressed the radical skepticism of his author, ridiculing the Jesuit missionaries, doubting the veracity of the Bible, and promoting an enlightened, functionalist view of sexuality. Lahontan was no admirer of the Sun King; his work was published in Holland and London but banned in France, and he lived the remainder of his life in exile from his native land. Chateaubriand, once a follower of Rousseau and then an exile from the French Revolution, makes his Chactas a countersatiric response to Lahontan's Adario. Arriving at Versailles for his audience with the king, Chactas questions the virtue of the palace's builders and, in lines consistent with edifying reflections on classical ruins, delivers an oblique prophecy of the revolution a century hence:

> Was this palace, of which you are so proud, built by command of the Spirits? Has it cost neither sweat nor tears? Were its foundations laid in wisdom, the only solid ground to build upon? . . . Under the veil of smiles, it seems to me that this hut is the hut of slavery, care, ingratitude and death. Do you not hear a doleful sound issuing from these walls, as though it were echo repeating the sighs of the people? Ah! how loud would here be the noise of weeping, should it ever begin to break forth! (*The Natchez* 1:147–48)

He later visits the "hut" of a starving peasant and reflects, "I had then, for the first time, an idea of European degradation in all its deformity. I saw man brutalized by indigence, amidst a famished family, not enjoying the advantages of society, and having lost those of nature" (1:192). But immediately thereafter, Chactas happens to meet "a man who has reconciled me with men" (1:194), a "chief of prayer" who turns out to be priest and author François Fénelon. In the eight-page dialogue that follows, Fénelon corrects Chactas's "prejudices," explains the necessity of agriculture and the arts, and insists that "virtues are emanations from the Almighty . . . necessarily more numerous in the social than in the natural order, the state of society which brings us nearer to the Deity is consequently a superior state to that of nature" (1:203).

Chactas's whirlwind tour of Paris briefly introduces him to La Fontaine and La Bruyere; Racine, Molière, and Boileau; Locke, Newton, and Leibniz; and many others, all conveniently identified in notes, but it is Fénelon who refutes the moral superiority of this enlightenment Man of Nature. Fénelon's *Aventures de Télémaque* was the model for texts of political (re)education such as he here provides for Chactas, and it employed the conceit of a visit back in time to meet with sages and leaders of the past. *Télémaque* also strongly influenced Lahontan (Carpenter 129). The contrast between Lahontan's and Chateaubriand's use of Fénelon parallels the conflict between Adario and Chactas over the planned revolt of the Natchez. Adario is the skeptic who rejects European society and urges the Natchez to attack; Chactas, a Christianized apologist for colonization, attempts to quell the uprising.

To see the Natchez uprising as a revolution entailed putting the French in the role of counterrevolutionary colonial oppressors, and because French Louisiana never got the chance to become a postcolonial nation, such a plot was not available for a rescripting of the Natchez Massacre in the service of a Louisiana national literature, as it was for Metacom's and Pontiac's rebellion in the historiography of the United States. French writers first developed the "plot" of the Natchez Massacre to help justify their reprisals against the Indians and then to invite a sympathetic identification with them; finally, however, the conspiracy's political dynamic was complicated by the French loss of Louisiana and the revolution of 1789. The uprising that was once so meaningful for French colonial writers is now an obscure memory for North Americans. Nowadays, many of the tourists visiting the Grand Village of the Natchez Indians near Natchez, Mississippi, come from France.

CHAPTER 7

The Pueblo Revolt of 1680 demands our attention as the most successful native uprising against colonial invaders in the history of North America. In August of that year, the peoples of the mud-brick towns known by the Spanish word for village, from Taos in the north to Jemez, Acoma, Zuni, and Hopi in the high desert west of the Rio Grande, rose up against the Spanish colonizers who had established themselves after Juan de Oñate's *entrada* in 1598. More than four hundred Spaniards were killed, including twenty-one of the province's thirty-three missionaries, out of a total population of some three thousand. Spanish survivors fled to the provincial capital of Santa Fe, where an estimated twenty-five hundred Indian warriors held them in siege for more than a week, cutting off the town's water supply, launching burning missiles over the palisades, and taunting their former oppressors with mockeries of the Latin Mass. On 21 August Governor Antonio Otermín finally battled his way out of Santa Fe and led a retreat downstream to El Paso. The Spanish were kept out of the pueblos for twelve years thereafter, until soldiers and settlers led by Diego de Vargas reoccupied Santa Fe and solidified alliances with a few pueblos that had not joined the revolt.

In its time, this revolt and reconquest on the northern frontier summoned up a good measure of military effort and heroic passion in New Spain. The lurid martyrdom of the Franciscan missionaries killed by the Indians in the uprising followed the sort of Manichaean drama that was used to raise political support and pious contributions for the cause of conversion. New Mexico in the seventeenth century had not yielded significant profits from gold or silver mines, but it had offered a population of Indian souls in the pueblos who were agricultural, sedentary, and therefore more promising as laborers and as Christian converts than the nomadic hunter-gatherers found elsewhere in the region—for example, the Apaches, who frequently harassed Pueblo villages. The missionary cause had sustained the colony during the seventeenth century and inspired the *reconquista* in the eighteenth. Carlos Sigüenza y Góngora, Mexico City's leading intellectual, compared by scholars to his contemporary, Cotton Mather, in Puritan Boston, responded early in 1693 to the news of Vargas's reconquest by publishing a tract, *Mercurio*

Volante con la noticia de la recuperacion de las Provincias del Nuevo Mexico conseguida por Don Diego de Vargas (The Flying Mercury with an account of the recovery of the provinces of New Mexico won by Don Diego de Vargas). Translator Irving Leonard describes the work as "journalistic in nature" and as among the "rudimentary newspapers" that anticipated the development of a periodical press in Mexico in the 1700s (14). Its style is indeed the polar opposite of epic. The narrative pays no heroic attention to the Pueblo leaders. Sigüenza y Góngora did allow that the Indians worked for fourteen years "to plot a revolt with the greatest secrecy ever known" (55), but he was not concerned with demonizing the mastermind behind the plot, as Cotton Mather had done to Metacom. Sigüenza y Góngora wrote simply that the siege of Santa Fe was accomplished by "two thousand apostates, led by Alonso Catiti and another no less rascally Indian called Popé" (56). Popé has in the ensuing three centuries become a major Indian tragic hero, but his mystique was very slow to develop. Gaspar Perez de Villagrá had been inspired to write an epic poem based on his experiences during the initial Spanish *entrada* into the Pueblo lands in 1598–99, but no Spanish soldier-poet wrote one about Popé and the Pueblo Revolt or about Vargas's retaliation. The resistance of the Araucana Indians, immortalized in Ercilla's epic poem, was much more successful and long lasting than that of the Pueblo Indians and became a more powerful nationalist epic for Chile than the Pueblo Revolt has ever become for New or old Mexico. Nineteenth-century Spanish American creoles in Mexico, Lima, or Caracas perceived Santa Fe in 1680 as quite distant from their nationalist consciousness and their revolutionary concerns. And from the perspective of historians and literati in the United States in the early 1800s, Spanish colonial New Mexico was even more distant and unfamiliar than French Louisiana, in part because until the end of the eighteenth century Spanish colonial officials generally prohibited travel through their territories by non-Spaniards and censored or suppressed the publication of some histories and travel narratives about these areas. No tragedies, epics, or verse romances were written in English about the Pueblo Revolt. And although later editions of Samuel Drake's compendium of Indian biography and history included a brief account (based on the French edition of Le Page du Pratz's *Histoire de la Louisiane*) of the 1729 Natchez uprising led by a chief whom Drake called "Grand Sun," Drake made no mention at all of the Pueblo Revolt.

Representations of the events of August 1680 nonetheless have followed many of the historiographic plots and patterns traced in earlier chapters. And although it has taken 300 years rather than just 150, the Pueblo Revolt has recently been interpreted in much the same manner as King Philip's War was in the 1820s—that is, as a harbinger of American postcolonial independence and as a bold statement of indigenous sovereignty that Anglos can now embrace as their own. Recent museum exhibitions and Web sites have referred to the Pueblo Revolt as the "First American Revolution."[1] School curricula have been created to study it, and American history textbooks and literature anthologies that long gave short shrift to Spanish and native populations in the colonial period now include sections on New Mexico that highlight the Pueblo Revolt (Weber, *What Caused* 16 n. 6). Students and teachers in the United States today likely find it easier and more inviting to study the Pueblo Revolt than the other Native American uprisings examined in this book because the Pueblo culture continues to thrive. The Natchez villages were destroyed by the French retaliations of the 1730s, and the people and their language ultimately merged into Chickasaw, Cherokee, and other tribal communities. Tecumseh's Shawnee and Metacom's Wampanoag likewise can scarcely be found in the regions where they led wars of resistance. But the Pueblo peoples and their villages have endured Oñate's and Vargas's attacks and four centuries of Hispanic and Anglo colonialism. Their heroic resistance and distinct culture makes a much more satisfying object for the cathartic ambivalence of modern Americans than do Pontiac and Tecumseh, who although more recent may seem more distant.

I have shown in previous chapters how the rebellions of American Indians against colonization have been portrayed according to certain dramatic plots, not only by the writers of formal histories but even in the documents left by the participants. These historiographic tropes are not simply misrepresentations of native history by imperialist historians. Native resistance has also had its own traditions and patterns. Accounts of the Pueblo Revolt support both of these themes, most of all in one singular detail: the method used to coordinate the attacks by Indians in at least a dozen pueblos, speaking at least six distinct languages and separated by hundreds of miles. Historians' essential documentary source for the revolt is the record of a series of interrogations by Spanish authorities of Pueblo Indians who were either captured in the aftermath of the uprising or remained loyal to the Spanish. One of these transcripts, from 18 December 1681, records the words of an Indian named Juan, who explains how the leader of the uprising planned the surprise attack: "Asked how the said Indian, Popé, convoked all the people of the kingdom so that they obeyed him in the treason, [Juan] said that [Popé] took a cord made of maguey fiber and tied some knots in it which indicated the number of days until the perpetration of the treason. He sent it though all the pueblos as far as that of La Isleta" (Hackett and Shelby 2:234). The number of knots in the ropes made from maguey or yucca plants (a common source of fiber in the native Southwest) serve the same function as the bundle of sticks (*buchettes*) that

French writers claimed the Natchez had prepared and distributed to their allies in preparation for the attack on Fort Rosalie in 1729. The conspiratorial mastermind, Popé (often spelled today in a more indigenous style as "Po'pay," since "Pope" seems unbearably ironic), is identified as the source both of the cords and of the concept of using them. Popé, like Pontiac, was regarded as the mastermind of an allied Indian revolt yet remains an enigmatic figure whose true influence historians debate.

In the preceding chapter, I show that the earliest French accounts of the Natchez uprising make no mention of the counting sticks and that subsequent historians introduced this story of the *buchettes* and of the fateful theft of a few sticks from one of the bundles as a means both to suggest that the Indian conspiracy was much wider than other evidence might indicate and to imply that the Indians were ill equipped to carry out such a well-organized attack. The Pueblo Revolt also follows this "plot" against the colonizers; indeed, the use of tokens to count down the days until an uprising represents a curious motif in the histories of native rebellions in North America from Christopher Columbus to Tecumseh. The recurrence of this trope raises acute questions about the reliability of some of the sources used by colonial historians and suggests that the strategy of resistance and/or the narrative plot that accounts for it may have spread through the unwritten folk communication networks of both native and European peoples on the continent and surfaced in historical documents at widely separated times and places.

The first appearance of the trope that I have found is from Columbus's third voyage, when he returned to Hispaniola in August 1498 and found that the settlement he had left there two and a half years earlier was in turmoil. As frequently happened in the Spanish colonies, the soldiers had split into factions. Roldán, the man Columbus had appointed *alcalde mayor* (chief justice) of the outpost, was in revolt against Columbus's brother, Bartolomé, who had been appointed *adelantado* (commandant, literally "leader"). Roldán apparently had sought the alliance of a native leader:

> Guarionex, the chief cacique of that province, undertook with Roldán's aid to lay siege to the town and fortress and kill the Christians who guarded it. To accomplish this he assembled all the caciques subject to him and secretly agreed with them that each should kill the Christians in his province. Because the area cultivated by each Indian is not large enough to support many people, the Christians were obliged to disperse into bands or companies of eight or ten to a district; this gave the Indians hope that by a surprise attack upon the Christians they might succeed in wiping them all out. Their only way of reckoning time or anything else being on their fingers, the Indians agreed to launch the attack on the first

day of the next full moon. After Guarionex had instructed the caciques about this, the principal one among them, desiring to gain honor by what he conceived to be an easy feat, and being in any case too poor an astronomer to know for sure the first day of the full moon, attacked the Christians before the appointed day. He was repelled and forced to flee, and when he sought a haven with Guarionex, he was instead put to death for prematurely revealing the conspiracy. (Colón 196)

Except for the fingers of the hand, this story mentions no tokens to represent the days before the attack. This difference only accentuates the supposed weakness of the Indians' intellect, which is, after all, the reason they need to use such tokens. According to a prejudice that still endures today, American Indians and other primitive peoples are believed to have been so innumerate that they could not keep an accurate count even of a series of fewer than thirty days. As primitives, the Indians were incapable of abstract thought, and the only way for them to measure time was to use tokens that stood in an isomorphic relation to the number of days. But this notion is a savagist myth. If the average Indian was numerate enough to count a bundle of sticks sent to him by the grand conspirator, why would he need to use them to represent the series of days? After all, the calendrical and astronomical methods devised by the Maya more than a thousand years ago were much more accurate and sophisticated than those used in Europe at the time. And although North American tribes did not share the Aztec or Maya calendars, ample evidence indicates that these tribes kept accurate count of days in the cycles of the moon. Still, according to the common Eurocentric prejudice, Indian conspirators simply cannot count, and even when they use token sticks or knots to help keep track, the potential loss or theft of the tokens renders the method prone to error. Thus, the most consistent detail about this emplotment of native revolt is its comical failure.

The second significant detail is how in the final analysis the technique of counting tokens is more or less irrelevant. Le Petit's and Le Page du Pratz's reports of the Natchez uprising show how the arrival of a valuable shipment of supplies at the French post tempted the Natchez to abandon the count and to launch the attack a few days earlier (Le Petit) or later (Le Page du Pratz). This plot twist alienated the Choctaw, who felt they had been double-crossed by allies who asked for help but then acted alone when they saw the chance to get more loot for themselves. But it also renders the entire story of the token sticks both superfluous and unverifiable. Similarly, in this story of a revolt against the leadership of Christopher Columbus, the faulty count of the unnamed cacique is fatal for him but ultimately inconsequential for the rebellion. Roldán had also recruited for his revolt many malcontented Spaniards by promising them the gold and slaves for which all were so impatient, and they were not liable to become confused about the date of the attack. Columbus was eventually forced to negotiate with Roldán and his faction (Morison 564–68). The quoted narrative comes from the biography of Columbus by his son, published in Italian in 1571, and the younger Columbus of course favored his father and uncle. Roldán is the chief villain of this story, and the failed conspiracy of the native leader, Guarionex, is highlighted as a fortunate event that preserved for a time the admiral's rule over the island. The uprising's failure hints that although the Indians are potentially much more powerful than the Spaniards, they do not pose a serious threat, and their innumeracy is even exploited by Roldán, who appealed to them as their protector: "With this pretext [Roldán] took an even greater tribute from them, making a single cacique named Manicaotex pay him a calabash filled with gold dust worth three marks every three months. . . . As my readers may wonder why I reduced gold marks to calabash measure, I should explain that I do it to show that in such cases the Indians, having no weights, dealt by the measure" (Colón 197). The natives' innumeracy not only helps to prevent a coordinated resistance to European domination but facilitates the theft of their land's wealth, and the entire story contributes to Columbus's goal of promoting a fantasy of enormous quantities of gold available in the lands he has discovered.

In New Mexico in 1680, the careful count of days leading up to the surprise attack was also disrupted. Let us turn now to the most important of the Spaniards' postrevolt interrogations, that of a Keres Indian named Pedro Naranjo, also taken in December 1681.

> At the summons of an Indian named Popé who is said to have communication with the devil, it happened that in an estufa (kiva) of the pueblo of Los Taos there appeared to the said Popé three figures of Indians who never came out of the estufa. They gave the said Popé to understand that they were going underground to the lake of Copala. He saw these figures emit fire from all the extremities of their bodies, and that one of them was called Caudi, another Tilini, and the other Tleume; and these three beings spoke to the said Popé, who was in hiding from the secretary, Francisco Xavier, who wished to punish him as a sorcerer. They told him to make a cord of maguey fiber and tie some knots in it which would signify the number of days that they must wait before the rebellion. He said that the cord was passed through all the pueblos of the kingdom so that the ones which agreed to it might untie one knot in sign of obedience, and by the other knots they would know the days which were lacking; and this was to be done on pain of death to those who refused to agree to it. As a sign

of agreement and notice of having concurred in the treason and perfidy they were to send up smoke signals to that effect in each one of the pueblos singly. The said cord was taken from pueblo to pueblo by the swiftest youths under the penalty of death if they revealed the secret. Everything being thus arranged, two days before the time set for its execution [11 August], because his lordship had learned of it and had imprisoned two Indian accomplices from the pueblo of Tesuque, it was carried out prematurely that night, because it seemed to them that they were now discovered; and they killed religious, Spaniards, women, and children. (Hackett and Shelby 2:246–47)

In this testimony and a few other sources, the fully heroic figure of Popé emerges, replete with a prophetic vision to inspire his people and a ruthless authority to punish dissenters. We shall further analyze his character and role later in the chapter. First, however, let us follow the countdown from 9 to 13 August.

The shroud of secrecy which Popé enjoined on his followers evidently did not hold. On 9 August 1680, messengers from a number of pueblos, including San Marcos, San Cristóbal, and La Ciénega, came and warned Governor Otermín that a revolt was imminent. In a statement dictated that day, the governor recorded an ominous realization "that the Christian Indians of this kingdom are convoked, allied, and confederated for the purpose of rebelling, forsaking obedience to his Majesty, and apostatizing from the holy faith; and that they desire to kill the ecclesiastical ministers and all the Spaniards, women, and children, destroying the whole population of this kingdom" (Hackett and Shelby 1:3). On 10 August, Fray Juan Pio's mission at Tesuque Pueblo was attacked, and the friar barely escaped to Santa Fe. At the same time, two Indian boys, Nicholas Catua and Pedro Omtua, were captured while running through the desert carrying ropes with knots in them. When interrogated in Santa Fe, the boys gave 13 August as the day the rebellion was to begin. Otermín then had them executed. Yet even before the thirteenth, when an army of Indian warriors besieged Santa Fe, Otermín learned of attacks on missionaries at Taos and Picuris and on soldiers near Santa Clara and elsewhere. The well-known letter that Otermín wrote to Fray Francisco de Ayeta on 8 September seems designed to deflect any accusation that he, like Commandant Chépar at Fort Rosalie, had failed to predict or prevent the Indian revolt: "The cunning and cleverness of the rebels were such, and so great, that my efforts were of little avail. To this was added a certain degree of negligence by reason of the uprising not having been given entire credence" by those in outlying pueblos (Hackett and Shelby 1:95).

Because the pueblos and the Spanish settlements were widely dispersed, it really was not necessary for all the Indians to attack on precisely the same day. News of an attack at Taos in the north on one day would not reach San Marcos or Isleta in the south until the next day at the earliest, so Indian warriors might strike there a day later without losing the advantage of surprise. Moreover, given the small number of Spanish soldiers at each settlement and the time needed to send for reinforcements, the advantage of surprise was not important. Historians of the revolt have calculated that Indians capable of bearing arms outnumbered the Spaniards in New Mexico by fifty or sixty to one (Weber, *Spanish Frontier* 47, 75), yet nonetheless they have devoted close, even obsessive attention to the precise sequence of this calendar and its correspondence to the knotted cords. In his lengthy introduction to a collection of translated documents regarding the revolt, Charles Hackett has written that "the knotted cord was primarily a means of notifying the pueblos of the date determined upon. . . . For every day that passed while the cord was in the process of circulation, one knot was taken out in order to avoid confusion in the matter of the date" (xxvii). Writing in *The Patriot Chiefs*, Alvin Josephy Jr. has claimed that "Popé dispatched his knotted maguey cords to the excited villages, calling for a concerted uprising on August 11th, 1680, but slyly sending a later date, August 13th, to several Christian chiefs whose loyalty he questioned" (89). Others have suggested that the 13 August date supplied by the two captured messengers was their own clever effort to deceive their torturers and save the rebellion. The accounts of the precise logistics of the messengers and their knotted cords strain credulity. In his prizewinning book on colonial New Mexico, Ramón Gutierrez contends that "on August 9, 1680, Popé dispatched two messengers to all the pueblos with knotted cords indicating that only two days remained" (132) and that after the two messengers were apprehended and interrogated by Otermín, "Tesuque's Indians learned of this, and fearing that all might be lost immediately dispatched runners to the confederated pueblos informing them that they should rebel the next day" (132–33). David Weber, another leading historian of the Spanish colonial Southwest, concurs that on 9 August, "when Pueblo leaders learned that their plans had been betrayed, they moved the attack up a day" (*Spanish Frontier* 135). For Peter Nabokov, the fact that another cadre of runners would have been able to depart on 9 or 10 August and reach all of the allied pueblos by 11 August offers evidence of the amazing long-distance running achievements of American Indians. All these claims seem exaggerated. It is more than one hundred miles as the crow flies from Tesuque to Acoma, sixty from Acoma to Zuni, and another hundred from there to Shungopovi in Hopi land. Could messengers truly have reached all of these pueblos within twenty-four hours? For the uprising to succeed, the

Indians needed only to carry news of it to the next pueblo before any surviving Spaniard might arrive to sound the alarm. Knotted cords might have been useful as symbols of resistance, as concrete corroboration of a village's
spoken promise to take part in the revolt, but surely would not have been necessary as a practical timing device, because it was not really necessary for all the attacks to occur on the same day.

So what are we to make of counting tokens and of what we might call the "surprise attack betrayed"? Should the recurrence of this trope in the accounts of Indian uprisings lead us to doubt the accuracy of all the colonial histories in which it appears, including the primary documents about the Pueblo Revolt where it plays such a pivotal role? Such skepticism may seem warranted, given how closely the trope reinforces Eurocentric prejudices about the innumeracy of primitive peoples. Yet even recent studies of the Pueblo Revolt by native scholars such as Joe Sando and Alfonso Ortiz affirm the story of the knotted cords. The trope seems so attractive, so romantic, that few wish to question it. And the kind of postcolonial critique that might be eager to puncture such myths, to brand them as manifestations of Eurocentric prejudice, can instead embrace the myths as long as they are recast into less obviously racist terms. For example, in *The Conquest of America*, Tzvetan Todorov characterizes the difference between Aztec and Spanish cultures by asserting that "there exist two major forms of communication, one between man and man, the other between man and the world. . . . The Indians cultivate chiefly the latter, the Spaniards the former" (69). Although Todorov does not mention the Pueblo Revolt, the trope of the tokens is a perfect example of this communication "between man and world." His savagist semiotic theory about Native Americans is all the more astonishing because it is not a matter of literacy, since the Aztecs did use a form of writing. Todorov's statement implies that the Indians were incapable of sending a simple verbal or written message to their allies instructing them to attack on a certain day and that they therefore had to rely on the "world"-ly, concrete symbol of the sticks or knots. Todorov goes to the remarkable extreme of saying that "for the Aztecs, signs automatically and necessarily proceed from the world they designate" and that one effect of their communication system is "a certain incapacity of the Aztecs to dissimulate the truth" (89). This would suggest that, as in Chateaubriand's representation of the Natchez uprising, the Indians would feel obliged to follow the count of the sticks even if they knew that it was faulty because some of the sticks had been stolen. So even though Todorov does not discuss the specific trope of the counting tokens, it is clearly consistent with his theory, which regards the Spanish as holding a distinct advantage as a result of their ability to deceive the Aztecs with signs. Sending an allied Indian spy to steal a token stick from the bundle, as Chateaubriand's Céluta did, would have been a logical strategy for Cortés or Otermín to use to foil an uprising.[2]

The trope of the token sticks and of what we might call the "surprise attack betrayed" seems to have appealed to colonial settlers and soldiers because it assuaged their nervous anxiety about native resistance by suggesting that although the Indians might try to band together to attack the colonizers, they were too primitive to actually pull off such an attack. Colonial commanders such as Périer and Otermín who had suffered Indian rebellions on their watch also had an interest in affirming the trope because it could suggest that even more damaging revolts had been averted. Colonial literature had a vested interest in exaggerating the conspiratorial schemes of Indian chiefs insofar as such stories enhanced the achievements of colonial leaders who defeated these conspiracies. It is no surprise that such a tale occurred again in the literature about Tecumseh, and I will anticipate the topic of the next chapter to discuss it here. In the summer and fall of 1811, Tecumseh left his Indiana base on a series of long journeys to recruit warriors for his cause. Historians disagree about just how far he went and how many nations he spoke to, but several men later claimed to have heard him speak to the Creeks (Muskogees) and the Seminoles in the Southeast. An account of Tecumseh's visit to the Seminole Indians appeared in the biographical sketch of Tecumseh's brother, Tenskwatawa, in Thomas McKenney and James Hall's History of the Indian Tribes of North America, published in 1836, and was quoted by Benjamin Drake (Life 143–44):

> [Tecumseh] had been down south, to Florida, and succeeded in instigating the Seminoles in particular, and portions of other tribes, to unite in the war on the side of the British. He gave out that a vessel, on a certain day, commanded by red-coats, would be off Florida, filled with guns and ammunition, and supplies for the use of the Indians. That no mistake might happen in regard to the day on which the Indians were to strike, he prepared bundles of sticks—each bundle containing the number of sticks corresponding to the number of days that were to intervene between the day on which they were received, and the day of the general onset. The Indian practice is to throw away a stick every morning—they make, therefore, no mistake in the time. These sticks Tecumseh caused to be painted red. It was from this circumstance that in the former Seminole war, these Indians were called "Red Sticks." (McKenney 46–47)

This is the trope of the counting sticks at its most absurd. The idea that Tecumseh could synchronize his native allies and the British suppliers (the Creeks in fact got ammunition from the Spanish fort at Pensacola) by sending bundles of sticks overland for hundreds of miles is preposterous. Unless

Tecumseh could know exactly how many days the messengers would spend en route, how could he know how many sticks to put in each bundle?

Yet for McKenney and Hall in the 1830s, Tecumseh's reputation seemed grand enough to sustain such a tall tale. After all, Tecumseh's call to arms, white settlers' desire for Creek lands, and the War of 1812 all coincided to create in 1813–14 a devastating conflict known as the Red Stick War. The warriors who were inspired by Tecumseh and several Creek prophets to defy their traditional chiefs and attack Fort Mims in August 1813, killing 250 Anglos, called themselves Red Stick Creeks. The origin of this name is uncertain. In the two most recent and comprehensive histories of the Creek Wars, Joel Martin and Claudio Saunt attribute the term to the color of the clubs these warriors carried and describe their uprising as part of a nativist movement that, like Neolin's and Tenskwatawa's, rejected European influences such as alcohol and even cattle and salt (Saunt 257–59; Joel Martin 129). They do not link these sticks to the counting tokens, as McKenney and Hall did. However, in his history of the Creek rebellion, George Stiggins describes the method of counting tokens, the only early-nineteenth-century Native American source that I have found who does so. The account comes amid the planning for the Fort Mims attack.

> The day was set for all the forces to concentrate at the mouth of Flat Creek, and they sent the broken days to all the towns (the broken days is a bundle of broken parts of twigs about four inches long every piece for one day tied carefully in a bundle one of the sticks is thrown away at sun rise every day to the last which is the day appointed) the leaders of different towns on an appointed day collected their warriors and every town separately and held a war dance, and after it was over they started on different routs for the mouth of Flat Creek, in the county of monroe, where they were to concentre their whole force and number them, which they did seven hundred and twenty six effective warriors. ("Creek Nativism" 162)

Stiggins was in the military and stationed at Fort Mims but (like Dumont de Montigny) was fortunate enough to be absent on the day of the attack. As a mixed-blood and as an agent who worked with the U.S. Indian bureaucracy, Stiggins deeply regretted the revolt. He goes to great lengths to explain how one of its métis leaders, William Weatherford, who later married Stiggins's sister, Mary, had been unwillingly swept up in the rebellion and forced to become one of its leaders. This passage about the "broken days" is presented in an offhand manner, as if many of his readers would have already been familiar with the technique. It is not attributed to any master conspirator, it has no obvious spiritual component, and, perhaps most significant, it does not fail. No theft of sticks undermines the planning, and in any case it appears that the purpose of the bundles of sticks is not to coordinate the date of attack, for the warriors have no difficulty counting. They enumerate themselves, after all, at 726. The surprise attack betrayed is a trope of imperialist savagism, but the use of isomorphic tokens was in fact a Native American semiotic technique.

A century prior to Stiggins's history, the anonymous French author of a journal of the Chickasaw war of 1739–40 wrote of how Choctaw allies of the French organized various war parties: "The method for counting the days in such cases is peculiar: they give to the chief of the party a certain number of sticks, keeping [a bundle of] the same number, and instruct him to throw out one each day" (Journal de la Guerre 84; my translation). The journalist does not connect this technique to the Natchez uprising ten years earlier and appears to be a source independent of Dumont. The transcripts of Pueblo Indian witnesses telling the Spaniards about the cords of maguey fibers are also trustworthy, I believe, for these were native people speaking soon after the event. Moreover, Nabokov has pointed out that several other Indian nations used knotted cords for more peaceful countings of days: "The eastern Pomo called such cords damalduyik, or 'day count,' and did not use them for periods longer than five days; the Chemehuevii had messengers called 'bringers of the knotted string' " (13). Still, this does not prove that they were used in the Pueblo Revolt, and Nabokov and other anthropologists have also observed that "there is scanty mention of the major war [of 1680] in Indian oral tradition" (13; see also Weber, What Caused 8). However, at least one member of a participating tribe has affirmed the tradition that the revolt was organized by the distribution of the knotted strings. Edmund Nequatewa's 1936 Truth of a Hopi tells the story of the revolt from the perspective of the Hopi pueblo of Shungopovi, where laborers had in the seventeenth century built a church for a Franciscan priest who then abused his welcome by demanding sexual favors from young Hopi girls. A runner was sent to the neighboring village, and "the chief at Awatovi sent word by this boy that all the priests would be killed on the fourth day after the full moon. They had no calendar and that was the best way they had of setting the date. In order to make sure that everyone would rise up and do this thing on the fourth day the boy was given a cotton string with knots in it and each day he was to untie one of these knots until they were all out and that would be the day for the attack" (44).

Nabokov's Indian Running is devoted in large part to documenting the 1980 tricentennial commemoration of the Pueblo Revolt, for which the Hopi and Pueblo tribes organized a relay run from Taos to Hopi, departing on 5 August and arriving five days later.[3] The relay baton consisted of a medicine bag containing, among other objects, a knotted cord made of rawhide rather than maguey or cotton string. Nabokov affirmed the importance of the messenger runners but did not commit himself on the question of the authenticity of the knotted cords. Herman Agoyo, then the executive director of the Eight Northern Pueblos, told Nabokov, "Somebody must have brought in the knotted string but nobody remembers, there aren't any legends" (31). The account by Nequatewa suggests that the Hopi may have remembered better, but his tale of the young boy at Shungopovi who needed the knotted string to ensure an accurate count of just four days is very much a "bottom-up" perspective on the revolt. The unnamed chief of the neighboring village Awatovi is only another intermediary, not the mastermind of the plot. In spite of Charles Hackett's claim to the contrary, it seems most likely that the knotted strings, like the "broken days," were used as a symbol of each village's commitment to joining the revolt, not as a means of counting the days until it occurred. An attempt to further clarify the role of the knot tokens in the Pueblo Revolt must lead back to Popé, for he was the source of the knotted cords, and according to Naranjo's testimony, Popé claimed to have received the idea from the three Indians who magically appeared in the kiva. The figure of Popé, even more enigmatic and sinister than Tecumseh or Metacom, is at the center of contemporary debates over the memory of the Pueblo Revolt.

Spanish colonial sources reveal a few additional facts about Popé and his life before 1680. In 1675, Popé was a medicine man at San Juan Pueblo when Spanish Governor Juan Francisco Treviño launched a campaign against such "witches" and "sorcerers." Popé was among forty-seven shamans who were arrested, flogged, and sold into slavery. But outraged Indian warriors descended on the governor's house in Santa Fe and demanded the release of these prisoners, and Treviño had no choice but to comply. Popé then relocated to Taos and began organizing his nativist rebellion, with a spiritual message that resembled the later ones of Tenskwatawa and Neolin. The interrogation transcripts explain that he commanded his followers to "separate from the wives whom God had given them in marriage and take those whom they desired. In order to take away their baptismal names, the water, and the holy oils, they were to plunge into the rivers and wash themselves with amole" (Hackett and Shelby 2:247). Naranjo and other witnesses thus suggested a spiritual struggle between two religious faiths. The Indian named Juan contended that Popé had said "that the devil was very strong and much better than God" (2:235). The millenarian message also included the goal of restoring the Pueblo people's independence from Spanish tools and goods: "Living thus in accordance with the law of their ancestors, they would harvest a great deal of maize, many beans, a great abundance of cotton" (2:248), not the wheat and barley that had been introduced from Europe.

Gutierrez has emphasized the spiritual nativism in the revolt while recognizing that this Manichaean struggle was just the sort of martyrdom tale that
suited the Franciscan missionaries and may even have prompted some of
them to provoke a native revolt that might bring about their own martyrdom.
Spiritual nativism also suits the tastes of some Anglo-Americans today who
idealize and even try to practice Indian religions. But Popé was no cuddly
New Age shaman. He murdered his son-in-law, Nicolas Bua, out of fear that
the man might betray his conspiracy. The testimony of Pedro Naranjo asserted that the knotted cords were a solemn pact distributed "on pain of
death to those who refused to agree to it" (2:246), and other interrogations
also suggested that some Indians went along with the plan more out of fear
of Popé than respect for his program or hope for its success.

No nineteenth-century Indian tragedy or epic poem was written with
Popé as its hero, no romantic historian such as Parkman or Prescott immortalized his revolt. But his image has nonetheless recently come to resemble
those of the Indian tragic heroes examined in earlier chapters. And the most
controversial piece of this puzzle is the suggestion that Popé, like St. Cosme,
Tecumseh, and Logan's father, Shickellamy, may have been by birth a mixed-
blood. A 1962 article by New Mexico historian and Franciscan priest Angelico Chavez questions the authenticity of Popé's prophetic vision and even
of Popé himself. Chavez spent years researching parish records in the state
and wrote the definitive genealogical history of the leading Spanish families
of the colony. His article draws on this research to present an account of five
generations of the Naranjo family. As we saw, the source of the key primary
account of Popé among the interrogations from December 1681 was an old
man of eighty who signed his name on the deposition as Pedro Naranjo.
Chavez believes this may be a pseudonym for or possibly a brother of Domingo Naranjo, who is identified in the genealogical records, and that
Pedro/Domingo Naranjo was in fact Popé. Otermín thus had the grand
conspirator in his custody and did not realize it. Chavez identifies Domingo Naranjo as the son of two servants of a soldier named Alonso Martin
Naranjo, with the father a black slave named Mateo and the mother one of
three sisters from Tepeaca in the valley of Mexico. The identities of these two
parents help to account for details in the testimony about Popé, who was
described as a large black man with yellow eyes. Chavez also asserted that
the names of the three spirits whom Pedro said came to Popé in the kiva
sound more like Nahuatl than Pueblo words and pointed out that Copala, the
lake the three figures named as their destination, was a mythical place in the
imagination of sixteenth-century colonists of New Spain, somewhat like the
Seven Cities of Cibola. Moreover, Indians captured and questioned by Otermín on 20 August, just after the revolt, claimed that they "had the mandate

of an Indian who lives a very long way from this kingdom, toward the north, from which region Montezuma came, and who is the lieutenant of Po he yemu; and that this person ordered all the Indians to take part in the treason and rebellion" (Chavez 88; Hackett and Shelby 1:15–16). Popé, then, was Poheyemu's representative, and Chavez chose this title for his article. According to the Aztec myth well known to Spanish colonizers, including Villagrá, Moctezuma's nation traced its origins to the Seven Caves of Aztlan, located in a northern region, possibly the Upper Rio Grande Valley. Otermín believed these captives were mocking him and had them put to death. As we have seen in the previous chapters, Indian rebels have often consciously mimicked the colonizers' myths and ideals in fomenting resistance against them, and colonizers have often projected their political dreams onto the figures of the Indian rebels.

The figure of Popé as Chavez deconstructs him is hardly the stuff of which romantic postcolonial dreams are made. If Chavez's identification of Popé and the genealogy of his family is accurate, it poses a handicap to modern efforts to enshrine the leader of the Pueblo Revolt as a revolutionary defender of Native American sovereignty. Instead of a Pueblo shaman turned revolutionary genius spreading a message of tribal renewal and dispatching swift messengers with knotted cords of maguey fibers, we have a mixed-blood slave who concocted a tale of divine revelation that convinced Indians to kill the Spaniards who had enslaved him and who then, when recaptured by the Spaniards, cleverly dissimulated his role in the uprising to escape punishment. The subsequent generations of the Naranjo family also fail to add any luster to their reputation. Lucas and Josephe Naranjo, sons of Domingo, were interrogated the day after Pedro and joined the Spaniards in their retreat downriver toward El Paso. However, on 8 January 1682, they fled back to the northern pueblos. In 1696, Lucas was implicated in another revolt by the Tewas, which killed five more Franciscan priests. Josephe alerted the Spaniards and then killed his brother and delivered his head to Don Vargas. This secured for Josephe the favor of the Spaniards and eventually the titles of *alcalde mayor* of Zuni and of war captain of all the Indian troops fighting with the Spanish in New Mexico. In 1701, Josephe claimed to have foiled another uprising by Zuni and Hopi Indians who were passing around a knotted thong. Jemez Pueblo native Joe Sando, author of a number of books and articles about the Pueblo people and now director of the Indian Pueblo Cultural Center in Albuquerque, has called Josephe "a traitor to his people" (230). Josephe's grandson, José Antonio Naranjo II, also ingratiated himself with the Spaniards and was trying to get an appointment as a military commander of Spanish as well as Indian troops when his mixed-blood heritage was exposed and he was stripped of his command. Chavez's findings are not beyond doubt, of course. Judgments about the Nahuatl origin of names as set down by scribes who most likely understood neither Nahuatl nor the local Pueblo languages are particularly tenuous.[4] Alfonso Ortiz has proposed a likely Pueblo word behind one of the three deities whom Pedro Naranjo named as inspiring Popé, and Sando, likely following Ortiz, explains that Otermín cited "Poheyemo" as the divine instigator of the revolt only because the Pueblo Indians who were interrogated about its leader gave the name of mythical northern sky spirit as a distraction or a joke (65–66).

As the most successful Indian rebellion in North American history, the Pueblo Revolt imparts a magical aura to the knotted maguey fibers and to the man who created them. Spaniards, Indians, and Anglos in New Mexico all share a belief in this magic, even as each culture is otherwise very careful to distinguish its supernatural devices—be they electronic machines, saints' relics, or medicine bundles—from those of the other two. If Popé was in fact a mixed-blood who rose to power in Pueblo society, he was a hybrid whose humble origins may have helped to disguise him. But we will never know for certain. Much like Pontiac, the stature of Popé and his leadership has been the subject of debate among academic historians. The actual importance of his role as a leader and organizer of the rebellion is in dispute. Van Hastings Garner has pointed to a number of less successful uprisings at various pueblos and has asserted that "there is little evidence marking Popé as a unique Indian leader beyond the fact that the Revolt of 1680 was a success. . . . Much of the misinterpretation of the Revolt of 1680 can be attributed to an overemphasis on the contribution of this one man and singling out his conspiracy as the cause of the Revolt" (Weber, *What Caused* 71). Others emphasize the role played by nomadic Apaches, whose raids the Spanish had helped the Pueblos to repel but who may have joined with their traditional enemies in attacking the Spanish in August 1680.

Nonetheless, outside academia, Popé is rising in stature as an Indian hero. By 1997 plans were under way for a statue of him to be erected in the National Statuary Hall Collection in the U.S. Capitol, the second of the two New Mexico figures among one hundred represented there. In support of this honor, Popé's reputation is being refurbished. In a story about Popé and the statue, the *Albuquerque Journal* quotes Sando as saying that Chavez's theory about Popé was "entirely wrong," that he "made it up" (Weber, *What Caused* 14). Jemez Pueblo sculptor Cliff Fragua has crafted the statue, which shows on Popé's back the scars from the flogging he received after his arrest by Governor Treviño. As a monument to Native American resistance, the statue might help respond to the statues of Juan de Oñate at Alcalde, New Mexico, and the one planned for El Paso, Texas. Popé was to be installed in

2002, but according to the Web site of the Architect of the Capitol, as of February 2005 he still had not taken his place. The statue may thus be embroiled in the controversy over Popé's heritage and authenticity.

The controversy about Popé and the history of the Pueblo Revolt bears comparison with a recent controversy among historians studying Denmark Vesey and the 1822 slave rebellion in Charleston, South Carolina. In June of that year, 128 black men were put on trial for conspiracy in a revolt allegedly organized for 14 July by Vesey, a fifty-five-year-old free black carpenter. Many confessed to their involvement, and thirty-five were hanged. Several prominent Charlestonians as well as the state's governor, Thomas Bennett, criticized the court proceedings as tainted and biased against the defendants, but the trial transcripts, together with a published *Official Report* on the affair that appeared soon after the court sentences were handed down, constitute the main source for historians studying the incident. As interest in African American history has grown since the 1960s, many scholarly studies of Vesey and his uprising have been published, as have various editions of the trial documents. In 1999 alone there appeared two new biographies of Vesey and an updated edition of the trial record. The controversy broke out in a 2001 review essay on those three books, written by Johns Hopkins historian Michael P. Johnson and published in the *William and Mary Quarterly*, the leading journal of early American history. The journal then published nearly seventy pages of responses and commentaries in its April 2002 issue. Johnson had gone to South Carolina to reexamine the trial documents, and although he confirmed the earlier claims that the accused were tried before a kangaroo court, he broke sharply from what he called "this heroic interpretation of Vesey" as a revolutionary freedom fighter and militant defender of African American slaves. Johnson described myths and contradictions in historians' accounts of Vesey, detailed faulty transcriptions of the documents published by scholars, and concluded that "Vesey and the other condemned black men were victims of an insurrection conspiracy conjured into being in 1822 by the court, its cooperative black witnesses, and its numerous white supporters and kept alive ever since by historians eager to accept the court's judgments while rejecting its morality" (971). He drove home the point by mocking other scholars' romanticization of Vesey as a giant strongman of deep black complexion who planned to lead an exodus of freed slaves to St. Domingue after his revolt succeeded. Because the alleged revolt was foiled by the mass arrests, its potential scale is uncertain, but the revisionist theory suggests that like the Natchez uprising, the Vesey conspiracy was exaggerated or even invented by the white colonizers who were its targets. And like Popé and the Pueblo Revolt, Vesey was portrayed first as a demonic visionary by those who sought to punish him and later as a rebellious hero by those who embraced his cause. Prominent Boston abolitionist Thomas Wentworth Higginson published an essay on Vesey in the *Atlantic Monthly* in 1861, and his rebellion featured prominently in the 1943 book *American Negro Slave Revolts* by pioneering African American historian Herbert Aptheker.

The histories of the Indian resistance actions we are studying in this book are not told in trial transcripts, and the relationship between Anglo-Americans and Indian leaders cannot be equated with whites' relationship to antebellum black slaves, but the lesson to learn from the comparison is that whereas historians and students today may assume that their education and predilections sharply differentiate them from the colonizers who contended with Indian rebellions and slave revolts some two centuries ago, the two groups' desires and motives may coincide. The prosecutors who condemned Vesey and dozens of other black men imagined a possible rebellion that they feared and sought to prevent, while today nearly all who study the incident admire Vesey and wish to imagine the possible success of his rebellion. The colonial soldiers who fought against Metacom or Popé feared his power, and the villagers and missionaries targeted by the Indian warriors saw themselves as righteous martyrs and innocent victims. Those examining the Indian rebels from a safe spatial or temporal distance cast them as the victims and martyrs. The paired emotions of fear and pity do not in fact differentiate the attitudes of the colonials from the moderns as much as tie them together into a common tragic emplotment of history. Colonizers feared the backlash of those whom they oppressed, but a repressed sense of justice often led them to pity their victims. The cathartic ambivalence in this tragic view of history allows for a working-out of this repression by reversing the poles of domination and indulging in a sympathetic affirmation for slaves or Indians. Sympathetic identification with the rebel is highly infectious, and the attractions of martyrdom can be so powerful that some of Vesey's coconspirators may well have confessed to a conspiracy that had not existed due to intimidation or out of a sense of solidarity or admiration for the alleged conspirator (see Paquette). Whereas those men were tried by a corrupt court in Charleston, the theater most often served as the setting for such reversals in the representation of Indian resistance, and though no tragedies were written starring Popé or Denmark Vesey, the figures of Metamora and Spartacus capture the same sort of rebel hero.

Popé was arrested by Governor Juan Francisco de Treviño in 1675 and was therefore the only one of our eight Indian rebel heroes to be tried and sentenced by a colonial court of law. It is significant that his crime was not treason or rebellion but witchcraft, which even more than treason constitutes a projection of the fears of the accusers and invites the sympathy of modern minds seeking to reject past superstitions, as events in Salem, Massachusetts, less than twenty years later amply prove. The weakness of Spanish control in Santa Fe at the time forced Treviño to release Popé. The kangaroo court's verdict against Vesey could not be overturned so easily. But the figures of Indian resistance and rebel slave nonetheless run parallel in American history.

CHAPTER 8 / TECUMSEH

> He was called the Napoleon of the west; and so far as that title was
> deserved by splendid genius, unwavering courage, untiring perseverance,
> boldness of conception and promptitude of action, it was fairly bestowed
> upon this accomplished savage. He rose from obscurity to the command
> of a tribe to which he was alien by birth. He was, by turns, the orator, the
> warrior, and the politician; and in each of these capacities, towered above
> all with whom he came in contact.
> —Judge James Hall, qtd. in Benjamin Drake,
>   *The Life of Tecumseh and of his Brother the Prophet* (1841)

> The general [Isaac Brock] used to call Tecumseh "the Wellington of the
> Indians."
> —Ferdinand Brock Tupper, *The Life and Correspondence of*
>   *Major General Sir Isaac Brock, K.B.* (1847), qtd. in Carl F. Klinck,
>   *Tecumseh: Fact and Fiction in Early Records* (1961)

In Tecumseh, the figure of the Indian resistance leader as hero
reached its apogee. His resistance to U.S. expansion, his alliance with the
British in the War of 1812, and the nativist movement he led with his brother,
Tenskwatawa, the Shawnee Prophet, all combined to make him the most
influential Indian rebel in the history of North America. As the literary topoi
of the heroic Indian chief proliferated in the 1820s, Tecumseh was therefore
the most obvious, most recent figure to whom they might be applied. More
epic poems, verse romances, historical novels, and biographies were written in the nineteenth century about Tecumseh than about any other Indian
leader—more even than about Metacom.

However, as the epigraphs to this chapter suggest, Tecumseh's efforts as
an ally of the British in the War of 1812 introduced a twist that we have not
encountered with Metacom, Logan, or even Pontiac. I have sought in previous chapters to show that in frontier colonial wars there was no consistent
or absolute opposition between red and white peoples or their interests, that
people of mixed-blood and cross-cultural identities played important roles,
and that the greatest challenge of native resistance was maintaining a solid

alliance among various tribes or nations, any of which might have reasons to ally with colonizers. But with Tecumseh, we for the first time find an Indian leader and his warriors fighting with one colonial power against another. Pontiac had fought in the same region and in defense of the French colonial cause, but he did not have the formal support of the French and did not fight alongside their soldiers, since France had already conceded defeat in the Seven Years' War. Tecumseh, conversely, applied colonial realpolitik and expressed his people's interest in a new manner that complicated any simple portrayal of the Indian resistance leader as an anti-imperial republican. To his ally, Isaac Brock, a fallen hero of the Anglo-Canadian side in the War of 1812, Tecumseh was the Indians' greatest leader, and this compliment became even greater than Brock knew when, a year after his death at Queenston, Ontario, Wellington led the British in the defeat of Napoleon at Waterloo, Belgium. For James Hall, Tecumseh embodied the same leadership qualities as Napoleon, the demogogic leader who had brought Europe to the brink of destruction and whose imperialist designs seemed to confirm U.S. Federalists' suspicions about the French during their revolution. In Benjamin's Drake's book, however, the "Indian Napoleon" was presented sympathetically as a friend. The epithet was widely used. Colonel William Stanley Hatch, an officer under General William Hull (who fought ineffectively against Tecumseh at Detroit in 1812), commented that Tecumseh's "face [was] oval rather than angular; his nose handsome and straight; his mouth beautifully formed, like that of Napoleon I, as represented in his portraits" (qtd. in Klinck 162). B. B. Thatcher likewise called Tecumseh "the INDIAN BONAPARTE" (Indian Biography 2:225).

The immensity of the Tecumseh legend and the volume of historical and literary material about him require that this chapter have a more limited scope than the studies of the five native uprisings and their leaders in chapters 2–6. Because Tecumseh has been the subject of several lengthy biographies, I shall not trace the entire story of his life and his battles for native sovereignty.[1] Nor will it be possible to discuss or even mention all of the literary works about him, a corpus that continued to grow into the twentieth century. Instead, this chapter will take the form of two essays.

The first will document, following on the case of the token sticks analyzed in the previous chapter, the ways that legends about Tecumseh followed the tropes of the Indian tragic hero and elements of the emplotment of Indian uprisings. There is a certain self-consciousness to these accounts. By 1810, when Tecumseh first met the man who would become his nemesis, William Henry Harrison, eyewitnesses were well aware of the phenomenon of the heroic Indian chief, and they tried to rise to the occasion by adapting their descriptions of Tecumseh and transcriptions of his speeches to the mold of tragic, stoic valor. Moreover, Harrison was certainly aware of how political leaders could capitalize on the stature of these Indian leaders, and he succeeded magnificently, riding his frontier battlefield record all the way to the White House.

Second, I will turn from Harrison and the U.S. historical perspective to the Canadian side of the Tecumseh legacy. We saw in chapter 2 how the tragic resistance of Moctezuma and Cuauhtémoc and the brave defiance of Xicoténcatl became "native" material for an epic narrative of the origins of Mexico as a nation. In chapter 3 we saw how Metacom became emblematic of resistance to British colonization and thus offered a foundation for the historiography of the American Revolution. Here I shall examine how Tecumseh, as the martyred hero of battles to protect Upper Canada against a U.S. invasion, became a symbol for an emergent Anglo-Canadian nationalism, particularly in the writings of John Richardson, who fought alongside Tecumseh in his final battle at Moraviantown (near Windsor, Ontario). Richardson is virtually unknown to U.S. literary scholars, but he has earned the label "Canada's first novelist" by virtue of a pair of novels he published in 1832 and 1840 based on Pontiac's rebellion and on the War of 1812. And Richardson, like Dumont de Montigny, also wrote a verse epic, Tecumseh: A Poem in Four Cantos (1828) about the Indian hero of the war in which he fought. This chapter therefore follows two Anglo-American men who built political or literary careers on their association with the Indian hero Tecumseh—his U.S. adversary, Harrison, and his Canadian ally, Richardson.

Tecumseh and Harrison

As a Shawnee, Tecumseh belonged to the tribe that had contributed most to the native defense of the Ohio Valley in the years following the 1763 British declaration that the Alleghenies should form the western limit for colonial settlement. The Shawnee under Cornstalk made up the majority of the warriors who faced Lord Dunmore at Point Pleasant in 1774, and Tecumseh's father, Pukeshinwa, was killed in that battle. Shawnee also predominated among the fighters who defeated Arthur St. Clair on 4 November 1791, killing more than six hundred soldiers, although the Miami leader, Little Turtle, is considered to have been the war chief for the battle. When Kentucky promotional tracts such as John Filson's Adventures of Colonel Daniel Boon celebrated the pastoral utopia of the Ohio Valley and at the same time warned of the dangers of the "dark and bloody ground," they were referring to the Shawnee and their hunting grounds. Boone's narrative told of how during a brief and painless captivity he had been adopted by a Shawnee family and how the "Shawanese King took great notice of me, and treated me with profound respect, and entire friendship, often entrusting me to hunt at liberty" (219). Had Boone identified this "Shawanese King" by name, the story would be more credible, and one might be able to study his appropriation of Native American heroism in a specific way comparable to that of Robert Rogers rather than in a general way, as Richard Slotkin has presented Boone's mythopoeic regeneration through the violence of Indian warfare.

After Pukeshinwa's death, Tecumseh's older brother, Cheesekau, became the head of a family of siblings that included a sister, Tecumpease, and a brother, Laulewaasikaw or Lalawethika, who later came to be known as Tenskwatawa and as the Shawnee Prophet. Although both trader John Johnston and French-Ottawa métis Anthony Shane, two of the key eyewitness sources for Benjamin Drake's biography, claimed that Tecumseh, the Prophet, and another brother named Kumskaukau were triplets, it is more likely that Tecumseh was born several years before the other two, perhaps as early as 1768 (Drake, *Life* 63; Sugden 23). The family lived at Piqua (Pekowi), an important Shawnee town that was forced to relocate several times during the 1770s and 1780s, shifting northwest across modern Ohio. George Rogers Clark led an attack on one of these sites that served as the basis for the concluding scenes of Robert Montgomery Bird's *Nick of the Woods*. In spite of this violent history, Tecumseh's biographers have represented his fatherless childhood at Pekowi in idyllic, child-of-nature terms. In *Tecumseh: A Life* (1997), John Sugden describes the Pekowi near Springfield, Ohio, as "an ideal playground for a boy of Tecumseh's spirit. He could explore swamps, scale the cliffs behind the town, or cross the cornfields to ford the river and set up ambuscades in the timbered ridges" (31). John Oskison, an Oklahoma Cherokee and a successful novelist and journalist in the 1930s, begins his biography, *Tecumseh and His Times* (1938), by linking this scene of Pekowi with the account of Shawnee life in Boone's narrative:

> Tecumseh longed for the opportunity to distinguish himself in conflict. His inspiration came from stories of raids told by his father and by Cheesekau. He saw them come in from forays on the Ohio, or into Kentucky, decked as warriors, scalps tucked under the twist of buckskin at their waists, leading their prisoners to the Piqua council house. As a lad of ten, he may have seen the party of forty warriors that took Boone with them from Old Chillicothe, the Shawnees' principal town on the Little Miami River. (30)

Oskison goes on to point out that just as Boone claimed that he was an instrument of God ordained to settle the wilderness, the Shawnee saw their wars of resistance as sanctioned by the Master of Life to defend their homelands.

Other legends carried the identification between Tecumseh and earlier leaders even further. In 1824–25, the *Cincinnati Literary Gazette* serialized an anonymous story about Tecumseh that claimed that his father, Onewequa, was the son of Shickellamy, the father of Logan. Benjamin Drake in his biography and Thomas McKenney and James Hall in their sketch of the prophet both included a story reportedly told by Laulewasikaw about his grandfather's marriage to the daughter of a colonial governor who had met him at a council in "one of the southern cities, either Savannah or Charleston." The governor's daughter "conceived a violent admiration for the Indian character; and having determined to bestow herself upon some 'warlike lord' of the forest, she took this occasion to communicate her partiality to her father," who selected this "handsome man and expert hunter" as a husband for his daughter (McKenney 37). Their children included Pukeshinwa, who after his father's death was raised for a time by the governor (Benjamin Drake, *Life* 63–65). Some Shawnee groups had lived in the South, and many people believed that Tecumseh's grandfather was a Creek, so the tale may be true. The Natchez/Creek George Stiggins also emphasized the links between the Shawnee and Creek nations, though he did not mention this colonial governor as an ancestor of Tecumseh. This story suggested that the rebellious spirit of Tecumseh, like the Natchez Sun St. Cosme, might owe something to his mixed blood and the elite status of his parentage. Or perhaps, as with the claim that Opechancanough was the son of a Spanish Jesuit missionary to Virginia, the notion of a full-blood Indian leader organizing a widespread coalition against colonizers was too frightening or too unlikely for prejudiced historians to accept.

Tecumseh's grandfather may have married an Englishwoman, but Tecumseh, in sources that present him as a severe and stoic Indian warrior, had no time for romantic dalliance. He in fact married a woman much older than himself and had just one son, Paukeesaa (Pugeshashenwa), who survived the removal to Oklahoma and spawned descendants who were acquaintances of Oskison in his youth (although Oskison identified him by the name Nathahwaynah). Thus, Oskison could dedicate his biography to "all Dreamers and Strivers for the integrity of the Indian race, some of whose blood flows in my veins; and especially to the Oklahoma Shawnee friends of my boyhood" (v). Nineteenth-century literary portrayals showed Tecumseh refusing the marriage offers of younger women, even those whose family legacy might have added luster to his anticolonial project. Since he and his brother had met in 1807 with a traveling band of Shakers, who praised the prophet's doctrines of sobriety and self-control (see Sugden 138–42), it is conceivable that Tecumseh absorbed a philosophy of sexual abstinence from them, but more likely it is part of the tradition of martial, republican virtues among the

Indian tragic heroes. In G. H. Colton's epic poem, *Tecumseh; or, The West Thirty Years Since* (1842), a late but comparatively polished contribution to the genre, the hero meets at Mackinac a maiden who introduces herself.

> Omeena is great Pontiac's daughter [actually granddaughter]
>
> . . . .
>
> this Pontiac's name
> Leads me to conflict, glory, fame—
> That star shall be Tecumseh's guide!
> Will Pontiac's daughter be his bride? (141)

Omeena then gives her knight Tecumseh a quest: she will marry him only when there are no palefaces remaining on the Wabash River. Moreover, her father, Kenhattawa, says to Tecumseh: "A maid of Pontiac's matchless line / Might never meet embrace of thine" (143). The romance subplot serves mainly as additional motivation for his heroic uprising, as Tecumseh announces

> though Pontiac's name be great,
> Who bowed not to the foe but Fate,
>
> . . . .
>
> Tecumseh's name in many a clime
> Shall mightier be through coming time. (144)

In James Strange French's novel, *Elkswatawa; or, The Prophet of the West* (1836) ("Elkswatawa" was a variant spelling of Tenskwatawa), Pontiac's young granddaughter proves even less of a distraction from Tecumseh's republican virtues. French, like a few other authors of Indian plays and romances in the 1830s, names some of his characters after Indians in John Tanner's narrative. Miskwabunokwa (the Ojibwa name of Tanner's first wife) comes seeking Tecumseh's hand in marriage, and her mother, Netnokwa (the name of Tanner's adoptive mother), insists that Pontiac's blood flows in her daughter's veins. Both Pontiac and the real Netnokwa were Ottawas. But Tecumseh, whom French has just compared to Hannibal, has no time for romance, he says, because he is going on the warpath.

These literary contributions to the Tecumseh myth stand in contrast to a more folkloric myth that probably arose long after the hero's death. The Galloway family had moved to the Little Miami River near Xenia, Ohio, in 1798, and patriarch James Galloway offered information to Drake for his biography. "For many years following 1797, Tecumtha maintained unbroken friendly relations with his host and family and continued to be a welcome guest at the Galloway home" (123), according to *Old Chillicothe: Shawnee and Pioneer History*, a book published at Xenia in 1934 by William Galloway, a descendant of James and a resident of the town. Local interest in colonial history was intense during this era (the Logan Elm historical park was dedicated at around the same time), and much of Galloway's book was devoted to proving that the site of Old Chillicothe, in modern Oldtown, Ohio, just north of Xenia and some fifty miles northwest of modern Chillicothe, was the Shawnee village of Pekowi, the birthplace of Tecumseh. Photos of several plaques and monuments embellish his case. The book also includes a thirty-five-page appendix of tribal history and autoethnography by Thomas Wildcat Alford, a friend and informant of Galloway's who claimed to be Tecumseh's great-grandson. But the most intriguing sections tell the legend of a romance between the Shawnee leader and Rebecca Galloway, James's daughter. Here the stoic republican of the nineteenth-century tragedies and epics is softened into a sentimental lover. Rebecca, we learn from three separate accounts of the courtship, recited daily prayers with Tecumseh, listened to his complaints about the injustice of U.S. land purchases, and read literature to him to help improve his English. As one might expect of an Indian tragic hero, "Hamlet was a character admired by Tecumtha" (124). Their courtship also involved Tecumseh giving Rebecca canoeing lessons on the Little Miami River. In 1807, when he was forty and she sixteen, Tecumseh asked James Galloway for his daughter's hand in marriage. As Rebecca considered her suitor, "she knew that this man bore within him a rising power, dangerous to her people and fateful to his own. Her thoughts continued to dwell on the possibility that this incident of love might, in some way, be made to change impending events. . . . If she gave consent to his honorable suit, could the power of this unusual man be turned from war and enlisted in the arts of peace?" (136). In this legendary romance, the actual sexual politics of *métissage* in North America are swept under the rug, and in their place we find a fantasy of assimilation resembling Oceana's symbolic inheritance of the indigenous sovereignty of Metamora. Like Metamora, Tecumtha (as Galloway spells his name) gives Rebecca a talisman to protect her from the imminent uprising: "Taking up the calumet he had given her father, confirming the pact of peace and friendship between her family and his people, he said: 'You and your family need have no fear from my race'" (137). A photo of this calumet appears in the book, along with the note that it was used again in a renewal of the "pact" in 1926. Yet the pact ultimately protects only the Galloway family, not the white settlers as a whole, for Tecumseh decides he cannot abide by her demand that "she would accept him if he would adopt her people's mode of life and dress" (137), and he withdraws his marriage proposal. The legend is the basis of an annual historical pageant that is still performed today in Chillicothe. Richard White sees it as evidence of white America "cannibalizing [Tecumseh] for the same reasons that Algonquians [and Iroquoians, I would add] ate the hearts of their admired enemies, America absorbed Tecumseh" (*Middle Ground* 519). By incorporating Tecumseh's heroism and converting it into familiar and acceptable cultural terms, Americans denied the unfamiliar aspects of the intercultural middle ground that had created him and on which his resistance struggle was fought.

Whether the heroic image of Tecumseh represents genuine admiration for the resistant Indian leader or a cannibalistic assimilation of a threatening cultural Other must remain a matter of opinion. Many elements of the legend can be interpreted in either way. The dichotomy between alterity and assimilation is in fact often false, particularly when it can be shown that stories of what is Other—the magical, the spiritual, or the Indian—are after all not so different from familiar Euro-American ideas. In some biographical portraits of Tecumseh and his brother, the Shawnee Prophet, the two men are split along this dichotomy: "Tenskwatawa became the ultimate other, the alien savage" (519), writes White, emphasizing that whereas Tecumseh's death made him amenable to tragic heroism, the prophet's nativist message, his persecution of rivals as witches, and then his fall from grace and his support for Shawnee removal to Oklahoma all made him less appealing to sympathizers of the Indian cause.

Most observers agree that the 1810 battle of Tippecanoe marked the intersection of the two brothers' contrasting trajectories. Before that time, the prophet's reputation and message had spread widely (as far as the Winnipeg area) but Tecumseh remained little known.[2] Even in 1812, Isaac Brock referred to him in a letter as "a Shawnee chief, Tecumset, brother to the Prophet" (qtd. in Klinck 141). One of Tecumseh's tragic flaws was to be absent from the battle at Tippecanoe. He was recruiting warriors in the South at this time, and his brother seems to have accidentally incited the battle and then offered no military leadership to complement his spiritual message: "Prior to the assault, the Prophet had given assurances to his followers, that in the coming contest, the Great Spirit would render the arms of the Americans unavailing, that their bullets would fall harmless at the feet of the Indians" (Benjamin Drake, *Life* 152). But this magical charm was ineffective. Much the same message was attributed to Nemattenow before the Jamestown Massacre of 1622. In fact, the notion of a magical shield against colonizers' bullets is a key part of the nativist tradition of resistance. At the tragic climax of the Wounded Knee uprising on 19 December 1890, James Mooney reports that "Yellow Bird, a medicine-man, had been walking about among the warriors, blowing on an eagle-bone whistle, and urging them to resistance, telling them that the soldiers would become weak and powerless, and that the bullets would be unavailing against the sacred 'ghost shirts,' which nearly every one of the Indians wore" (117–18). George Stiggins's history of the attack on Fort Mims explains how a Creek nativist prophet, Paddy Walsh, "urged as an omen for them to know by of their being successfull in their assaut . . . that the four men he should select for that purpose he would make invulnerable and proof against a white mans bullet" (164). When this magical armor proves worthless and half of the Creek warriors are killed or wounded, the survivors "rose in fury at night against the prophet and leading man Paddy Walsh" ("Creek Nativism" 167). The authenticity of these reports is more solid than those employing the trope of the counting sticks and the surprise attack betrayed, but from the point of view of colonial soldiers, the tropes served much the same purpose. The rebellious Indians would be easy to defeat because they lacked European knowledge and technology and relied instead on superstitions. Benjamin Drake also writes that when Tenskwatawa's promises proved false, he was so discredited that surviving warriors threatened to put him to death (*Life* 154).

Another of the notable stories about Tenskwatawa involves his early exchanges with William Henry Harrison before Harrison faced Tecumseh. In 1808 the Prophet sent a messenger to explain that his movement sought to eliminate whiskey from native life and that he had resisted recent British invitations to take up the tomahawk and fight on their behalf. Moses Dawson wrote in 1824 that "the subtlety and address of this fellow was so profound, that he completely deceived the Governor [Harrison] and impressed him with the opinion, that the influence which he had obtained over the Indians, would be advantageous to the cause of humanity, rather than of a mischievous tendency" (qtd. in Klinck 50). Dawson's comment may be colored by hindsight, and evidence also indicates that Harrison had feared the prophet's growing influence. Early in 1806, Harrison addressed Delaware followers of the Shawnee Prophet, telling them to "demand of him some proofs at least of his being the messenger of the Deity. If God has really employed him, he has doubtless authorized him to perform some miracles, that he may be known and received as a prophet. If he is really a prophet, ask of him to cause the sun to stand still—the moon to alter its course" (Dawson 83–84; Benjamin Drake, *Life* 90). A few weeks later, on 16 June 1806, an eclipse of the sun answered Harrison's challenge, enabling the Prophet "to carry conviction to the minds of many of his ignorant followers, that he was really the earthly agent of the Great Spirit" (Benjamin Drake, *Life* 91). Although Benjamin Drake suggested that Tenskwatawa knew of the pending eclipse and R. David Edmunds explains that astronomers traveling in the area could have informed the Indians of it (*Shawnee Prophet* 48), some my-thologists, including Alvin Josephy (149–50), have presented the incident as a miracle of the Shawnee Prophet.[3]

By linking native revolts to natural phenomena that, unlike the eclipse, could not have been predicted, historians both of Tecumseh's time and of our own have emplotted these uprisings with epic grandeur. In September 1811, during one of Tecumseh's southern recruiting trips, a comet appeared, a celestial echo of the translation of Tecumseh's Shawnee name as "shooting star." Sugden suggests that this phenomenon aided his cause: "No Creek could be blamed for believing that this man had truly been favored by the spirits"; however, as he also points out, "in November the visibility of the comet declined," coinciding with the lost battle at Tippecanoe, so the omen seems to have been an ill one for the Indian cause (246–47). Both McKenney and Hall's biography and Stiggins's history mention the comet but make much more of the influence Tecumseh derived from having predicted the enormous New Madrid earthquake of 12 January 1812. According to Stig-gins, in a September 1811 address to Creeks at Tuckabatchee, Alabama, Tecumseh said that "if he was to beat the white people in his intended conflict with them and obtain his desire, they would know it by the following sign, That he would assend to the top of a high mountain in about four moons from that time And there he would whoop three unbounded long whoops slap his hands together three times and raise up his foot and stamp it on the earth three times and by these actions call forth his power and thereby make the whole earth tremble" ("Creek Nativism" 147; McKenney 47 also has Tecumseh saying "stamp the ground with my foot"). In fact Tecumseh's major battles did not occur until well after the January 1812 earthquake, but for the Creeks "the earthquake happening so near the time that Tecumseh [told them] was to convince them of his power and truth, by his actions on the mountain to shake our globe, they were certain that the shaking was done by him, their conviction of the event left no room to doubt any thing he had said of the successful irruption of the Indians against the white people" (Stiggins, "Creek Nativism" 150). The stereotype of Indian peoples as being in closer communication with the earth and heavens was active even in the 1820s and 1830s, and this notion was also closely allied to the prejudice that Indians were in thrall to superstitions, omens, and au-guries, that they lived in an archaic manner suitable to archaic literary genres. Hence, in his epic poem *Tecumthe* (1824), a work similar in plan but weaker in execution than Richardson's poem, George Longmore enumer-ates omens foretelling the Indians' defeat—in waterfalls, owls' flights, meteors, and lightning bolts—that the Prophet Tenskwatawa seeks to re-describe as auspicious.

Sly to perceive, and swift to turn
His thoughts to what he might discern,
Once more, he raised his voice in song,
Which soon was chorus'd by the throng,
And in his gestures wild, essay'd
To calm the fear each sign had swayed;
But in his features were express'd,
The labourings of an anxious breast. (32)

Whereas Euro-American historiography has used the trope of the token sticks and the interpretation of celestial omens to attribute primitive or superstitious practices to the Indians, these stories often reflect Euro-Americans' own folklore and belief in portents. Edwin James reported having learned from John Tanner that the Ojibway and Cree "have the opinion common among ignorant white people, that the appearance of a comet is an indication that war is to follow" (Tanner 322).

In the accounts of speeches at key meetings between Tecumseh and his nemesis, William Henry Harrison, we also can perceive the echo chamber of colonial mimicry. Although Homi Bhabha's oft-cited concept of mimicry was coined to describe the manner in which colonized Indians of the Asian subcontinent learned to imitate the language and fashions of the British, on the American colonial frontier I see the process as more mutual. Harrison's speeches mimicked the figural style of Indian oratory, so popular since Logan's speech and before, and Tecumseh's and the prophet's speeches mimicked the political rhetoric of American postcolonial unity and independence. It is impossible to be sure if the rhetorical genius of either man was genuine—there was plenty of room for revision and embellishment by the various translators, scribes, and historians on whom we must rely for the Indians' words. Tecumseh spoke always in Shawnee, and the most important negotiations with Harrison were not recorded by fluent bilingual or mixed-blood interpreters who might offer more reliable transcriptions. Harrison wrote his dispatches to Washington with an eye to protecting his position, and his biographers wrote in support of a man whose political success might later benefit them and their region. The exchanges at Vincennes in August 1810 are the most dramatic in Tecumseh's career, but reports of these speeches in various documents differ widely. Many are mere paraphrases. We can be fairly certain, however, that Harrison continued the habit of referring to the United States as the "seventeen fires" and the president as the Indians' "father." An address Harrison sent to Tecumseh and the Prophet in July by an interpreter named Joseph Barron warned that he was aware of a pantribal conspiracy and that you have been in some measure successful as I am told they are ready to raise the tomahawk against their father; yet their father, notwithstanding his anger at their folly, is full of goodness, and is always ready to receive into his arms those of his children who are willing to repent, acknowledge their fault, and ask for his forgiveness. . . . What can a few brave warriors do, against the innumerable warriors of the 17 fires. Our blue coats are more numerous than you can count. Our hunters are like the leaves of the forest, or the grains of sand on the Wabash. (Dawson 153; Klinck 64)

Tecumseh parried this rhetoric of the U.S. president as patriarchal Christian God with a rhetoric of republican deism, and, in a more original flourish, by describing the U.S. president in the terms of Native American leadership. Tecumseh insisted that treaties which surrendered huge tracts of Indiana and Ohio lands, such as the one signed at Greenville in 1795, were invalid because no single village or tribal chief could sign away sovereignty over lands that belonged collectively to all Indian peoples. While multitribal alliances and pan-Indian consciousness had also been a hallmark of Pontiac's rebellion and of the nativist spirituality of Neolin, this sense of pan-Indian land sovereignty was innovative. The Prophet likewise mimicked Harrison's rhetoric, insisting that the movement was one of unity, that "those Indians were once different people; they are now but one" (Benjamin Drake, Life 108), much as the thirteen and now seventeen fires had joined in a union. As Oskison wrote, conscious of the damage done by the Dawes Allotment Act and the recent attempt to restore tribal sovereignty through the Indian Reorganization Act of 1934, "The Indians regarded the whole as their common property, to be hunted over by all; and any Indian could build his home and cultivate his garden and fields wherever he liked. . . . Tecumseh, of course, knew what was going on. . . . He knew the essential validity of their communal title" (85).

The eyewitness accounts of Tecumseh and his orations reflect not only an innovative and defiant concept of pantribal sovereignty but also a stoic republican's reluctance to fight. One of the most consistent elements of the Tecumseh legend is the humane treatment of prisoners captured by his warriors or by British soldiers. Although the defeated General Hull complained that the Indians had plundered the fort at Detroit after his August 1812 surrender, the British and Americans agreed that Tecumseh was not responsible. When Americans were massacred after the battle of River Raisin in January 1813, Tecumseh was not present. And in the spring of 1813, when Tecumseh led Indian warriors alongside the British troops under Matthew Elliot and Henry Proctor to besiege Fort Meigs, his humane virtues emerged in full. Benjamin Drake's biography devotes a long passage to reports that General Proctor had promised Tecumseh that, if victorious, the Indians would have William Henry Harrison as their prisoner; however, he noted, "To suppose then, that [Tecumseh] really intended to permit General Harrison, or those who fought with him on the Wabash, to be burned, would have been at variance with the whole tenor of his life" (*Life* 180). Tecumseh, his biographers maintained, had also opposed his brother's persecution of dissenters as witches. Longtime captive Stephen Ruddell, who had been brought up alongside Tecumseh at Pekowi, reported that even as a young warrior he had recoiled from the practice of torturing prisoners (Benjamin Drake, *Life* 68–69). Thus, in Colton's poem, Tecumseh prevents the Ottawa chief, Kenhattawa, from torturing the white heroine, Mary, and in George Jones's tragedy, *Tecumseh and the Prophet of the West*, he several times defies his brother's orders to torture captives.

Richard Emmons's *Tecumseh; or, The Battle of the Thames, a National Drama*, includes the most complex portrayal of Tecumseh's humane virtues. The play was commissioned in 1836 as campaign propaganda for Senator Richard Johnson, candidate for vice president on the Democratic ticket alongside Martin Van Buren, who had been vice president during Andrew Jackson's second term. Emmons no doubt got the assignment because he had in 1827 published *The Fredoniad; or, Independence Preserved: An Epic Poem on the Late War of 1812*. In four volumes consisting of 33,380 lines in heroic couplets, this work narrated every battle of the war and celebrated every hero including Johnson, replete with apotheoses and heavenly interventions. Even more than Barlow's *Columbiad*, upon *The Fredoniad* we moderns may lay blame for destroying the potential appeal of any U.S. national epic. But the Van Buren–Johnson campaign nonetheless gave Emmons a chance to try his hand at a more popular genre of nationalist historical literature, the Indian tragedy. The final scene was all set, for Johnson claimed to be the man who had killed Tecumseh at the battle of Moraviantown on 5 October 1813 (figure 8.1). Through the 1830s the question of the truth of this claim raged in the columns of U.S. newspapers, most of which had partisan editorial stances anyway. Benjamin Drake, who in 1840 was employed to coauthor a campaign biography for Harrison, Van Buren's Whig opponent, devoted a chapter at the end of his biography of Tecumseh to disproving Johnson's claim.[4] The true circumstances of Tecumseh's death and the location of his grave had became so bound up with politics and mythology as to be impossible to determine. What is of interest to us is how both Johnson and Harrison managed to capitalize on their common foe's heroic reputation even after they had become political adversaries. Van Buren defeated Harrison for president by a close margin in 1836, and then Harrison defeated Van Buren by a landslide in 1840.

Emmons echoes other writers in portraying Tecumseh's protests against torture. His second act opens with the British general, Proctor, paying Indian warriors for the scalps of Americans. When Maypock (a corruption of the name of Pottawatomie shaman and war chief Main Poc) presents the scalps of a bride and groom and their infant, Tecumseh breaks down in tears. Maypock had already called Tecumseh a "squaw" in front of his brother, the Prophet, and in this scene Maypock raises his tomahawk to strike the hero. As he says afterward, however, "My arm fell dead—fell nerveless. He, from a low, dwarf shrub, seemd at once an oak" (14). The hackneyed image of the hero as an oak resonates with accounts that Johnson slew Tecumseh near "the large trunk of a fallen tree" (Klinck 211), which later served as a landmark for eyewitnesses of the death of Tecumseh. Jones's play even put the "large prostrate and withered Oak tree" on stage as a prop (act 5, scene 2). Maypock and the Prophet later begin to torture Edward, an American taken captive by the British and the lover of Lucinda in the play's romantic subplot, but the Indians are forced to flee when Tecumseh approaches. Although Emmons's Tecumseh appears dignified and virtuous compared to his brother, to Maypock, and to the "hair-buyer" Proctor and his ignorant Canadian soldiers, Tecumseh nonetheless does not speak in the elevated style written for the heroes of most Indian tragedies. His lines are in a semiliterate pidgin English: when told of his adversary, Johnson, Tecumseh grunts in anticipation, "Me feel my sinews swell—me watch—me keep my eye awake—to see—to trail—to hunt him in the battle" (9). Emmons does not even allow Tecumseh an eloquent dying speech after he is shot by Johnson. The traditional curse on his victorious foes is delivered in the briefest possible manner: "Great Spirit! Thy Red Children's cause avenge. Thick curses light upon the white man's head! . . . I die—the last of all my race" (39). When Emmons's play was performed in Baltimore, Johnson's supporters mounted an exhibit including an outfit supposedly worn by Tecumseh and a pistol owned by Johnson. Johnson's triumphalist appropriation of Tecumseh's power was strongly fetishistic, relying on a chain of material evidence supporting his claim to have dealt the deathblow some twenty-three years before. Tecumseh was little more than another scalp in Johnson's bag.

Harrison's exploitation of Tecumseh's heroic image was more subtle or at least maintained an elevated tone more in keeping with the literary traditions we have followed. Harrison capitalized on the ambivalence of catharsis toward the Indian tragic hero. He or his handlers sensed that it might be possible for voters to adore Tecumseh and admire his nemesis as well. The

1 Col. Johnson heroically defending himself against the attack of an Indian Chief.
2 The American Infantry firing upon a body of the enemy on the left
3 A dismounted Dragoon personally engaged with one of the enemy
4 The cavalry pursuing the retreating savages across the hills.

FIGURE 8.1. "A View of Col. Johnson's Engagement with the Savages (commanded by Tecumseh) near the Moravian Town, October 5, 1812 [1813]." Richard Johnson is on horseback at center left. Tecumseh is at far right "rallying his men, and encouraging them to return to the attack," according to the legend. Frontispiece from Henry Trumbull, *History of the Discovery of America* (1830).

d by Tecumseh)near the Moravian Town, October 5, 1812.

5 Tecumseh rallying his men, and encouraging them to return to the attack.
6 A savage in the act of scalping a wounded drummer of the American Infantry.
7 The savages pursued by the cavalry, retreating to a swamp on the left.
8 The enemy (rallied by their commander Tecumseh) returning to the attack

texts of speeches exchanged by the two leaders at Vincennes and elsewhere, reprinted in many versions in many different publications, were a foundation of Harrison's statesmanlike reputation. Tecumseh's orations, translated from the Shawnee, did not reduce him to the level of pidgin English, as Emmons did in his play, but raised him to the heights of Indian oratory popularized by Logan and others. Harrison's mimicry of Indian rhetoric—metaphors such as "seventeen fires"—only enhanced the gravity of his address. Neither man could maintain such elevated rhetoric without an equal level of dignity from the other.

Historians of the presidency identify Harrison's 1840 campaign as pioneering the techniques of modern campaigns by avoiding substantive issues and manipulating ideological symbols and associations to promote a candidate's popular appeal. Harrison, the scion of an aristocratic Virginia family, was cast as a frontier populist, the "log cabin and hard cider" candidate. These images had first been formed around Andrew Jackson, the first president born west of the Alleghenies. But by 1840, Jackson's legacy also included his Indian removal policy and his bloody wars against the Seminoles in Florida, which had aroused strong opposition and against which Samuel Drake's and B. B. Thatcher's Indian Biographies and Indian tragedies such as Metamora so eloquently dissented. Thus, the Harrison campaign combined frontier populism with Indian heroism, repeating Jackson's symbolic strengths while avoiding his policy liabilities. One step was to hire Benjamin Drake, who had already struck this balance in his successful 1838 biography of Black Hawk. Drake teamed up with Charles S. Todd to write Sketches of the Civil and Military Services of William Henry Harrison, published in Cincinnati in 1840. A preface declares forthrightly that the book was "written at the request of the Harrison committees in Cincinnati and Louisville, and is published under their sanction." In contrast to Emmons's puff piece for Johnson and in spite of the well-known campaign slogan mentioning Harrison's running mate along with his most famous battlefield victory, "Tippecanoe and Tyler too," Drake and Todd's biography does not present its subject as an Indian fighter. The battle of Tippecanoe is narrated in just a few pages, and the emphasis is on rebutting charges that Harrison's poor choice of a campsite for his troops made possible a surprise attack by the Indians that inflicted many casualties. The August 1810 conference at Vincennes also receives only a brief treatment, and Harrison's well-known speeches are not reprinted; his main accomplishment there was to have secured a promise from Tecumseh "to put a stop to that cruel and disgraceful mode of warfare which the Indians were accustomed to wage against women and children, and upon their prisoners . . . and it is due to the memory of Tecumthe to add, that he faithfully kept his promise" (31). Harrison is portrayed as a restrained, rational, republican. Drake and Todd later quote Harrison's speech on the floor of the U.S. House in which he censured Andrew Jackson's conduct of the Seminole Wars by evoking the fall of the Roman republic: "General Jackson will be faithful to his country; but I recollect that the virtues and patriotism of Fabius and Scipio, were soon followed by the crimes of Marius and the usurpation of Sylla" (118). Harrison's campaign biography thus distanced him from Jackson, the architect of Indian removal, and located him firmly within the tradition of ethical virtues associated with Indian resistance leaders and Roman republicans.

Harrison also took the high road of classicism in publishing his 1840 book, *Discourse on the Aborigines of the Valley of the Ohio*. It was based on a lecture delivered two years earlier to a historical society in that state and was published, says its preface, to demonstrate "the scholar-like habits of General Harrison during his retirement from public life." It opens with a jeremiad against "the accumulation of riches" and "a decline in patriotism" attributable to "the great increase in the works of fiction," the reading of which has made the elite men of America "deficient in the knowledge of the history of their own country" (5). He goes on to praise the Greek custom of presenting to "their youth the examples of the heroic achievements of their ancestors" (6). But the text is not an edifying biography of himself or of his Indian foe. Harrison's title echoed those of two previous books written by prominent men about the legendary Mound Builders, New York Governor DeWitt Clinton's *Memoir on the Antiquities of the western part of New York* (1818) and Caleb Atwater's *Description of the Antiquities Discovered in the State of Ohio and Other Western States* (1820). Those texts contributed to the myth of the Mound Builders as a great civilization that had vanished in prehistoric times and been replaced by the primitive Indians. Harrison's book supported that myth and added to it certain details that had the effect of cleaning up his own reputation as a man who had spearheaded the expropriation of Indian lands in Ohio and Indiana territories from the 1790s through the 1810s. He first argues that these Mound Builders were related to the Aztecs, were the "ancestors of Quitlavaca and Gautimosin" (12) or Cuauhtémoc, and vanished for unknown reasons centuries earlier, leaving the Ohio Valley adorned with their earthworks and fortifications but devoid of any human population. He then goes into a long explanation of why central Ohio was not part of the ancestral lands of the Iroquois, as "the late De Witt Clinton, of New York" (15) had argued, or the property of Tecumseh's people, for "the Shawanese came from Florida and Georgia about the middle of the eighteenth century" (28). It was instead the land of the Miamis, the tribe whose chiefs, among them Little Turtle, received the largest share of the annuities apportioned for its purchase by the treaties concluded at Greenville and thereafter. The only reference to the famous meeting with his nemesis at Vincennes is Harrison's claim that he presented this history of the tribe at that meeting "to resist the pretensions advanced by the far-famed Tecumthey to an interference with the Miamis in the disposal of their lands. However galling to this chief the reference to these facts might have been, he was unable to deny them" (29). Rather than take credit for defeating Tecumseh in battle, Harrison preferred to challenge Tecumseh's sovereignty over the lands for which he fought.

In the foreword to his biography, Oskison compared Tecumseh to the legendary founders of the Iroquois Confederacy, Deganawida and Hiawatha, and remarked on the ironic contrast between his legacy and that of his U.S. foe: "While Harrison is almost forgotten and his record clouded, this Shawnee warrior, orator, statesman, and patriot has grown in stature" (viii). The Indian author and his subject eagerly heaped historical revenge on Harrison, who in his book had belittled both Tecumseh and the Iroquois and who died soon thereafter, just a month into his term as president. Harrison seems to have been aware that the prestige of Tecumseh the Indian hero might end up working against his presidential candidacy. Certain lines in *Discourse on the Aborigines of the Valley of the Ohio* critique, in the most elevated language Harrison could muster, the foundations of the Indian tragic hero phenomenon. He refutes "an erroneous opinion" that the Indians of North America "are supposed to be Stoics, who willingly encounter deprivations. The very reverse is the fact" (32). Indians are epicureans, he claims, pleasure-loving and gluttonous and avoiding martial exploits whenever possible. He also takes issue with Alexander Pope's assertion, in the prologue to Addison's *Cato*, that republican tragedies such as that work might change the " 'savage natures' of tyrants":

> Miserable indeed, would be the situation of mankind, if that were their reliance to escape oppression. But I conceive that the operation, as well of tragedy as history itself, is more direct. Instead of palliating and lessening the evil when it shall have existence, their great object is (and such is certainly their effect) to prevent its occurrence. Instead of softening the hearts of tyrants, to harden those of the people against all tyrants and usurpers . . . and to warn them of the insidious means by which their confidence is obtained, for the purpose of being betrayed. (8)

Although this passage addresses a long-standing question about tragedy and the *Discourse* mentions "Tecumthey" only twice, it is quite plausible, I think, to read these comments as a rejoinder to those who had read Thatcher's chapters about Tecumseh in the early editions of *Indian Biography* or had seen a performance of Emmons's tragedy and who believed that such works might soften the hearts of the tyrannical U.S. leaders who continued to attack and

displace Indian peoples. Harrison suggests that the function of these tragedies and histories is not to convert the rulers to a more humane Indian policy
but to warn the populace about usurpers, by which he means not Andrew
Jackson or himself but Indian leaders such as Tecumseh and the Shawnee
Prophet whose nativist movements and allegiance with the Anglo-Canadians
he saw as a betrayal of the tribes they claimed to unite.

Harrison's remarks here are oblique, but much more solid evidence also
shows that contributors to the Indian tragedy genre conceived of their works
as a check against tyranny. As we have seen with regard to *Metamora*, most
critics today are inclined to see such plays as an endorsement of Indian
removal, but in that play and in works about Tecumseh I see evidence to the
contrary. George Jones's *Tecumseh and the Prophet of the West, An Original Historical Israel-Indian Tragedy, in Five Acts* (1844) weighed in directly on the issue to
which Harrison alluded. This Indian drama was perhaps the most preposterous in the entire genre. Jones had already published *The Original History of
Ancient America*, one of a number of nineteenth-century tracts purporting
to explain the origins of the Native American peoples and of the Mound
Builders. Jones, like many others, subscribed to the theory of the Indians as
descendants of the Lost Tribes of Israel, and so he inserted into Tecumseh's
speeches lines affirming this theory in spite of the damage it did to his hero's
historical authenticity. Jones also used the preface to his play for a shrill
attack on critics of his earlier book. Following this, however, he explained
that tragedies about rebels against tyranny "instruct us as to the means
employed by those Scorpions of the human family, to obtain their enven-
omed and poisonous power." Although this line could be read as concurring
with Harrison's statement quoted earlier, the action of the play makes it clear
that although the Prophet might have been a tyrant, Tecumseh was a rebel
fighting to protect the freedom and sovereignty of his people from the
tyranny of the United States. He aligns his struggle with those of Pontiac and
Metacom and even invokes "Brave Kosciusko! leader of the Poland Chiefs"
(36). As an "Israel-Indian" tragic hero, Tecumseh can even claim divine
support for his sovereignty: "Indian believe! / Tradition claims the Book to
be their own!" (28). He even accuses Harrison and the Americans of per-
secuting Indians, as Christ had been persecuted:

The Red-man only is cast forth: for him
The Pale-face hath but one cry,—and like that,—
Which, howl'd throughout your Holy-City's walls,
(When bloody thongs unflesh'd His sacred bones,)
Did drive Mes-shé-hah, thy Great Prophet,—to the Cross,—
'Tis—: Crucify him! (37)

Jones was one of only a few contributors to the literature of heroic Indian leaders to make this analogy between the native victims of U.S. imperialism and the Savior crucified by Roman imperialists. Heretical as it may be, it also concurs with René Girard's theory of the sacrificial victim. By the time Jones wrote, Harrison had also died, and by offering praise to both Tecumseh and to his nemesis, Jones's play proposes a symbolic resolution to the cycle of warfare between them and perhaps also to the continuing Indian wars in the trans-Mississippi West. Moreover, in act 5, scene 1, the prophet is stabbed to death by Melindah, the maiden who had offered herself to Tecumseh, in revenge for the Prophet's having ordered the death of her mother, Net-nokwa. The Shawnee Prophet is a villain in Jones's play, but the Manichaean opposition between the brothers only enhances their reciprocal dependence. Tecumseh and the Prophet actually shared the dual roles of sacrificial victim and of heroic leader. Tenskwatawa was, after all, a prophet who claimed divine revelation. His prophetic vision (recorded by Trowbridge, as we shall see) resembles that of Pontiac's tale of the Indian of the Wolf tribe and McCullough's copy of Neolin's map, and his doctrines of temperance and abstinence were, like Neolin's, influenced by Protestant missionaries. Yet with the failed battle of Tippecanoe, the Shawnee Prophet abdicated his leadership in favor of his brother, who assumed the mantle both of military hero and sacrificial martyr. Tenskwatawa lived on obscurely until 1836 and "lies buried somewhere under modern Kansas City, Kansas" (Edmunds, *Shawnee Prophet* 187), while Tecumseh was sacrificed to the benefit of John-son's and Harrison's political careers and to the cause of Canadian national-ism. Harrison wrote, in the manner of a Cortés drunk on his own power, that Tecumseh was "one of those uncommon geniuses which spring up oc-casionally to produce revolutions, and overturn the established order of things. If it were not for the vicinity of the United States, he would, perhaps, be the founder of an empire that would rival in glory Mexico or Peru" (qtd. in Benjamin Drake, *Life* 142). Yet Tecumseh, in spite of the "vicinity of the United States," did find his legacy appropriated by a great nation, much as postcolonial Mexico embraced Cuauhtémoc, Chile the Araucana, and Peru Atahualpa. The nation is Canada.

Tecumseh and Richardson

In the final chapter of his biography of Tecumseh, John Sugden provides a fine survey of the many literary works about him and comments that "com-pared to their Canadian counterparts American writers were reluctant to see Tecumseh as a subject of serious literature" (398). In support of this claim he lists titles of many dime novels and juvenile adventure stories published in the United States in the century after the hero's death. Frivolous as those works may be, Drake's biography, the dramas by Emmons and Jones, and Colton's epic poem—all published in the United States during the thirty years after the battle of Moraviantown—can be taken seriously as literary works in the most respectable genres of the day. Perhaps their authors took themselves too seriously, for the genres of verse epic and Indian drama had by 1840 become too grandiloquent and too formulaic to maintain the respect of U.S. readers and theatergoers, who were by then all too familiar with the conventions and sentiments of the Indian chief as tragic hero. Canada, however, offered a fresh start. For the national literary history of Canada, the battles of the War of 1812 and the heroic role of Tecumseh were foundational. The Anglophone population there numbered less than fifty thousand in 1800 but grew quickly after the War of 1812. Upper Canada, or Ontario, which swelled first with loyalist refugees from the American Revolution and then with Scots and British immigrants, was the scene of Tecumseh's heroic exploits and was destined to become the new nation's agricultural heartland. John Richardson was well aware of this potential. He wrote in his 1847 autobiography, *Eight Years in Canada*, that he had been Canada's "first and only author" and that he had made Tecumseh Canada's first Indian hero. Richardson's first published writing, which appeared just prior to his epic poem, *Tecumseh*, was a series of five articles that appeared from December 1826 to June 1827 in London's *New Monthly Magazine* under the title "A Canadian Campaign, by a British Officer." He revised and expanded this war narrative after returning to Canada in 1838 and published the new version in 1842 in *New Era*, a newspaper he had started in Brockville, Ontario, and then again as a book. The Legislative Assembly of Upper Canada provided a grant to support the book's publication, and a preface explained that *War of 1812* would be the first installment in a series of schoolbooks for Canadians "on the gallant deeds performed by their Fathers" (Duffy, "John Richardson" 108; Richardson, *Tecumseh* xv). He also published his epic poem, *Tecumseh*, both as a book and in his newspaper and in the book's introduction proclaimed that he intended to place the last copy of the print run "under the foundation stone of the Monument to be erected to that celebrated Warrior" (xxi), a monument that was never built. So whereas Robert Rogers never found a safe spot to build his postwar career or a monument to Pontiac and Joseph Doddridge promoted Logan as a heroic founder only for his region of western Pennsylvania, Richardson went for broke by invoking his Indian hero on behalf of all Canada. Unfortunately, he also went broke doing it. The issue of the *New Era* in which the fourth canto of *Tecumseh* appeared was the paper's final one. In October 1849 Richardson was forced to move to New York City to seek his livelihood from U.S. publishers issuing reeditions of his works.

A fundamental paradox of the genre of epic is that although each tribe, empire, or nation can use its epic to legitimate its heroic founders and
unique origins, the genre is perhaps the most imitative in all of literature. When writing *Tecumseh, a Poem in Four Cantos*, Richardson was living in England and may have been unfamiliar with *Yamoyden* or other recent verse epics about American Indians. He chose instead as his models some of the most prestigious forms and poets of the time, ottava rima stanzas and a romantic historical persona in the manner of Scott and Byron. Nonetheless, the ways in which Richardson chose to revise his hero's historical actions in the battles of September and October 1813—battles in which Richardson had fought—followed some of the major conventions of Indian tragedy as it was forming in the United States in the 1820s and 1830s. Tecumseh in the poem has a son named not Paukeesaa but Uncas, who must have been named for the same Mohegan as in Cooper's hit novel of 1826 even though Richardson claimed to have begun the poem in 1823. In the first canto, which portrays the victory of American Commodore Oliver Hazard Perry over the British fleet at the battle of Put-In Bay, Uncas feels

> a secret dread,
> A dark foreboding of some agony
>
> .   .   .   .
>
> was it but to die
> For him, that honor'd Sire.
>
> .   .   .   .
>
> How would he fly to meet death's rudest shock! (canto 1, stanza 41)

Sure enough, in the second canto Uncas's grandfather (presumably his maternal grandfather, since Pukeshinwa had died in 1774) is brought his grandson's dead body and told

> But not in vain does he, that sweet boy lie;
> His death has spar'd the life-blood of his Sire;
> The rifle-ball, sent whizzing from on high,
> Warm'd in his heart, and quench'd his bosom's fire;
> The wound unerring he had flown to meet,
> Else had the Chief fall'n lifeless at his feet. (canto 2, stanza 32)

As in other Indian tragedies, the hero's son precedes him in death. Uncas is killed off and leaves his father to be the last of his race, although the real Tecumseh's son survived his father and perpetuated his line even after the Shawnee, including the prophet, were removed to Oklahoma. "And none remain'd of all his Father's line / Save he—The Prophet of the brow divine" (canto 4, stanza 18), Tecumseh muses as he surveys the battle ranks at the

Thames on the morning of the battle of Moraviantown (called the battle of the Thames in some histories), a line that anticipates his death and points to his brother, the Shawnee Prophet, as the only survivor of Pukeshinwa's line, although the prophet is mentioned only once earlier in the poem. Tecumseh's self-sacrificing republican ethic at first forswears grieving or revenge. When a harpy-like fiend sacrifices an American prisoner to avenge the spirit of Uncas, Tecumseh deplores this barbaric act and arrives just too late to stop it. Tecumseh's humane treatment of white prisoners is, as we have seen, consistent with his reputation in historical works. By the fourth canto, however, Richardson's Tecumseh has become more of a romantic Satan-hero who feels

> the hate that mock'd at suffering or toil,
> For with his Uncas' death-pang snapp'ed the tie
> Which bound him latest to humanity. (canto 4, stanza 21)

He thus welcomes his own death, a sacrifice that amounts to another favor to his American foes.

Epic traditions also prompted Richardson to begin each canto with pastoral landscape descriptions, such as the evocation of Indian hunting and games in an apostrophe that opens, "All these, oh Erie! were thy scenes of yore" (canto 2, stanza 16). Furthermore, Richardson follows a pattern used in *Yamoyden* and *Metamora*, comparing his Indian hero's final struggle to that of a great mammal extinguished by human hunters or by their beneficent God.

> Not the wild mammoth of Ohio's banks
> Dash'd fiercer splashing thro' the foaming flood,
> When his huge form press'd low the groaning ranks
> Of giant oaks which deck'd his native woods,
> Than rag'd Tecumseh through the deep phalanx
> Of deadliest enemies, soon bathed in blood,
> Whose quivering scalps, half-crimsoned in their gore,
> The dusky Warrior from the white-men bore. (canto 1, stanza 30)

In a note to these lines, Richardson references Thomas Jefferson's *Notes on the State of Virginia*, where Jefferson cites a Shawnee tale about the last mammoth driven out of the Ohio and Wabash by "the Great Man above," who intervened to prevent the giant creature from destroying all the Indians' game (see Gordon Sayre, "Mammoth"). In this manner, Richardson reiterates the vanishing Indian cliché that attributes the demise of native peoples to the inevitable course of a beneficent Nature. But the end of the poem suggests a more critical angle to the simile linking Tecumseh with an extinct beast. The American soldier who kills him is identified only as "The Chief," the same term used for Tecumseh himself. While a note to the 1828 edition glosses this chief as Richard Johnson, the 1842 Canadian edition omits this note. Both the note and the final stanzas of the poem denounce the American soldiers for their savage, bestial treatment of Tecumseh's body as a relic or fetish: "a hundred foemen" descend on the body and

> Like famished blood-hounds to the corse they cling,
> And bear the fallen hero's scalp away.
>
> . . . .
>
> Wild hell-fiends all—and reveling at his death,
> With bursting shrieks and pestilential breath. (canto 4, stanza 42, and a
>   note repeated a story that Kentucky militiamen "tore the skin from off
>   his bleeding form, and converted it into razor-straps!!!" 113)

With a bullet in his bosom, Tecumseh cannot deliver the customary curse on the white man, but Richardson delivers on his behalf a curse on those who desecrated his body: "May they who left him thus e'er howl, and creep / As vile through life, as cruel in that hour," and may death "blast the promise which their creeds impart" (canto 4, stanzas 43–44) of a heavenly rest in the afterlife. Like the Pennsylvanian Doddridge, Richardson saw proper funereal customs and respect for the dead as fundamental to a civilized society and used this principle to differentiate the values of his region from those of the savage white "long knives" to the south.

Both his military and his literary experiences provided Richardson with an animus against the United States. At the battle of Moraviantown, where Tecumseh was killed, Richardson was captured by the Americans and taken as a prisoner to Frankfort, Kentucky, where he was held for a year, often in shackles. When he returned to the United States in 1849 to try to recover his fortunes by republishing his novels for the larger U.S. market, he was forced to abridge them of their anti-American language but nevertheless derived so little profit from their sales that he died in penury just three years later. These novels—Wacousta; or, The Prophecy: A Tale of the Canadas (London, 1832) and its sequel, The Canadian Brothers; or, The Prophecy Fulfilled (Montreal, 1840)—focus on the history of Pontiac and Tecumseh and the two wars fought around Detroit. Wacousta has become canonized as the first great novel in Canadian literature: Dennis Duffy declares that it "seems virtually the sole reason for the survival of its author's name" ("John Richardson" 108). The two novels portray much more of Richardson's participation in the battles around Lake Erie than the epic poem did and necessitate a brief survey of his biography and the plots of the two books.

Richardson was born in 1796 in Queenston, Ontario (later the site of the most heroic Canadian battle of the war of 1812), and raised in Amherstburg (Moraviantown), the site of Tecumseh's death. His maternal grandfather was John Askin, a prominent fur trader based in L'Arbre Croche on Lake Michigan, later based in Michilimackinac and in Detroit, and still later the partner of Robert Rogers in an Albany, New York, general store. Askin's first wife was an Ottawa woman, but John's grandmother was probably his second wife, a French-Canadian woman. In 1802, when the United States demanded an oath of loyalty from Askin, who was living on large landholdings near Detroit, he refused and crossed the river to take up residence in British territory. John Richardson lived with his grandfather during some of these years and later returned to the Detroit area when his father was appointed surgeon to the Queen's Rangers at Fort Malden. Richardson thus passed his childhood in fur trade and military families during the buildup to the War of 1812, and in June of that year he and his brother enlisted in the Forty-first Regiment as gentleman volunteers. A year and a half later, he was festering in the Kentucky prison.

In *Wacousta* and its sequel, Richardson drew on his experiences and those of his grandfather's family to create frontier romances that mimicked many features used by Cooper but added lurid gothic scenes that are closer to Neal's *Logan: A Family History*. Much like Cooper, Richardson followed a habit of not providing characters' names until many pages after they first appear and of including dorky characters who exist purely for comic relief, such as the bad punster Middlemore in *Canadian Brothers*. Less like Cooper, sex, miscegenation, and even cannibalism were not so taboo for Richardson as to be excluded from his fiction. Again like Cooper and even more like Scott, the novels' plot arises out of a family rivalry that crosses the boundaries of language and empire. Family lineages connect the two novels, just as Richardson's family history linked the Detroit of Pontiac's rebellion with that of Tecumseh and the War of 1812.

The family rivalry begins in Scotland during the Highland Rebellion of the 1740s, in which the villain, Reginald Morton, was a British officer and where he became friends with a colleague, Captain de Haldimar. On a ramble through the sublime highland scenery, Morton meets the beautiful Clara Beverley, who is living with her father on an isolated farm. They fall in love and are about to marry when Morton's regiment is posted elsewhere. When he returns, he finds that his fiancée has married de Haldimar instead. De Haldimar attempts to squelch his rival by drumming up grounds for his court-martial, so Morton renounces Britain and begins a lifelong vendetta. First, as Morton tells it in *Wacousta*, "the rebellion of forty-five saw me in arms in the Scottish ranks" (394), then he joined the French army in Quebec so that he could fight against de Haldimar in the Seven Years' War. After the

British victory, de Haldimar is promoted to colonel and appointed commandant at Detroit, where his sons, Charles and Frederick, serve under him.

Reginald Morton then continues his vendetta by transforming himself into
Wacousta, a renegade alter ego known to Ponteac (as Richardson spells his
name) and the natives as the brilliant and devious "pale warrior." As we saw
in chapter 4, Richardson's version of the siege of Detroit relegates Ponteac to
a secondary role behind this villain, whose lycanthropic transformation adds
inches to his height, gives his complexion a "swarthy hue," and renders him
"repulsive, from the perpetual action of those fierce passions which have
since assailed my soul" (368). The climactic event in the first volume of
Wacousta comes when de Haldimar orders the execution of a soldier named
Frank Halloway, who turns out to be Reginald Morton's nephew, also named
Reginald, living under an assumed identity. As Halloway/Morton is shot at
the Bloody Bridge, site of a famous battle in Pontiac's war, his wife, Ellen,
intones the prophecy referred to in the title, a curse on the de Haldimar
family ("the destruction of your accursed race" [124]) and then joins forces
with Wacousta. By the end of the novel, Wacousta kills Charles de Haldimar
and his sister, Clara, but Frederick survives and produces another generation, which appears in *The Canadian Brothers*.

Although Richardson does acknowledge the French-English and British-
American rivalries that pervade Canadian history and uses as his settings the
major frontier wars in 1763 and 1812, the gothic vendettas pursued by his
villains are less racial or national than personal and familial. And the conflict
and contrast between the Wacousta and de Haldimar lines resemble in some
ways the two sides of Richardson's family, the maternal side with John Askin
and his Indian wife versus the paternal lineage of English officers who
recoiled from the intercultural middle ground that came so easily to the fur
traders. The de Haldimars of the first novel are carried on by their descendants, Henry and Gerald Grantham, the titular brothers of the sequel. Their
mother, Isabella de Haldimar, is the daughter of Frederick from the first
novel. Their father, Major Grantham, has been recently killed in an apparent
hunting accident by a man named Jeremiah Desborough, the villain of the
second novel, who is revealed to be the son of Ellen Halloway and one of the
two Reginald Mortons. Without any overt crossracial unions, Richardson
imbues his villains with all the savage Indian stereotypes of Cooper's and
Bird's novels while deflating his Indian characters, Ponteac and Tecumseh,
into one-dimensional figures who support either the villain, Wacousta, or
the good guy, General Brock. In texts by U.S. writers such as Bird's *Nick of the
Woods* and James Seaver's *Life of Mary Jemison*, the archetype for the cultural
traitor villain was Simon Girty, a boyhood captive of the Seneca and later a
frontier interpreter who fought with the British in the Revolutionary War.

Jeremiah Desborough constitutes a British-Canadian response to Girty (who appears in The Canadian Brothers as Simon Gattrie, a harmless and good-natured servant of the British). Desborough is introduced as one of a class of "adventurers from the United States, chiefly men of desperate fortunes, and even more desperate characters, [who] had, through a mistaken policy, been suffered to occupy the more valuable portion of the country" (1:80)—that is, Upper Canada. Although Desborough swears fealty to Britain at the outbreak of the war, he is actually a traitor working as a spy for the United States. He employs his daughter, Mathilda, who has been adopted by the American Major Montgomerie, to seduce Gerald Grantham. When Gerald is taken to Kentucky, he meets Desborough in a log cabin, where he is feasting on the arm of an Indian he has killed, a scene that satirizes the Boone-ish ideal of Kentucky frontiersmen so dear to the mythic U.S. self-image. A subsequent episode involves Gerald and Mathilda in a weak imitation of the "Kentucky tragedy," a real-life scandal of love and murder better known from Edgar Allan Poe's Politian and William Gilmore Simms's Beauchampe (see Duffy, "John Richardson's Kentucky Tragedies"). Wacousta and Desborough are villains because they have crossed beyond the palings of respectable Anglo-Canadian society, as represented by its fragile forts at Detroit and Amherstberg, to join with Indian, French, or U.S. enemies.

Richardson's narrow partisanship produced frontier novels that portrayed Indians no more accurately than did those by his American contemporaries Cooper, Bird, and Simms. But because he knew Tecumseh, it is worth looking closely at his portrayal of the great Indian hero in his epic poem and in The Canadian Brothers. We have seen how Richardson demonstrated an acquaintance with the key motifs of the Indian tragic hero, and when Tecumseh is introduced at a council at Fort Malden in The Canadian Brothers, the novel seems to convey these motifs from Richardson's perspective: "Never did the noble Indian appear to greater advantage than on this occasion. . . . That ardor of expression in his eye . . . could not fail to endear him to the soldier hearts of those who stood around, and to inspire them with a veneration and esteem, not even surpassed by what they entertained for their own immediate leader" (1:173–74). Tecumseh proved himself worthy of this respect, for according to Richardson's poem and novel and in the estimation of many historians, the battle of Moraviantown occurred where it did only because Tecumseh insisted on fighting the Americans rather than retreating. After Perry's victory on Lake Erie cut the British supply lines from Fort Niagara, Henry Proctor ordered the abandonment of Fort Malden and began a long retreat along the north side of the lake. If for Americans the climactic scene of Tecumseh's heroic eloquence is his August 1810 address to Harrison, for Canadians it is his reproach of Proctor on 18 September 1813.

The text of the speech was first published by Richardson in his 1826–27 narrative of the war and was later reprinted by Benjamin Drake and others. Perhaps because it was already so familiar by 1840, Richardson chose not to include it verbatim in his novel but simply referred to "the indignation of Tecumseh" in stating "what many of the English officers most religiously believed also, although their tongues dared not of course give utterance to the thought" (2:188). In the speech, Tecumseh uses the paternal epithet that Pontiac had resisted so strongly but begins by rebuking the British for abandoning their Indian allies in the Revolutionary War: "The war before this, our British father gave the hatchet to his red children when our old chiefs were alive. They are now dead. In that war, our father was thrown upon his back by the Americans, and our father took them by the hand without our knowledge, and we are afraid our father will do so again at this time" (Klinck 184; Benjamin Drake, *Life* 188). He then skewers the general as a coward: "You always told us you would never draw your foot off British ground; but now, father, we see you are drawing back, and we are sorry to see our father doing so without seeing the enemy. We must compare our father's conduct to a fat animal, that carries its tail upon its back, but when affrighted, it drops it between its legs and runs off" (Klinck 185). Proctor was later court-martialed for his actions, and the text of the speech appears in the transcripts of those hearings. Tecumseh's rebuke thus hit home both emotionally and legally. To Richardson and other Anglo-Canadians fighting in the battle, Tecumseh's rebuke of Proctor implies a declaration of independence from Britain and its colonial leaders, even if Richardson was otherwise loyal to Britain and its values. This independence is also symbolized in the testimony Drake receives from Anthony Shane that before his final battle, Tecumseh "laid aside his British military dress, and took his place in the line, clothed only in the ordinary deer-skin hunting shirt" (193), a costume not merely Indian but that of a common warrior rather than the dandified ostrich plumes that he had earlier sported as war chief.

Tecumseh's tragic fate was to die fighting not for the cause of the Indian peoples' freedom and sovereignty but for that of the white Anglophones of Upper Canada. He therefore became not a foe of imperialism but an ally, which ironically made him less well suited to the imperial literary form that was Indian tragedy. Tecumseh's death fits the formula of *Metamora* and other Indian tragedies only when viewed from the perspective of his U.S. foes. From the Canadian perspective, the catharsis of his tragedy lacks the political ambivalence that is so important to the overall effect. When Tecumseh first appears in *The Canadian Brothers*, he says that he dislikes the British as "a people to whom he owed all the misfortunes of his race, and for whom he had avowed an inextinguishable hostility of heart and purpose; but unless when this might with strict propriety be exercised, the spirit of his vengeance extended not, and not only would he have scorned to harm a fallen foe, but his arm would have been the first uplifted in his defence" (1:56–57). His hatred of whites is thoroughly repressed by the necessity of his alliance with the British against the Americans, and the "strict propriety" of his behavior removes all fear from the British reception of him. Tecumseh as an Indian tragic hero in Richardson's work is too domesticated to play the fierce role familiar in U.S. literature.

No Man Is an Island

Let me conclude with these famous lines about the character who may today be the best-recognized Native American in English dramatic literature:

Miranda: Abhorrèd slave,
> Which any print of goodness wilt not take,
> Being capable of all ill! I pitied thee,
> Took pains to make thee speak, taught thee each hour
> One thing or other. When thou didst not, savage,
> Know thine own meaning, but wouldst gabble like
> A thing most brutish, I endowed thy purposes
> With words that made them known. But thy vile race,
> Though thou didst learn, had that in't which good natures
> Could not abide to be with. Therefore wast thou
> Deservedly confined into this rock, who hadst
> Deserved more than a prison.

Caliban: You taught me language, and my profit on't
> Is, I know how to curse. The red plague rid you
> For learning me your language! (*The Tempest* act 1, scene 2, lines 351–64)

Like the audiences of the Indian tragedies, Miranda pities Caliban, and like the playwrights of those tragedies, she teaches him to speak. Yet her gift is no act of generosity. As Eric Cheyfitz has written, "Miranda images Caliban as speaking no language. The translation in this case can only go one way. Miranda's language cannot be alienated in Caliban's if Caliban possesses none. So it is only Caliban who is left to be alienated, or translated (thus imperialism fantasizes the univocality of its own power)" (163). Caliban complains that the only thing he has gained from the English language is the ability to curse his fate and his oppressors. Such are the curses delivered in the dying speeches by Metamora, by Tempal and Cotumbo in Villagrá's epic, and by Tecumseh in the literary works we have just examined. This well-known scene from *The Tempest* raises again the question of whether the

Indian tragedies and the other literature of Indian resistance really convey anything of the Native American experience of colonization. Caliban's lines, like those of Metamora and Ponteach, were written and performed by Anglophone actors. Caliban's island is often read as being modeled on Bermuda, for Shakespeare wrote the scenes of the tempest and shipwreck using lines from accounts of the wreck there of the *Sea Venture* in 1609 as it carried members of the Virginia colony to Jamestown. Yet Bermuda was uninhabited. Caliban's existence there and that of his mother, Sycorax, are a mythical creation.

Some of the most influential books of colonial American studies, such as Peter Hulme's *Colonial Encounters*, Eric Cheyfitz's *The Poetics of Imperialism*, and Leo Marx's *The Machine in the Garden*, analyze *The Tempest* as a work that distills the early European colonizers' reactions to America and its natives and that marks America's entry into the canon of English literature. Such use of *The Tempest* reinscribes the myth of native America as being without its own literatures, languages, and cultures, even though critics who so use it often claim to be challenging this imperialist myth. Cheyfitz's Native American voices are twentieth-century authors N. Scott Momaday and Leslie Marmon Silko, to whom he devotes a few pages. Hulme introduces his book as a Marxist critique of imperialism, as following a model of radical history involving "the rediscovery of native sources that offer a different and revealing light on colonial events and issues." But he then claims that in his chosen venue, the Caribbean, the "only evidence that remains[is] the very European texts that constitute the discourse of colonialism" (8). The Caribs, the likely cultural or etymological origin for the cannibals and thus for Caliban, were exterminated before European explorers made any substantive account of their lives or language. This makes Hulme's study rather solipsistic. The "extended Caribbean" on which he focuses includes Virginia and should include Spanish Florida and French Louisiana as well, with their native peoples and languages. Yet Hulme eschews native sources from those regions and languages even though they offer more than do the English documents. His introduction includes a perfunctory problematizing of the literary standards of canon and genre but then claims that "the texts studied here largely chose themselves" (9). To analyze as Hulme does how *The Tempest* and *Robinson Crusoe* express the ideologies of English imperialism is all too easy a postcolonial critical project, for it takes place on mythical uninhabited islands where no indigenous language is heard and only a solitary Friday or Caliban appears to aid or to challenge the colonizers' work.

In this study, I have ignored until now *The Tempest* and other canonical works of English literature and sought instead to draw attention to obscure dramas, epics, and poems such as *Ponteach*, Richardson's *Tecumseh*, and Dumont's mock epic "Poème." These works were written in established European genres that were in many respects imperial forms, designed to limit the agency of the rebel heroes they portrayed. Yet in these texts, Indian leaders such as Pontiac, Tecumseh, the Natchez Suns, and the Shawnee Prophet speak, in words written by men who knew them in the flesh. And in the speeches of these native leaders recorded by eyewitness interpreters such as Robert Navarre, these men speak to us even more directly. These voices need to be listened to. The question of translation remains important and vexing, as we have seen, but it is a question not only of language but of genre, not only of cultural Otherness but of our imperialist traditions. U.S. literature and scholarship since the time of Logan have too often ignored or narrowly confined the texts of Indian oratory, even when the words of men such as Tecumseh and the Shawnee Prophet offer so much more than stoic monologues.

In 1820, Michigan's territorial governor, Lewis Cass, hired twenty-year-old C. C. Trowbridge as a private secretary. In and around Detroit in 1824, Trowbridge compiled a manuscript on "Shauwanoa [Shawnee] Traditions" based in part on interviews with Shawnee chief Black Hoof and with Tenskwatawa, the Shawnee Prophet. This manuscript, along with a similar ethnography of the Miami (Twightwee), "Meearmeear Traditions," was not published until the 1930s and remains little known. According to Erminie W. Voegelin, the pioneering ethnohistorian who coedited these works, it is fairly certain that Tenskwatawa was among Trowbridge's major informants and quite possible that his translator was Paukeesaa, Tecumseh's son. The Shawnee origin myth with which Trowbridge begins his text offers a valuable riposte to Shakespeare's *Tempest* and to the manner in which it has been read as a fundamental text of American literature. It opens with the creation of humankind: "When the Great spirit made this Island he thought it necessary to make also human beings to inhabit it, and with this view he formed an Indian." As in many Native American creation stories, this Great Spirit is not burdened with the solemn infallibility of the Christian God: in his first effort at making humans, he sees he has erred in "misplacing the privates to the forehead instead of the middle of the body," and in the "second formation he placed the privates under the arm of a man, and of a woman, and seeing this would not do he became vexed and threw away the different members of the body" (Trowbridge 1). When he finally succeeds in forming a man and woman who can copulate, he then gives them hearts, ears, tongues, and teeth; sets their life span at two hundred years; and reminds them to "tell your children all that I have told you that it may be transmitted to the latest posterity" (2). Finally, he informs them, "You are now about to go to the Island which I have made for you, and which rests upon the back of a great turtle that carries it as a load. You must call this Turtle your grand-father" (2). This Turtle island cosmology is common among northeastern

natives (see Brotherston, *Book* 174–92). But this version is distinctive for the way it accounts for the independent existence of Europeans. For at the moment the Shawnee ancestors are ready to take residence on their island,

> The Great spirit then opened a door, and looking down they saw a white man seated upon the ground. He was naked, and destitute of hair upon his head or his body and had been circumcised. The great Spirit told them that this white man was not made by himself but by another spirit who made and governed the whites & over whom or whose subjects he had no control. That as soon as they reached their Island and had got comfort-ably situated, this great white spirit would endeavor to thwart his designs, and would certainly exert himself to change the period of their existence from 200 years to a shorter time. (3)

Much as Pontiac did in the story of the Wolf Indian, Tenskwatawa's narrative here confounds the terms of political and of divine sovereignty over human "subjects." The remaining five pages of the cosmogony consist of a complex account of the origins of the various bands of the Shawnee tribe, including the Tshilikauthee (Chillicothe), Piccaway (Pekowi), and Kishpookoo. This section makes a shift characteristic of epics from a universal genesis to a more territorial perspective. The white man is left stranded by the narrative, for although in the following section the Shawnee bands move among vari-ous islands on the turtle's back, this island is not mentioned again. It is not clear whether the primordial Shawnee ever contended with this naked Pros-pero. Nonetheless, the passage is arresting, for this circumcised white man claims, like Prospero, a mandate of sovereignty that the Shawnee Great Spirit cannot challenge, yet, like Caliban, he is an isolate, a projection of the racial-cultural Other as seen through Shawnee eyes, quite different from Shakespearean eyes.

No man is an island, and no island since creation could have had a native population of just one man. Shakespeare's *Tempest* has been so appealing for literary critics because it stages the colonial encounter in starkly iso-lated terms that, though profound, are thoroughly contrived and portray the imagination of European explorers rather than of American settlers or native peoples. In act 2, Stephano finds Caliban, plies him with liquor, and boasts of the lucre to be gained by exhibiting him as an exotic curiosity, as Native Americans were often exhibited in Europe in the sixteenth century. Return-ing to Stephano in act 3 to seek his assistance in a rebellion to overthrow Prospero, Caliban speaks of the fetishistic power of written language:

Remember
First to possess his books; for without them
He's but a sot, as I am, nor hath not
One spirit to command. (act 3, scene 2, lines 95–98)

As we have seen, writing and books did not in fact enchant or enthrall the natives, for Neolin and Pontiac contrived their own books and texts as tools to resist the colonizers. If *The Tempest* reflects the history of Native American resistance, it does so through Prospero, not Caliban. Prospero is the victim of a court conspiracy in Italy and has a paranoid fear of falling victim again to an indigenous uprising, even though his magical powers (emblematized by his books) enable him to foresee and prevent

that foul conspiracy
Of the beast Caliban and his confederates
Against my life. (act 4, scene 1, lines 139–41)

Caliban's resistance is, like the storm that shipwrecks Prospero's foes on the island, part of a well-plotted masque, a magical fantasy of power much like the conspiracy that Governor Périer imputed to the Natchez and the vicious retaliation he led thereafter. Indigenous resistance in the play—and often in history—is a semiconscious projection of the colonizers' anxieties about their power. Prospero even hints that Caliban, somewhat like Popé, may be Prospero's son, "this thing of darkness / I Acknowledge mine" (act 5, scene 1, lines 275–76).

The Shawnee Prophet tried to organize magical-spiritual assistance for a campaign of resistance to European imperialism, and he too may have had an apocalyptic vision of its outcome. Trowbridge took down from his interviews with the prophet Shawnee beliefs about the "Sacred Fire." The Great Spirit told them that from their original homeland on Shawnee River,

They would go to Weeyukewaa wee Theeepee, Mad River [a literal translation] and thence to the Mississippi, where they would remain a short time and where they would discover something coming towards them (the whites), which would make them very poor and miserable. They moved to the Mississippi where they saw the prediction verified. In all these travels they took with them the sacred fire, and now that they see the settlements of the whites progressing so rapidly that [they] look forward to a time when it will be necessary for them to endeavour to retransmit the sacred fire to Shawnee river. Twelve men will be deputed to carry this fire, who, when they have arrived at Shawnee river, will open the fire and put to the test the power of the whites, in four years the fire will become visible to all the world. Then the Indians grown desperate by a consciousness that their end is approaching will suffer the fire to burn and to destroy the whites, upon whom they will call, tauntingly, to quench it. The same persons who have now the care of the fire at the Mississippi will be the bearers of it to Shawnee river. Twelve days (years) after the destruction of the world by this fire the Great spirit will cause it to be reformed & repeopled, but they don't know what description of persons will inhabit it. (56)

This prophecy from 1824 looks ahead twelve years, during which time Tenskwatawa was removed with his people across the Mississippi and finally died in Wyandotte County, Kansas. Shawnee beliefs in a millennial return of Tenskwatawa and Tecumseh persisted into the twentieth century (Sugden 389). Such prophecies of a second coming of the Indian hero, of a final judgment against colonial dispossession, are not so much indigenous protests as intercultural ripostes in an ongoing hybrid genre of colonial contestation. We should not discount Indian millenarianism because it appears to be influenced by Protestant millenarianism. We should not discount Indian tragedy because it sometimes reads like bourgeois melodrama. The genre of millennial prophecy, like that of epic, belongs to no one culture and has loaned its forms to both colonizers and to natives as they have constructed the intercultural narratives of native resistance in American history. Perhaps the curses and prophecies of these native seers and heroes may be heard once again in North America.

NOTES

CHAPTER ONE

1. Samuel Drake, *Aboriginal Races* 663–64. Black Hawk was received with similar honors and excitement on a second tour with a rival chief, Keokuk, in 1837. In Boston, they heard an address by the Governor Edward Everett at the statehouse and were presented with ceremonial swords in front of a crowd of thirty thousand (Benjamin Drake, *Great Indian Chief* 140–41).

2. See Volney 356–63. The case of Little Turtle took some more complicated turns after 1798. As Gregory Dowd has shown in *A Spirited Resistance*, Little Turtle became an "annuity chief" who received payments from the United States to the tribes, in his case the Miami, which agreed to remain neutral in subsequent nativist movements and wars of resistance, such as that of Tecumseh and his brother, Tenskwatawa, the Shawnee Prophet. But I refer here to the events of the 1790s, before Tenskwatawa articulated his message.

3. Brian Dippie's *The Vanishing American: White Attitudes and U.S. Indian Policy* is probably the best book devoted to the trope, but he focuses on later-nineteenth- and early-twentieth-century materials. Among the many expressions parallel to Jackson's speech here, see Parkman 732.

4. It is ironic that in his chapter on "Imperialist Nostalgia," Rosaldo discusses the fieldwork of William Jones, a brilliant Harvard-trained anthropologist who, like Rosaldo, studied the Ilongot of the Philippines. Jones was born among the Mesquakie Indians of Iowa, descendants of the Sauk tribe led by Black Hawk, and wrote several stories and ethnographic monographs about his people. For a critical analysis of Rosaldo's sentimentality, see David Johnson; for more on Jones, see Schmitz 1–45.

5. The choice of Wallace is an unusual one yet must have been well motivated. As a Scot like Ossian, Wallace represents a people distinct from the English, who sought to dominate his land as they later did North America, but this difference was not so extreme as to be indissoluble, for by the nineteenth century Scotland and England were conjoined as Britain, and Doddridge imagines a similar blending of settlers and natives in western Pennsylvania.

6. Although he uses "religion" with an anthropologist's breadth and never once mentions Christ in the book, Girard is a devout Catholic and seems to me to have been influenced in his theory by a vision of Christ's sacrifice. However, his faith seems to have been orthodox enough that in an interview published in his *Things Hidden since the Foundation of the World* he insisted that Christ's death was nonsacrificial.

7. Over the same century or so and probably by coincidence, the number of hier-

archical chiefdoms commanding large regions of native North America, such as Powhatan's in Tidewater Virginia, had declined.

8. Samuel Gardner Drake was not related to and should not be confused with Benjamin Drake, the Cincinnati-based author of successful biographies of Black Hawk and Tecumseh that will be important sources in chapter 8. The two shared a sympathy for the Native American leaders about whom they wrote but differed in their regional allegiances. While Benjamin was part of a nascent western literati, Samuel was a New Englander through and through. He owned the "Antiquarian Book-Store" in Cornhill, Boston, and published reeditions of early New England histories and relations such as those of Benjamin Church and William Hubbard, a popular history of the witchcraft crisis, an anthology of captivity narratives, and a massive history of Boston. At his death, his estate included a library of nearly twelve thousand books.

9. Another competing history of the Indian wars is Henry Trumbull's *History of the Discovery of America*, which first appeared in 1810 and was revised and reprinted more than a dozen times through the 1840s. Richard Slotkin has called it "the most popular anthology of Indian war narratives in the nineteenth-century" (432), but I feel Slotkin erred in according it greater importance that Drake's and Thatcher's works. Trumbull excluded the history of seventeenth-century colonies other than New England, and although in later editions he expanded the section on western frontier battles to include Tecumseh and Black Hawk's War, much of this material was simply copied from other sources. Trumbull had neither the scholarly approach nor the revisionist sympathy for the Indians that characterized both Samuel and Benjamin Drake and Thatcher. Trumbull's account of the Pequot War, for example, makes no apologies for the Mystic massacre or for the death of Miantonomo, two key events examined in chapter 3. *History of the Discovery of America* represents a procolonialist outlook that faded in the 1830s as the phenomenon of the Indian tragic hero rose.

10. Whereas Drake and Thatcher have received benign neglect from modern scholarship, McKenney and especially Hall have aroused conflicting opinions. Richard Drinnon adopted the subtitle for his *Facing West: The Metaphysics of Indian Hating and Empire Building* from Herman Melville's adaptation of Hall's short story, "The Indian Hater," in chapters 25–27 of *The Confidence-Man*. Drinnon equates Judge Hall with his character, Colonel James Moredock. But Edward Watts counters that Drinnon and others have "misread Hall's depiction of the 'Indian Hater' as an endorsement of Moredock's racist pathology" (134) and that "Drinnon's comments on Hall seem to have little connection to the facts of Hall's life" (246 n. 10). Watts also documents Hall's collaborations with Benjamin Drake. Melville captures the irony and contradictions between enemy and hero, hatred and admiration. The Confidence-Man in his guise as the Cosmopolitan says just before the story, "When I think of Pocahontas, I am ready to love Indians. Then there's Massassoit, and Philip of Mount

Hope, and Tecumseh, and Red-Jacket, and Logan—all heroes. God bless me; hate Indians? Surely the late Colonel John Moredock must have wandered in his mind" (140).

11. Anthologies of Native American oratory were in the twentieth century just as successful for U.S. publishers as Indian biographies in the tradition set by Drake and Thatcher. Such titles include Clements; Vanderwerth; Mintz; Armstrong; Calloway; Hoxie. Most of these collections include not only speeches but also some excerpts from ethnographic works by Euro-Americans and written texts by natives.

12. On the chanson de mort as an English literary fad in this period, imitated by William Wordsworth and Charlotte Smith, see Ellison 98–100. On the more serious manner in which missionary martyrs contributed to the genre, see Gordon Sayre, "Communion."

13. The *Narrative* of John Tanner, who was taken captive in Kentucky as a young boy and lived for thirty years among Ojibwa and other natives of the North Woods, offers a rare look at how Indians reacted to such pretentious speeches. Tanner recalls an address by Lord Selkirk, the leader of a Scots emigration scheme who attempted to put a stop to violent clashes between rival fur traders and their Indian allies, that opens, "My children, the sky which has long been dark and cloudy over your heads, is now once more clear and bright. Your great father beyond the waters, who has ever, as you know, nearest his heart the interests of his red children, has sent me to remove the briars out of your path that your feet may no more bleed." According to Tanner, "The Indians answered with the usual promises and professions, and being about to leave the fort that evening, they stole every horse belonging to Lord Selkirk and his party" (220–21).

14. Rudolph Kaiser's article reveals how the version of the speech most often used to support environmentalist causes was actually composed by a white documentary filmmaker in the early 1970s.

15. Books promoting the idea include Barriero; Grinde; Johansen. For a critical analysis, see Ed White, "Challenge"; and a group of articles in the *William and Mary Quarterly* 53:3 (1996).

CHAPTER TWO

1. "Montezuma" is the common English spelling of the Mexican leader's name, but primary sources in Spanish and specialists in the field use a variety of other spellings, including "Motecuhzoma" and "Moteucçoma." Except in quotations from other sources, I will use "Moctezuma." The name "Aztec" is commonly used for his empire, but specialists prefer "Mexica." "Nahua" or "Nahuatl" is the name of the language spoken by the Mexica and some other city-states in the region and still spoken today by some.

2. The Mexica followed a fifty-two-year cycle, or calendar round, enumerated by four symbols—Rabbit, Reed, Flint, and House—in combination with the numbers one

through thirteen. The year 13 Rabbit was followed by the year 1 Reed, and then 2 Flint, and so on. On painted documents, years were indicated by a number of dots around an icon of the rabbit, reed, flint, or house.

3. To cite an example familiar to Anglo-American readers, think of Cabeza de Vaca's apologetic and self-justifying preface to the king in his *Naufragios* ("Castaways").

4. Compare this history of the mestizo nobility of Mexico, well explained in an essay by Donald Chipman, to the lineage of Pocahontas and John Rolfe in Virginia. As Robert Tilton has observed, the aristocratic First Families of Virginia were proud to claim descent from Pocahontas's only son, Thomas Rolfe, even as the colony and later state prohibited miscegenous marriages between whites and Africans or Native Americans. In New Spain, where blood quantum was calculated even more obsessively, Moctezuma's offspring also enjoyed an exemption, an aristocratic status that precluded the usual racial prejudices.

5. Among native tales of dreams and auguries of the arrival of Europeans, see Joseph Jeremy's account in the 1894 *Legends of the Micmacs* (Mulford 152–53), David Cusick's 1831 history of the Iroquois, or the account in the *Maya Books of the Chilam Balam*, which echoes the Quetzalcoatl myth in many respects. And as Lafaye has observed (190), South American native cultures nurtured syncretic legends of indigenous deities whose messages were associated with the myth of apostolic visits to the New World in the time of Christ.

6. By the time that Durán was writing, during the reign of Philip II, the Spanish monarch no longer exercised power through spectacular public appearances but minimized his public role in favor of bureaucratic control represented by the royal seal.

7. The leading proponent of Aristotle's theories in sixteenth-century Spain was Ginés de Sepúlveda, who engaged in a famous debate with Bartolomé de las Casas at Valladolid in 1550 concerning the status of the Indians.

CHAPTER THREE

1. The Indian removal bill passed in the spring of 1830 after lengthy debate by a vote of 101–97 in the House of Representatives and 28–20 in the Senate. Opposition to Indian removal was strongest in the Northeast, where the threat of violent competition for lands was a thing of the past. As we will see, works such as Lydia Maria Child's *The First Settlers of New England; or, Conquest of the Pequods, Narragansetts, and Pokanokets* (1829) include a strong critique of Indian removal and of European colonialism in general. To interpret *Metamora* or the other Indian dramas of the early 1830s as ideologically proremoval is to silence the strong dissent of the many literary and political figures who opposed Jackson's policy.

2. Typology as employed in seventeenth-century New England referred to the biblical hermeneutic that read events and individuals in the Old Testament as prefiguring those in the New, such as Moses and Jesus. Some Puritan writers, such as Cotton Mather, extend the method to readings of history and of "providential," or divinely

guided, events of their time. The literati of 1820s New England were schooled in this methodology and expected their readers to recognize its application in the service of a new civil religion of nationalist historiography.

3. King Philip's War also has a richer modern historiography than any of the other Indian wars of resistance studied in this book. I have depended particularly on two fine books: Francis Jennings's *The Invasion of America: Indians, Colonialism, and the Cant of Conquest* (1976) brought the imperatives of the new Indian history to colonial New England and proved that the dour Puritans were scarcely less rapacious and deceitful toward Indians than nineteenth-century U.S. soldiers at Sand Creek and Wounded Knee. Jill Lepore's *The Name of War: King Philip's War and the Origins of American Identity* (1998) applied the methods of cultural studies to interpret how the war and the literature and monuments it inspired inform notions of Indian and of American national identity. Jennings and Lepore immersed themselves in archival records of Plymouth, Providence, and other colonies, and I shall quote their findings frequently.

4. The treaty recounts how Massassoit and Wamsutta had declared themselves loyal to the king and to Plymouth and then has Philip express his penance in familiarly Puritan language: "I having of late, through my indiscretion and the naughtiness of my heart, violated and broken this covenant with my friends, by taking up arms with evil intent against them, and that groundlessly, and being now deeply sensible of my unfaithfulness and folly, desire at this time solemnly to renew my covenant" (qtd. in Hutchinson 1:238).

5. Sedgwick oddly chooses the name Oneco for the Pequot who marries Faith Leslie even though he was allied to the traitor, Uncas, who had facilitated the massacre of Pequots at Mystic in 1637.

6. For an alternative account of why Apess claimed to be a descendant of King Philip, see Velikova.

7. As Karen Kupperman has pointed out to me, both "Squanto" and "Hobomok" are names for evil Manitous in Algonquian languages of New England. In giving out these names to the Plymouth colonists they befriended, were these men laying a kind of curse on the English?

8. Perhaps the most interesting part of the prophet's history of the tribe is this passage alluding to the origin story of the Delaware tribe's ancient migration from the Northwest as recorded in John Heckewelder's *History, Manners, and Customs of the Indian Nations Who Once inhabited Pennsylvania* (1819) and later in Samuel Rafinesque's transcription of the hieroglyphic text of the *Walam Olum.*

> Where now are the race in their might who came forth,
> To destroy and to waste, from the plains of the north?
> As the deer through the brake, mid the forests they sped,
> The tall trees crashed round them; earth groaned with their tread;
> He perished, the Mammoth,—in power and in pride,

And defying the wrath of YOHEWAH he died!
And say, what is man, that his race should endure,
Alone through the changes of nature secure?
Where now are the giants, the soil who possest,
When our fathers came down, from the land of the west?

The detail about the Mammoth recalls Cornelius Mathews's *Behemoth: A Legend of the Mound Builders* (1839). This is the earliest reference that I have found to such a prehistory (see Gordon Sayre, "Mammoth").

9. See James Wallace; Mitchell; Person; Arch; Opferman. Opferman presents evidence that although Cooper denied having read Sedgwick's *Hope Leslie*, he actually did so, and he copied some aspects of its plot in writing *Wept*.

10. McConachie has written of the three plays that "traditional justice is tyrannical; greed, cruelty, and injustice are built into the traditional order and nothing but its complete overthrow will make any difference. . . . Forrest's vehicles pit the people against all forms of patrician power" (99). All three heroes die, but their rebellions were fully justified, as the existing order was illegitimate. The other two plays were also products of prize competitions sponsored by Forrest.

11. Scholars have also speculated on the influence of a Choctaw chief, Pushmataha, an ally of Andrew Jackson's during the War of 1812 with whom Forrest lived briefly during a visit to New Orleans in the mid-1820s. Forrest's biographer, William Alger, describes the friendship in erotic, homosocial terms (Lepore 201).

CHAPTER FOUR

1. In *War under Heaven*, Dowd lists a larger set of causes for Indian resistance: "The British sense of hierarchy, the poor conditions of trade, the demand for the return of captives, and the destruction of the hunting economy" (86); nevertheless, all of these reasons redound on British intransigence toward native demands to continue the practices of the French.

2. For other conspiracy fears, see George Croghan's story paraphrased in Peckham 95–96 (not included in the published version; see Croghan); Anthony Wallace, *Death* 115. Wallace is inclined to give the Seneca more credit than Pontiac for the rebellion. By contrast, Joseph Doddridge, the memorialist of Logan and focus of a section in the next chapter, sees no influence from the French or from other tribes: "They fought for their native country. They engaged in the terrible war of 1763 with a view to recover from the possession of the white people the whole of the western settlements" (*Notes* 9).

3. By "postcolonial" I do not mean to imply that Pontiac's speeches should be read using the critical terms that have emerged in the analysis of contemporary postcolonial literary figures but that his political leadership should be considered according to some of the challenges faced by postcolonial states, from the United States to the postcolonial nations of Africa and Asia in the twentieth century.

4. I use the Lakeside Press edition of this text, and even though its editor, Milo Milton Quaife, doubted the attribution to Navarre, later scholars including Peckham have reaffirmed it. The original French text and page opposite translation appear in Burton. Dowd describes the appearance and composition of the manuscript in *War under Heaven* (6, 282), and although he concludes that "Navarre does seem to be the most likely author," he avoids referring to the document by Navarre's name.

5. The biblical-style "ye" pronoun that the Master of Life uses is the product of the translator, R. Clyde Ford. The French original uses the polite form of the second person, "vous." The term "Master of Life" is, however, a literal translation of the French "Maître de la Vie."

6. Contrast this text to scenes where natives described the Great Spirit to Christian missionaries, appealing to a principle of religious toleration in response to the missionaries' insistence on conversion. See, for example, how another nativist, the "Assinsink Prophet," Wangomend, addresses David Zeisberger at Goschgoschnenk on the Ohio in 1767 (Zeisberger 28).

7. The continuation of this passage from Morris includes an interesting geopolitical connection between Pontiac's rebellion and the Natchez uprising: ". . . containing the most improbable falsehoods, though beginning with a truth. The writer mentioned the repulse of the English troops in the Mississippi, who were going to take possession of Fort Chartres, blamed the Natchez nation for their ill conduct in that affair, made our loss in that attack to be very considerable, and concluded with assuring him, that a French army was landed in Louisiana, and that his father (the French king) would drive the English out of the country." The grain of truth was that an English detachment led by Major Arthur Loftus, sent from Pensacola to take possession of the Illinois country from the French, had been attacked at Tunica Bend near Natchez in March. At the end of his journal, Morris offers a scarcely credible explanation: the Natchez attack was actually meant to save the English from total annihilation by the French and was conceived of as revenge against the French for their genocidal campaign against the Natchez in the 1730s. See also Parkman 752–53; Alvord and Carter 250.

8. The Navarre manuscript calls him a "Sauvage Loup" or "Wolf Indian." The Wolf or Munsey were one of the three tribes or clan totems of the Delaware or Lenape nation, along with the Turtle (Unami) and the Turkey (Unalachtgo) (Heckewelder, *History* 52). This, together with the resemblance of the vision to Neolin's prophecy, was the rationale for Schoolcraft to translate this as "An Indian of the Lenapee tribe" in the opening line of his "Paradise Opened to the Indians." See also Dowd, *War* 31. In his discussion of the speech (101–5), Dowd contends that the Wolf Indian was Neolin, that Pontiac was explicitly repeating a prophetic vision that Neolin had related to his followers.

9. As we shall see in the chapter on the Natchez, books about North America by Charlevoix and Le Page du Pratz were translated and published with the same

purpose but were abridged and annotated to inoculate the texts against the possibly seditious opinions of their French authors.

10. One British officer commented, "The Indians consider him as their God" (Cuneo 262). Cuneo does not cite the source, however.

CHAPTER FIVE

1. See Gustafson chap. 3, esp. 115.

2. William Holmes McGuffey, the creator of the series, was an Ohioan. The Logan speech appeared in the fourth and fifth of the six readers (1837, 1844, 1848) arranged by grade level. The emphasis is on pronunciation and oratory, as nothing is included alongside the speech to explain who Logan was or the context for his oration. Such explanation may not have been necessary because the speech was so widely recognized.

3. Michael Cresap was the son of Thomas Cresap, a prominent Marylander who in the so-called Conojacular War of 1731–34 had defended the province's efforts to assert control over land in the Susquehanna Valley that Pennsylvania also claimed.

4. Parkman vol. 2, chaps. 14–15 (701–30). John R. Dunbar edited a collection of the pamphlets as *The Paxton Papers*. Amid this literature, the publication of the Logan speech can be read as an effort to give a tragic voice to the victims of Conestoga and to gain a moral and literary high ground in the back-and-forth of sordid frontier terrorism. Although I find Merritt's account of the controversy persuasive, other recent scholarship has emphasized the plight of the back settlers and regarded their protest as a grassroots antiimperial effort comparable to Pontiac's. See Dowd, *War* 175, 211; Ed White, "Backcountry."

5. Draper 158. This biography of Logan is from the Draper manuscripts at the Wisconsin Historical Society.

6. Coming less than a year before the outbreak of the Revolutionary War, the battle of Point Pleasant has been regarded as significant for colonial military fortunes. Theodore Roosevelt praised the valor of the backwoods militia compared to the British-led troops of the Seven Years' War: "In all the contests waged against the northwestern Indians during the last half of the eighteenth century there was no other where the whites inflicted so great a relative loss on their foes. . . . It rendered possible the settlement of Kentucky, and therefore the winning of the West" (1:240).

7. See Sandefur 291; Seeber, "Critical Views" 143–45. More recently, Thomas McElwain has attempted to retranslate the speech into Oneida or Cayuga. However, it is also possible that Logan spoke in either English or Shawnee.

8. The text appeared as follows in the *Virginia Gazette*: "The following is said to be a message from Captain Logan (an Indian Warrior) to Governor Dunmore, after the battle in which Col. Charles Lewis was slain, delivered at the treaty. 'I appeal to any white man to say that he ever entered Logan's cabin but I gave him meat; that he ever came naked but I clothed him. In the course of the last war, Logan remained in his cabin an advocate for peace. I had such an affection for the white people, that I was

pointed at by the rest of my nation. I should have ever lived with them, had it not been for Colonel Cressop, who last year cut off, in cold blood, all the relations of Logan, not sparing women and children: There runs not a drop of my blood in the veins of any human creature. This called upon me for revenge; I have sought it, I have killed many, and fully glutted my revenge. I am glad there is a prospect of peace, on account of the nation; but I beg you will not entertain a thought that any thing I have said proceeds from fear! Logan disdains the thought! He will not turn on his heel to save his life! Who is there to mourn for Logan?—No one.'" A third version, first published in New York on 16 February 1775, is quite close to Jefferson's. For a comparison of the versions, see Seeber, "Critical Views" 142–46; Sandefur.

9. The warrior's custom of leaving his symbol inscribed on a war club left by the body of his victim was documented by Heckewelder (*History* 327) and used in *Yamoyden*.

10. We have already seen in chapter 3 that in novels of the 1820s such as *Hobomok* and *The Wept of Wish-ton-Wish*, cross-blood children were either erased from the narrative or had their Indian heritage effaced through their education. Moreover, those familiar with the subsequent history of Indian wars might not regard the adoption of Logan's orphaned nephew as a philanthropic gesture; see Flood.

11. Doddridge also published an undated broadside, "An Elegy on His Family Vault," in which the lyric persona asks,

> Then let their offspring, mindful of their claims,
> Cherish their honor in the lyric band—
> O save from dark oblivion's gloomy reign,
> The brave, the worthy, fathers of our land.

12. Doddridge's earlier book, *Treatise on the Culture of Bees* (1813), in some ways anticipates his views on assimilation and colonization of the Indians: according to his daughter, Narcissa, he was among the first to advocate colonizing rather than killing bees to procure their honey.

13. Sawvel's biography claimed that Outalissi, the noble Indian of Thomas Campbell's popular verse romance "Gertrude of Wyoming," was based on Logan. Campbell quotes Logan's speech in a note, but the only connection with Outalissi is that the latter says in one line, "not a kindred drop of blood runs in my veins" (58).

CHAPTER SIX

1. The term "massacre" is politically loaded. In what follows, I shall use "uprising" rather than "massacre" or "revolt" or "rebellion" to clarify that the native peoples acted to defend their lands and were not the subjects of any sovereign political power. For the number of French lives lost in the initial uprising, see Delanglez, "Natchez Massacre" 631–32; Rowland, Sanders, and Galloway 1:123–26.

2. For example, at the time of King Philip's War, some New England Puritans believed that all the Indians were planning to drive them back into the sea. William Hubbard

wrote, "There was a Design of a general rising of the Indians against the English, all over the Countrey, (possibly as far as Virginia, the Indians there making Insurrection this same year)" (2:92–93), referring to Bacon's Rebellion.

3. Bridenbaugh advances the claim that Spaniards had captured Opechancanough. Most other historians doubt this, however, and it appears to fit a pattern that attributes Indian revolts to part-European leaders, as if to deny that Native Americans would be capable of planning such a conspiracy.

4. Le Mercure de France, September 1731, printed an account of the uprising by Antoine-Alexis Périer de Salvert, the governor's brother, and the 1731 installment of the Jesuit organ Lettres Edifiantes, vol. 20, included the narrative by Father Mathurin le Petit.

5. The Importance and Advantage of Cape Breton (London: Knapton, 1746) qtd. in O'Neill, introduction to Charlevoix, Charlevoix's Louisiana xiv.

6. For more on Le Page du Pratz, see Joseph Treagle's introduction to the reprint of the English translation of History of Louisiana; Dawdy. I sometimes shorten his name to "Le Page," as he signed it in at least one colonial document. For more on Dumont, see Delanglez, "Louisiana Poet-Historian." Dumont's prose manuscript reveals that he left Natchez in January and therefore that his narrative of the events leading up to the uprising in the "Poème" and in the Mémoires Historiques is not an eyewitness report.

7. The first volume was finally translated in 1938 as part of the Works Progress Administration's writers project, but this mimeograph typescript is even rarer than the French original. Because the published English translation of Le Page du Pratz is abridged and those of Dumont are unreliable, I have translated all quotations myself. Most of my quotations from Le Page can be found in my online translation of key sections of the Histoire de la Louisiane at <http://darkwing.uoregon.edu/gsayre/LPDP.html>. Some of the text on the site was adapted from the English translation and some from Swanton. For ease of reading, I have omitted the French originals of the quotations, although they are included in Gordon Sayre, "Plotting the Natchez Massacre."

8. In collaboration with Shannon Dawdy and Carla Zecher, I am currently engaged in a project to edit and publish this manuscript. The work will involve a close comparison with Le Page du Pratz's articles and book, Dumont's poem and book, and other published and unpublished sources that may bring answers to questions about Natchez ethnography and colonial history.

9. Pocahontas was baptized and christened Rebecca in an allusion to Genesis 25, where Rebecca bore two sons, one white and one red. In Girard's provocative reading of the biblical scene, Rebecca's idea of covering Jacob's neck and hands with goatskin so that his blind father, Isaac, would mistake him for his savage, hairy, hunting brother marks the moment of sacrificial substitution: "The animals thus interpose themselves between father and son" (Violence 5). In Le Page du Pratz's rewriting, the colonist becomes the surrogate victim, the Stinkard and the goat,

but he also offers a different solution to the violence of the sacrificial crisis, as we shall see.

10. Perhaps the true, unstated reason for Le Page's refusal was that he was already in a relationship with his Chitimacha slave/spouse, herself the daughter of an influential father with ties to the Natchez.

11. The title of this section, which translates as "this bloody tragedy," is from Dumont, *Mémoires historiques* 1:235. He used the same words to describe the Natchez uprising; see 2:141.

12. The French Fort Rosalie was located near the Grand Village of the Natchez, the site of the central temple of the nation and home of the Grand Soleil and preserved today as a historical site on the south edge of the city of Natchez. However, the degree of authority of the Grand Village and the Grand Soleil over other villages during the 1720s is uncertain. Archaeologists Ian Brown and Karl Lorenz believe that the Flour (Farine) and Tioux villages just across St. Catherine's Creek from the Grand Village were pro-French, while the villages of White Apple (Pomme Blanche or often simply Pomme), Grigra, and Jenzenaques, located about ten miles to the northeast, were pro-English and followed the authority of their own Suns, who may have instigated the uprising against the French (Ian Brown 185; Lorenz 100). The French sources often do not specify which village a certain Sun hails from, complicating the task of determining the leaders of the uprising.

13. The quotation literally translates as "take the French by a hit of a string." Dumont's account, like Le Page's, begins with an ethnographic intent; chapter 26 is titled "Ceremonies Observed on the Funeral of a Great Chief." His relation to the events is unclear, however. The start of the chapter explains, "I will make use of an account that has been communicated to me by a Frenchman, who in 1725 was a witness to these ceremonies" (1:208), but then he proceeds to narrate it in the first person. Later, a speech by Yakstalchil is addressed to "he who was speaking to him in my name" (1:231). Dumont may not have been in Natchez in 1725: Delanglez believes, based on the manuscript, that Dumont arrived "in the latter part of 1727" ("Louisiana Poet-Historian" 41). It seems unlikely that this surrogate is Le Page du Pratz or that Dumont copied his account from Le Page's manuscript, however, for Dumont's version includes details missing from Le Page, such as the names of sacrificial victims and the dates (1–5 June) on which the ceremonies occurred. Conversely, however, Dumont's manuscript does not include the narrative of the funereal rites of Serpent Piqué. It describes in detail the mortuary sacrifice in a generalized ethnographic manner and then in a separate description of the annual feast of the corn describes Serpent Piqué and the tattoo he wore, an elaborate serpent circling his body from mouth to foot. The moniker "Tattooed Serpent" was more likely an emblem of tribal authority than the name of an individual.

14. Dumont and Le Page give conflicting accounts of the names and titles of the two Suns. Dumont identifies Yakstalchil as the second war chief of the Flour Village and

Serpent Piqué or Obalalkebiche as the "grand Chef" (civil chief) of the Grand Village (*Mémoires historiques* 1:208–9). It seems more likely that Yakstalchil was the Grand Soleil of the Grand Village, as Le Page reports.

15. Although Stiggins's account has been published in book form, in that edition the text is cleaned up and broken into chapters and subheadings; consequently, I quote from the first published version, which was edited by Nunez.

16. Dumont was something of a hypochondriac, referring to his health and the means by which he was cured of illnesses even more frequently than Le Page does. Dumont reports, for example, that rattlesnake fat makes a good salve for rheumatism (*Mémoires historiques* 1:109), praises the skills of the native "Alexis" (a word derived from the Creek *alikchaki* for healer) at curing many injuries, often using Spanish moss (1:172), and sometimes even extols tattoos as a therapeutic tool ("Poème," 405–6). His manuscript autobiography also includes several colorful accounts of how he cured himself of various ailments. Le Page, for his part, wrote that shortly after arriving in Natchez, he had been laid up for months with sciatica in his thigh and found a cure only when he went to a Natchez healer on the recommendation of Serpent Piqué. Thus Le Page, like the patients of La Glorieuse, owed his health and perhaps his life to the Natchez.

17. Another manuscript in the Ayer Collection at the Newberry—to my knowledge not examined by other historians of the Natchez uprising—offers another appearance of the trickster Taotal. The four-volume manuscript, Ayer MS 293, dated 1732, is a transcription by a priest named Bobé, a chaplain at Versailles, of various reports from the French colonies. At the end of the fourth volume (386–93) is a "Relation of the most remarkable events of the massacre that the Indian nation of the Natchez made upon the detachment at that post." It records the February 1730 retaliation against the Natchez, which went awry because most of the Natchez, after being besieged in the old fort, escaped across the Mississippi. This speech by Taotal, spelled "lactale" in the manuscript, explains how the escape happened: "I come here to assure you on behalf of my great chief, and all my nation, that we have remorseful hearts for what we did to the French in burning their houses, which we wish to help them rebuild. But, as they have also killed many people, and ruined our lands with this war, one might call it even. We wish for the future only that we might walk together in the same path as the French, and to this end here are seven rabbits that I have brought, in anticipation of more from our hunters who have all gone out hunting for a feast for the French, and as the female chief has been informed by your commandant that you are eating off of the dirt without plates, here are eighteen small plates and two large ones which she gave to me for presents so that you might dine as befits a chief such as yourself." A note clarifies that these eighteen brass plates had been pillaged from the French and adds that "during the time that this tricky fellow was making this harangue and giving the presents to Sr. de Loubouy," the Natchez were sneaking out of the fort.

18. Curiously, the word "valeur" appears thirteen more times in the remainder of chapter 26 of Dumont's work but not again after this in the account by Le Page, who has the favorite wife and Ette-Actal saying instead, "Ta vie t'est donc chère" and "la vie m'est chère" (life is dear to me or to you). Swanton, in his translation of Dumont, glosses over the puzzle of "de valeur" by translating it in several different ways: "It is very grievous," "It is precious," "is dear," "It is well," and "is of importance," even though the context cannot always so specify the meaning. Swanton even uses the phrase "it is well" twice in two lines, first to translate "de valeur" and then to translate "il est bon que" (Dumont, *Mémoires historiques* 1:234). Comparing the two authors is equally inconclusive. As we have seen, in the speech of the favorite wife of the Grand Soleil to Taotal/Ette-Actal, "de valeur" apparently means "dear." But in the opening line of her speech thanking the French for intervening to save her life, the idiomatic signification applies. She says in Dumont, "Votre père est mort; c'est beaucoup de valeur" (*Mémoires historiques* 1:220; "it is very grievous," in Swanton) and in Le Page du Pratz, "Il est bien fâcheux que votre père est mort" (*Histoire* 3:50). Neither writer gives a transliteration of the actual Natchez word. Dumont indicates that the Tioux war chief was speaking the Mobilien lingua franca, so it is unclear whether the Natchez speakers using the idiom were speaking French, Mobilien, or Natchez. Moreover, Dumont does not describe the funeral of Serpent Piqué in his manuscript and in the "Poème" discusses the practice of mortuary sacrifice only in a general, ethnographic manner. Hence Le Mascrier may have copied this scene from du Pratz's article in the April 1752 *Journal Oeconomique*, 151, where he also used the paradoxical term "de valeur (bien fâcheuse)." Of course, Dumont may also have added new insights in the published text that he had not employed in his manuscripts.

19. St. Cosme, the Natchez Sun named after a French missionary, is not mentioned at all in Le Page's account of the death of Serpent Piqué, but Dumont reports Brontin saying that when he first went to see the grief-stricken Grand Soleil, "St. Côme had arrived before me, and told me that he had not dared take the gun out of the hands of the great war chief" (*Mémoires historiques* 1:229). Thus, St. Cosme appears eager for his relative to die, possibly so that St. Cosme can take over as Grand Soleil.

20. The French text of the play is available at <http://www.centenary.edu/french/houmma/>. Bossu published two books, in 1768 and 1777, based on his two brief stints in Louisiana. Much of the material in them was copied from other published sources, including Le Page du Pratz. This story about the Colapissa father and son appears to have spread widely: it was also included in the anonymous *Boy's Book of Indian Battles and Adventures* (63–66).

21. This name is spelled variously in the primary documents: "Chépart" by Le Page du Pratz; "Chopart" by Dumont; and "Etcheparre," "de Chepar," and "Detchéparre" elsewhere. I have decided to follow Chinard and Chateaubriand's spelling, "Chépar."

22. Dumont's "Poème" says later,

> The last Sun of White Apple
> Who for a previous peace had been decapitated
> By this blow could find his death retaliated. (319)

23. Moreover, a local headman, Orou, invites Diderot's French chaplain to take to bed one of his daughters, much as the Grande Soleille asks Le Page du Pratz to marry her daughter, a Natchez princess.

24. The French original directly quotes this conversation, while the English translator turns it into indirect discourse and abridges it; see Le Page du Pratz, History 86–90.

25. Bibliothèque Nationale manuscript fr 2550, 115–16. That the document dates from 1728, before the uprising, is of course significant. I am grateful to George Milne, who found and transcribed the document and shared his work with me, and to Carla Zecher, who also transcribed it. Pénicaut says that in 1733 Bienville saw St. Cosme among the enslaved Natchez being sent to St. Domingue (70). Jennifer Lamonte of Harvard University has also explored this possible paternity of the Natchez rebel in a conference paper and shared her findings with me. In an e-mail exchange, Patricia Galloway has suggested that the missionary may have been St. Cosme's godfather and namesake but not biological father. The issue is confounded by Charlevoix's history of the uprising and the French retaliation, which states that in January 1731 Périer met with "a Natché named St. Côme, a son of the woman Chief, and who consequently would have succeeded the Sun" (Charlevoix's Louisiana 116). St. Côme claims that "the prime mover in all the mischief had been killed in the first siege," a year earlier, but Charlevoix maintains that "another called the Flour Chief (Chef de la Farine) was the real author of the massacre of the French, but Saint Côme had wished to throw the fault on another" (117).

26. In his 1768 Nouveaux Voyages en Louisiane, Bossu copied some of this episode from Le Page du Pratz but omitted any mention of Bras Piqué or of the counting sticks. Bossu wrote only that an unnamed young Natchez woman, motivated by her love for a French soldier named Macé or Massé, informed him of the conspiracy. He told Chépar but was put in irons.

27. My quotations from Les Natchez are from the 1827 English translation, which was published by the same publisher as the French. However, the English version was abridged, omitting the titles of the twelve books and some of the most ridiculous parts of the epic, such as book 4.

CHAPTER SEVEN

1. The Vermont Law School held a September–October 2001 exhibition under the title "The First American Revolution: The Pueblo Revolt of 1680." See also the Web site created by Bernadett Charley Gallegos, a San Juan Pueblo/Hopi, at <http://members.aol.com/chloe5/pueblos02.html> (February 2005).

2. The accounts of the conquest of Mexico do include a related trope suggesting that

Indian women would easily betray a planned attack on the colonizers. In Bernal Díaz's *Discovery and Conquest of Mexico*, a Cholulan woman, the wife of a cacique, goes secretly to Doña Marina (Malinche) to warn her of the planned attack on the Spaniards, only to have Malinche betray the woman and the plan to Cortés (176). As we saw in chapter 5, legends surrounding Pontiac's surprise attack on the British fort at Detroit in 1763 also told of a woman who betrayed the plans to the British commandant, Gladwin.

3. Sioux Indians have organized a similar annual pilgrimage in commemoration of the Wounded Knee uprising of 1890. Each December they ride on horseback 350 miles over two weeks, from Mobridge, South Dakota, to Wounded Knee.

4. The Spanish sources are currently getting a fresh look. The National Endowment for the Humanities has funded an effort by the Cibola project at the Center for Romance Studies at the University of California, Berkeley to retranscribe and retranslate the copies of New Mexico records held at various Spanish colonial archives.

CHAPTER EIGHT

1. I have relied most extensively on Sugden's 1997 biography and on Edmunds's separate biographies of Tecumseh and of the Shawnee Prophet. The most useful source for studying the literature and legends about Tecumseh, however, is Carl Klinck's *Tecumseh: Fact and Fiction in Early Records*, a sourcebook containing more than a hundred short excerpts from primary documents, many of which are in manuscript archives or are very rare. Benjamin Drake's biography is the most excerpted source in Klinck's collection, and although he worked a quarter century after Tecumseh's death, Drake interviewed eyewitnesses who gave his work an authenticity that modern scholars cannot match. Klinck also coedited the John Norton's too rarely cited narrative and edited the reprint of Richardson's *The Canadian Brothers* that I cite in this chapter.

2. See Tanner 144–47. This is one of the most often cited accounts of the prophet's message, but Tanner describes his reaction to this and later self-proclaimed prophets as highly skeptical. His account may be colored by the decline in Tenskwatawa's stature during the 1820s, when Tanner set down his narrative.

3. This episode represents a reversal of a common trope whereby a colonizer uses his knowledge of astronomy to manipulate colonized peoples. One early instance appears in the histories of Columbus's voyages. He used his foreknowledge of a 29 February 1504 eclipse to compel Taino Indians in Jamaica to continue supplying his men with food (Morison 654).

4. Moreover, later editions of Benjamin Drake's *Life of Black Hawk* have an appendix by James Hall that claims that Black Hawk was at the battle of Moraviantown and witnessed Tecumseh's death in an attack by Johnson's regiment, though without confirming that Johnson was the man who shot him. It is interesting that Hall had also written a campaign biography of Harrison for the 1836 election.

WORKS CITED

Aeschylus. *The Persians*. Translated by Anthony J. Podlecki. Englewood Cliffs, N.J.: Prentice-Hall, 1970.

Alger, William Rounseville. *Life of Edwin Forrest, the American Tragedian*. 2 vols. Philadelphia: Lippincott, 1877.

Alvord, Clarence, and Clarence Carter, eds. *Illinois Historical Collections*. Vol. 10, *The Critical Period*. Springfield: Illinois State Historical Library, 1915.

The American Pioneer, a Monthly Periodical, Devoted to the Objects of the Logan Historical Society. Cincinnati: Williams, 1842–43.

Anonymous. "Azakia: A Canadian Story." *American Museum*, September 1789, 193–98.

———. *The Boy's Book of Indian Battles and Adventures, with Anecdotes about them*. New York: Miller, 1861.

———. *Journal de la Guerre du Micissippi contre les Chicachas, en 1739 et finie en 1740*. New York: Shea, 1859.

———. "Relation de ce qui s'est passé de plus remarquable sur le massacre, que la nation sauvage des Natchez a fait à la garnaison du Poste . . ." In *À la Substitution des Valdées proche Solevre en Suisse*. 1732. Ayer MS 293, Newberry Library, 4:386–93.

———. "Tecumseh." *Cincinnati Literary Gazette*, 9 October 1824, 14 May 1825, 16 June 1825.

———. *Xicoténcatl: An Anonymous Historical Novel about the Events Leading Up to the Conquest of the Aztec Empire*. Translated by Guillermo I. Castillo-Feliú. Austin: University of Texas Press, 1999.

Apess, William. *On Our Own Ground: The Complete Writings of William Apess, a Pequot*. Edited by Barry O'Connell. Amherst: University of Massachusetts Press, 1992.

Arch, Stephen Carl. "Romancing the Puritans: American Historical Fiction in the 1820s." *ESQ* 39:2–3 (1993): 106–31.

Aristotle. *Poetics*. In *Critical Theory since Plato*, edited by Hazard Adams, 47–66. San Diego: Harcourt Brace Jovanovich, 1971.

Armour, David A., ed. *Treason? at Michilimackinac: The Proceedings of a General Court Martial Held at Montreal in October 1768 for the Trial of Major Robert Rogers*. Mackinac Island, Mich.: State Park Commission, 1967.

Armstrong, Virginia, ed. *I Have Spoken: American History through the Voices of the Indians*. Chicago: Sage, 1971.

Arnold, Laura. " 'Now . . . Didn't Our People Laugh?' Female Misbehavior and Algonquian Culture in Mary Rowlandson's *Captivity and Restauration*." *American Indian Culture and Research Journal* 21:4 (1997): 1–28.

Atwater, Caleb. "Description of Antiquities Discovered in the state of Ohio and other Western States." *Transactions of the American Antiquarian Society* 1 (1820): 98–200.

Axtell, James. "The Power of Print in the Eastern Woodlands." *William and Mary Quarterly*, 3d ser., 44:2 (1987): 301–9.

Bacon, James. *The American Indian; or, Virtues of Nature*. London: Harrison, 1795.

Bank, Rosemarie K. *Theatre Culture in America, 1825–1860*. New York: Cambridge University Press, 1997.

Barlow, Joel. *The Columbiad*. Philadelphia: Conrad, 1809.

Barnett, Jim. *The Natchez Indians*. Natchez: Mississippi Department of Archives and History, 2002.

Barriero, José, ed. *Indian Roots of American Democracy*. Ithaca, N.Y.: Akwekon Press, 1992.

Bartram, John. *Observations on the Inhabitants, Climate, Soil, Rivers, Productions, Animals, and other matters worthy of Notice. Made by Mr. John Bartram, in his Travels from Pennsylvania to Onondago, Oswego, and the Lake Ontario, in Canada*. 1751; Rochester, N.Y.: Humphrey, 1895.

Baym, Nina. "How Men and Women Wrote Indian Stories." In *New Essays on the Last of the Mohicans*, edited by H. Daniel Peck, 67–86. New York: Cambridge University Press, 1992.

Beatty, Charles. *Journals of Charles Beatty*. University Park: Presbyterian Historical Society/Penn State University Press, 1962.

Behn, Aphra. *Oroonoko; or, The Royal Slave*. 1688; New York: Norton, 1973.

Bell, Michael Davit. *Hawthorne and the Historical Romance of New England*. Princeton: Princeton University Press, 1971.

Bergland, Renée. *The National Uncanny: Indian Ghosts and American Subjects*. Hanover, N.H.: Dartmouth College/University Press of New England, 2000.

Berkhofer, Robert. *The White Man's Indian: Images of the American Indian from Columbus to the Present*. New York: Knopf, 1978.

Bernal, Ignacio. "Durán's Historia and the Crónica X." In Diego Durán, *History of the Indies of New Spain*, 565–77. Norman: University of Oklahoma Press, 1994.

Bhabha, Homi. *The Location of Culture*. New York: Routledge, 1994.

Bienvenu, Germain. "Another America, Another Literature: Narratives from Louisiana's Colonial Experience." Ph.D. diss., Louisiana State University, 1995.

Bird, Robert Montgomery. *Nick of the Woods; or, The Jibbenainosay: A Tale of Kentucky*. 1837; New York: American Book, 1939.

Black Hawk. *Life of Ma-Ka-Tai-Me-She-Kia-Kiak or Black Hawk*. Edited by Donald Jackson. 1833; Urbana: University of Illinois Press, 1990.

Bossu, Jean-Bernard. *Nouveaux Voyages aux Indes Occidentales*. 1768. Reprinted as *Nouveaux Voyages en Louisiane*, edited by Philippe Jacquin. Paris: Aubier Montaigne, 1980.

Bourne, Russell. *The Red King's Rebellion: Racial Politics in New England, 1675–1678*. New York: Oxford University Press, 1990.

Bowden, Henry Warner. "Spanish Missions, Cultural Conflict, and the Pueblo Revolt of 1680" (1975). In *What Caused the Pueblo Revolt of 1680?*, edited by David Weber, 23–40. Boston: Bedford/St. Martins, 1999.

Bradford, William. *Of Plymouth Plantation, 1620–1647*. New York: Modern Library, 1981.

Brading, David A. *The First America: The Spanish Monarchy, Creole Patriots, and the Liberal State, 1492–1867*. Cambridge: Cambridge University Press, 1991.

Brain, Jeffrey P. "La Salle at the Natchez: An Archaeological and Historical Perspective." In *La Salle and His Legacy: Frenchmen and Indians in the Lower Mississippi Valley*, edited by Patricia K. Galloway, 49–59. Jackson: University Press of Mississippi, 1982.

Bridenbaugh, Carl. *Jamestown, 1544–1699*. New York: Oxford University Press, 1980.

Brotherston, Gordon. *The Book of the Fourth World: Reading the Native Americas through Their Literature*. Cambridge: Cambridge University Press, 1992.

———. *Painted Books from Mexico: Codices in U.K. Collections and the World They Represent*. London: British Museum Press, 1995.

Brougham, John. *Metamora; or, The Last of the Pollywogs* (1847). In *Staging the Nation: Plays from the American Theatre, 1787–1909*, edited by Don B. Wilmeth, 101–23. Boston: Bedford, 1998.

———. *Po-ca-hon-tas; or, The Gentle Savage* (1855). In *Dramas from the American Theatre, 1762–1909*, edited by Richard Moody, 397–421. New York: Houghton Mifflin, 1966.

Brown, Charles Brockden. *Edgar Huntly; or, Memoirs of a Sleepwalker*. 1799; Harmondsworth: Penguin, 1988.

Brown, Ian W. "An Archaeological Study of Culture Contact and Change in the Natchez Bluffs Region." In *La Salle and His Legacy: Frenchmen and Indians in the Lower Mississippi Valley*, edited by Patricia K. Galloway, 176–93. Jackson: University Press of Mississippi, 1982.

Buell, Lawrence. *New England Literary Culture: From Revolution through Renaissance*. New York: Cambridge University Press, 1986.

Burk, John. *The History of Virginia, from its First Settlement to the Present Day*. 4 vols. Petersburg, Va.: Dickson and Pescud, 1804–16.

Burton, M. Agnes, ed. *Journal or Narration of Pontiac's Conspiracy in 1763*. Detroit: Speaker-Hines, 1912.

Butor, Michel. "Chateaubriand et l'Ancienne Amérique." *Nouvelle Revue Française*, no. 132 (1963): 1015–31; no. 133 (1964): 63–77; no. 134 (1964): 230–50.

Cabeza de Vaca, Alvar Nuñez. *Castaways*. Translated by Frances M. López-Morillas. Berkeley: University of California Press, 1993.

Calloway, Colin G., ed. *Our Hearts Fell to the Ground: Plains Indian Views of How the West Was Lost*. Boston: Bedford/St. Martin's, 1996.

Campbell, Thomas. *Gertrude of Wyoming: A Pennsylvanian Tale, and Other Poems*. 1809; Oxford: Woodstock, 1991.

Canizares-Esguerra, Jorge. *How to Write the History of the New World: Histories, Epistemologies, and Identities in the Eighteenth-Century Atlantic World*. Stanford, Calif.: Stanford University Press, 2001.

Carpenter, John. *Histoire de la Littérature Française sur la Louisiane de 1673 à 1766*. Paris: Nizet, 1966.

Carrasco, David. *Quetzalcoatl and the Irony of Empire: Myths and Prophecies in the Aztec Tradition*. Rev. ed. Boulder: University Press of Colorado, 2000.

Carver, Jonathan. *The Journals of Jonathan Carver and Related Documents, 1766–1770.* Edited by John Parker. St. Paul: Minnesota Historical Society Press, 1976.

———. *Travels through the interior parts of North-America in the years 1766, 1767, and 1768.* London: the author, 1788.

Charlevoix, Pierre-François-Xavier. *Charlevoix's Louisiana: Selections from the History and the Journal.* Edited by Charles E. O'Neill. Baton Rouge: Louisiana State University Press, 1977.

———. *Journal Historique d'un Voyage Fait par Ordre du Roi dans l'Amérique Septentrionale.* Edited by Pierre Berthiaume. 2 vols. Montreal: Presses de l'Université de Montréal, 1994.

———. *Journal of a Voyage to North America.* 1761; Ann Arbor, Mich.: University Microfilms, 1966.

Chateaubriand, François-René. *Atala; or, The Love and Constancy, of Two Savages in the Desert.* Translated by Caleb Bingham. Boston: Carlisle, 1802.

———. *Atala-René.* Paris: Garnier Flammarion, 1964.

———. *Les Natchez.* Edited by Gilbert Chinard. Baltimore: Johns Hopkins Press, 1932.

———. *The Natchez.* 3 vols. London: Colburn, 1827; reprint, New York: Fertig, 1978.

———. *Travels in America.* Translated by Richard Switzer. Lexington: University of Kentucky Press, 1969.

Chavez, Angelico. "Pohé-yemo's Representative and the Pueblo Revolt of 1680." *New Mexico Historical Review* 42:2 (1962): 85–126.

Cheyfitz, Eric. *The Poetics of Imperialism: Translation and Colonization from "The Tempest" to "Tarzan."* Expanded ed. Philadelphia: University of Pennsylvania Press, 1997.

Child, Lydia Maria. *The First Settlers of New England; or, Conquest of the Pequods, Narragansetts, and Pokanokets.* Boston: Monroe and Francis, 1829.

———. *Hobomok and Other Writings on Indians.* Edited by Carolyn L. Karcher. New Brunswick, N.J.: Rutgers University Press, 1986.

Chinard, Gilbert. *L'Amérique et le Rêve Exotique dans la Littérature Française au XVIIième et au XVIIIième Siècle.* Paris: Hachette, 1913.

———. *L'Exotisme Américain dans l'Oeuvre de Chateaubriand.* Paris: Hachette, 1918.

Chipman, Donald. "Isabel Moctezuma: Pioneer of Mestizaje." In *Struggle and Survival in Colonial America,* edited by David G. Sweet and Gary B. Nash, 214–27. Berkeley: University of California Press, 1981.

Church, Thomas, and Benjamin Church. "Entertaining Passages Relating to Philip's War" (1716). In *So Dreadfull a Judgment: Puritan Responses to King Philip's War, 1676–1677,* edited by Richard Slotkin and James K. Folsom, 395–464. Middletown, Conn.: Wesleyan University Press, 1978.

———. *The History of Philip's War, Commonly Called the Great Indian War, of 1675 and 1676.* Edited by Samuel G. Drake. 2d ed. Exeter, N.H.: Williams, 1829; reprint, Bowie, Md.: Heritage, 1989.

Claiborne, John Francis Hamtramck. *Mississippi as a Province, Territory, and State, with Biographical Notices of Eminent Citizens.* 1880; Spartanburg, S.C.: Reprint Company, 1978.

Clavigero, Francisco Javier. *The History of Mexico*. Translated by Charles Cullen. 2 vols. London: Robinson, 1787; reprint, New York: Garland, 1979.

Clements, William M. *Oratory in Native North America*. Tucson: University of Arizona Press, 2002.

Clendennin, Inga. *Aztecs: An Interpretation*. Cambridge: Cambridge University Press, 1991.

Clifford, James. "On Ethnographic Allegory." In *Writing Culture: The Poetics and Politics of Ethnography*, edited by James Clifford and George E. Marcos, 98–121. Berkeley: University of California Press, 1986.

Colden, Cadwallader. *The History of the Five Indian Nations Depending on the Province of New York in America*. 1727, 1747; Ithaca: Cornell University Press, 1964.

Colón, Fernando. *The Life of the Admiral Christopher Columbus by His Son Ferdinand*. Translated by Benjamin Keen. New Brunswick, N.J.: Rutgers University Press, 1992.

Colton, George Hooker. *Tecumseh; or, The West Thirty Years Since: A Poem*. New York: Wiley and Putnam, 1842.

Cooper, James Fenimore. *The Wept of Wish-ton-Wish: A Tale*. Boston: Houghton Mifflin, n.d.

Cortés, Hernán. *Letters from Mexico*. Translated and edited by Anthony Pagden. New Haven: Yale University Press, 1986. Originally published as *Cartas de relación de la conquista de la Nueva España* (1519–26).

Crèvecœur, J. Hector St. John de. *Letters from an American Farmer and Sketches of Eighteenth-Century America*. Edited by Albert Stone. 1782; Harmondsworth: Penguin, 1986.

Croghan, George. "Croghan's Journal: May 15–September 26, 1761." In *Early Western Travels, 1748–1846*, edited by Reuben Gold Thwaites, 1:126–66. Cleveland: Clark, 1904–7.

Cuneo, John. *Robert Rogers of the Rangers*. New York: Oxford University Press, 1959.

Cusick, David. *Ancient History of the Six Nations*. 1831; Lockport, N.Y.: Niagara County Historical Society, 1961.

Dawdy, Shannon. "Enlightenment from the Ground: Le Page du Pratz's *Histoire de la Louisiane*." *French Colonial History* 3 (2003): 17–34.

Dawson, Moses. *Historical Narrative of the Civil and Military Services of Major-General William Henry Harrison and a vindication of his character and conduct as a statesman, a citizen, and a soldier; with a detail of his negotiations and wars with the Indians, until the final overthrow of the celebrated chief Tecumseh, and his brother the Prophet*. Cincinnati: Dawson, 1824.

Deering, Nathaniel. *Carabasset: A Tragedy, in Five Acts*. Portland, Maine: Colman, 1830.

Deffebach, Louis. *Oolaita; or, The Indian Heroine*. Philadelphia: the author, 1821.

Dekker, George. *The American Historical Romance*. New York: Cambridge University Press, 1987.

Delanglez, Jean, S.J. *The French Jesuits in Lower Louisiana*. Washington, D.C.: Catholic University of America, 1935.

——. "A Louisiana Poet-Historian: Dumont dit Montigny." *Mid-America* 19:1 (1937): 31–49.

——. "M. Le Maire on Louisiana." *Mid-America* 19:2 (1937): 124–54.

———. "The Natchez Massacre and Governor Périer." *Louisiana Historical Quarterly* 17:4 (1934): 631–41.

Deloria, Philip. *Playing Indian.* New Haven: Yale University Press, 1998.

Díaz del Castillo, Bernal. *The Discovery and Conquest of Mexico, 1517–1521.* New York: Farrar, Straus, and Cudahy, 1956. Originally published as *Historia verdadera de la conquista de la Nueva España* (1632).

Diderot, Denis. *Supplément au Voyage de Bougainville.* Paris: Garnier Flammarion, 1972.

Dippie, Brian. *The Vanishing American: White Attitudes and U.S. Indian Policy.* Middletown, Conn.: Wesleyan University Press, 1982.

Doddridge, Joseph. "An Elegy on His Family Vault." *An American Time Capsule: Three Centuries of Broadsides and Other Printed Ephemera.* <www.memory.loc.gov>. 16 June 2004.

———. *Logan, the Last of the Race of Shikellemus, Chief of the Cayuga Nation.* Buffaloe Creek, Va.: Sala, 1823.

———. *Notes on the Settlement and Indian Wars Of the Western Parts of Virginia and Pennsylvania from 1763 to 1783, Inclusive, together with a Review of the State of Society and Manners of the First Settlers of the Western Country with a Memoir of the Author by His Daughter, Narcissa Doddridge. Republished with the Addition of New and Valuable Material by John Ritenour and Wm. T. Lindsey.* Pittsburgh: n.p., 1912.

———. *Treatise on the Culture of Bees.* St. Clairsville, Ohio: Armstrong, 1813.

Dowd, Gregory Evans. "The French King Wakes Up in Detroit: 'Pontiac's War' in Rumor and History." *Ethnohistory* 37:3 (1990): 254–78.

———. *A Spirited Resistance: The North American Indian Struggle for Unity, 1745–1815.* Baltimore: Johns Hopkins University Press, 1992.

———. "Thinking and Believing: Nativism and Unity in the Ages of Pontiac and Tecumseh." *American Indian Quarterly* 16:3 (1992): 309–35.

———. *War under Heaven: Pontiac, the Indian Nations, and the British Empire.* Baltimore: Johns Hopkins University Press, 2002.

Drake, Benjamin. *The Great Indian Chief of the West; or, Life and Adventures of Black Hawk.* 1838; Cincinnati: Queen City, 1855.

———. *Life of Tecumseh, and of his brother, The Prophet; with a Historical Sketch of the Shawanoe Indians.* 1841, 1858; New York: Kraus, 1969.

Drake, Benjamin, and Charles Todd. *Sketches of the Civil and Military Services of William Henry Harrison.* Cincinnati: James, 1840.

Drake, Samuel G. *The Aboriginal Races of North America; comprising Biographical Sketches of Eminent Individuals, and An Historical Account of the Different Tribes from the Discovery of the Continent to the Present Period.* 15th ed. New York: Hurst, 1880.

———. *Biography and History of the Indians of North America; comprising A General Account of them, and Details in the Lives of all the most distinguished chiefs, and others who have been noted, among the various Indian nations upon the continent. Also, A History of their Wars; their manners and customs, and the most celebrated speeches of their orators.* Boston: Perkins; New York: Carvill; Philadelphia: Grigg and Ellio, 1834.

——. *The Book of the Indians of North America; comprising details in the lives of about five hundred chiefs and others, the most distinguished among them.* Boston: Drake, 1833.

——. *Indian Biography, containing the lives of more than two hundred Indian chiefs: also, others who have rendered their names conspicuous in the history of North America. Giving at large their most celebrated speeches, memorable sayings and numerous anecdotes; and a History of their wars. Much of which is taken from manuscripts never before published.* Boston: Drake, 1832.

——, ed. *The History of King Philip's War, by the Rev. Increase Mather, D.D. Also, a History of the Same War, by the Rev. Cotton Mather, D.D. To which are added an Introduction and Notes.* Albany, N.Y.: Munsell, 1862; reprint, Bowie, Md.: Heritage, 1990.

——, ed. *Indian Captivities; or, Life in the Wigwam.* Boston: Drake, 1839.

Draper, Lyman C. "Logan—The Mingo Chief, 1710–1780." *Ohio Archaeological and Historical Publications* 20 (1911): 137–75.

Drinnon, Richard. *Facing West: The Metaphysics of Indian-Hating and Empire-Building.* Minneapolis: University of Minnesota Press, 1980.

Dryden, John. *The Indian Queen and The Indian Emperour; or, The Conquest of Mexico by the Spaniards.* In *Works of John Dryden*, edited by Edward Niles Hooker and H. T. Swedenborg, vols. 9, 10. Berkeley: University of California Press, 1956–2000.

Duffy, Dennis. "John Richardson." In *Canadian Writers and Their Works: Fiction Series*, edited by Robert Lecker, Jack David, and Ellen Quigley, 1:107–48. Downsview, Ont.: ECW, 1983.

——. "John Richardson's Kentucky Tragedies." *Canadian Review of American Studies/Revue Canadienne des Études Américaines* 22:1 (1991): 1–21.

Dumont de Montigny. "Établissement de la Province de la Louisiane: Poème Composée de 1728 à 1742." Edited by Marc de Villiers. *Journal de la Société des Américanistes de Paris*, n.s., 23:2 (1931): 273–440.

——. *Historical Memoir on Louisiana.* Translated by Olivia Blanchard. Baton Rouge: Works Progress Administration, Survey of Federal Archives in Louisiana, 1938.

——. "Historical Memoirs of M. Dumont." Vol. 5 of *Historical Collections of Louisiana; embracing many rare and valuable documents relating to the natural, civil, and political history of that state.* Edited and translated by Benjamin Franklin French. New York: Wiley and Putnam, 1853.

——. *Mémoire de Lxx Dxx officier ingénieur, Contenant Les Evenements qui se sont passés à la Louisiane depuis 1715 jusqu'à present. Ainsi que les remarques sur les moeurs, usages, et forces de diverses nations de l'Amérique Septentrionale et de ses productions.* 1747. Ayer MS 257, Newberry Library, Chicago.

——. *Mémoires historiques sur la Louisiane contenant ce qui y est arrivé de plus mémorable depuis l'année 1687 jusqu'à présent: avec l'établissement de la colonie françoise dans cette province de l'Amérique Septentrionale sous la direction de la Compagnie des Indes: le climat, la nature, & les productions de ce pays; l'origine et la religion des sauvages qui y l'habitent, leurs moeurs et leurs coutumes, &c.* 2 vols. Paris: Bauche, 1753.

Dunbar, John R., ed. *The Paxton Papers.* The Hague: Martinus Nijhoff, 1957.

Dunn, Richard S. "John Winthrop, Jr., and the Narragansett Country." *William and Mary Quarterly*, 3d. ser., 13:1 (1956): 68–86.

Durán, Diego. *Book of the Gods and Rites and the Ancient Calendar*. Translated by Fernando Horcasitas and Doris Heyden. Norman: University of Oklahoma Press, 1971.

——. *The History of the Indies of New Spain*. Translated by Doris Heyden. Norman: University of Oklahoma Press, 1994.

Du Ru, Paul. *Journal of Paul du Ru*. Translated by Ruth Lapham Butler. Fairfield, Wash.: Ye Galleon, 1997.

Dussel, Enrique. *The Invention of the Americas: Eclipse of the Other and the Myth of Modernity*. Translated by Michael D. Barber. New York: Continuum, 1995.

Eastburn, James Wallis, and Robert Charles Sands. *Yamoyden, a tale of the wars of King Philip: in six cantos*. New York: Clayton and Kingsland, 1820.

Edmunds, R. David. *The Shawnee Prophet*. Lincoln: University of Nebraska Press, 1993.

——. *Tecumseh and the Quest for Indian Leadership*. Boston: Little, Brown, 1984.

Ellison, Julie. *Cato's Tears and the Making of Anglo-American Emotion*. Chicago: University of Chicago Press, 1999.

Emmons, Richard. *Tecumseh; or, The Battle of the Thames, a National Drama*. Philadelphia: n.p., 1836.

Ercilla, Alonso de. *La Araucana*. 2 vols. Madrid: Editorial Castalia, 1979.

Fairchild, Hoxie. *The Noble Savage: A Study in Romantic Naturalism*. New York: Columbia University Press, 1928.

Faulkner, William. *Collected Stories of William Faulkner*. New York: Random House, 1934.

Fausz, J. Frederick. "Opechancanough: Indian Resistance Leader." In *Struggle and Survival in Colonial America*, edited by David G. Sweet and Gary B. Nash, 21–37. Berkeley: University of California Press, 1981.

Felman, Shoshona, and Dori Laub. *Testimony: Crises of Witnessing in Literature, Psychoanalysis, and History*. New York: Routledge, 1991.

Fiedler, Leslie. *Love and Death in the American Novel*. Rev. ed. New York: Anchor, 1992.

Filson, John. "The Adventures of Col. Daniel Boon." In *American Lives: An Anthology of Autobiographical Writing*, edited by Robert F. Sayre, 211–26. Madison: University of Wisconsin Press, 1994.

Fliegelman, Jay. *Declaring Independence: Jefferson, Natural Language, and the Culture of Performance*. Stanford, Calif.: Stanford University Press, 1994.

——. *Prodigals and Pilgrims: The American Revolution against Patriarchal Authority, 1750–1800*. New York: Cambridge University Press, 1982.

Flood, Renée Sansom. *Lost Bird of Wounded Knee: Spirit of the Lakota*. New York: Scribner, 1995.

Franklin, Benjamin. *A Narrative of the Late Massacres*. In *The Heath Anthology of American Literature*, 3d ed., edited by Paul Lauter, 1:733–45. Boston: Houghton Mifflin, 1998.

Frazier, Ian. *Great Plains*. New York: Farrar, Straus, Giroux, 1989.

French, James Strange. *Elkswatawa; or, The Prophet of the West. A Tale of the Frontier*. New York: Harper, 1836.

Frye, Northrup. *Anatomy of Criticism*. Princeton: Princeton University Press, 1957.

Fuchs, Barbara. *Mimesis and Empire: The New World, Islam, and European Identities*. New York: Cambridge University Press, 2001.

Fuentes, Patricia de, ed. and trans. *The Conquistadors: First-Person Accounts of the Conquest of Mexico*. Norman: University of Oklahoma Press, 1993.

Furtwangler, Albert. *Answering Chief Seattle*. Seattle: University of Washington Press, 1997.

Galbreath, C. B. "The Logan Elm." *Ohio Educational Monthly*, November 1923, 2–7.

Galloway, Patricia K. *Choctaw Genesis, 1500–1700*. Lincoln: University of Nebraska Press, 1995.

Galloway, William. *Old Chillicothe: Shawnee and Pioneer History: Conflicts and Romances in the Northwest Territory*. Xenia, Ohio: Buckeye, 1934.

Gardener, Lion. "Leift Lion Gardener his Relation of the Pequot Warres." *Collections of the Massachusetts Historical Society*, 3d ser., 3 (1833): 131–64.

Gaul, Theresa Strouth. " 'The Genuine Indian Who Was Brought upon the Stage': Edwin Forrest's *Metamora* and White Audiences." *Arizona Quarterly* 56:1 (2000): 1–27.

Girard, René. *Things Hidden since the Foundation of the World*. Research undertaken in collaboration with Jean-Michel Oughourlian and Guy Lefort. Translated by Stephen Bann and Michael Metteer. Stanford, Calif.: Stanford University Press, 1987.

——. *Violence and the Sacred*. Translated by Patrick Gregory. Baltimore: Johns Hopkins University Press, 1977.

Giraud, Marcel. *A History of French Louisiana*. Vol. 5, *The Company of the Indies, 1723–1731*. Translated by Brian Pearce. Baton Rouge: Louisiana State University Press, 1991.

Goddu, Teresa. *American Gothic*. New York: Columbia University Press, 1997.

Gookin, Daniel. "An Historical Account of the Doings and Sufferings of the Christian Indians in New England, in the Years 1675, 1676, 1677." *Transactions of the American Antiquarian Society* 8 (1905): 423–534.

Gould, Philip. *Covenant and Republic: Historical Romance and the Politics of Puritanism*. New York: Cambridge University Press, 1996.

——. "Remembering Metacom: Historical Writing and the Cultures of Masculinity in Early Republican America." In *Sentimental Men: Masculinity and the Politics of Affect in American Culture*, ed. Mary Chapman and Glenn Hendler, 112–24. Berkeley: University of California Press, 1999.

Gravil, Richard. "Regicide and Ethnic Cleansing; or, Edmund Burke in *Wish-ton-Wish*." *Symbiosis: A Journal of Anglo-American Literary Relations* 4:2 (2000): 187–204.

Gray, Edward. "The Making of Logan, the Mingo Orator." In *The Language Encounter in the Americas, 1492–1800: A Collection of Essays*, edited by Edward G. Gray and Norman Fiering, 258–77. New York: Berghahn, 2000.

Grimsted, David. *Melodrama Unveiled: American Theatre and Culture, 1800–1850*. Chicago: University of Chicago Press, 1968.

Grinde, Donald A., Jr. *The Iroquois and the Founding of the American Nation*. San Francisco: Indian Historian Press, 1977.

Grose, G. Donald. "Edwin Forrest, *Metamora*, and the Indian Removal Act of 1830." *Theatre Journal* 37:2 (1985): 181–92.

———. "Here Come the Indians: An Historical Study of the Representations of the Native American upon the North American Stage, 1808–1969." Ph.D. diss., University of Missouri–Columbia, 1979.

Gustafson, Sandra. *Eloquence Is Power: Oratory and Performance in Early America*. Chapel Hill: Omohundro Institute of Early American History and Culture/University of North Carolina Press, 2000.

Gutierrez, Ramón. *When Jesus Came, the Corn Mothers Went Away: Marriage, Sexuality, and Power in New Mexico, 1500–1846*. Stanford, Calif.: Stanford University Press, 1991.

Hackett, Charles, and Charmion C. Shelby, eds. *Revolt of the Pueblo Indians of New Mexico and Otermin's Attempted Reconquest*. 2 vols. Albuquerque: University of New Mexico Press, 1942.

Hall, Gwendolyn Midlo. *Africans in Colonial Louisiana: The Development of Afro-Creole Culture in the Eighteenth Century*. Baton Rouge: Louisiana State University Press, 1992.

Hall, James. *A Memoir of the Public Services of William Henry Harrison, of Ohio*. Philadelphia: Key and Biddle, 1836.

Harrington, James. *The Commonwealth of Oceana; and, A System of Politics*. Edited by J. G. A. Pocock. New York: Cambridge University Press, 1992.

Harrison, William Henry. *Discourse on the Aborigines of the Valley of the Ohio*. Boston: Tucker, 1840.

Hartog, François. *The Mirror of Herodotus: The Representation of the Other in the Writing of History*. Translated by Janet Lloyd. Berkeley: University of California Press, 1988.

Hawthorne, Nathaniel. "The Grey Champion" (1835). In *Hawthorne: Tales and Sketches*, 236–43. New York: Library of America, 1996.

Heckewelder, John. *History, Manners, and Customs of the Indians Who Once Inhabited Pennsylvania and the Neighboring States*. 1817; New York: Arno Press/New York Times, 1971.

———. *A Narrative of the Mission of the United Brethren among the Delaware and Mohegan Indians, from Its Commencement, in the Year 1740, to the Close of the Year 1808*. 1820; New York: Arno Press/New York Times, 1971.

Herodotus. *The Histories*. Translated by Aubrey de Sélincourt with introduction by A. R. Burn. Harmondsworth: Penguin, 1954.

Honour, Hugh. *The New Golden Land: European Images of America from the Discoveries to the Present Time*. New York: Pantheon, 1975.

Horan, James D. *The McKenney-Hall Portrait Gallery of American Indians*. New York: Crown, 1972.

Hoxie, Frederick, ed. *Talking Back to Civilization: Indian Voices from the Progressive Era*. Boston: Bedford/St. Martin's, 2001.

Hubbard, William. *A Narrative of the Troubles with the Indians In New-England, from the first planting thereof in the year 1607, to this present year 1677, but chiefly of the late Troubles in the two last years, 1675 and 1676: To which is added a Discourse about the Warre with the*

Pequods in the year 1637. 1677. Reprinted as *The History of the Indian Wars in New England from the First Settlement to the Termination of the War with King Philip*, in 1677, edited by Samuel G. Drake. 2 vols. New York: Kraus, 1969.

Hulme, Peter. *Colonial Encounters: Europe and the Native Caribbean, 1492–1797*. London: Routledge, 1992.

Hunter, Charles E. "The Delaware Nativist Revival of the Mid–Eighteenth Century." *Ethnohistory* 18:1 (1971): 39–49.

Hutchinson, Thomas. *The History of the Colony and Province of Massachusetts Bay*. Edited by Lawrence Shaw Mayo. 3 vols. Cambridge: Harvard University Press, 1936.

Iberville, Pierre Le Moyne d'. *Iberville's Gulf Journals*. Translated and edited by Richebourg Gaillard McWilliams. Tuscaloosa: University of Alabama Press, 1981.

Ingersoll, Thomas N. "Free Blacks in a Slave Society: New Orleans, 1718–1812." *William and Mary Quarterly*, 3d ser., 48:2 (1991): 173–200.

Irving, Washington. "Philip of Pokanocket." *Analectic Magazine*, n.s., 3 (1814): 502–15.

Jacob, John J. *A Biographical Sketch of the Life of the Late Captain Michael Cresap*. 1826; New York: Arno Press/New York Times, 1971.

Jacobs, Wilbur R. *Dispossessing the American Indian: Indians and Whites on the Colonial Frontier*. New York: Scribner, 1972.

Jefferson, Thomas. *Notes on the State of Virginia*. Edited by Frank Shuffleton. Harmondsworth: Penguin, 1999.

Jennings, Francis. *The Invasion of America: Indians, Colonialism, and the Cant of Conquest*. New York: Norton, 1976.

Johansen, Bruce E. *Forgotten Founders: Benjamin Franklin, the Iroquois, and the Rationale for the American Revolution*. Ipswitch, Mass.: Gambit, 1982.

Johnson, David E. "Descartes's Corps." *Arizona Quarterly* 57:1 (2001): 113–50.

Johnson, Edward. *Wonder Working Providence of Sions Saviour in New England (1654) and Good News from New England (1648)*. Delmar, N.Y.: Scholars' Facsimiles and Reprints, 1974.

Johnson, Michael P. "Denmark Vesey and His Co-Conspirators." *William and Mary Quarterly*, 3d ser., 58:4 (2001): 915–71.

Jones, Eugene H. *Native Americans as Shown on the Stage, 1753–1916*. Metuchen, N.J.: Scarecrow, 1988.

Jones, George. *Tecumseh, and the Prophet of the West, An Original Historical Israel-Indian Tragedy, in Five Acts*. London: Longman; New York: Harper; Paris: Klincksieck; Berlin: Dunker, 1844.

Josephy, Alvin M., Jr. *The Patriot Chiefs: A Chronicle of American Indian Leadership*. New York: Viking, 1961.

Kaiser, Rudolph. " 'A Fifth Gospel, Almost': Chief Seattle's Speech(es): American Origins and European Reception." In *Indians and Europe: An Interdisciplinary Collection of Essays*, edited by Christian F. Feest, 505–26. Aachen: Herodot, 1987.

Keen, Benjamin. *The Aztec Image in Western Thought*. New Brunswick, N.J.: Rutgers University Press, 1971.

Kenny, James. "Diary of James Kenney." *Pennsylvania Magazine of History and Biography* 37 (1913): 1–47, 152–201.

Kibbey, Ann. *The Interpretation of Material Shapes in Puritanism: A Study of Rhetoric, Prejudice, and Violence.* Cambridge: Cambridge University Press, 1986.

Kinietz, W. Vernon. *John Mix Stanley and His Indian Paintings.* Ann Arbor: University of Michigan Press, 1942.

Klinck, Carl F., ed. *Tecumseh: Fact and Fiction in Early Records.* Englewood Cliffs, N.J.: Prentice-Hall, 1961.

Krupat, Arnold. *Ethnocriticism: Ethnography, History, Literature.* Berkeley: University of California Press, 1992.

——. *For Those Who Come After: A Study of Native American Autobiography.* Berkeley: University of California Press, 1985.

——. *Native American Autobiography: An Anthology.* Madison: University of Wisconsin Press, 1994.

Kupperman, Karen. *Settling with the Indians: The Meeting of English and Indian Cultures in America, 1580–1640.* Totowa, N.J.: Rowman and Littlefield, 1980.

Lafaye, Jacques. *Quetzalcoatl and Guadalupe: The Formation of Mexican National Consciousness, 1531–1813.* Translated by Benjamin Keen. Chicago: University of Chicago Press, 1976.

Lafitau, Joseph-François. *Mœurs des Sauvages américains comparées aux mœurs des premiers temps.* Paris: Saugrain l'ainé et Charles Estienne Hochereau, 1724. Published in English as *Customs of the American Indians Compared with the Customs of Primitive Times.* Translated and edited by William Fenton and Elizabeth Moore. 2 vols. Toronto: Champlain Society, 1974.

Lahontan, Louis-Armand de Lom d'Arce, Baron de. *New Voyages to North America.* Edited by Reuben Gold Thwaites. 1703; Chicago: McClurg, 1905.

Lame Deer, John (Fire). *Lame Deer Seeker of Visions.* Edited by Richard Erdoes. New York: Simon and Schuster, 1972.

Lamonte, Jennifer. " 'You Are the Son of a French Man': Women, Kinship, and Nurturing of Identity in Colonial Louisiana." Paper presented at Colonial Louisiana: A Tricentennial Symposium, Biloxi, Miss., March 1999.

Leonard, Irving A. *Books of the Brave: Being an Account of Books and of Men in the Spanish Conquest and Settlement of the Sixteenth-Century New World.* Cambridge: Harvard University Press, 1949.

Léon-Portilla, Miguel. *The Broken Spears: The Aztec Account of the Conquest of Mexico.* Boston: Beacon, 1992.

Le Page du Pratz, Antoine. *Histoire de la Louisiane.* 3 vols. Paris: De Bure, Veuve Delaguette, et Lambert, 1758. Published in English as *The History of Louisiana, or of the Western Parts of Virginia and Carolina.* London: Becket, 1774; reprint, Baton Rouge: Louisiana State University Press, 1983.

——. "Mémoire sur la Louisiane" (series). *Journal Oeconomique; ou, Mémoires, Notes, et Avis, sur l'Agriculture, les Arts, le Commerce,* September 1751–February 1753.

Le Petit, Mathurin. "Letter from Father le Petit, Missionary, to Father d'Avaugour, Procurator of the Missions in North America." In *Lettres édifiantes et curieuses écrites des missions étrangères par quelques Missionaires de la Compagnie de Jesus*, edited by J. du Halde. Paris: Le Clerc, 1731. Reprinted in *The Jesuit Relations and Allied Documents*, edited by Reuben Gold Thwaites, 68:120–223. Cleveland: Burrowes, 1896–1901.

Lepore, Jill. *The Name of War: King Philip's War and the Origins of American Identity*. New York: Knopf, 1998.

Levin, David. *History as Romantic Art: Bancroft, Prescott, Motley, and Parkman*. Stanford, Calif.: Stanford University Press, 1959.

Liebersohn, Harry. *Aristocratic Encounters: European Travelers and North American Indians*. Cambridge: Cambridge University Press, 1998.

Longmore, George. *Tecumthe, a Poetical Tale: In Three Cantos*. Edited by Mary Lu MacDonald. 1824; London, Ont.: Canadian Poetry Press, 1993.

Lorenz, Karl. "A Re-Examination of Natchez Sociopolitical Complexity: A View from the Grand Village and Beyond." *Southeastern Archaeology* 16:2 (1997): 97–112.

Loskiel, George Henry. *History of the Mission of the United Brethren among the Indians in North America*. Translated by Christian Ignatius La Trobe. 2 vols. London: Brethren's Society for the Furtherance of the Gospel, 1794.

Lott, Eric. *Love and Theft: Blackface Minstrelsy and the American Working Class*. New York: Oxford University Press, 1993.

Loudon, Archibald, ed. *A Selection of Some of the Most Interesting Narratives of Outrages Committed by the Indians in Their Wars with the White People*. 1808; New York: Arno, 1971.

Mackenthun, Gesa. *Metaphors of Dispossession: American Beginnings and the Translation of Empire, 1492–1637*. Norman: University of Oklahoma Press, 1997.

MacLeod, William Christie. "Natchez Political Evolution." *American Anthropologist* 26:2 (1924): 201–29.

———. "On Natchez Cultural Origins." *American Anthropologist* 28:2 (1926): 409–13.

Macomb, Alexander. *Pontiac; or, The Siege of Detroit. A Drama, In Three Acts*. Boston: Colman, 1835.

Madrid, José Fernández. *Atala y Guatimoc (Tragedias en Verso)*. Bogotá: Biblioteca Aldeana de Columbia, 1936.

Marmontel, Jean François. *Les Incas; ou, La destruction de l'empire de Pérou*. Amsterdam: Changuion, 1777.

Martin, Scott C. "Interpreting *Metamora*: Nationalism, Theater, and Jacksonian Indian Policy." *Journal of the Early Republic* 19:1 (1999): 73–101.

Martin, Joel W. *Sacred Revolt: The Muskogees' Struggle for a New World*. Boston: Beacon, 1991.

Mason, Jeffrey D. "The Politics of *Metamora*." In *The Performance of Power: Theatrical Discourse and Politics*, edited by Su-Ellen Case and Janelle Reinelt, 92–110. Iowa City: University of Iowa Press, 1991.

Mather, Cotton. *Magnalia Christi Americana; or, The Ecclesiastical History of New-England, from*

its first planting in the year 1620, unto the year of Our Lord, 1698. 2 vols. Hartford:
    Andrus, 1820.

Mather, Increase. "A Brief History of the Warr with the Indians in New England"
    (1676). In So Dreadfull a Judgment: Puritan Responses to King Philip's War, 1676–1677,
    edited by Richard Slotkin and James Folsom, 79–152. Middletown, Conn.:
    Wesleyan University Press, 1978.

Mayer, Brantz. Tah-gah-jute; or, Logan and Captain Michael Cresap. Baltimore, n.p.,
    1851.

McConachie, Bruce. Melodramatic Formations: American Theatre and Society, 1820–1870.
    Iowa City: University of Iowa Press, 1992.

McConnell, Michael. A Country Between: The Upper Ohio Valley and Its Peoples, 1724–1774.
    Lincoln: University of Nebraska Press, 1992.

McCullough, John. "A Narrative of the Captivity of John McCullough, Esq." In A
    Selection of Some of the Most Interesting Narratives of Outrages Committed by the Indians in
    Their Wars with the White People, edited by Archibald Loudon, 1:52–301. New York:
    Arno, 1971.

McElwain, Thomas. " 'Then I Thought I Must Kill Too': Logan's Lament: A 'Mingo'
    Perspective." In Native American Speakers of the Eastern Woodlands: Selected Speeches and
    Critical Analyses, edited by Barbara Alice Mann, 107–22. Westport, Conn.:
    Greenwood, 2001.

McIntosh, John. The Origin of the North American Indians: with a faithful description of their
    manners and customs . . . including various specimens of Indian eloquence as well as historical
    and biographical sketches of almost all the distinguished nations and celebrated warriors,
    statesmen and orators, among the Indians of North America. New York: Nafis and Cornish,
    1843.

McKenney, Thomas. Biographical Sketches and Anecdotes of Ninety-five of 120 Principal Chiefs
    from the Indian Tribes of North America. Washington, D.C.: Bureau of Indian Affairs,
    1967.

McKenney, Thomas, and James Hall. History of the Indian Tribes of North America, with
    Biographical Sketches and Anecdotes of the Principal Chiefs. Edited by Frederick Hodge.
    1836; Edinburgh: Grant, 1933–34.

McWilliams, John P. The American Epic: Transforming a Genre, 1770–1860. New York:
    Cambridge University Press, 1989.

Medina, Louisa. Nick of the Woods: A drama, in three acts. New York: Samuel French, n.d.

Melville, Herman. The Confidence-Man: His Masquerade. Evanston, Ill.: Northwestern
    University Press/Newberry Library, 1984.

Merrell, James H. The Indians' New World: Catawbas and Their Neighbors from European
    Contact through the Era of Removal. New York: Norton, 1989.

——. Into the American Woods: Negotiators on the Pennsylvania Frontier. New York: Norton,
    2000.

——. "Shickellamy, 'A Person of Consequence.' " In Northeastern Indian Lives, edited by
    Robert S. Grumet, 227–57. Amherst: University of Massachusetts Press, 1996.

Merritt, Jane T. *At the Crossroads: Indians and Empires on a Mid-Atlantic Frontier*. Chapel Hill: University of North Carolina Press, 2003.

Mintz, Steven, ed. *Native American Voices*. St. James, N.Y.: Brandywine, 1995.

Mitchell, Domhnall. " 'Acts of Intercourse': Miscegenation in Three Nineteenth-Century American Novels." *American Studies in Scandinavia* 27:2 (1995): 126–41.

Montejo, Victor. *Testimony: Death of a Guatemalan Village*. Willimantic, Conn.: Curbstone, 1987.

Moody, Richard. *America Takes the Stage: Romanticism in American Drama and Theatre, 1750–1900*. Bloomington: Indiana University Press, 1955.

——. Introduction to *Metamora; or, The Last of the Wampanoags*. In *Dramas from the American Theatre, 1762–1909*, edited by Richard Moody, 199–204. New York: Houghton Mifflin, 1966.

——. "Lost and Now Found: The Fourth Act of *Metamora*." *American Literature* 34:3 (1962): 335–64.

Mooney, James. *The Ghost Dance Religion and the Sioux Outbreak of 1890*. Edited and abridged by Anthony F. C. Wallace. 1896; Chicago: University of Chicago Press, 1965.

Morison, Samuel Eliot. *Admiral of the Ocean Sea: A Life of Christopher Columbus*. Boston: Little, Brown, 1942.

Morris, Michael P. *The Bringing of Wonder: Trade and the Indians of the Southeast, 1700–1783*. Westport, Conn.: Greenwood, 1999.

Morris, Thomas. "Journal of Captain Thomas Morris of His Majesty's XVII Regiment of Infantry." In *Early Western Travels, 1748–1846*, edited by Reuben Gold Thwaites, 1:301–28. Cleveland: Clark, 1904–7.

——. *Miscellanies in Prose and Verse*. London: Ridgway, 1791.

Morton, Sarah Wentworth. *Ouâbi; or, The Virtues of Nature: An Indian Tale in Four Cantos*. Boston: Thomas and Andrews, 1790.

Motley, Warren. *The American Abraham: James Fenimore Cooper and the Frontier Patriarch*. Cambridge: Cambridge University Press, 1987.

Mulford, Carla, ed. *Early American Writings*. New York: Oxford University Press, 2002.

Murdock, James. *The Stage; or, Recollections of Actors and Acting from an Experience of Fifty Years*. Philadelphia: Stoddard, 1880.

Murray, David. *Forked Tongues: Speech, Writing, and Representation in North American Indian Texts*. London: Pinter, 1991.

Murray, Laura. "The Aesthetic of Dispossession: Washington Irving and the Ideologies of (De)Colonization in the Early Republic." *American Literary History* 8:2 (1996): 205–31.

Nabokov, Peter. *Indian Running: Native American History and Tradition*. Santa Fe, N.M.: Ancient City, 1981.

Nabokov, Peter, and Dean Snow. "Farmers of the Woodlands." In *America in 1492*, edited by Alvin Josephy, 119–46. New York: Vintage, 1991.

[Neal, John]. *Logan: A Family History*. 4 vols. Philadelphia: Carey and Lea, 1822.

Nelson, Dana D. *National Manhood: Capitalist Citizenship and the Imagined Fraternity of White Men*. Durham, N.C.: Duke University Press, 1998.

——. *The Word in Black and White: Reading "Race" in American Literature, 1638–1867*. New York: Oxford University Press, 1993.

Nequatewa, Edmund. *Truth of a Hopi and Other Clan Stories of Shung-Opovi*. Edited by Mary-Russell F. Colton. Flagstaff: Northern Arizona Society of Science and Art, 1947.

Norton, John (Teyoninhokarawen). *Journal of a Voyage, of a Thousand Miles, Down the Ohio; from the Grand River, Upper Canada;—Visit to the Country of the Cherokees:—Through the States of Kentucky and Tennessee: and an Account of the Five Nations, Etc. from an Early Period, to the Conclusion of the Late War between Great Britain and America*. Edited by Carl Klinck and James Talman. Toronto: Champlain Society, 1970.

Noyes, James O. "Logan and the Home of the Iroquois." *Knickerbocker* 53:5 (1859): 554–67.

O'Donnell, James H. "Logan's Oration: A Case Study in Ethnographic Authentication." *Quarterly Journal of Speech* 65:2 (1979): 150–56.

Opferman, Susanne. "Lydia Maria Child, James Fenimore Cooper, and Catharine Maria Sedgwick: A Dialogue on Race, Culture, and Gender." In *Soft Canons: American Women Writers and Masculine Traditions*, edited by Karen L. Kilcup, 27–47. Iowa City: University of Iowa Press, 1999.

Orians, G. Harrison. "The Angel of Hadley in Fiction: A Study of the Sources of Hawthorne's 'The Grey Champion.'" *American Literature* 4:3 (1932): 257–69.

Ortiz, Alfonso. "Popay's Leadership: A Pueblo Perspective." *El Palacio* 86:2 (1980–81): 18–23.

Oskison, John. *Tecumseh and His Times*. New York: Putnam, 1938.

The Oxford Companion to American Literature. By James D. Hart. 4th ed. New York: Oxford University Press, 1965.

Palfrey, John Gorham. Review of *Yamoyden* by James Wallis Eastburn and Charles Sands. *North American Review* 12:1 (1821): 466–88.

Paquette, Robert L. "Jacobins of the Lowcountry: The Vesey Plot on Trial." *William and Mary Quarterly*, 3d ser., 59:1 (2002): 185–92.

Parkman, Francis. *The Conspiracy of Pontiac and the Indian War after the Conquest of Canada*. 1851; New York: Library of America, 1991.

Pearce, Roy Harvey. *Savagism and Civilization: A Study of the Indian and the American Mind*. Baltimore: Johns Hopkins University Press, 1965.

Peckham, Howard H. *Pontiac and the Indian Conspiracy*. Princeton: Princeton University Press, 1947.

Pénicaut, André. *Fleur de Lys and Calumet: Being the Pénicaut Narrative of French Adventure in Louisiana*. Translated and edited by Richebourg Gaillard McWilliams. 1953; Tuscaloosa: University of Alabama Press, 1988.

Person, Leland S., Jr. "The American Eve: Miscegenation and a Feminist Frontier Fiction." *American Quarterly* 37:5 (1985): 668–85.

Peterson, Merrill. *Thomas Jefferson and the New Nation*. New York: Oxford University Press, 1970.

Plutarch. *Lives of the Noble Greeks*. Edited by Edmund Fuller. New York: Dell, 1959.

Pocahontas. Directed by Mike Gabriel and Eric Goldberg. Disney, 1995.

Pocahontas II: Journey to a New World. Directed by Tom Ellery and Bradley Raymond. Disney, 1998.

Poe, Edgar Allan. *Poetry, Tales, and Selected Essays*. New York: Library of America, 1984.

Prescott, W. H. *History of the Conquest of Mexico*. 2 vols. New York: Hurst, 1843.

Prévost, Abbé de. *Le Philosophe Anglais; ou, Histoire de Monsieur Cleveland, fils naturel de Cromwell*. Vol. 2 of *Oeuvres de Prévost*. Edited by Jean Sgard. 1731–39; Grenoble: Presses Universitaires de Grenoble, 1978.

Prucha, Paul. *The Great Father: The United States Government and the American Indians*. Lincoln: University of Nebraska Press, 1984.

Quaife, Milo M., ed. *The Siege of Detroit in 1763: The Journal of Pontiac's Conspiracy and John Rutherfurd's Narrative of a Captivity*. Chicago: Lakeside, 1958.

Quint, David. *Epic and Empire: Politics and Generic Form from Virgil to Milton*. Princeton: Princeton University Press, 1993.

Rabasa, José. *Writing Violence on the Northern Frontier: The Historiography of Sixteenth-Century New Mexico and Florida and the Legacy of Conquest*. Durham, N.C.: Duke University Press: 2000.

Racine, Jean. *Phaedre*. Translated by Richard Wilbur. 1677; San Diego: Harcourt Brace Jovanovich, 1984.

Rafinesque, Samuel. *Walam Olum; or, Red Score, the Migration Legend of the Lenni Lenape or Delaware Indians*. 1833; Indianapolis: Indiana Historical Society, 1954.

Raynal, Guillaume-Thomas. *Histoire des Deux Indes*. 3d ed. 4 vols. Geneva: Pellet, 1780.

Richardson, John. *The Canadian Brothers; or, The Prophecy Fulfilled: A Tale of the Late American War*. 1840; reprint, Toronto: University of Toronto Press, 1976.

——. *Tecumseh; or, The Warrior of the West: A Poem, in Four Cantos*. 1828. London, Ont.: Canadian Poetry Press, 1992.

——. *Wacousta; or, The Prophecy: A Tale of the Canadas*. 1832; Ottawa, Ont.: Tecumseh, 1998.

Richter, Daniel. *Facing East from Indian Country: A Native History of Early America*. Cambridge: Harvard University Press, 2001.

Rigal, Laura. "Framing the Fabric: A Luddite Reading of Penn's Treaty with the Indians." *American Literary History* 12:3 (2000): 557–84.

Roach, Joseph. *Cities of the Dead: Circum-Atlantic Performance*. New York: Columbia University Press, 1996.

Rogers, Robert. *A Concise Account of North America*. 1765; New York: Johnson Reprints, 1966.

——. *Diary of the Siege of Detroit in the War with Pontiac*. Edited by Franklin B. Hough. Albany, N.Y.: Munsell, 1860.

——. *Journals of Major Robert Rogers*. 1765; New York: Johnson Reprints, 1966.

——. *Ponteach; or, The Savages of America: A Tragedy*. Edited by Allan Nevins. 1766; Chicago: Caxton Club, 1914.

———. "Rogers's Michilimackinac Journal." *Proceedings of the American Antiquarian Society* 28 (1918): 224–73.

Rogin, Michael Paul. *Fathers and Children: Andrew Jackson and the Subjugation of the American Indian.* New York: Knopf, 1975.

Roosevelt, Theodore. *The Winning of the West.* 4 vols. New York: Putnam, 1894–97.

Rosaldo, Renato. *Culture and Truth: The Remaking of Social Analysis.* Boston: Beacon, 1989.

Rowland, Dunbar, and A. G. Sanders, eds. and trans. *Mississippi Provincial Archives, French Dominion.* Vols. 1–3. Jackson: Mississippi Department of Archives and History, 1927.

Rowland, Dunbar, A. G. Sanders, and Patricia K. Galloway, eds. and trans. *Mississippi Provincial Archives, French Dominion.* Vols. 4–5. Baton Rouge: Louisiana State University Press, 1984.

Rowlandson, Mary. *The Sovereignty and Goodness of God.* Edited by Neal Salisbury. Boston: Bedford, 1997.

Rutherfurd, John. "Mr. John Rutherfurd's Journal in a Letter to Sir John Nisbet, New York, 1763." In *The Siege of Detroit in 1763: The Journal of Pontiac's Conspiracy and John Rutherfurd's Narrative of a Captivity,* edited by Milo M. Quaife, 219–74. Chicago: Lakeside, 1958.

Sabin, Edwin L. *Boys' Book of Indian Warriors and Heroic Indian Women.* Philadelphia: Jacobs, 1918.

Sahagun, Bernardino de. *Florentine Codex: General History of the Things of New Spain.* Edited and translated by Arthur J. O. Anderson and Charles E. Dibble. 13 vols. Santa Fe, N.M.: School of American Research/University of Utah Press, 1950–82.

St. Cosme, Jean-François Buisson. "Letter of J. F. Buisson St. Cosme, Missionary Priest, to the Bishop." In *Early Voyages Up and Down the Mississippi,* edited by John Gilmary Shea, 61–85. Albany, N.Y.: Munsell, 1861.

Sandefur, Ray H. "Logan's Oration—How Authentic?" *Quarterly Journal of Speech* 46:3 (1960): 289–96.

Sando, Joe. *Pueblo Nations: Eight Centuries of Pueblo Indian History.* Santa Fe, N.M.: Clear Light, 1992.

Sargent, Mark L. "Thomas Hutchinson, Ezra Stiles, and the Legend of the Regicides." *William and Mary Quarterly,* 3d ser., 49:3 (1992): 431–48.

Saunt, Claudio. *A New Order of Things: Property, Power, and the Transformation of the Creek Indians, 1733–1816.* Cambridge: Cambridge University Press, 1999.

Savage, Sarah. *Life of Philip, the Indian Chief.* Salem, Mass.: Whipple and Lawrence, 1827.

Sawvel, Franklin B. *Logan, the Mingo.* Boston: Badger, 1921.

Sayre, Gordon M. "Communion in Captivity: Torture, Martyrdom and Gender in New France and New England." In *Finding Colonial Americas: Essays Honoring J. A. Leo Lemay,* edited by Carla Mulford and David S. Shields, 50–63. Newark: University of Delaware Press, 2001.

———. "Le Page du Pratz's Fabulous Journey of Discovery: Learning about Nature Writing from a Colonial Promotional Narrative." In *The Greening of Literary*

Scholarship: Essays on Literature, Theory, and the Environment, edited by Steven
Rosendale, 26–41. Iowa City: University of Iowa Press, 2002.

——. "Les Sauvages Américains": Representations of Native Americans in French and English
Colonial Literature. Chapel Hill: University of North Carolina Press, 1997.

——. "The Mammoth: Endangered Species or Vanishing Race?" Journal for Early Modern
Cultural Studies 1:1 (2001): 63–87.

——. "The Mound Builders and the Imagination of American Antiquity in Jefferson,
Bartram, and Chateaubriand." Early American Literature 33:3 (1998): 225–49.

——. "Plotting the Natchez Massacre: Le Page du Pratz, Dumont de Montigny,
Chateaubriand." Early American Literature 37:3 (2002): 381–413.

——, ed. American Captivity Narratives. Boston: Houghton Mifflin, 2000.

Sayre, Robert. Thoreau and the American Indians. Princeton: Princeton University Press,
1977.

Scheckel, Susan. The Insistence of the Indian: Race and Nationalism in Nineteenth-Century
American Culture. Princeton: Princeton University Press, 1998.

Schmitz, Neil. White Robe's Dilemma: Tribalism and American Literature. Amherst: University
of Massachusetts Press, 2001.

Schoolcraft, Henry Rowe. Algic Researches: North American Folktales and Legends. Mineola,
N.Y.: Dover, 1999.

Schwartz, Stuart, ed. Victors and Vanquished: Spanish and Nahua Views of the Conquest of
Mexico. Boston: Bedford/St. Martins, 2000.

Sears, Priscilla. A Pillar of Fire to Follow: American Indian Dramas, 1808–1859. Bowling
Green, Ohio: Bowling Green University Popular Press, 1982.

Sedgwick, Catharine Maria. Hope Leslie; or, Early Times in the Massachusetts. Edited and
introduction by Mary Kelley. New Brunswick, N.J.: Rutgers University Press, 1987.

Seeber, Edward D. "Critical Views on Logan's Speech." Journal of American Folklore
60:236 (1947): 130–46.

——. "Diderot and Chief Logan's Speech (Frontières de Virginie)." Modern Language Notes
60:3 (1945): 176–79.

Seelye, John. Beautiful Machine: Rivers and the Republican Plan, 1755-1825. New York:
Oxford University Press, 1991.

——. Memory's Nation: The Place of Plymouth Rock. Chapel Hill: University of North
Carolina Press, 1998.

Shields, David S. "Moving the Rock." In Finding Colonial Americas: Essays in Honor of J. A.
Leo Lemay, edited by Carla Mulford and David S. Shields, 387–402. Newark:
University of Delaware Press, 2001.

Sigüenza y Góngora, Carlos de. The "Mercurio Volante" of Don Carlos de Sigüenza y Góngora:
An Account of the First Expedition of Don Diego de Vargas into New Mexico in 1692.
Translated, introduction, and notes by Irving A. Leonard. Los Angeles: Quivira
Society, 1932.

Silverberg, Robert. Mound Builders of Ancient America. Greenwich, Conn.: New York
Graphic Society, 1968.

Slotkin, Richard. *Regeneration through Violence: The Mythology of the American Frontier, 1600–1860.* Middletown, Conn.: Wesleyan University Press, 1973.

Smith, John. *The Complete Works of Captain John Smith (1580–1631).* Edited by Philip Barbour. 3 vols. Chapel Hill: Institute for Early American History and Culture/University of North Carolina Press, 1986.

Smith, Russell. *Harrington and His "Oceana": A Study of a Seventeenth-Century Utopia and Its Influence in America.* New York: Octagon, 1971.

Smith, Seba. *Powhatan: A Metrical Romance, in Seven Cantos.* New York: Harper, 1841.

Smith, William, and Thomas Hutchins. *Historical Account of Bouquet's Expedition against the Ohio Indians, in 1764.* 1765; Cincinnati: Clarke, 1868.

Sollors, Werner. *Beyond Ethnicity: Consent and Descent in American Culture.* New York: Oxford University Press, 1986.

Sophocles. *Oedipus Tyrannus.* Translated by Luci Berkowitz and Theodore F. Brunner. New York: Norton, 1970.

Southey, Robert. "Oliver Newman." In *The complete poetical works of Robert Southey, LL.D. (later poet laureate) Collected by himself.* New York: Appleton, 1846.

Soyinka, Wole. *Death and the King's Horseman.* London: Methuen, 1982.

Steele, Ian K. *Warpaths: Invasions of North America.* New York: Oxford University Press, 1994.

Stiggins, George. *Creek Indian History: A Historical Narrative of the Genealogy, Traditions, and Downfall of the Ispocoga or Creek Indian Tribe of Indians.* Edited by Virginia Pounds Brown. Birmingham, Ala.: Birmingham Public Library Press, 1989.

———. "A Historical Narration of the Genealogy, Traditions and Downfall of the Ispocaga or Creek Tribe of Indians, Written by One of the Tribe." Edited by Theron A. Nunez Jr. as "Creek Nativism and the Creek War of 1813–1814." *Ethnohistory* 5 (1958): 1–47, 131–75, 292–301.

Stone, John Augustus. *Metamora; or, The Last of the Wampanoags.* In *Staging the Nation: Plays from the American Theatre, 1787–1909,* edited by Don B. Wilmeth, 60–98. Boston: Bedford, 1998.

Strong, Pauline Turner. *Captive Selves, Captivating Others: The Politics and Poetics of Colonial American Captivity Narratives.* Boulder, Colo.: Westview, 1999.

Sugden, John. *Tecumseh: A Life.* New York: Holt, 1997.

Surrey, N. M. Miller. *Calendar of Manuscripts in Paris Archives and Libraries Relating to the History of the Mississippi Valley to 1803.* 2 vols. Washington, D.C.: Carnegie Institution of Washington, Department of Historical Research, 1926–28.

Swanton, John R. *Indian Tribes of the Lower Mississippi Valley and Adjacent Coast of the Gulf of Mexico.* Smithsonian Bureau of American Ethnology Bulletin vol. 43. Washington, D.C.: U.S. Government Printing Office, 1911.

Tanner, John. *A Narrative of the Captivity and Adventures of John Tanner (U.S. Interpreter at the Saut de Ste. Marie) during Thirty Years Residence among the Indians in the Interior of North America.* Edited by Edwin James. 1830; reprint, Minneapolis: Ross and Haines, 1956.

Taussig, Michael. *Mimesis and Alterity: A Particular History of the Senses*. New York: Routledge, 1994.

Thatcher, B. B. *Indian Biography; or, An Historical Account of those Individuals who have been distinguished among the North American Natives as Orators, Warriors, Statesmen, and Other Remarkable Characters*. 2 vols. New York: Harper, 1832.

——. Review of *The Fall of the Indian, with other poems*, by Isaac McLellan Jr. *North American Review* 33:73 (1831): 407–49.

——. *Tales of the Indians, being prominent passages from the history of the North American natives*. Boston: Wiatt and Dow, 1831.

Thevet, André. *André Thevet's North America: A Sixteenth-Century View*. Translated by Roger Schlesinger and Arthur P. Stabler. Kingston, Ont.: McGill–Queen's University Press, 1986.

Thwaites, Reuben Gold, ed. *The Jesuit Relations and Allied Documents*. 73 vols. Cleveland: Burrowes, 1896–1901.

Thwaites, Reuben Gold, and Louise Phelps Kellogg, eds. *Documentary History of Dunmore's War, 1774: Compiled from the Draper Manuscripts*. Madison: Wisconsin Historical Society, 1905.

Tilton, Robert. *Pocahontas: The Evolution of an American Narrative*. New York: Cambridge University Press, 1994.

Todorov, Tzvetan. *The Conquest of America*. New York: Harper and Row, 1984.

Tompson, Benjamin. "New England's Crisis." In *So Dreadfull a Judgment: Puritan Responses to King Philip's War, 1676–1677*, edited by Richard Slotkin and James K. Folsom, 213–33. Middletown, Conn.: Wesleyan University Press, 1978.

Tooker, Elizabeth, "The Constitution and the Iroquois League." *Ethnohistory* 35:4 (1988): 305–36.

Trowbridge, Charles Christopher. *Shawnese Traditions*. Edited by Vernon Kinietz and Erminie W. Voegelin. Ann Arbor: University of Michigan Press, 1939.

Trumbull, Henry. *History of the Discovery of America: of the Landing of the Pilgrims at Plymouth, and of their most remarkable Engagements with the Indians in New England, from their first arrival in 1620, until the final subjugation of the natives in 1679. To which is annexed the particulars of almost every important engagement with the savages in the United States and territories; including the defeat of Generals Braddock, Harmer, and St. Clair, the Creek and Seminole War, etc.* 1810; Boston: Clark, 1840.

Usner, Daniel. *American Indians in the Lower Mississippi Valley: Social and Economic Histories*. Lincoln: University of Nebraska Pres, 1998.

Vanderwerth, W. C., ed. *Indian Oratory: Famous Speeches by Noted Indian Chieftains*. Norman: University of Oklahoma Press, 1971.

Varela, Félix. *Jicoténcal*. Edited by Luis Léal and Rodolfo J. Cortina. Houston: Arte Publico, 1995.

Vaughan, Alden T. " 'Expulsion of the Salvages': English Policy and the Virginia Massacre of 1622." *William and Mary Quarterly*, 3d ser., 35:1 (1978): 57–84.

Vega, Garcilaso de la. *The Florida of the Inca*. Translated by John Grier Varner and Jeannette Johnson Varner. Austin: University of Texas Press, 1951.

———. *Royal Commentaries of the Inca, and General History of Peru*. 2 vols. Translated by Harold V. Livermore. Austin: University of Texas Press, 1966.

Velikova, Roumiana. " 'Philip, King of the Pequots': The History of an Error." *Early American Literature* 37:2 (2002): 311–35.

Villagrá, Gaspar Perez de. *Historia de la Nueva México, 1610*. Translated and edited by Miguel Encinias, Alfred Rodríguez, and Joseph P. Sánchez. Albuquerque: University of New Mexico Press, 1992.

Villiers du Terrage, Marc de. "La Louisiane de Chateaubriand." *Journal de la Société des Américanistes de Paris*, n.s., 46:1 (1924): 125–67.

Volney, Constantin-François. *A View of the Soil and Climate of the United States*. Translated by Charles Brockden Brown. 1804; New York: Hafner, 1968.

Walker, Cheryl. *Indian Nation: Native American Literature and Nineteenth-Century Nationalisms*. Durham, N.C.: Duke University Press, 1997.

Wallace, Anthony F. C. *Death and Rebirth of the Seneca*. New York: Knopf, 1970.

———. *Jefferson and the Indians: The Tragic Fate of the First Americans*. Cambridge: Harvard University Press, 1999.

Wallace, James D. "Race and Captivity in Cooper's *Wept*." *American Literary History* 7:2 (1995): 189–209.

Walsh, Dennis P. "Many Metamoras: An Indian Drama in the Old Northwest." *Old Northwest* 12:4 (1986): 457–68.

Watts, Edward. *An American Colony: Regionalism and the Roots of Midwestern Culture*. Athens: Ohio University Press, 2002.

Webber, Samuel. *Logan: An Indian Tale*. Cambridge, Mass.: Hilliard and Metcalf, 1821.

Weber, David J. *What Caused the Pueblo Revolt of 1680?* Boston: Bedford/St. Martins, 1999.

———, ed. *The Spanish Frontier in North America*. New Haven: Yale University Press, 1992.

Welles, Lemuel Aiken. *The Regicides in Connecticut*. New Haven: Tercentenary Commission of the State of Connecticut and Yale University Press, 1935.

Wertheimer, Eric. *Imagined Empires: Incas, Aztecs, and the New World of American Literature, 1771–1876*. New York: Cambridge University Press, 1999.

White, Ed. "The Backcountry and the City: Feelings of Structure in Early America." Unpublished manuscript, 2003.

———. "The Challenge of Iroquois Influence." *American Quarterly* 52:1 (2000): 179–88.

White, Hayden. "The Noble Savage Theme as Fetish." In *First Images of America: The Impact of the New World on the Old*, edited by Fredi Chiapelli, 1:121–35. Berkeley: University of California Press, 1976.

———. *Tropics of Discourse: Essays in Cultural Criticism*. Baltimore: Johns Hopkins University Press, 1978.

White, Richard. "The Fictions of Patriarchy: Indians and Whites in the Early Republic." In *Americans and the Early Republic*, edited by Frederick E. Hoxie, Ronald Hoffman, and Peter J. Albert, 62–84. Charlottesville: University Press of Virginia, 1999.

——. *The Middle Ground: Indians, Empires, and Republics in the Great Lakes Region, 1650–1815.* Cambridge: Cambridge University Press, 1991.

Wickman, Patricia R. *Osceola's Legacy.* Tuscaloosa: University of Alabama Press, 1991.

Williams, William Carlos. *In the American Grain.* New York: Boni, 1925.

Wilmeth, Don. *Staging the Nation: Plays from the American Theater, 1787–1909.* Boston: Bedford, 1998.

Winthrop, John. *The History of New England from 1630 to 1649. By John Winthrop, esq., first governor of the colony of Massachusetts Bay.* Edited by James Savage. 2 vols. Boston: Little, Brown, 1853.

Wogan, Peter. "Perceptions of European Literacy in Early Contact Situations." *Ethnohistory* 41:3 (1994): 407–29.

Wolcott, Roger. "A Brief Account of the Agency Of the Honourable John Winthrop, Esq; In the Court of King Charles the Second, Anno Dom. 1662. When he Obtained for the Colony of Connecticut His Majesty's Gracious Charter." In *Poems of Roger Wolcott, Esq, 1725,* 19–78. Boston: Club of Odd Volumes, 1898.

Wolf, Eric. *Europe and the People without History.* Berkeley: University of California Press, 1982.

Wood, Stephanie. *Transcending Conquest: Nahua Views of Spanish Colonial Mexico.* Norman: University of Oklahoma Press, 2003.

Woods, Patricia Dillon. *French-Indian Relations on the Southern Frontier.* Ann Arbor, Mich.: UMI Research Press, 1979.

Wyman, William Stokes. Introduction to *Creek Indian History: A Historical Narrative of the Genealogy, Traditions, and Downfall of the Ispocoga or Creek Indian Tribe of Indians,* by George Stiggins, 13–20. Birmingham, Ala.: Birmingham Public Library Press, 1989.

Zagarell, Sandra. " 'Expanding America': Lydia Sigourney's *Sketch of Connecticut,* Catharine Sedgwick's *Hope Leslie.*" *Tulsa Studies in Women's Literature* 6:2 (1987): 225–45.

Zeisberger, David. "David Zeisberger's History of Northern American Indians." Edited by Archer Butler Hulbert and William Nathaniel Schwarze. *Ohio Archaeological and Historical Publications* 29 (1910): 1–173.

INDEX